Hong Kong Confidential

Hong Kong Confidential

Life as a Subversive

David T. K. Wong

BLACKSMITH BOOKS

Hong Kong Confidential
ISBN 978-988-77928-9-5

Published by Blacksmith Books
Unit 26, 19/F, Block B, Wah Lok Industrial Centre,
37-41 Shan Mei Street, Fo Tan, Hong Kong
Tel: (+852) 2877 7899
www.blacksmithbooks.com

Also by David T. K. Wong:

Memoirs

Hong Kong Fiascos: A Struggle For Survival (2015)
Adrift: My Childhood in Colonial Singapore (2015)

Novels

The Embrace of Harlots (2011)
The Evergreen Tea House (2003)

Short story collections

Collected Hong Kong Stories (2016)
Chinese Stories in Times of Change (2009)
Connections: Stories of East Asia (2001)
Hong Kong Stories (1996)
Lost River and Other Stories (1990)

CONTENTS

CHAPTER I

Interregnum

AFTER LOSING A SERIES of wars during the 19th century, China had to make reparations, confer privileges and cede territories to foreign countries under the terms of "unequal" treaties. In the case of Britain, one of the territories surrendered under a series of treaties comprised the 400 square miles of land making up the Crown Colony of Hong Kong. The bulk of that area, however, was only on a 99-year lease on land called the New Territories.

In January of 1943, while the Second World War was still raging, Britain and China signed a further treaty pledging friendship, which abrogated the provisions of previous treaties between them — except for the retention of the colony of Hong Kong. The future of that territory was to be further negotiated after the end of World War II.

By the time the war ended, however, the internationally recognised Chinese government under General Chiang Kai-Shek was already locked in a bitter struggle for power with Chinese Communist rebels under the leadership of Chairman Mao Tse-Tung. The negotiations projected to be held between Britain and China were therefore left in limbo.

It was during that politically unsettled interregnum that I returned to Hong Kong in the spring of 1947. I had been born there but I had been taken by my mother to live in Canton when I was about three. By the time of my return, I was already 18, short of money and with no visible means of support. I was also weighed down by a variety of psychological baggage.

Before my return, I had gained a Cambridge School Leaving Certificate in Singapore. I had been living there since before I was six, having been consigned to live with my paternal grandparents after the collapse of my parents' marriage.

My grandfather was a doctor, trained at the then Hong Kong College of Medicine. Soon after his graduation in 1900, however, he secured an appointment as a medical officer in the British Colonial Service and was fortuitously assigned to Singapore, then a part of the Straits Settlements. That was why he happened to live there.

Though my grandfather was officially a British Crown servant, he had spent a significant part of his time supporting revolutionary activities against the corrupt and ineffective Ching Dynasty in China. He got involved because he was a good friend of Dr. Sun Yat-Sen, the revolutionary leader advocating change, unity and renewal for the country.

Because my grandfather had shared Dr. Sun's belief in the need for China to pull itself together and end its humiliations at the hands of foreign powers, he devoted his efforts to raising funds among overseas Chinese to support the revolution. After a number of failed attempts, the revolution finally succeeded in 1911. But the country, unfortunately, remained politically almost as fractured and divided as before.

When I was growing up, my grandfather had been pretty tight-lipped about his clandestine activities. He made little mention of Chinese history or politics. In any case, I had been too young to be interested in such topics. I had far more immediate and vexing existential puzzles of my own — why my parents had separated and why my mother had given me up while retaining my younger brother? I felt instinctively that brothers ought to grow up together and that children ought to be with their parents. I could not fathom why I had to be split away in such an incomprehensible fashion.

My brother, Tzi-Choy, admittedly had a more felicitous name than my own.

His name meant "talented son" or "gifted child" whereas mine only meant "strange son" or "unusual child". Thus I grew up with a thirst to uncover the reasons for the unexplained goings-on within my own family. No adult had ever given me a satisfactory reason for my fate. Not my grandparents, my father nor my many aunts and elders. They all seemed deliberately evasive. I smelt a rat.

I soon suspected that my mother must have rejected me because I had some unspeakable defect and for which she felt ashamed. Perhaps I had an incurable disease, for I certainly could not put on weight however much I ate. Leaving me with my grandfather, a doctor, made sense in that case. But what was the disease afflicting me? I simply could not find out.

So, with those unresolved suspicions hanging around my neck after completing my secondary education, I made it known within the family I intended to head for Canton, where my mother was living with my younger brother. I had not seen either of them for almost 13 years. In the meantime, my mother had also acquired a new husband. They lived in a street called Six Two Three Road. That latter fact, coupled with my determination to go there, somehow caused my grandfather to start telling me about certain aspects of Chinese history.

He explained that the street where my mother lived had been named to commemorate the slaughter in 1925 by French and British machine-gunners of cadets from the Whampoa Military College and other demonstrators trying to cross the two bridges leading to the foreign concessions on the island of Shameen. The island was located at the western side of the city.

My grandfather then went on to describe the many other massacres of Chinese by the British — in Shanghai, in Hong Kong and in other parts of China — and to explain why our countrymen had to overthrow the Ching Dynasty and end such oppressions. Sadly, after the overthrow of the Manchus, China failed to produce the calibre of leaders the country needed.

After listening to my grandfather's narratives, I began to understand better his attachment to his country and why he had committed himself to revolution. He was then 73 and I got an impression that, in recounting the past, he was somehow trying to indicate he had done all he could and that the responsibility for rejuvenating China now rested with my generation.

I found that slightly unnerving. Was he expecting me to pick up where he had left off? I was not sure. I had only just got out of secondary school. What could I do? If I had any ambition at all, it was only to continue my education at a university somewhere.

* * *

The Kwangtung provincial capital of Canton had a reputation for being "the mother of revolutions" because it had hatched more insurrections and rebellions than any other city in China. When I set eyes on it after the war, that reputation seemed well-deserved. The place indeed reeked of corruption and political divisions.

Sing-song houses, gambling dens, black market dealerships in UNRRA supplies and shady restaurants with hidden agendas lined the front of its harbour. Spiralling inflation, grinding poverty, economic chaos and criminal enterprises affected virtually every walk of life. Everything and everyone appeared capable of being bought or sold — if the price was right. The need to restore the country's dignity seemed almost palpable, just waiting for the right patriots to answer the call. Yet the inhabitants of the city appeared more concentrated on just surviving the economic chaos, staying ahead of the rampant inflation and avoiding being caught up in the raging civil war.

One look at Six Two Three Road was enough to tell me that the glory previously associated with heroic deaths was transient and overrated. How could a string of numbers, indicating a half-forgotten date, do sufficient honour to the dozens who had forfeited their lives there 22 years earlier?

Meeting my mother and brother again also proved something of an anticlimax. Neither turned out to be as warm and welcoming as I had expected. The reunion seemed stiff and formalised, like a meeting between distant relatives. The only surprise was that my mother and her doctor husband had produced a jolly baby daughter as a half-sister for me.

I was soon to discover for the first time hitherto unknown traits in my mother's personality. I found her very practical and down-to-earth and not much interested in politics or national issues, notwithstanding that in the days before I was born she had worked in a secretarial capacity in the office of Borodin, that notorious Russian Comintern agent sent to China to foment revolution.

The circumstances at her home in Six Two Three Road indicated a diminishing economic status. Whatever resources she and her husband might have accumulated had fallen victim to spiralling inflation. If I had previously entertained hopes of my mother financing my further education, those hopes quickly evaporated.

Stuck for a direction for my future, I sounded my mother out on the prospect of enrolling in the Whampoa Military Academy. It would be my contribution towards national reconstruction and advancement, I claimed. She responded with ridicule. She suggested I should learn typing and shorthand instead. I saw some justice in her response. Although I was 18, I was physically little more than a bag of skin and bones, weighing in at a mere 102 pounds! Hardly the right material for a military career.

Her reaction naturally doused me like a bucket of ice water poured unceremoniously over my head. It hurt my pride that my own mother should see so little prospect for me. A depressing clerical life loomed before my mind's eye. Pushing pens and filling in ledgers was hardly the life I wanted. My heart sank. I realised that if I wanted a better fate, I would have to find it for myself. And certainly at a place less chaotic and more promising than Canton. On that basis I boarded a train for the short journey to Hong Kong.

* * *

The British Crown Colony represented a sea change. In 1947, the Hong Kong dollar was much more stable than Chinese currency. Neither did the city display Canton's filth and disorder and its air of impending doom. Yet the colony also had its own edginess, apprehensions, anomalies and antagonisms. More than 98% of its population were Chinese; but the real political power and commercial wealth rested in the hands of a small elite group of European rulers and Chinese merchants.

Since I was desperately short of money, I wasted no time seeking out relatives and family friends to help me find a job. It was not easy. I had no qualifications apart from a School Leaving Certificate. I managed in the end to land a probationary appointment as cub reporter with the *South China Morning Post*, the colony's leading English-language newspaper.

A probationer's pay, however, was pitched at starvation levels — a mere HK$150 per month or roughly 80 American cents per day at the then prevailing rate of exchange! The amount was just about sufficient for two modest meals per day, in the form of either two bowls of *wonton* noodles or two plates of barbecued pork and rice.

But the low pay was not what upset me most. It was the sharp discrepancy in the terms of employment between local journalists and expatriate ones. The latter not only got higher salaries but also housing and holiday packages. I had spent more than four years as a refugee in Australia during the war, predominantly among Europeans, and I could not see that they, as a racial group, were inherently superior to any other race. So why should they be automatically paid more and treated better in Hong Kong? What was equally surprising was that the local employees within the newspaper seemed to accept such disparities without much ado.

As I set about my duties, covering everything from magistrate courts to fires and accidents, from social galas and charity balls to the funerals of the great and the good, it came to me that racial discrimination was an all-pervading fact of life in the colony. As a Chinese, I resented deeply that I should be regarded as inferior simply because of my race. It riled me more effectively than my grandfather's accounts of historical massacres of Chinese by foreigners. It pricked more directly upon my skin.

It became progressively obvious that enormous gulfs of ignorance separated the bulk of the population from the tiny foreign ruling elites, not only where language, race, culture and habits were concerned but also in the nurturing of competing myths and concepts of *amour propre*.

Under such circumstances, different outlooks and approaches to everyday issues were bound to arise. How could a hawk gliding far up in the heavens have the same point of view as a worm burrowing through the mud flats below? Even a person living in an airless tenement bunk space, where the communal night-soil bucket would be replaced only once every two or three days, could not entertain the perspectives of someone subsisting in a squatter hovel, without electricity, running water or latrine facilities, and exposed to the quotidian whims of wind, rain and fire.

The growing squatter problem had been staring everyone in the face, yet no coherent policy had been put in place by the administration to tackle it. On Christmas night of 1953, a fire broke out at Shek Kip Mei squatter area and by morning it had left two dead, 53,000 homeless and many unemployed.

It took that misfortune to force the government to embark on an emergency housing programme. Remarkably, for a small place like Hong Kong, within a year and a bit all the victims had been re-housed in a resettlement estate. That demonstrated what a government could be capable of if the will and the determination existed. That project marked the beginning of the colony's public and subsidised housing programme now covering more than half the population. But the demand for affordable housing remains today as great as ever.

Homeless former residents of the Shek Kip Mei squatter area after the fire of December 1953.
Photo: *South China Morning Post*

Another illustration of the potential for mutual misunderstandings between rulers and the ruled could be found in the way hawkers were dealt with. According to one official estimate at the time, in excess of 75,000 people were earning their livings through hawking after World War II. That meant a quite significant part of the population was dependent upon that rudimentary form of economic activity.

Since time immemorial, the Chinese had been primarily an agrarian nation, living relatively plain and simple lives. Should the need for some extra money arise, it was customary for people to set up pitches on the roadsides of nearby towns and villages to sell produce, products or snacks. Or to trade their skills in juggling, fortune-telling, toy-making or whatever in return for a coin or two. It was not too dissimilar to market days in some of the smaller European towns.

After the British took over, however, they wanted to bring system and order and to prevent thoroughfares from becoming obstructed. They introduced licensing for hawking, separating that activity into different types — fixed pitches of specified sizes at specified locations, for example, and another on an itinerant basis. Thus new offences such as obstruction and hawking without a licence — or with the wrong type of licence — came into being.

Sometimes the regulations contradicted one another. While itinerant hawking licences were provided, such hawkers were forbidden to call out to indicate their presence or to create noise to peddle their wares.

I recalled when I was a boy living in Blair Road in Singapore, I always kept an ear open for the arrival of various hawkers — the tock-tock signals struck on bamboo sticks by the noodle sellers, the ting-a-ling of the ice popsicle man, the high-pitched cries of the sharpener of knives and scissors, and the different call signs of the Indian seller of nuts, the fruiterer, the olive man and so forth. Without making a noise, how could any itinerant hawker make his presence known? So the courts ended up seeing daily parades of bewildered folks being fined or otherwise punished for unwittingly committing various breaches of the law.

So far as officialdom was concerned, it was just trying to produce a public good for a people predisposed to being disorderly, noisy and disorganised. But for the hawkers affected, it came across as foreigners trying to stop them from making an honest living.

When more strange and arcane offences were added to the statute books — like loitering with intent, larceny by finding and possession of an implement fit for an unlawful purpose — even the most competent court interpreters had difficulty explaining them to baffled defendants. That provided further sources for resentment and disaffection and the rise of irredentist sentiments.

It was therefore unsurprising that in October of 1946, the authorities appeared taken aback by an outbreak of anti-foreign rioting in Kowloon after a peanut seller had been killed during a hawker clearance operation in Yaumati. Disturbances flared spontaneously and spread rapidly to other parts of Kowloon. Foreigners and the police were stoned wherever they appeared. It was days before the authorities could re-establish control.

The authorities might have anticipated trouble if they had been more conscious of the anger building up for months over hawker clearances. Any cursory examination into Hong Kong's colonial history would reveal many more instances of absence of understanding between the ruling elites and the common people.

Towards the end of 1964, for another later example, the local demand for Chinese to be made a second official language — which had been brewing for some time — reached a critical mass. But such a demand, if met, would create a number of legal and technical problems which were outside the bureaucracy's comfort zone. So instead of offering a degree of accommodation, the government sought to stifle or downplay the demand, branding it as "an intellectual exercise" by "frustrated intellectuals". It was left to civil society to take the lead for change. The Catholic Church, for instance, began using Chinese for Mass in 1965. It was not till 1972 that the government, with ill-grace, conceded to making Chinese a second official language.

Another example of the ham-fisted way the administration dealt with public opposition could be found in the way it handled a proposal for a five-cent increase in First Class Star Ferry fares in 1966. The arrest of a solitary peaceful protester for staging a fast at the Star Ferry concourse, and thus causing a minor obstruction, provided the spark igniting three days of rioting. One person was killed, 1,800 were arrested and 258 sent to gaol as a consequence. A subsequent Commission of Inquiry ascribed one of the causes of the riots to the distrust existing between the government and the population at large.

* * *

It might be appropriate at this point if I were to make a foolhardy attempt to encapsulate in a few short paragraphs some of the enduring traits of a people as old and complex as the Chinese. They have the distinction of being the only continuous civilisation from ancient times which has survived more or less intact to the present day.

They are a people who are highly individualistic, eccentric, creative, hard-working and rambunctious. Yet they are bound by history, rituals, customs, family and clan ties which curbed their more individualistic inclinations. That rendered them difficult to stereotype. My justification for this attempt, however inadequate and skimpy it might be, is that the overwhelming number of Hong Kong people are an offshoot of that dominant racial stock. So to understand them requires some grasp of the origins of their behaviour, culture and values.

The Chinese had once been described as a people "poor in possessions but rich in sentiments and discriminating tastes". To get a feel of their character, it is essential to explore how they had been shaped by circumstances and how their social and philosophical systems have evolved over the millennia.

Of foremost importance to the Chinese was the influence of Confucius, a teacher who lived between 551 and 479 B.C. His period was a chaotic time of feudal city states and patriarchal societies, arranged in hierarchies according to age, sex and class distinctions.

Confucius believed in the fundamental goodness and teachability of human beings, that they could cultivate virtue and ethics through personal and communal endeavours. Unlike Aristotle, he held that man was not just a reasoning being but was also a reasonable one.

Hence he worked out a system of propriety and restraint, of moderation and of knowing one's place. He assigned a moral duty on those in higher positions to look after those below them, as would be the case for a king over his subjects and for a head of household over his family. Those in lower positions should in turn repay those who looked after them with loyalty and obedience.

In respect of the virtues of the individual, Confucius emphasised certain inherent qualities which he called human-heartedness and righteousness. The latter revolved around what ideally *ought* to be done. In other words, in every society there would be things which ought to be done because they were morally the right things to do. A person might do those things for non-moral reasons, but if so then he could only be acting for profit and not righteousness.

By 100 B.C. Confucius and his teachings had become so revered that his countrymen regarded him as The First Teacher and his ideas were accepted as national orthodoxy. Around that time, the famed Chinese imperial examination system also began, whereby entry into the ranks of government depended not upon noble birth or wealth but on passing periodic examinations based upon the Confucian classics.

During the Tang Dynasty, under the Emperor Tai Tsung, an official edition of the Confucian classics was prepared, together with the numerous commentaries which had been made upon them. Confucianism was thus reaffirmed as the official teaching of the state.

Legend has it that Confucius had a slightly older contemporary by the name of Li Erh, who ridiculed Confucius when they met, berating him for his arrogance, ingratiating manners and excessive ambition. Li Erh has come down to us as Lao Tzu or the Old One, the putative author of the *Tao Te Ching*, a slender two-part volume embodying the philosophy known as Taoism.

Taoism is not easy to explain. The very first sentence of the *Tao Te Ching* had tested the ingenuity of commentators and translators for centuries. It is now generally translated as: "The Tao which can be spoken of is not the eternal Tao." Lao Tzu then went on to obscure the concept further, by saying that the Tao concealed itself by being nameless, shadowy and indistinct. He believed the Tao to be a force behind everything existing in the world. It could not be categorised, sliced up or placed under a microscope. It could only be intuited. Man was an integral part of the Tao, so he was like an eye that could see but could never see itself.

At its heart, Taoism is concerned with the survival of the common man, whom it believed to be innocent and ought to be living in harmony with Nature and leaving things alone. If people would only follow their own nature, then a social order would emerge by itself. In short, to act through non-action, because every tiniest thing was interconnected, each following its own nature. "The Tao does nothing, yet nothing is left undone." To be proactive might inadvertently upset the harmony of the Tao. It would be better for people to curb ambition, avoid seeking fame and position, slow down the tempo of their lives and not despise working with their hands.

Confucianism and Taoism in due course produced a reaction in another group of thinkers known collectively as the Legalists. That short-lived school was embodied in Han Fei, who committed suicide in 236 B.C.

Whereas Confucius held that man was born good and Lao Tzu that he was born innocent, the Legalists held he was born evil. Hence man had to be forced to obey a fixed set of rules, regardless of his social or political status. The rule of law might sound beguiling but if man was a rascal, who could draw up laws which would not benefit rascals? And of course the more laws the more law-breakers.

After a brief attempt to bring an elaborate system of law into practice, social and economic affairs of the country ground to a halt. It would appear that modern advocates of the rule of law had not studied thoroughly enough what had happened in China a couple of thousand years ago. Law without the human touch would be both unworkable and unenforceable. In many countries today, legal processes have become so complicated, convoluted, time-consuming, expensive and open to abuse that it is arguable whether justice could really ever be served.

While both Taoism and Confucianism dealt with the problems of earthly existence and on finding human happiness and contentment in an inhospitable world, they left unfilled in the Chinese psyche a spiritual gap about eternity and the afterlife. Confucius, when asked about death, gave the terse and celebrated answer which, in pidgin English, went as follows:

"Don't know life, how know death?"

When Buddhism first came to China is a matter of dispute but it was a few centuries after Confucius and Lao Tzu. One Taoist legend has it that Lao Tzu went to India and influenced Buddhism before it came to China. In any event, its offer of a Nirvana after the pain and vicissitudes of earthly life gradually rendered it a major factor in Chinese civilisation. Today, it is quite noticeable that for every Taoist temple still standing in China there are probably at least ten Buddhist ones.

Buddhism's concept of karma, of a person's deeds forming a chain of causes and effects stretching well into the future, found ready acceptance among the Chinese. It did them a power of good by making them conscious that death needed not to be the end of their being but only one aspect of an extended process. Whatever people did in their present existence would determine what they would become in the future. That belief made them kinder, more peace-loving and more inclined towards becoming vegetarians. It also drove them to engage in charitable acts in order to store up merit for their next reincarnation.

None of those strands of philosophy touched upon above would appear very suitable preparation for vaulting into the bare-knuckled struggle for profits and fame under the quasi-capitalistic arena currently prevailing in Hong Kong. Indeed, commerce had been frowned upon since ancient times and merchants had been relegated to the lowest level in society. That was because merchants and traders — unlike farmers and artisans — produced nothing while seeking to make gains from trading the products of others. They therefore came to be generally viewed as corrupt, treacherous and selfish.

Notwithstanding such seeming anomalies, most Chinese have woven some elements of those schools of thought into their personalities, emotional make-up and everyday conduct. They would seek whatever enjoyment or happiness there might be on hand, be it through sipping tea, playing chess or *mah-jong*, picking their teeth, keeping caged canaries, practising *tai chi*, eating melon seeds or fiddling with their toes. Bits of each philosophy would also be reflected through family custom and common habit. For example, when I was a boy, I quickly got accustomed to the family cook serving up Buddhist vegetarian dishes on the first and fifteenth day of each lunar month, although my family was supposed to be Christians.

Close behind philosophies, another important element in the make-up of the Chinese was their preoccupation with food. They have remained completely catholic in this regard, more so than most nations. They would eat everything that moved and a lot more that did not. In some parts of China, snakes were popular; and in other parts, dogs. Because famines used to be such a recurring feature of life, the Chinese had also tried assuaging their pangs of hunger with grass, tree bark and boiled mud.

Some believe that certain foods eaten determined virility. For instance, it is a historical fact that all Chinese dynasties had been founded by noodle-eaters from the north, with no dynasty ever being established by a rice-eater from south of the Yangtse River.

Dr. Sun Yat-Sen, a southerner, had inspired and led the Revolution of 1911, but soon discovered the unforgiving reality that a man with words could never prevail against one with guns. In the interests of national unity, he stepped aside as President of the fledging republic in favour of the northern warlord Yuan Shih-Kai. But Yuan — who incidentally had failed twice in Imperial Examinations — had other ideas. He had set his heart on establishing another dynasty with himself as its first emperor, until a timely death in 1916 put paid to his ambition.

In addition to that general picture, the Chinese have also developed a wry sense of humour, rather akin to the British one. They are known for their intelligence, their innovative cast of mind and their capacity for hard work when that proved necessary. Their social structure and upbringing have foisted upon them a family-oriented outlook in spite of any individualistic inclination they might have. That also created in them an aversion to poking their noses into other people's business.

* * *

The Chinese in Hong Kong have inherited many of the basic characteristics of their compatriots from the mainland. But since they are largely immigrants, they also bring the complications of geographic and dialectic attachments with them. Most are Cantonese, with roots in Kwangtung Province, but sizeable segments had originated from Kwangsi, Fukien, Kiangsu, Chekiang, Shanghai and places farther afield.

The fact that they all looked pretty much alike and shared a common written language and an aloof and self-satisfied manner, have often led foreigners to take them to be the same. In truth, they are often divided into factions and cliques, and further separated by class, education, politics, religion, wealth, family background, clan attachments, sex and varying money-grubbing motives.

Outsiders might also consider the Chinese to be over-attached to the concept of face. It might be just a more openly ritualised form of politeness not uncommon among Eastern races. For instance, some cultures would say "yes" when they actually mean "no". It was the way in which the "yes" was expressed that told the true response. The Chinese possibly set a greater store in subtlety than others.

Yet, as an all-pervading social practice, face is not easy to explain, especially to foreigners. The best I can do is to quote from Dr. Lin Yu-Tang, an eminent Chinese scholar, who wrote a book entitled *My Country and My People* more than 80 years ago.

Dr. Lin said: "Face cannot be translated or defined. It is like honour and is not honour. It cannot be purchased by money, and gives a man or a woman a material pride. It is hollow and is what men fight for and what women die for. It is invisible and yet by definition exists by being shown to the public.

It exists in the ether and yet can be heard, and sounds eminently respectable and solid. It is amenable, not to reason but to social convention. It protracts lawsuits, breaks up family fortunes, causes murders and suicides, and yet it often makes a man out of a renegade who has been insulted by his fellow townsmen, and it is prized above all earthly possessions. It is more powerful than fate and favour, and more respected than the constitution. It often decides a military victory or defeat, and can demolish a whole government ministry. It is that hollow thing which men in China live by."

A Chinese should be able to relate easily to what Dr. Lin had described. He would almost certainly have come across instances of a family going into debt to lay on a wedding feast or a stylish funeral in order to preserve face. I doubt, however, whether very many foreigners would plumb the true depths of silliness to which the Chinese could descend in their pursuit of face.

Dr. Sun Yat-Sen, the Father of Republican China, had likened the Chinese nation to a tray of sand, lacking cohesion and unity. I would characterise those in Hong Kong as more like a heap of beans, thrown together haphazardly inside a shop-worn gunny sack of foreign colonialism.

Within that sack, each retained an individual existence, jostling for whatever opportunities there might be for survival or profit or advancement. Such competitive contacts often generated more friction than warmth; good fellowship was left to providence or chance. Should that colonial gunny sack ever split, they would probably spill all over the place, with each pursuing his individual self-interest, ranging from the noble to the profane.

I am unsure whether a reader is left much wiser about the Chinese race after these brief paragraphs. Perhaps Sir John Bowring, the Governor of Hong Kong from 1854 to 1859, had put his finger neatly on that issue when he declared: "We rule in ignorance, they obey in blindness."

I sometimes wonder whether, for some perverse reason, those gulfs of ignorance had been kept deliberately unbridged by both the rulers and the ruled. Left apart, both might find it easier to nurse misconceptions and illusions about each other. Closer contact might reveal the unsettling reality of a common humanity. In that case, how could relationships continue to be conducted on a basis of inequality and lack of mutual respect?

* * *

My joining the *South China Morning Post* in 1947 marked the beginning of more than 70 years — and still counting — of a working life carried out in a variety of callings. Out of that total, 35 years had been spent in Hong Kong, including nearly 21 years as an Administrative Officer in the colonial government.

When I was first admitted to that select cadre in 1961, it comprised only 84 officers, with 28 in what was described as superscale officers, that is, those running secretariat branches or departments, and the rest on time-scale. Naturally the overwhelming majority in that corps were expatriates, with local officers coming to only slightly more than half a dozen.

Given the antipathies I have expressed towards foreign occupation, and given my grandfather's influence during my upbringing, ending up as a colonial civil servant must appear to readers as grossly incongruous. Those considerations had, indeed, left me with a problem as uncomfortable as a dog bothered by fleas. I have tried to explain some of my reservations and feelings in the two earlier volumes of these family memoirs, in *Adrift* and in *Hong Kong Fiascos*.

The present volume will deal with some of the further dilemmas I faced as I continued to serve as an Administrative Officer for another 10 years, till 1981.

I should re-emphasise, however, that my integration into the colonial civil service at various levels had been rendered more rewarding than I had expected because of a succession of very kind, able, knowledgeable, dedicated and enlightened British superiors. Each of them, in his own way, had taught me a great deal, not only about what bureaucratic ropes to manipulate and what pitfalls to avoid, but also about the sense of integrity and duty which should be at the heart of discharging public responsibilities. I should add that throughout my career in the Administrative Service, I had only ever worked once directly to a local superior. That was because there were very few Chinese officers senior to myself.

That single occasion proved a thorough pleasure though it lasted for just a few short months before I was reassigned. That superior was Eric Ho. We shared many common attitudes which had enabled us to remain firm friends long after both of us had retired.

* * *

In the autumn of 1970, the administration decided — for some reason not altogether clear to me — to pack me off to Oxford on a Queen Elizabeth House Fellowship. I assumed someone must have decided that I was becoming, under the influence of Sir John Cowperthwaite, too agnostic over many of the more orthodox tenants of that pseudo-science known as economics and needed some re-indoctrination in free market dogma.

I have used the term "pseudo-science" deliberately because economics has struck me as a discipline too full of imprecisions, with far too many of its practitioners attempting to bamboozle the public over the reliability of their dodgy analyses and forecasts. I had arrived at that point of view due in no small measure to working for Sir John as his Assistant Economic Secretary. Sir John had been the Financial Secretary of Hong Kong since 1961 and had been the chief architect of the colony's sturdy and workable financial and economic structure.

In my humble opinion, he was one of the greatest and most practical-minded economists of his day. Many have praised him as a dyed-in-the-wool free marketeer. But, in my opinion, that would be too simplistic a view. He allowed a free market only in spheres where he thought it would be in the interest of Hong Kong to have one.

One could as easily make the case that he was a central planner by selecting a different set of facts. For example, all the public transport facilities were either state-owned or operated by private monopolies subject to profit-limitation clauses. The electricity companies, the gas company, the telephone service and the international cable operations were likewise regulated. Road-building, water supplies and postal services were carried out by government departments.

Rice imports worked under a quota system and virtually all the other foodstuff imported from China — fruits, vegetables, eggs, meat and fowl — were being brought in by a China-appointed cartel subjected to a profit limitation regime imposed by the Chinese authorities.

As for exports from the colony, textiles and garments were dominant. They made up some 40% of domestic exports by value and provided employment for 41% of the industrial workforce. Most of those exports were subjected to quota restrictions imposed by importing countries. Taken overall, Hong Kong could hardly be said to conform with the widely held myth of being a free-wheeling *laissez-faire* economy.

Under Sir John's tutelage, I had acquired a healthy scepticism over economic myths and over many of the over-dressed theoretical formulations favoured by politicians, academics and media gurus. Instead of using complicated mathematical formulae or econometric models to tackle economic problems, Sir John had merely used common sense, fair play and a constant reviewing of the facts on the ground.

When I was offered the Fellowship, however, the thought of digging into more of the lamer economic obscurities was far from my mind. Instead I saw Oxford as a temporary respite, not only from bureaucratic memos in the office but also an intractable tangle of sexless domesticity and responsibilities at home.

I had never previously been to Oxford, although I had read a fair amount about its dreamy spires, its bleached ancient stones, its grimacing gargoyles, secluded cloisters and its history of intellectual ferment. There was a flow in the language of the likes of Walter Pater and Edward Thomas that I found beguiling. One of them had spoken about the place being marked by "the unction of antiquity".

Thus long before I even got there, I was already entertaining notions of loitering in the churchyard of Holy Cross, as Byron had done, or putting on a ridiculous straw hat for an afternoon in a punt. Or indulging in some amusement, like studying Etruscan tomb pottery or pronouncing on the virtues of cold soups, as the Shakespearean scholar William George Clark had ventured after a visit to Spain.

Oxford turned out to be much more than I had anticipated. I soon discovered that all that was required was a short stroll from Carfax to be delivered into some splendid idioms in green, usually enhanced by a gently flowing rivulet or stream. Before I knew it, I would find leaves expiring around me, dropping as softly as autumnal sighs. They would fall from trees whose names I had to recall from memories of other places and other times.

Tall poplars and priestly yews, pale birches and thoughtful elms. Here and there, grey beeches and venerable oaks would interlace branches like holding hands. Any stream nearby would be fringed by willows, leaning this way and that. And around their timbered feet, rank grasses would grow with impish delight, livened occasionally by splashes of yellow toadflax. Paths might weave unsteadily across verdant swathes, as if they had been trampled by people in happy inebriation.

Such encounters left a catch in my heart, as if I had stumbled upon a succession of hallowed places. Something soul-restoring would scent the air, like an elusive spirit teasing an idling painter or poet. My mind would drift to Blake's line about seeing a world in a grain of sand.

The very next moment, lines by the Chinese poet Li Shang-Yin would also re-surface in me. Li had written a thousand years before Blake, about seeing a world in a grain of millet. What common sentiments could be shared across both time and space!

Other thoughts would take me back to the Wordsworth of my boyhood.

> "One impulse from a vernal wood
> May teach you more of man,
> Of moral evil and of good
> Than all the sages can."

Those musings soon took me even farther back, to the more elevated beauty of China's five sacred mountains highlighted by a Chinese tutor I had when I was a boy in Singapore. He told me about those mountains when he was teaching me the *Three Character Classic*. He said there were vantage points on those mountains where one could experience the meeting of Chinese poetry and painting. At the time, I did not know sufficiently of either to grasp what he was driving at. By the time I had gained an appreciation, political obstacles and restrictions had intervened to deny me access to even a single one of those mountains.

* * *

Those solitary walks around Oxford inevitably reignited my longing for communion with Nature, a longing that formed an inevitable part of every Chinese soul. The woods at Oxford had something mysterious and healing about them. They filled me with a sense of wonder and liberation. It was as if I had miraculously sloughed off all the trammels of official protocol, the restraints on social behaviour and the shackles of family responsibilities. Half a world away, the oppression of the tight concrete canyons of Hong Kong, made up more gracelessly and more sharp-edged than the geometrical constructions in New York or Chicago, could no longer confine me. Even the air in the woods seemed perfumed by freedom.

It was, of course, only a trick of the mind, a momentary delusion. I was already 41 and was unambiguously unfree. Moreover, more than half of my biblical allotment of three score and ten — which my maternal grandfather used to tell me about — had been used up to no apparent purpose. That passage of time had brought me neither a realistic goal in life nor even a clear direction of travel.

In retrospect, the period after the end of World War II appeared almost idyllic by comparison. There had been a semblance of hope and potential, even if human courage was sometimes in dreadfully short supply. At the bungalow of my Eighth Grandaunt on Tsing Yee Island, I could hear birdsong at the break of dawn, see honey bees and butterflies during the day and be entertained by the chirping of cicadas and the glitter of fireflies at night. Even within the brashness of the city itself, banyan trees could still provide shade along parts of Pedder Street and Nathan Road.

Now, Tsing Yee Island had disappeared and the city had turned itself into little more than a jungle of structures made of concrete, glass and steel, tied together with dark strips of macadam. The notion of lining roads with trees was about as dead as the dodo. The noises of pile-drivers, jackhammers, car horns and angry engines polluted every livelong day; garish neon signs erupted like unsightly rashes with the advent of darkness. Now, contrary to the glossy advertisements paid for by both the government and the tourism trade, the place was just turning into a piece of counterfeit China, catering to the manufactured predilections of wide-eyed visitors, while recurring rumours of impending disasters lurked within the hearts of locals.

* * *

It soon became abundantly clear that Oxford was quite the wrong place for me to be at that time of life. It left me with too much leisure to reflect and worry about the future. Those hushed and tranquil Oxford nights, which should have brought refreshing rest, brought instead mainly fitful sleep. My mind was filled with too many memories of missed opportunities, dubious choices, delusions, defeats and loves won and lost. They rushed back like so many sub-atomic particles, colliding with one another, only abruptly to change substance and form before flying off in unpredictable directions. Could they in fact be alerting me to the incongruities and schizophrenia gumming up my own life?

What was I, after all, but a second-class flunkey serving both foreign masters and a life sentence for an ill-advised marriage? Everything was a muddle. I had accepted an appointment from the British Crown. But my salary was being paid by Hong Kong taxpayers and not Whitehall. Common sense and logic dictated that whoever paid the piper ought to be calling the tune. But the payers could not. Dr. Sun Yat-Sen had repeatedly warned against allowing foreigners to play off one section of our nation against another. Had I not now been reduced to just another pawn in that dismal game?

Trying to serve two masters was problematic enough without race and heritage being thrown into the mix. The Communist rulers of China might have their reasons for leaving a sliver of Chinese land under foreign sovereignty but their decision could not absolve me, a Chinese, from my duty to both my nation and my fellow countrymen. How could I stand with folded arms when white occupiers advanced policies I considered inimical to Chinese values? Someone had to object to cultural imperialism.

My father had to endure repeated humiliations during the Japanese occupation of Singapore. He had to demean himself every day before Japanese Army officers at the Blue Willow Restaurant, just so that he could lay his hands on enough leftover food to keep 10 members of our family alive.

Unlike my father, I did not *have* to work for occupiers. I had other options. I could quit and, indeed, I would be able to support my family in far better style if only I were prepared to join that shifty, abacus-clicking commercial fraternity.

Had the great Six Dynasties poet, Tao Yuan-Ming, not already set an example for me to follow? Had he not resigned in disgust after serving for 10 years as an official because he was no longer willing to "bow like a servant in return for five bushels of grain"?

Whenever an Emperor was weak and his court corrupt, a righteous official had to humanise rash edicts and protect citizens from excessive taxes. Simply walking away had to be an abandonment of responsibility or an act of self-indulgence. I was, without equivocation, an official of some sort. But what sort?

Confucian ethics required an official to be a *fu mu guan*, in other words, to be someone who would look after the welfare of his charges like a father and mother. I was only one of a handful of Chinese Administrative Officers. If I were to quit, one more Chinese voice would be removed from the scene. The fate of ordinary citizens would then be more than ever in the hands of foreigners and their colonial stooges, of commercial profiteers and "running dogs".

Apart from the example of Tao Yuan-Ming, I had another role model much closer to hand — Sir John Cowperthwaite. He had distinguished himself throughout his career by standing up for the interests of Hong Kong — in so far as the colonial system and international politics allowed — rather than to obey blindly whatever British politicians and the mandarins in Whitehall might want him to do.

Among his many successful tussles with London had been those concerning access rights to Britain for Hong Kong textiles, limiting local contributions to British defence costs, ending the requirement to hold reserves in sterling and gaining greater control over the colony's civil aviation landing rights. Those successes had been achieved away from the limelight and the glare of publicity, for Sir John was a very shy man. He preferred to work anonymously, as befitting every good civil servant.

If Sir John, an expatriate British civil servant without roots in the colony, could fight so hard on Hong Kong's behalf, could a native son like myself throw in the towel without a fight?

Sir John was due to retire in mid-1971. By the time I returned from Oxford, he would probably be gone. I became fearful over the forthcoming loss of his masterful economic touch and was doubtful if his successor would command either the stature or the inclination to fight for the people of Hong Kong as Sir John had done.

Moreover, the existing Governor, the genial and laid-back Sir David Trench, would also be retiring towards the end of 1971. The kind of satrap Whitehall might send to oversee the end-time of colonialism was fraught with uncertainties. It would be a period when the city would be especially in need of all the stability it could get.

Those considerations weighed upon me during my stay at Oxford as I tried to figure out how I ought to live out the rest of my life. No easy resolution came to mind. The future seemed more tangled than ever in contradictions and anomalies. Yet, somehow, through that mental fog, I dimly perceived that I was far too exposed and vulnerable on too many fronts. I decided I had to pull myself together before I got back.

* * *

In the event, in spite of my misgivings and reservations, I was to remain in the Administrative Service after Oxford until 1981. That period coincided roughly with the governorship of Sir Murray MacLehose.

Now that some 35 years have passed since Sir Murray ended his governorship, perhaps historians ought to do a more forensic and dispassionate assessment of his achievements and failures. It should be remembered in this context that every colonial Governor was by definition an autocrat. At the same time, it should also be remembered that following the formation of the United Nations, a consensus was arrived at whereby those who ruled over non-self-governing territories should do so as trustees, for the benefit of their wards. Britain had subscribed to that consensus.

With those considerations in mind, what did Sir Murray actually leave behind? Just the flamboyance of a seasoned diplomat and the warm words propagated through his public relations machine? Or improvements to the traditions and structures of a long-established administration? Did he pursue policies in the short-term political interests of Britain or in the long-term interests of the people he ruled over? He turned out to be, at the end, the longest-serving Governor in 150 years.

My direct contacts with Sir Murray had been fairly limited, though I could not avoid many of the indirect effects of his decisions. I have revealed in this volume my honest opinions concerning a number of his policies. Much of what I have recounted had never previously been recorded, let alone put into the public domain.

Obviously, others may not share my assessments on Sir Murray, for he had been well liked locally and highly thought of in Whitehall. He was elevated to the peerage after his retirement. But if historians were ever to do an objective analysis of his tenure, then I think what I have written in this volume ought to be taken into account. The people of Hong Kong deserve to make up their own minds on where the truth should actually lie.

* * *

When I left the Administrative Service in 1981, it was on premature rather than normal retirement. I had applied for it, but with considerable ambivalence. My reasons for leaving had been several. Prominent among them was my need for more money to fulfil the wishes of my sons to be further educated in North America. I simply could not afford to do that on my civil service salary.

I had either to frustrate them or to find an enhanced income.

After retiring, I took up a position as managing director in an international trading company called Li & Fung (Trading), which had its headquarters in Hong Kong. The company had originally been founded in Canton in 1906. It moved to Hong Kong after World War II. My subsequent years in the private sector will form the subject for the next volume of these memoirs.

That next volume will also detail how I met one day, quite by chance, a teenage member of the Communist Youth League on the Great Wall of China. Within two hours of that meeting, I had proposed marriage.

But it took about 18 months of hard work to persuade her family and the Chinese Communist Party to allow us to tie the knot. And it took many more months to persuade the Chinese officialdom — right up to the Politburo level — to issue my wife with a one-way exit visa so that she would be granted permanent residential status in Hong Kong.

All this may amount to another case of the ordinary facts of life being much stranger than fiction!

CHAPTER 2

Fresh Beginnings

WHEN I RETURNED TO Hong Kong from Oxford at the end of spring in 1971, I found myself promoted to Staff Grade C in the Administrative Service. I was at the same time appointed to a post in the Secretariat for Chinese Affairs with the title of "City District Commissioner for Hong Kong."

What was foremost in my mind, however, was not official advancement but the grasping of the long-avoided nettle of my failed marriage. It was necessary not only to end one of my vulnerabilities but also to arrange for some civilised break from Man-Ying and to secure the care and well-being of our children. Yet such moves were fraught with financial and custodial implications I could not completely get my head around.

On the financial side, I had already gained a tenuous independence back in 1968, after I had become eligible for subsidised government quarters. But, following the *Singapore Herald* débâcle, I had no savings to speak of. My only income was my civil service salary. The prospect of supporting two households after separation was daunting.

However, right after my return from Oxford, my mother-in-law forced my hand by deciding to leave for America to rejoin her husband. The loss of her calming presence around the home left me with no other choice.

But before I could act after my mother-in-law's departure, another unexpected development occurred. The "one-foot-kick" who had come over with the family from Wise Mansion gave notice she was quitting. Her excuse was that the size of the Palm Court apartment was too large for her to manage on her own. There was a semblance of truth in the assertion because my mother-in-law used regularly to lend a hand with housework.

Man-Ying had no such inclinations. I was unwilling, however, to disclose that the size of the family was about to shrink in order to retain her services. So it came down to finding a suitable replacement.

A friend recommended a Cantonese peasant woman from Vietnam by the name of Ah Duen. She was around 50 and was short, sturdy and barely literate. She had come to the colony as a refugee because she had relatives in the New Territories. She had been helping them on their farm and had never worked as a domestic before. But she was willing to learn. I liked her honest looks and hired her on the spot.

She turned out to be a real brick, though her culinary skills were too far removed from *cordon bleu* standards to rate a mention. Nonetheless, she could concoct a kind of Vietnamese spring roll that the boys greatly favoured. She was also good at keeping an eye on them whenever I had to be away. She stayed with the family for 10 years, till I left government service.

Once Ah Duen had proved herself reliable and capable of helping to look after the children, I initiated a conversation with Man-Ying. I asked whether we could disengage with a minimum of fuss; I found her as every bit as keen as myself in bringing an end to our nominal marriage.

British laws on divorce were by no means as flexible as Ching dynastic laws. The grounds were limited to five. We eventually decided to live apart for a number of years, to demonstrate to a court that our marriage had irretrievably broken down.

Custody of the children was another issue. I thought my wife might want to have the eldest boy, for he had always been her favourite. Having been separated from my brother, Tzi-Choy, during my childhood, I had wanted to keep the children together. It turned out my wife did not want any of them;

so I got all three. It was better than splitting them up, though I was not sure how I could possibly bring them all up.

Since Man-Ying was aware of the loss of my savings because of the *Singapore Herald* misadventure, she generously offered to move out and forego maintenance. She suggested instead that I should rebuild the educational fund for the children. The divorce settlement provided her access to the children four times a week, if she so desired. I was so grateful for her generous approach that I reciprocated by giving her free visiting rights to the children at any time, so long as she left before I returned from work. She could also have them for at least one day each weekend, or even for the entire weekend.

In that way, 11 years of a hapless marriage came to an end. It was then that I discovered how difficult it was to explain to children in terms they could apprehend why their parents' marriage had failed and why their mother had to leave them. I could do no better than to leave most of the explaining to Man-Ying. My only hope was that she would do it in such a way as to minimise their trauma.

As for explaining to friends and colleagues, I resorted to a quite ungallant ploy. Around that time, I was about to go into partnership with Fung Hon-Chu to acquire a Jockey Club subscription horse. So I told everybody that as a civil servant I could not afford to support both a wife and a horse. Therefore, one or the other had to go!

* * *

The Secretariat for Chinese Affairs had long been regarded in government circles as the main conduit for communication between the administration and the urban Chinese population. My arrival in that secretariat coincided with some major changes in its leadership, structure and responsibilities. Not all the changes, however, struck me as well conceived.

One of the more commendable changes was the introduction of a City

District Officer scheme to make the government more accessible to — and more in touch with — the urban citizenry. The scheme was based on an arrangement which had long been in existence in the more rural New Territories.

After the Peking Convention of 1898, when a lease of that territory was made to Britain for 99 years, a District Officer scheme based on what had been tried in other parts of the British Empire was introduced. District Officers were supposed to be a manifestation of government at the grassroots level, providing authoritative father figures for settling minor disputes, extending pastoral care and drawing the attention of the central authorities to local deficiencies. That concept meshed well with the traditional Chinese view that officials should act as "parents" to citizens.

As Hong Kong's urbanisation increased, it became apparent that there was no effective means of tapping in a similar way into the aspirations and needs of urban and immigrant population. It had occurred to David Trench when he was Deputy Colonial Secretary in the mid-1950s that a means had to be found. Therefore, when he returned as Governor in 1964, it was no surprise that he would try to give reality to an urban scheme similar to the one in the New Territories.

But he came up against a long-serving Secretary for Chinese Affairs who staunchly believed that the best way to improve communications would be through expanding his existing channels. It was a more indirect approach, of gathering comments and feedback through contacts with the office bearers of the 400 or so traditional Chinese organisations like clansmen groups, kaifong associations, temple trustees and so forth. Needless to say, opinions from those sources had to be biased towards those with vested interests and not necessarily those reflecting the worries of the common man.

For more than a century, the Secretariat for Chinese Affairs had operated as a quasi-independent entity, physically removed from what some had regarded as "the ivory tower" of the Colonial Secretariat. Such an arrangement gave the

Secretary for Chinese Affairs a powerful voice within the bureaucracy, for he alone could claim to speak for all Chinese. It inevitably spawned jealousies, rivalries, back-biting and personality clashes between the staff of the two bureaucracies.

The concept of having a body of officials devoted to garnering urban Chinese opinion at the street level was not flawed in theory. It failed in practice, however, because there was a dearth of Chinese officers with the right talent and of the right seniority, coupled with a shortage of British officials with the linguistic, cultural and personality traits to engage with ordinary citizens. Racial and cultural differences also separated the rulers from the ruled, the occupiers from the occupied. Many political sensitivities were side-stepped or overlooked as a result.

Yet, given the irredentist sentiments bubbling across China following the end of World War II, it was unrealistic to expect that similar feelings stirring in Hong Kong could be smothered merely through economic progress alone, through its so-called "trickle-down" effects.

As I have already explained in Volume 2 of this family memoir, the contacts cultivated by the Secretariat for Chinese Affairs tended to be focused on English-speaking Chinese from traditional organisations and the more affluent classes, that is, mainly from the commercial and professional sectors. They generally stayed aloof from politics, for the status quo was quite congenial to them. They were the main beneficiaries of political stability and the prevailing free-wheeling commercial ethos.

The common man was largely left out of account. For him, the everyday image of a governmental presence took either the form of a predatory policeman or a bossy hawker control inspector. The need for change became increasingly urgent as corruption became more prevalent and as the gap between the rich and the poor widened. A better way of taking the public pulse was needed.

But the sitting Secretary for Chinese Affairs could not be persuaded. Sir

David Trench, in his characteristically laid-back and non-confrontational way, allowed his idea to be placed in cold storage, at least until after the Secretary in question had retired in 1966.

By then, however, the Star Ferry riots of 1966 came along g and the Cultural Revolution erupted in China. Instead of the administration gaining credit for the City District Officer scheme as a forward-thinking move, many members of the public saw it as a belated and panicky reaction to those unfortunate events.

The scheme itself involved the creation of two City District Commissioners, one for Hong Kong Island and one for Kowloon, with each overseeing a number of City District Officers to be drawn mainly from the Administrative Officer corps. I was made the Commissioner for Hong Kong.

City District Offices were deliberately located in the midst of commercial and shopping areas, with frontages similar to adjacent commercial enterprises. Their decor was customer friendly. Each was equipped with a public enquiry counter at which anyone could ask for help, information or explanations of government policies. Complaints about failures in government responsibilities were also entertained. Each office was staffed with a complement of liaison personnel who went out to observe situations on the ground and to report back. Every approach by the public had to be logged and pursued to the best of each City District Officer's ability, before referring the more complicated problems to higher authority.

As Commissioner, I had responsibility for four City District Offices. My own office, however, was physically separated from theirs. I had my own small staff at Hysan Avenue, a three-minute walk from the former Leighton Road home of my Eighth Granduncle. By then, No. 33 and the other buildings along that road had all been demolished and rebuilt. My granduncle and his family had moved into new flats at Tai Hang.

While the City District Office scheme was being installed, other changes also took place. It was decided that the former Secretariat for Chinese Affairs should be dismantled, with the Secretary being moved into the Central Secretariat, as just another policy Secretary. The word "Chinese" in the title would also be replaced by the word "Home".

That change was presumably to remove from the title the condescending imputations of dealing with "natives" or "the indigenous" or "lesser breeds without the law". The Secretary would also lose his former independence and be stripped of line functions. The liaison and other work, together with the new responsibilities under the City District Officer scheme, would instead be assumed by a new Director for Home Affairs.

* * *

My new posting filled me with misgivings. I was conscious of a rising sentiment of rebellion, particularly among the young, as they groped for some national ballast or cultural identity. There was also a re-awakening of the spirit of the May 4th Movement among local intellectuals, coloured to some extent by an undertone of racial resentment. Everybody seemed to be reaching for some form of emotional or national attachment which the colonial administration had singularly failed to foster.

Any Chinese reading *China's Destiny*, written by the country's wartime President, Chiang Kai-Shek, and first published in 1943, could hardly fail to feel aggrieved by his summary of bullying and humiliations inflicted upon the nation by foreign powers for a hundred years. Britain had been one of the chief aggressors. Deep personal and national resentments had therefore accumulated in many sections of the local population. With the defeat of Japan after World War II, there had to be an almost palpable urge to restore some dignity to the nation. The colonial remnant that was Hong Kong therefore appeared to be a place ripe for confrontation, unless the situation could somehow be defused.

The big picture was clear. Right across the Chinese political spectrum there was unease that Hong Kong was becoming only a side show in wider international politics. The Sino-British treaty signed in January of 1943 had provided for the relinquishing of extraterritorial and concession rights in China but a final settlement over Hong Kong was deferred till after the end of World War II. But that settlement did not take place due to post-war power politics and the start of China's own civil war.

It gradually came to be expected, however, that when the lease of the New Territories terminated in 1997, the place and its millions of inhabitants would be handed back to whoever might be in charge of China at that time. In the public psyche, the days of British rule appeared numbered. Those who thrived particularly on colonialism knew it too.

What policy ought Britain to pursue to prepare the more general population for that eventuality? Should it retain the tried and tested imperial policy of divide and rule or should it follow the spirit of the United Nations decision that all nations ruling over non-self-governing territories should rule as trustees for the benefit of the local inhabitants?

Both London and the local officialdom appeared keen to dodge such tricky and awkward questions. Indeed, an influential segment of the China-watchers in Whitehall smugly thought that Chinese leaders could be manipulated into extending British management over Hong Kong for another 50 years, in exchange for Britain's self-assessed excellence in public administration. Later, the British Prime Minister, Mrs. Margaret Thatcher, upon their recommendation, actually put forward such a flawed proposition. It got unceremoniously shot down by the Chinese leadership.

That *faux pas* illustrated the lack of understanding by many Westerners of how the Chinese nation and its leadership had been evolving. They apparently saw Chinese leaders as just a later version of the semi-ignorant opium-smoking and muddle-headed warlords their ancestors had bested repeatedly in the past. They imagined them as essentially peasant types, with cow-dung between their toes. They overlooked the fact that the latter day

Chinese leaders had been steeled in the crucibles of protracted wars and revolutions. A tougher bunch could hardly be found, enormously committed to restoring national pride and cultural identity.

The appropriate lessons were not drawn from developments in Hong Kong. For example, when the Star Ferry riots broke out in April of 1966, the administration was at a loss to understand why a five-cent increase in First Class ferry fares should have provoked such a violent response. The Commission of Inquiry which followed ascribed one of the main reasons for the riots to the significant gap in communication and understanding between the government and the people. But those findings washed over the consciousness of officialdom like water off a duck's back.

The following year, when the Cultural Revolution spilled over into the colony and the left-wing Federation of Trade Unions called for a general strike, the government was again surprised to find that thousands of its junior staff had joined left-wing unions and had answered the strike call.

I doubted if the government had any reliable figure on the number of other staff who had joined unions under the right-wing and equally irredentist Trade Union Council. That Council, for political reasons, had not joined the Federation's call for strike action. If its paymasters in Taiwan had called for a strike, it must remain a matter of speculation how many other government servants would have acted against their British employer.

An observer might well wonder why there should be so much disaffection. The history of a succession of British acts would suggest the answer. First of all, a declaration had been made way back that any British-born subject of the Chinese race would not be entitled to British consular protection whenever he or she happened to be under Chinese legal jurisdiction. That meant that only a sub-standard British citizenship could be conferred upon someone of the Chinese race.

Secondly, it had also been made plain by the passage of the 1962 Commonwealth Immigration Act that a British subject of the Chinese race would not automatically enjoy the right of other classes of British subjects to take up residence in Britain. Implicit in that Act was also the message that should anything untoward befall Hong Kong, no Chinese should expect to find the doors of hospitality open to him or her in the metropolitan country.

Thirdly, regulations covering recruitment into the civil service made obvious that any local candidate fortunate enough to be offered a post should not expect the terms and treatment extended to expatriates. The reasons were not spelt out, perhaps because they were truths already considered self-evident.

Add to those realities the random and recurring everyday slights and insults and it should be easy to understand why locals should feel little attachment to a British administration.

The educational system was geared to a Eurocentric narrative rather than the promotion of native history or culture. When I was a school teacher in the mid-1950s, instructing classes in European history along the lines set by the school syllabus, I could see that whenever I detailed the battles of the Napoleonic era — Ulm, Austerlitz, Eylau, Borodino, Leipzig *et al* — the minds of my students would shut down like shops on the eve of foreclosure. What was the point? Had there not been Far Eastern squabbles enough to draw from? They would be more digestible and of greater relevance to the Hong Kong young.

Geography was probably no different. Why keep going on about the voyages of Magellan or Cook when similar voyages had already been carried out by the eunuch Cheng Ho and his admirals in the early part of the Ming Dynasty? Those had been completed a hundred years or more before any European appeared on the scene. Did they not count?

The Eurocentric bias was even more pronounced in the fields of science and technology. Never mind going back to Chinese sources. Any European with a passing acquaintance with the scholarship of Joseph Needham and his monumental work, *Science and Civilisation in China,* must have got an inkling of the extent of China's contributions to the modern world. The First Law of Motion was discovered there some 2,000 years before Newton, for instance, and moveable type in printing had been in use 400 years before Gutenberg. Yet little attention was being paid to numerous such achievements and inventions in the classrooms of Hong Kong.

Another key point which was left unexamined and unappreciated was the firm linkage in Chinese culture between science and ethics. In the West there had been a steady separation of the two from the 17th century onwards. That separation opened a path for those without moral restraints to turn their hands at robber-baron capitalism and creating such horrors as nuclear bombs and weapons of mass destruction.

Today it remains highly doubtful whether political leaders would ever find the wisdom to re-evaluate a failing neoliberal economic order well on its way out. It was already devastating much of the world through exploitative economics, creating unacceptable inequalities in most societies, and blighting the lives of millions for the sake of profits for the few.

Conspiracy theorists could no doubt construct plausible explanations pointing to the well-established policy of divide and rule, of disdain for local cultures so often practised by the proponents of empire. The aim would be to produce rootless, pliant, partially de-culturised and semi-educated servitors for the needs of empire. The way to achieve this would be through an education system which would dampen nationalistic feelings and induce cultural amnesia.

I do not believe in such theories because I cannot conceive of any British administration in Hong Kong having the corporate intelligence and foresight to implement such a fanciful scheme. If such an outcome was achieved, it would more likely be due to the thoughtlessness, indolence, incompetence, ignorance and misplaced good intentions of those placed successively in charge of education since the colony was acquired.

It would not be difficult to parody a conversation, say, between a couple of Victorian dodderers in 19th century Hong Kong. Imagine them sitting in one of their exclusive clubs at sundown, sapped by tropical heat and rubicund with drink, sipping their second or third pink gin.

"We've got a thankless task here, old chap, trying to educate this lot," the first, a man of squire-like proportions wearing mutton chop whiskers would muse out loud. "They simply can't do what they've been told, you know. Been trying to teach them rugby all afternoon. No matter how many times you tell them to pass the ball backwards in heading for the opponents' goal posts, they keep tossing it forward. No respect for rules."

His drinking companion was a man more lean and less hirsute. He looked like one of those Pickwickian characters who kept turning up like a bad penny. He would mumble: "One-track minds, in all probability. Heathens are all alike."

"They just don't get the point of the game. They can't see that the greatest battles in life had to be won on the playing fields."

"Hmmm." The lean man would puff out his cheeks for a moment, as if he were cogitating a deep philosophical matter. "Yes, that's a tough one to get across," he conceded after a pause. "How in heaven's name did we ever learn, never to wonder why but just to do and die?"

"Why, at our splendid boarding schools, naturally," the squire-like man said, gazing soberly down his aquiline nose. "It was beaten into us, wasn't it? Toughening our moral fibre was what they called it."

"By Jove, yes! All that fagging, cold showers, kneeling in a draughty chapel, endlessly reciting the Recessional and getting six of the best when our masters wanted some light entertainment."

"Precisely," the bewhiskered man of ample girth agreed. "Inflict the punishments first and then leave the blighters to figure out why afterwards. We all had to be guilty of *something*. That teaches us to think, you see, forces us to nut things out, though that might take some years or decades to achieve.

Education nowadays is quite different. It's all about indoctrinating the young on how to make a living."

The lean man furrowed his brow for a moment. "Yes, I can see it all now," he declared, with sudden enthusiasm. "The rest of the world do not quite understand our methods. That's why we've acquired an empire upon which the sun never sets."

"Come to think of it, our rules can be a bit confusing. If you send a team out to get a ball from Point A to Point B, the ordinary yokel would try to do the job by passing the ball forward towards Point B, rather than backwards in the direction of Point A. It takes a lot of horse-sense to work that one out."

"Is it wise to even attempt to explain the rules to the locals? Why not just leave them confused? Otherwise, they might start to get restive."

"Well, perhaps you're right. Confusion does make our jobs easier. I'll drink to that."

With that the two well-intentioned gentlemen emptied their glasses and ordered another round.

* * *

That was probably how the educational approach was arrived at. Somewhere along the way, however, the notion of education being indoctrination got reversed into indoctrination being education, which was not at all true. But that muddle nonetheless became the ruling ethos. That would probably account for the long and inglorious record of education in Hong Kong.

For those interested in the details of the fiascos and cock-ups, such as the public burning of the Green Paper on Higher Education by excitable Baptist College students in 1977, the threatened march on Government House by girl students and teachers of the Precious Blood Golden Jubilee School in 1978 and other scandals, they could do no better than to read *Times of Change: A Memoir of Hong Kong's Governance*, written by my late friend and

Administrative Service colleague, Eric Peter Ho, published in 2005.

Ho's book is illuminating in another respect. It records instances where Sir Murray's peremptory style of governance often exacerbated problems. Though soft and deliberate in speech, the Governor was inclined to behave like a gunslinger in the Wild West when arriving at decisions — shoot first and ask questions afterwards.

* * *

Given my own reading of the portents — particularly after a period of quiet reflection at Oxford, away from the wishful-thinking and rapaciousness of the ruling elites — I had serious reservations as to whether I was the right person for conveying to the upper government echelons the unpalatable truths about "the great unwashed". It would be like trying to indicate to someone not very bright that he was suffering from halitosis or an unpleasant body odour. If the words were too subtle, the message would not be received. If they were too straightforward, the messenger might be regarded as disloyal, biased, mischievous, subversive or simply mad. It was an invidious task. I warned myself to tread cautiously.

* * *

When I arrived at the new Department in May of 1971, the re-allocation of responsibilities was still in a state of flux and a Director had yet to be appointed. The Secretary therefore remained in command. At the same time, a change in the Secretaryship took place. The new incumbent was an Administrative Officer by the name of Donald Luddington.

My first encounter with Luddington was a trifle unsettling. He was tall, hard-jawed and square-chinned, with the martial bearing of one totally committed to Queen and Country. That impression was heightened by an intimidating moustache known to aficionados as a handlebar or an imperial. Such a growth was far from common in Hong Kong in the 1970s. It conjured up in my mind an image of a drill sergeant berating foot soldiers as the lowest of the low. In such a presence, one could hardly resist the impulse to snap to attention and salute.

Luddington's appearance belied his agreeable nature, however. He was then 51. He had military credentials all right. He had been an officer in the Royal Armoured Corp, in charge of a unit of three tanks in Burma during the war. He had been mentioned in dispatches. Yet his speech was soft, slow, considered and not the least bit hectoring. I was to find him a thoroughly decent, practical and principled superior, who was easy to like and a pleasure to work for. He had a sense of humour and a common touch to boot. He had a Deputy somewhere, but for reasons not altogether apparent to me, he chose to deal directly with me.

Sir Donald Luddington

Our relationship was unusual in another respect. Whereas in the past I had always worked to superiors who were readily accessible and could be seen every day — for they would be just in the next room or in an office along the same corridor — I was located in a building far removed not only from Donald Luddington's but also from the headquarters of the Home Affairs Department. Even telephonic communications were trying because we had different schedules for meetings and inspections. Hence most important matters had to be dealt with through written memos.

* * *

Before I could really find my feet in the new job, an illegal student-led demonstration involving about 6,000 people took place at Victoria Park on the 7th July 1971. When the police tried to break it up, rioting occurred, and it spilled over into the shopping areas of Causeway Bay. Injuries were sustained and arrests were made at the park. Subsequently, prison sentences were handed down.

Tellingly, hardly a single Western media correspondent stationed in Hong Kong ever let out more than a peep about the democratic right of peaceful demonstration or of freedom of speech following the forceful dispersal of demonstrators at Victoria Park. According to President Franklin Roosevelt, the latter freedom was one of the Four Freedoms that the world had given up the lives of its citizens for during World War II.

As a consequence of the demonstration and the rioting that followed, both Donald Luddington and I were summoned to Government House by the Governor, Sir David Trench, on July 16th. I was quickly pitched into the deep end, with orders to initiate a dialogue with student organisations to calm things down.

The demonstration had arisen out of a dispute concerning five uninhabited islands and three rocky outcrops off Taiwan known collectively as the Diaoyu Tai islands. World attention had been drawn to the problem early in 1970, when America announced an intention to hand over control of those islands to Japan. Chinese students around the world mounted demonstrations opposing the move. In America alone, Chinese students groups formed in some 130 universities and colleges. Those in Hong Kong naturally followed suit.

I soon discovered that a number of the student organisations involved operated under the banner of the Hong Kong Federation of Students. Since the Federation, formed in 1968, was unregistered under the Societies Ordinance, it constituted an illegal outfit. I pointed out that there might be legal and public relations implications if a civil servant were to be seen holding discussions with its leaders. I was nonetheless authorised to do so at another meeting at Government House on August 13th.

The Diaoyu Tai demonstration at Victoria Park on 7 July 1971. Pictures on this and following pages courtesy of *South China Morning Post*

保衛
釣魚台

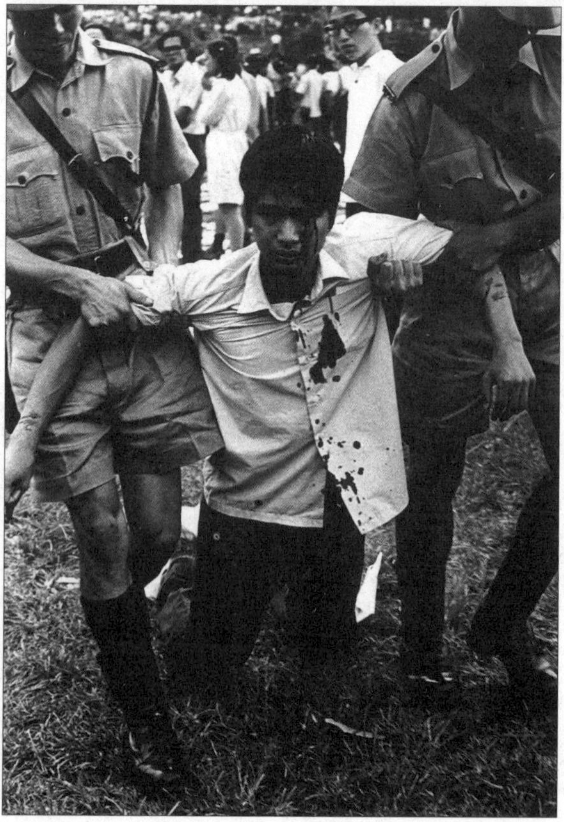

* * *

I had been pretty sketchy on the background to the dispute when I was first given the assignment. I began to trace its origins. It went back to the first Sino-Japanese War in 1894. China had lost that war and had been forced to sign the Treaty of Shimonoseki of 1895, ceding to Japan the island of Taiwan and its "subsidiary islands" as well as the Penghu group of islands.

From the Chinese perspective, historical records indicated that the Taiwan provincial authorities had for long exercised a theoretical oversight over the Diaoyu Tai islands. That had been recorded in Ming Dynasty guidebooks since 1403 and official documents of the Ching Dynasty had listed them as of strategic maritime importance since 1722. A record also existed of a Chinese landing on them in 1808, a full 76 years before the Japanese claimed to have discovered them. So in the Chinese mind, when they ceded Taiwan, they also ceded those "subsidiary islands".

To the Japanese, those islets were known as Senkaku Islands and they claimed they formed part of Okinawa. Both the Chinese and Japanese names for them referred to fishing, which had been the main activity around their waters for centuries.

Japan had desired those islands at least as far back as 1885, long before it formally went to war with China. It had planned an invasion to grab them but did not carry out the plan. In the midst of the First Sino-Japanese War, however, it did land troops on one of the islands in January of 1895 and erected a sovereignty marker there, before the Treaty of Shimonoseki was signed in April. After the treaty, it formally annexed those islands to Japan, which would appear unnecessary if the islands had been part of Okinawa all along.

After the annexation, a Japanese businessman bought four of the islands from the government and set up a tuna processing plant in 1900 because of the islands' rich fishing harvests. At the height of the venture, about 200 people had been employed. But the project proved uneconomical and it was wound up in 1940. The islands, now once again uninhabited, were then sold to the Kurihara family.

After World War II, Japan surrendered unconditionally. One of the terms imposed by the Allies was that all territories seized by Japan through its many wars of aggression had to be returned to their original owners. It should be noted that no Chinese representatives took part in the drafting of the peace treaty with Japan because the civil war then raging in China claimed the attention of both the warring factions.

Chinese of all political persuasions had assumed that when the country took back Manchuria and Taiwan, the subsidiary islands of Diaoyu Tai would be included in the reversion. But exercising control over those tiny islets hardly featured in the long list of priorities for those engaged in the civil war. There were no people or facilities there. Both sides were too busy pursuing their own battles for turf and power on the mainland.

Another of the terms imposed on Japan was that the United States could administer Okinawa for so long as it deemed necessary. The Americans accordingly built a number of military bases there. As occupiers, they followed that old imperialist practice of expelling inhabitants from any land they wanted and demanding extraterritorial rights. The latter is still a hot prevailing policy in Okinawa as well as in places like Afghanistan and Iraq. In addition, America imported some 7,000 Filipinas as sex workers to provide "recreation" for its servicemen stationed there. Displaced Okinawa families were encouraged to migrate to Latin America.

As part of that occupation, the Americans took over control of the Diaoyu Islands and used one of them as a firing and bombing range. It was uncertain whether they sought anyone's permission. Neither China nor Taiwan made an issue of it at the time. That island is today probably very badly contaminated, because of depleted uranium contained in the ammunition and bombs exploded there. But no one will know for sure until the site has been examined.

While the Chinese civil war settled into a messy stalemate, with the Communists in control of the mainland and the Nationalists holed up in Taiwan, under the protection of the United States Seventh Fleet, neither of the two Chinese regimes felt it opportune to pick an argument with America over the Diaoyu Islands.

Neither were either able to resolve militarily its own tussles over two sparsely populated archipelagoes called Matsu and Kinmen lying just a few miles off the Fukien coast. The uninhabited rocks of Diaoyu Tai, lying much farther away, were simply left as an issue for some other day.

In their contest over the Matsu and Kinmen islands, the opposing sides resorted to a fine and ancient Chinese military tradition. The two commands talked to each other through clandestine back channels. They both belonged to a sensible and practical race; no point shedding blood if some alternative *modus vivendi* could be arrived at, regardless of what their respective superiors might decide.

Thus a proposition along the lines of: "Why not shell me only on certain specified days of the week while I will shell you in return on other specified days? We could both preserve face, get on with our lives and not harm our people."

And so it was agreed. Today, there is no more shelling at either Matsu or Kinmen. Instead, tourist and trading boats ply happily between the two archipelagoes and to and from both the mainland of China and Taiwan.

* * *

Meanwhile, in Okinawa, the people grew restive under American occupation. They liked neither the nuclear weapons being stored on their island nor the heavy foreign military presence. The latter spawned bars, night clubs and cultural corruption, giving rise to increasing numbers of women being molested by Americans whom — because of extraterritorial protection — they could not be brought to book before local courts. That provided the bedrock of the island's continuing opposition to having American bases on its territory till the present day.

The island's standard of living was also slipping progressively lower, compared with the rising prosperity in the rest of Japan. A demand for independence gathered momentum and it came as a surprise to the United States that the people should elect in 1968 a leftist named Chobyo Yara as their Chief Executive, notwithstanding that Okinawa was still under American tutelage.

In Japan, misgivings increased as well. Many felt that Okinawa had become like an abandoned or orphaned child. Though Japan provided subsidies for the island, there was a large body of sentiment that the Okinawa people were drifting away from them. They wanted reunification and an end to American occupation.

In America, the political mood was changing too. The strategic and military importance of Okinawa had declined over the years. President Nixon wanted to get out of Vietnam and repair relations with China. Talks got underway for the reversion of Okinawa to Japan, with the Japanese agreeing to pick up the cost of US$320 million involved. It was eventually announced by America towards the end of 1970 that Okinawa would be returned to Japanese administration in May of 1972. The intention was that Diaoyu Tai would also be handed over as part of the package.

It was then that China came out to denounce the move as "illegal". Taiwan also lodged its claims of ownership. Those moves provided the spark for Chinese students to mount protests in defence of their nation's territorial integrity.

* * *

The demonstrations began first in China and among Chinese students studying in Western universities. It was an issue around which ordinary Chinese in Hong Kong of all shades of political opinion could unite. The first local demonstration in 1970 was small, consisting of only about 40 participants. By April of 1971, however, the number had swelled to several hundred.

It was perhaps fortuitous that the Diaoyu Tai issue should have erupted at roughly the start of the last generation to be born under the Union Jack in Hong Kong. They were growing increasingly restive about their future and their anomalous identity. Thus, when a "Defend the Diaoyu Tai Action Committee" was formed, many participated.

The Committee called for a demonstration on May 4th — a significant date in modern Chinese history — and it took place outside the American Consulate General. Notwithstanding its generally peaceful nature, the police made 12 arrests.

Those arrests somehow touched a patriotic nerve among the usually apolitical Hong Kong populace. Sympathy for the demonstrators mounted steadily. A boycott of Japanese goods soon started. Student leaders decided to hold a larger but peaceful demonstration on July 7th — another politically significant date — in Victoria Park, a public park in Causeway Bay. They had been keen to do so legally. Therefore they took pains to apply to the Commissioner of Police for permission.

The police, however, disliked the idea of anyone holding any demonstration at all. Keeping order at such events was too much like hard work. But they could not think of a plausible reason for refusing, at least not one which could bear much public scrutiny. So they resorted to the usual bureaucratic game of passing the buck, hoping that somebody else would carry the can. They told the students their application could not be considered because Victoria Park was under the jurisdiction of the Urban Council. For the application to be considered, they said, there must first be approval from the Urban Council for the use of the park. In short, they attempted a Pontius Pilate.

The bureaucrats at the Urban Services Department were flummoxed. They had never been called upon to decide a thing of this sort before. So when the students applied for permission as advised by the police, the Urban Services hierarchy did not fancy putting the matter before an unpredictable Urban Council. The redoubtable Mrs. Elise Elliott was there. They did realise, however, they were holding the short end of the stick. Being seasoned civil servants, they knew that some problems could resolve themselves if they could be held in abeyance for long enough. The students had asked for July 7th, why not first offer them alternatives to Victoria Park?

To that end, football stadia and other out-of-the-way sites were suggested to the students. They would be more comfortable at such sites, they suggested, some had seating capacity for many thousands. Shelter would also be available should the rains come. No need for disturbing other users of Victoria Park.

The student leaders rejected the alternatives. They wanted to be seen by the population at large. They wanted to arouse the public and to persuade them to join the protest.

What a pity, the Urban Services bureaucrats must have thought. The young had such inflexible ideas. But at least time had marched on and it was now July 6th. Surely, no reasonable person could expect the Urban Council to be convened for an emergency night session at the eleventh hour to consider such an issue?

The students were not amused. Their leaders felt they had been given the run-around, to frustrate their right to demonstrate peacefully. They decided to press ahead with the demonstration the following day, regardless of whether it was legal or not. In fact, the Urban Council had approved the use of Victoria Park that evening but the decision never got conveyed in time to the students. Notwithstanding that, over 6,000 participants turned up for what was still technically an illegal gathering.

The problem was now back on the lap of the Commissioner of Police.

The rule of law was at stake. The police had a clear duty to enforce the law. Agitators could not be allowed to hold illegal rallies whenever they chose. The crowds were ordered to disperse immediately.

When the orders were not obeyed, the riot squads moved in with batons swinging. The crowds scattered in confusion and terror. Those not fleet enough of foot were beaten, with six of them injured. Missiles were thrown at the police in return and rioting spilled out of the park into the shopping areas of Causeway Bay. Injuries to the person were sustained and cars and private properties were damaged. A total of 25 demonstrators were arrested.

It was following those unhappy circumstances that I was directed to open a dialogue with students and to try and defuse the situation. From the British point of view, it seemed pointless for students to be demonstrating on a political matter over which Britain had no control.

My brief was to find out what youth leaders were up to and to persuade them to desist from further unlawful activities. I had no authority to negotiate with them or to offer concessions. I was merely to calm their agitation, to report on their attitudes and to persuade them to remain good boys and girls.

* * *

In spite of the passage of more than 40 years, I can recount to a fair extent my involvement from 1971 onwards with some degree of precision. The reason was because I had fortuitously found among my old papers a copy of a nine-page confidential report I had sent to the Secretary for Home Affairs dated 8th October 1971. The reference number on the report indicated that it was the 51st report I had made on the subject up till that point.

I cannot explain why I had kept a copy of this particular report, except that it represented an interim summary in which I had made certain proposals for future action. All the reports I had made should be available in the files of the

Secretary for Home Affairs, unless those files had been removed to London or destroyed prior to the return of Hong Kong to Chinese sovereignty in 1997.

* * *

Getting a dialogue started with youth leaders proved quite difficult. Emotions were still raw after the injuries and arrests on July 7th. That created a certain *fin de siècle* air, as if the cusp of a tipping point had been reached. The resentments against the British were counterbalanced by the fears that the Cultural Revolution had unleashed. Complicating the political atmosphere were the anomalous emotional attachments of many members of Kuomintang affiliated organisations who had been chased out of China by the Communists. Nonetheless, though still smarting over their dispossession, they tended to be even more xenophobic than the Communists.

Previously, the end of the New Territories lease in 1997 had been taken as a likely curtain fall for British sovereignty. But more recent developments, like ping-pong diplomacy and a thaw in relationships between China and America, raised the possibility of that a finale might come much sooner. An unsettling ambivalence therefore rippled through the young. The British as least represented the devil they knew, whereas the Communists, consistently demonised in the Western mass media, stood as a more terrifying one that they did not know. Their colonial education had left them as unsatisfactory hybrids drifting between conflicting cultures and competing value systems.

Given such a mood, no youth leader wanted to be seen having a *tête-à-tête* with a government official *qua* government official. The various organisations they belonged to also had differences in agenda and political inclinations. It was only after much persuasion that I managed to convince a few of them to start talking to me on a strictly person-to-person basis. Once the ice had been broken, however, others were also prepared to come for tea.

The office bearers and leaders whom I met could be classified under three broad categories — those in university or post secondary college unions or in umbrella organisations like the Hong Kong Federation of Students; a small collection of precocious and overly idealistic secondary students; and committed activists in fringe organisations like the 70's Bi-Weekly and the Chong Kin Experimental College.

I talked to at least 50 student leaders during the course of the exercise, meeting a number of the more influential ones several times. Once a degree of personal rapport had been established, they generally spoke frankly, thoughtfully and often passionately.

It became evident very quickly that vast gulfs of misunderstanding existed between them and the colonial government. They entertained woefully mistaken notions of how the bureaucracy functioned and ascribed to it a fanciful degree of cunning and deviousness which bureaucrats wished they actually had. The students failed to appreciate that some official actions might merely be the result of individual ineptitudes or ham-fistedness; or based on a reading of reality every bit as flawed as their own.

They sought reassuring political certainties where none could be delivered. They predicated their actions on views about the future no more valid than those advanced by Nostradamus or one of the local *fung shui* masters. I had to keep reminding them that for more than a century Hong Kong had thrived on adapting to changes as they came. Very many more of those same challenges lay ahead. It was up to each generation to shape its own future.

Understandably, the youngsters were in a hurry. Because they had drawn mistaken inferences from actual happenings, they believed they could somehow really change the nature of their society. For instance, they interpreted the government's establishment of a Chinese Language Committee to study the demand for Chinese to be made a second official language as a direct result of their confrontational approach on the issue. They saw the illegal demonstration at Victoria Park as a continuation of that successful strategy.

Their thinking was often coloured by a romantic delusion that any gaol sentence served for their activism would automatically turn them into patriotic martyrs. It proved difficult to disabuse them. Their education had clearly failed to acquaint them to the real implications of the Stalinist show trials or, closer to home, the various rectification campaigns in China against erstwhile comrades who had not been nimble enough to shift with every change in political orthodoxy.

* * *

Of the three groups I had identified, my judgement was that the students in university or college unions were the least dangerous. Many had middle-class backgrounds and had absorbed — to some extent at least — the bourgeois values of making good, getting rich, not rocking the boat and becoming reputable citizens. Their participation in demonstrations was probably little more than a gesture to the idealism of their youth, a rite of passage, before settling down to a more humdrum money-grubbing life in commerce or one of the professions. They were essentially sheep trying to dress up as wolves for the sake of their own self-esteem.

The secondary students, on the other hand, were more difficult to handle. They appeared to come from less affluent backgrounds and, because they had not yet been humbled by experience, they tended to see the world in the simplistic hues of black and white. That rendered them more dogmatic and vulnerable to manipulation by rabble-rousers.

I could see the flame of rebellion burning more brightly in them than in many of the older students. I tried to water down their perceptions into varying shades of grey, but to no great avail. In order to play down their importance in the demonstrations, I deliberately made a point of not seeing them individually but only in groups of threes or fours.

Their radical frames of mind boded ill for the future. Unless their perceptions could be altered through the educational system or through youth work or sensible adult engagement, they could become a more confrontational generation of student leaders should they move into universities. It was a foregone conclusion that any advice I gave them to concentrate on their studies instead of joining demonstrations would go down no better than similar advice given by their parents or teachers.

The fringe groups presented the greatest challenges and concerns because they were sincere, active and rapidly gaining adherents. Members of the 70's Bi-Weekly, for instance, were by no means unintelligent people. The group had a hard core of a hundred-odd members, made up of university students, factory workers, clerks, musicians, shop assistants and citizens from other walks of life. But it was clearly an expanding organisation, along with others in the same mould.

Most members of such organisations regarded themselves as "revolutionaries" because they felt Hong Kong society to be so corrupt and unjust as to be beyond reform. They saw the widening wealth gap between the haves and the have-nots. They were prepared to lend comfort and support to anyone challenging the existing social order. They often intervened on the side of the underdogs in all manner of disputes, ranging from a strike by construction workers at the Cross Harbour Tunnel to the protests by squatters being cleared from their hovels at Tung Tau.

Members of such groups were often dedicated and committed. They would conduct discussion groups and long study sessions on specific topics in the evenings and on weekends. They also published magazines highlighting instances of corruption and injustice. They found ready favour among the underclasses because they raised bread-and-butter issues like the lack of affordable housing or the inadequacies in tackling the heroin trade and the increasing addiction it engendered. They believed in the rightness of their various causes and were not afraid to act. Therein lay their appeal to young people. They were prepared to act while the more traditional student union leaders often merely talked about social problems.

The fringe groups were not without their own mistaken notions and blind spots, however. For example, they took the lack of government response to the complaints published in their magazines as official admissions of their validity.

In reality, the top levels of officialdom were not even aware of the existence of most of their publications, for they were all written in Chinese. Until very late in the day, top officials paid little attention to what was written even in the main Chinese newspapers. They took scant notice of criticisms made in English also, such as a book by J. Walker called *Under the Whitewash* criticising various aspects of government policy. Trying to get that reality across to committed youngsters was like trying to chip away at a piece of granite with a toothpick.

One of the leaders of the 70's Bi-Weekly I had invited to tea went by the name of Mok Chiu-Yu. I remembered him particularly because a number of other student leaders kept pointing to his circumstances as a case of British unfairness and injustice.

Mok had studied to become a teacher. In 1969, he intervened in a dispute concerning some students at Chu Hai College who got expelled for criticising the administration of the college. Mok joined in a demonstration to demand an investigation into the grievances of the students. He was arrested and convicted for taking part in an illegal demonstration. Because of his conviction, the Education Department later refused to register him as a teacher.

Student leaders felt an injustice had been done because Mok had effectively been punished twice for the same offence. His hopes of becoming a teacher were dashed for standing by his principles. Recalling how I myself had been sacked from the *Hong Kong Standard* for no apparent reason, I had considerable sympathy for his plight. But there was nothing I could do except to refer his case to higher authorities.

While the government was in general turning a blind eye to the expansion of fringe groups — because it also had no firm vision of the future — those groups were catching the attention of the left-wing politicians and others. Offers of financial support had reportedly been made. The 70's Bi-Weekly group had plans for the imminent opening of a book shop to sell its pamphlets and publications but there was no indication where its financing came from. None of the leaders of the fringe group admitted to having taken funds from Communist organisations.

* * *

It would be tedious and repetitious if I were to attempt a summary of each of the dozens of conversations I had with different youth leaders, for many of them rehearsed the same topics with variations in tone, emphasis and arguments employed.

Many of the exchanges were conducted in Chinese though all reporting done by me had been in English. In order to give a tenor of those talks, I propose to create a fictional dialogue based on actual questions posed and answers given. The putative student leader would also be a composite of the various young men involved. I shall give him the fictional name of Kwan. It was significant that no female leader had emerged at that time among the youth.

* * *

Kwan was a skinny fellow, much like what I had been before my fellow student at Stanford, Mike Zinck, started me pumping iron. And the lad was clearly excitable. He seemed over-eager to get a government official within the cross-hairs of his verbal weaponry. I could read in his quick brown eyes a certain lust for confrontation and martyrdom.

"It's good that you've accepted my invitation to tea," I began, trying to set the tone. "Chinese tradition has it that it is always better to talk to opponents than to fight them. It seems students have some issues with the government; some young people have managed to get themselves hurt or sent to gaol. That is something I personally would not like to see. Government has asked me to initiate some conversations to get to the root of disaffection. So here I am. I don't want to mislead anybody, however. I have no power to approve or change anything; I am here only to listen to your views and perspectives and to convey them upwards."

Kwan wasted no time in venting his spleen over what had happened at Victoria Park. "I was beaten by batons; got bruises all over to prove it," he declared. "My girlfriend didn't quite get beaten but she got pushed around too. What need was there for the police to behave like fascists and to treat us like hooligans?"

His voice surprised me. It was strong and affecting, the kind which could sway impressionable crowds. I had not expected it to emanate from so unlikely a frame. If its potency were tempered by more knowledge and discipline, it would be capable of stirring trouble. I wondered if I could harness his anger and channel it in more constructive directions, as Hon-Kit had done with me when I was his age.

"Yes, it was a poor show by the police," I essayed casually. "I fear they're not very good at dishing out equal treatment for women."

"You think that's funny?"

"No, no, not at all. But wit is sometimes a useful diversion when one is on the defensive. As I understand the situation, the police gave the crowds several warnings to disperse. They did not. The assembly thus became an illegal one, which the authorities were obliged to break up."

Kwan emitted a derisive grunt. "That's very neat and tidy and legal, isn't it? The government gives us a run-around, knowing full well we wanted to hold a legal and peaceful demonstration on July 7th. It deliberately delayed things and then claimed it was too late to grant permission in time."

"Did you point out the significance of the date when you first applied for permission?"

"No, of course not. Everybody knows that date. The Brits make us learn their dates of significance. Why can't they respect *ours*?"

"The British are not required to study Chinese history. You can't blame them for not knowing the importance of July 7th. It's the fault of the applicants for not alerting them."

My guest stared at me from across the table and made a wry face. "I suppose it was our fault too that we got beaten and manhandled?"

"I did not say that. I was not there to form any judgement. According to official reports, some demonstrators started throwing missiles at the police. Then rioting broke out, spreading to Causeway Bay. Both public and private properties got damaged or destroyed."

"How are people supposed to react when they're being beaten, when they see their girlfriends being manhandled?"

"They could have obeyed police instructions and dispersed in an orderly manner. Or else, if they had a valid point to make, they could have made it non-violently, like Gandhi and his followers. That may not always work, of course, but at least they would have secured the moral high ground. Violence is never the answer."

Kwan snorted. "That's easy to say. Why are the Brits so set against a peaceful demonstration? We were not even demonstrating against *them*, only against the Japs and the Yanks. Isn't it bad enough that after the war our leaders — for whatever political or economic reason — had allowed them to hang on to this place under the terms of unequal treaties? Why must these foreigners now throw their weight around, to prevent us from expressing opinions on matters of national concern to us?"

"I don't think the British are against legal and peaceful demonstrations. Perhaps what they do not understand is why you and your friends want to demonstrate over Diaoyu Tai, an issue in which they are not involved and over which only international politics can resolve."

"Why are you defending them? Because you are a Crown servant enjoying fat perks denied to ordinary people? When the time comes, they'll dump you, you know, just like the rest of us."

"I'm not defending the British. I'm defending the orderliness of this city because my salary is being paid by Hong Kong taxpayers."

"But you're a Chinese. Don't you care if foreigners get back to their old stealing game with parts of our Motherland? Wouldn't expressing our outrage be the right and patriotic thing to do?"

"A wise Frenchman once said that being a patriot or a traitor — or vice versa — was just a matter of dates. A person could turn from one into the other with a simple change in the ruling regime. Loving one's country, like loving one's god, is growing rather out of fashion these days. I suppose there's no great harm in either, so long as one does not expect to be loved in return. I hope you and your friends are not allowing yourselves to be used by those with hidden agendas."

"What do you mean?"

I put on a sympathetic but cautious air before replying, not daring to go too far down that slippery road. "It is just that international politics are not always what they seem," I said. "Young people kick up a fuss about Diaoyu Tai and that might create a useful bargaining chip for those seeking to make deals behind the scenes."

"Is that the line the Brits are asking you to spread, to discourage us and throw us off stride?"

"No, no, that's not a government line. It's just some talk I'd picked up from friends attuned to diplomatic hypocrisies. Rumours have it China might be willing to play down the Diaoyu Tai issue in exchange for Japan's support for its bid to take over Taiwan's seat at the United Nations."

"Jesus! I don't believe it. Can you prove it?"

"No, I don't even know if it's true. But governments and states don't have any moral sense of right and wrong. Their concerns are power and expediency, securing what they conceive as imperative ends by whatever means necessary. But you don't have to take my word for it. As the old saying goes, rocks will emerge once the tide recedes. You will be able to see for yourself whether the rumour has any validity when the General Assembly meets later in the year."

"So the government message is just to be good little colonials and stop trying to be patriotic Chinese?"

"I didn't say that."

"What are you saying then?"

"What I'm trying to say is: Be careful and think things through. Laws are seldom perfect; often they're asinine. But they're all we've got. Legal procedures can also be complex and cumbersome but I'm ready to help you negotiate your way, if you want me to. I'm a public servant; I have to be at your disposal. But things should be done within existing rules. To do so may not make as much of a splash in the media as acting outside the law but in the long run it may be more productive. Why risk ruining anyone's future for what might turn out to be only an illusion?"

My young interlocutor snorted again. "Everything's an illusion, isn't it? Truth, justice, fair play, the whole bloody lot. The law's just a trap, to make criminals out of people who want to stand for principles. Do you think any of us wants a criminal record? We want visas to study abroad, to get decent jobs. But we are being frustrated all the time. Just look at Mok Chiu-Yu. You've heard of him, haven't you? He got a very raw deal."

"Yes, I've heard of his case."

"Then why don't you do something about it?"

"Look, I may have a fancy title but I have no authority to speak of, and I certainly have no authority to intervene."

"No authority to intervene," Kwan echoed derisively. "What kind of public official is one who does not stand up against injustice? In ancient times, didn't righteous officials send memorials to the emperor and resign in protest? Mok just asked for a fair investigation into why a college should expel students for criticising its administration. For that, he got sentenced for taking part in an illegal demonstration. Then, because of his conviction, the Education Department refused to register him as a teacher. Is that the kind of British justice you stand for?"

"Mok knowingly broke the law," I said, through gritted teeth. "People who break laws ought to be prepared for the consequences. That's why I am urging everybody to think before acting in hot blood. If Mok believes the Education Department has been wrong in denying him registration, he has a legal remedy. He can always apply to the High Court for a judicial review."

A rising note of indignation reverberated in Kwan's voice. "Who has time and money for that? Are there lawyers lining up to do *pro bono* work? They're all too busy clocking up their bloody hourly rates from rich corporate clients."

"Some of your colleagues said they intended studying law. Perhaps when they're qualified, they would go out and make a difference."

"You officials are all the same. You have nice excuses and evasions for everything, except for rectifying wrongs. Mok isn't the only victim, you know. There are plenty of others. Chan Yee-Hon from the Chinese University is another example. He's right now being prosecuted through the courts for what happened at Victoria Park. No wonder the Chinese character for 'official' includes twice the character for 'mouth'. How convenient it must be for officials to speak with different voices whenever it suits them."

I sighed, feeling a degree of disappointment as well as of culpability. "Officials are *not* all the same," I asserted. "You should learn to tell the difference. But you are also right in one respect. It *is* convenient sometimes to speak through two mouths — one to speak the truth to you and the other to speak a different truth to my masters. You may not believe me, but my sympathies might be closer to you students than you think. I want to help them — and you — so long as you all stay within the law. Try me. What have you got to lose? We are both intelligent people; we can betray each other only once. More than once and the game's up."

Kwan regarded me quizzically for a couple of seconds. "What *can* you actually do for us?" he asked.

"That depends on what you intend to do," I replied. "If you intend to stay peaceful and within the law, I will argue on your behalf within the government. I fear Fate has only given me the chance to deploy words, not to exercise power. I can't promise talking will bring you what you want; but I will at least try. If you don't follow the law, then I'll have to speak out against you. Are more demonstrations being planned?"

"They're being discussed."

"Well, you know where I stand. Please tell your colleagues and friends what my position is and my willingness to help. My door is always open, if they stay within the law. You can give them my number. Call me any time, if they want advice."

Kwan gave a nod and when I offered my hand at the end of the meeting, he seemed to have shaken it more firmly than when we first met.

* * *

On October 6th, two days before I wrote my summary report, an astonishing and unprecedented event — unrelated to the Diaoyu Tai protests — occurred. Some 300 off-duty nurses marched up to Government House and handed in a petition signed by most of the 3,600 nurses in government service demanding equal pay between men and women. It represented the first time in Hong Kong's history that a group of civil servants was to demonstrate openly against their employer.

That episode marked another instance of simply how out of touch the ruling elite was with the people it ruled over. The demand for equal pay for equal work had a long history, particularly in respect of discrimination on the basis of sex.

Some years back, under pressure, the government announced that it would seek to have equal pay between genders in place by 1975. But it singled out nurses for separate consideration. The nurses were unhappy. It went without saying that their overwhelming number were women.

The government then made it known, with the sort of crude cunning that would have made Machiavelli spin in his grave, that equal pay for nurses might be achieved by lowering the pay of the handful of male nurses to the level for women. The nurses, predictably, would have none of that. It was not lost on anyone that no whisper of eliminating the differential in pay between locals and expatriates might be similarly achieved.

In any event, the government unveiled on August 24th a unisex scale for nurses which had the effect of squeezing together the male and female scales. The nurses were furious. The general public and various social organisations came out on the side of the nurses. The result was the march on Government House on October 6th. On that same evening, the government announced it would think again.

Those who knew their Machiavelli must have reflected upon the Florentine's observation that the first method for estimating the intelligence of a ruler was to look at the men he had around him. And that insight remains as valid for the political classes of today as it had been when first advanced in the 15th century. Very few rulers, however, had the good fortune to have a Mencius or an Aristotle as an advisor.

* * *

Given that unexpected development, I thought it best to attend quickly to my own responsibilities. Hence my summary report of October 8th. I put in it a number of recommendations for future action. I pointed out that there were grave misunderstandings and misconceptions between the government and the younger generation. Many of those misunderstandings could be rectified or dispelled through honest and sympathetic engagement. Without engagement, mistaken ideas would gain root and disaffection would spread. The educated young were destined to become future leaders of Hong Kong. If positive messages from the government were not forthcoming or were being lost through default, they could turn much more disruptive in the years ahead.

But to engage meaningfully with the young, a senior and matured official would have to be appointed to deal with the young full-time. A Polonius would not do. He would have to participate more actively in the out-of-office-hours discussion groups to promote official points of view and to keep track of and to rebut flawed opinions expressed in youth publications.

It was not possible for that job to be done effectively on an *ad hoc* basis, as I was attempting to do as City District Commissioner. Engaging with the young was a patient and time-consuming business. To try doing the job while carrying out the responsibilities of another office would cause both jobs to suffer.

There would also need to be much more co-ordination between government departments. I was working in complete isolation, with no access to reports and attitudes of other departments or to the intelligence gathered by the Special Branch.

In my own mind, I would visualise a clear pattern of disaffection and identity crisis emerging. Each appeared like a harbinger of a future doom. Yet the leaders of society did not seem to recognise them as such and hence did not take the remedial actions to forestall that fate.

For the sake of simplicity, allow me to construct a simple summary, beginning with the 1966 Star Ferry riots during which one person was killed, 1,800 arrested and 258 sent to gaol. A Commission of Inquiry convened afterwards to look into the causes of the rioting drew attention to the "gap between the government and people in communication and understanding."

The following year, 1967, the spill-over of the Cultural Revolution in China brought another bout of rioting. This time, 52 people lost their lives and about 5,000 were arrested, with some 2,000 convicted of some type of crime. To the surprise of many in the government elite, when the left-wing trade unions called for a general strike to oppose the government, a large number of junior civil servants responded. Over 1,650 of them were sacked as a result.

Having been active as a trade unionist myself in the Senior Non-Expatriate Officers Association, I could testify to unhappiness felt at the senior levels as well. Many resented the government's discriminatory treatment as between expatriate and local officers.

In 1968, student unions formed the Hong Kong Federation of Students to press for some unclearly defined reforms. It operated illegally without proper registration for years. Yet the guardians of the rule of law remained fast asleep.

Then came the more massive and clearly nationalistic Diaoyu Tai demonstrations of 1970. Nurses soon took the cue to voice their own dissatisfactions and marched on Government House in 1971.

On that sequence of events, could anyone still proclaim that God was in His heaven and all was well with the world? For reasons unexplained to the ordinary man, it seemed a great many among the elite decision-makers still clung to a complacent attitude!

While those open manifestations of alienation and dissatisfaction were taking place, more fundamental changes were also destabilising society at various levels.

For instance, the virtue of frugality which had for thousands of years marked the Chinese character soon came under attack. Likewise the people's native propensity to save what little they could against hard times and the education of their children. Once the industrial and financial corporations noticed that Hong Kong was beginning to prosper against the odds, they quickly devoted huge efforts to fabricate artificial needs and stimulate consumption through advertising and marketing. Since the machines of the Industrial Revolution made mass production possible, it followed that their outputs had to be consumed to keep the cycle of profits rolling. Otherwise factories would go bankrupt.

Confucian philosophy used to hold teachers in high esteem. Children were taught that without a father there was no life and without a teacher there would be no wisdom. But the Eurocentric nature of colonial education, the decline in moral teaching through religious institutions and the advent of Western films like *Blackboard Jungle* and reality television shows created an environment for some very different and equivocal attitudes.

The growth of population within a limited geographical area naturally caused property prices to soar. That in turn impacted upon the ability of the general public to afford housing spacious enough to accommodate extended families. In ancient times, there used to be well over a hundred names to identify the precise kinships within the extended family. But with the pressure on space in Hong Kong — and not to mention the implementation of the "one-child" policy in China — hopes of returning to the traditional family structure were all but a memory.

Other measures also began crimping urban family life further. For instance, prior to World War II, building regulations provided for ceiling heights of 16 to 18 feet. But central air conditioning becoming available in new commercial buildings, an argument was advanced for ceiling height to be reduced to a minimum of ten feet. The rules were accordingly changed. But what about domestic buildings without central air-conditioning? Since the demand for affordable housing far outstripped supply, it would always remain a sellers' market. And who would be controlling the rapacious instincts of developers to add an extra floor or two by reducing the height of each floor?

All the while, the British occupying power did its best to duck the consideration of such complicated matters. It assumed that so long as economic progress kept making headway, a trickling down of wealth would theoretically occur. That would be sufficient to keep the population satisfied enough to remain politically divided and neutered.

Such developments and others left the young of the time with realities that were more and more adrift from the traditional aspirations and ideals. It was as if they were caught in a vortex of forces they could neither comprehend or influence, leaving them alienated, rootless, culturally eroded and without any meaningful collective purpose except the accumulation of wealth.

Wise leadership became sorely needed to prevent a disaffected generation from descending into rebellion or nihilism. But did the elites manage to rise to that challenge? That question has to be left to posterity to answer.

* * *

Shortly after submitting my report, the rumours of political horse-trading at the United Nations proved to be substantially correct. By the end of September, the organisation decided collectively that the decades-old fiction of representatives from Taiwan speaking on behalf of the Chinese nation should end. All seats in key U.N. organs should be occupied by nominees of the Communist mainland government. Japan supported the move.

Before my recommendations for dealing with the restive youth of the colony could be considered by the government, however, a new Governor in the person of Sir Murray MacLehose was installed in November to replace Sir David Trench. He was to serve a record-breaking ten-and-a-half-years in that post.

My suggestion for the appointment of a dedicated and senior official to further the dialogue with student and youth leaders was therefore left in limbo.

CHAPTER 3

Enter Sir Murray

WHEN I WAS IN THE MIDST of my dialogues with student leaders, Sir Murray MacLehose took over as Governor of Hong Kong in November of 1971. Sir Murray, aged 52, was the first career diplomat to be appointed to that position. Hitherto, Governors had emerged from the administrative ranks of the Colonial Service. Of course, gubernatorial appointments had always been the prerogative of Whitehall and the British government of the day. The millions living in colonies had no say whatsoever over the appointees.

Nonetheless, the decision to parachute in a diplomat to run Hong Kong at a transitional time did raise a few eyebrows, both within the bureaucracy itself and among the general public. Diplomats, by their very nature, were perceived to be talkers rather than doers. Was a talker the right choice at such a crucial juncture? A host of social, political and economic problems was coming to a boil and the termination of the New Territories lease in 1997 was already looming like Banquo's ghost over the territory.

In a sense, a talker was not unreasonable. Some cynic had once defined a diplomat as someone sent abroad to lie on behalf of his country. Talleyrand, that arch diplomatist known during his own era as "the Limping Devil", had asserted that speech had been given to man to enable him to disguise his thoughts. Only a contempt for glory, he added, could create a great man. But then, Talleyrand had also been variously regarded as an opportunist, racketeer, cynic, turncoat, weathercock and traitor. Where would Sir Murray come to rest among that range of judgements and expectations?

History was far from reassuring. Given the way British diplomats had a whole series of bungled initiatives to their names, like demarcating the McMahon Line in India, the carving up of the Middle East *à la* Sykes-Picot, the unholy mess in discharging the trusteeship in the Palestine Mandate, the ill-conceived conspiracy to seize the Suez Canal — to name but a few. No thinking Hong Kong Chinese could be very sanguine about a diplomat handling the many tricky issues pending the end of British imperial rule.

What was most worrying was that a segment of the British political class, including the so-called China-watchers, still clung to the delusion that British administrative control could be extended over Hong Kong after the end of the New Territories lease in 1997. In the circumstances, locals were unsure whether Sir Murray had been sent to lie on their behalf or to lie *to* them on Britain's behalf.

Sir Murray seemed ill-suited to run an alienated, politically divided and multi-dimensional enclave like Hong Kong. After soaking in the tepid bath of British diplomatic duplicity for the best part of his life, would he countenance the kind of arm-wrestling with Whitehall that Sir John Cowperthwaite had hitherto been doing? Or would Sir Murray, honouring Britain's trusteeship obligations, inject a fresher spirit of cohesion into a society where his predecessors had merely allowed an unsteady status quo to bumble along?

Of course, how to measure "success" often came down to a matter of definition. Churchill had once light-heartedly defined success as the ability to proceed from failure to failure without any loss of enthusiasm. By that sort of definition, British rule over Hong Kong could possibly be considered a resounding success.

Whatever Sir Murray might have been instructed to do or had himself planned to do was unknown. An examination of his record gave little away. He had done some work in China as a vice-consul early in his career and had

Sir Murray MacLehose. Photo: *South China Morning Post*

later served a short secondment to Hong Kong as Political Advisor. In the early 1960s, he had been the Principal Private Secretary to a heavy-drinking George Brown, the then British Foreign Secretary. Subsequently he was appointed first as ambassador to South Vietnam and then to Denmark, both rather middle-ranking posts.

I knew little about the life of diplomats. The accounts I have read about them, penned by the likes of Evelyn Waugh and Lawrence Durrell, and my own limited experiences with them had left me with an unfavourable impression of that entire breed. They struck me rather like ham actors in bad plays, sent on stage to deliver vapid lines from poor scripts or to strike outrageous postures. They appeared overly-attached to pomp and circumstance, often thin-skinned and protocol-ridden. Whether Sir Murray would run true to type or be conspicuously different, I could only wait and see.

* * *

Almost at once I got involved with the new Governor at first hand. Donald Luddington asked me to prepare a familiarisation programme for Sir Murray, to acquaint him with some of the specific problems affecting Hong Kong Island.

I drew up a programme which involved the Governor abandoning his gubernatorial car to go walking incognito through some of the seamier backstreets. He could then take in local realities at close quarters, passing himself off as just another foreign Joe doing the rounds. I could show him the older tenement bunk-houses, where accommodation was being rented out on the basis of individual bunk spaces on different levels, one on top of the other. He could also stop to chat with grannies doing piece work on pavements. Or to watch children playing in one of those mean little playgrounds, shoe-horned into the midst of the hostile steel and concrete high-rises spreading like plague through urban areas.

I would, of course, bring along a seasoned liaison officer to augment inadequacies in my own local knowledge, to guard against the Governor inadvertently shaking hands with a local triad boss or one of those madams operating neighbourhood whore-houses advertised, with that Chinese penchant for puns, as "one cage, one phoenix".

Should Sir Murray grow tired of walking, we could hop onto a bus or tram. He could then feel intimately the presence of the *hoi polloi*, overhear their gripes and inhale their odours of sweated toil. The experience might not exactly be on a par with Emperor Chien Lung travelling in disguise south of the Yangtse but the Governor would at least be moving among the citizenry like a fish in water, as the Chinese Communists consistently recommended to their cadres.

Of course, I did not justify my proposals in such indelicate terms. Nonetheless I was surprised when Government House accepted them without ado.

On the appointed day I waited with my liaison officer at the appointed place. My heart sank, however, when I saw the Governor approaching. It had nothing to do with the fact he was an imposing and patrician presence, standing at six-foot-three, or that he possessed a slightly comical Bob Hope kind of nose.

What disconcerted me was that the Governor had brought along Lady MacLehose, their bodyguard, a couple of press relations officers, and a government photographer or two. Together with myself and my liaison officer, all that was needed for a lively procession would be the trumpets and cymbals of a Chinese band. I could see at once that my original plan had gone for a burton. The anonymous familiarisation walk was being turned into a multi-photo opportunity for the new man in charge.

I was forced to make impromptu adjustments to the tour but we did get to talk to some lowly citizens and eventually to board a tram, with the entire entourage in train. The government photographers snapped happily away and their handiwork was soon distributed to the media.

A satirist at the *Hong Kong Standard,* going by the pseudonym of Yum Char, subsequently published one of the photographs by adding a mocking speech bubble.

As a public relations exercise, the tour went off well enough. Sir Murray was soft-spoken and courteous. The handful of citizens who got to meet him were amused. But I was unsure whether the Governor took in much about their day-to-day trials or their existential hardships.

* * *

The next initiative undertaken by Sir Murray took me by surprise, giving rise to more apprehension. Early in 1972, he decided to splash out HK$4.7 million of hard-earned taxpayer money to engage the management consultant firm of McKinsey & Company to review and reorganise the machinery of government. The bureaucratic grapevine was soon filled with agitated chatter

The tram ride. From the left: Sir Murray, Lady MacLehose, myself and the tram conductor.

about the need for "sophisticated forward planning" in "anticipation of future problems".

Many within the administration had misgivings about so peremptory a decision by Sir Murray, before he had, as it were, even put up his feet to warm his hose at Government House.

That the government machinery was musty and creaky in parts could not be gainsaid. The time I had spent under Sir John Cowperthwaite's tutelage had given me a healthy scepticism over the efficacy of any long-term planning. Also the absolute necessity for sufficient intellectual resources if plans were to stand a chance of being effectively implemented. But both long-term and short-term plans needed to spell out ultimate goals. The real question to be answered before any re-organisation had to be what the re-organisation was designed to achieve. Airy-fairy talk of greater efficiency was not enough. Greater efficiency to what ends?

For the sake of argument, if the aim was to maintain an unchallenged occupation, to curb people from upsetting the social order by demonstrating over one thing or another, then McKinsey & Company could not be the right people for the task. Far better to get Israeli consultants with extensive experience in crowd control and in imposing administrative detention without trial or *habeas corpus*.

At the other extreme, if the aim was to prepare the population for reunification with their homeland a quarter of a century down the road, that would involve major political decisions which could not be left to a commercial management company out to make a profit. It would require considerable engagement with local people clued up on local circumstances and a rapid increase in the number of talented local officers capable of implementing policies and operating the actual levers of power.

No doubt HK$4.7 million would buy a lot of management-speak, complete with a nice collection of organisational charts. But as any experienced manager would know, formal structures counted for very little in practice. It would be the calibre of people occupying the positions of command who would determine how an organisation would function.

Merely tinkering with technical arrangements without a root-and-branch rethink of the entire policy-making structure and taking into account the limited talent available for implementation would not be worth the money. Competent administrators could hardly be conjured out of thin air.

My views, naturally, came from the level of a worm's eye. My niche in the hierarchy was in the mudflats of the lower strata. But there was such a thing as the turning of the worm, which those occupied with theories and high strategies could ignore only at their own peril. Sir Murray's liberal dispensation of public funds at such an early stage of his tenure set me wondering if he had his priorities right. But I kept my reservations to myself.

* * *

McKinsey & Company eventually sent three wise men to earn its fees. I had no idea what their brief had been nor whom they had consulted during the course of their work. Had they been asked for the re-organisation to take account of the disharmonies revealed through the Star Ferry riots of 1966, the Cultural Revolution riots of 1967-68, the Diaoyu Tai demonstrations which began in 1970 and were then still on-going, the unprecedented march of the government's own nurses on Government House in 1971 and so on? I never found out.

I would be surprised if they had consulted very many Chinese officers because the top brass at the time had been virtually all expatriates. No local officer headed any of the key Secretariat branches. Certainly the views of a lowly officer like myself were never sought.

Neither did anyone attempt to answer that tantalising question about what the re-organisation was *for*. Without a straightforward answer the whole exercise would be just window dressing, like planting a new flower into the window-box without noticing that part of the window-frame had already been hollowed out by termites. And on closer examination, the new flower might even turn out to be plastic at that.

In 1973, McKinsey & Company duly produced a report grandly entitled: *The Machinery of Government: A New Framework for Expanding Services*. It was supposed to set out how decisions were supposed to be made and acted upon and the delineation of responsibilities between the centre and the front line departments.

One thing came through clearly, however. Before McKinsey there had been only three officers at the Secretary level — the Colonial Secretary, the Financial Secretary and the Secretary for Chinese Affairs. They were supposed collectively to be the voice of government. They were all members of the Executive Council.

After McKinsey, branch heads in the Secretariat were all upgraded to Secretaries, which meant that the voice became less distinct coming through yet another layer of bureaucracy. Not only would that extra layer provide more scope for bureaucratic in-fighting but it would also insulate the elites further from everyday realities. The people who had been doing those jobs merely continued to do them, but at much enhanced salaries, either on promotion or in acting pay.

A number of them were actually quite mediocre in my opinion, time-servers who had filled the shoes of more experienced and talented men, like Cowperthwaite, Baron and Todd, after they had retired. But those less competent successors had advanced nonetheless, like derelict sampans rising with an unseasonable tide. There had been a suspicion in some quarters that they had been the very people upon whom the McKinsey team had relied for material in framing their proposals.

If a stricter ethical standard were to be applied, such people would be in a conflict-of-interest situation and ought to have withdrawn themselves from direct involvement. The management firm was being paid enough to work things out for itself. No one saw fit to raise such an issue.

When the McKinsey report was completed, I was not given a copy nor was one even shown to me. I therefore happily assumed I was considered too insignificant to be concerned with such lofty stuff. But I did subsequently have to resolve certain important matters arising out of that report, matters which the three wise men had neglected to cover.

* * *

Meanwhile, I continued with my assignment to engage with student leaders over the Diaoyu Tai issue. As time went by, it became evident to the students that demonstrations were not going to deter America from its decision to hand over the disputed islands to Japan. America did claim, however, that it was completely neutral in that dispute and that it would be up to the parties concerned to sort out their differences.

The attitude of student leaders by then was turning more ambivalent. Their protests had not secured them the critical mass in support they had anticipated. The political horse-trading at the United Nations, which saw the Communists replacing the Kuomintang, had also muddied the local atmosphere. Yet most student leaders remained bound to their cause.

Perhaps a sense of their mood and defiance could be more easily conveyed if I were to present them again in the form of another made-up conversation with the mythical Kwan.

* * *

The young student leader was more subdued than when we had last met. "We went out and got beaten to make a point," he said. "But the public did not care enough to rally behind us. How can any patriotic Chinese not react to the Yanks and the Japs trying to steal another bit of our country again?"

"When a man has to struggle daily to feed himself or his family, it takes quite a lot to get him to quit work and forego pay to demonstrate for a distant and insubstantial ideal." I countered.

"Man cannot live by bread alone."

"I suspect those who advance such sentiments usually have full bellies. I've never known anyone who can stay hungry for very long. I certainly can't."

"So you think trying to enlist the masses is a lost cause?"

"Probably," I allowed. "For the present, at least. But then, there's always something very beguiling about lost causes. They often seem the only ones worth fighting for."

"Some of us have argued that way. We felt it our duty to act, to keep the protest going. But we haven't been able to agree on what to do next. Another mass rally, boycotting classes, a march through the town or something more dramatic."

"You'd be unlikely to get permission for a march when you didn't get one for demonstrating inside Victoria Park."

"We did, actually. But it came too late. Victoria Park is no longer a problem. Some Urban Councillors have told us they would support our campaign. Even if we fail, we must fail with dignity and not let the Yanks and the Japs get off scot-free."

"I'm not sure what you mean by failing with dignity."

Kwan gave me a puzzled look. "It means standing up for a principle, for an ideal, even though it might turn out to be what you've called a lost cause."

"I see. Tell me something: You were at Victoria Park last year and got beaten by policemen with truncheons. Did you find that experience less painful or more satisfactory than, say, being knocked down by a car in an accident?"

"You're not comparing the same thing!"

"I should have thought that the pain you felt, the bruises, the broken bones, *et cetera*, would have been more or less the same as being knocked down by a car. Yet, if you had been a victim of the latter, you would take pains to avoid it happening again, whereas in the case of the police beatings, you and your friends seem to be seeking more of the same. I'm just trying to understand why?"

"Surely you must see the difference! One is about choosing a side, making a stand; the other's pure accident."

"Young people should be more careful over allowing their actions to be driven by myths. There are many situations in life where a person finds himself with no side to choose."

"What are you trying to say?"

"Only what I have been trying to tell you all along. My orders are to dissuade you and your friends from further demonstrations. Nothing more than that."

"But I thought you were sympathetic to our stand. You promised you would help us."

"Only if you keep within the law, not to help you stir up trouble."

"We're not the ones stirring up trouble. It's the Yanks and the Japs. They think there's oil under the seas at Diaoyu Tai. That's why they want those islands. The Yanks pretend they're neutral. If a man happens upon a wallet that's not his and three people claim it, he wouldn't just hand it over to one of the three and tell them to sort things out themselves. The Yanks know that possession is nine-tenths of the law. So they're up to no good. If they were really neutral, they would have handed the item to some legal authority or to some disinterested third party to adjudicate."

I smiled indulgently, slowly shaking my head. "How can you be in a university and yet remain so naive?" I asked. "Nation states are not bound by what's fair or what conforms with moral scruples. They operate under imperatives like national security, civilising mission, promoting democracy, manifest destiny, high-sounding stuff like that. Their perceived ends justify their means, even though the ends seldom turn out as they have perceived them to be. There are always unforeseen circumstances and unintended consequences. That gives rise to the eternal conundrum over ends and means. Have you read a book called *America's Strategy in World Politics*, written by a Yale professor shortly after Pearl Harbour?"

"Never heard of it."

"Ah, another deficiency in our educational system. I suggest you get hold of a copy. Even as World War II was being furiously fought, the professor advocated that America should not beat Japan and Germany too comprehensively, because they would be needed later to counter the rise of China and Russia. He asserted there could be no security in being simply as strong as a potential enemy. To be really secure, a country had to be substantially stronger than any possible enemy.

"His ideas were later adopted by John Foster Dulles as American foreign policy and he became known as the godfather of containment. So you see, that is the way power games are played and how arms races and wars are created.

"Of course, the two Chinese claimants to Diaoyu Tai have not come forward with exactly clean hands. They knew that the Americans had been using one of the islands as a bombing and shooting range. If someone were using part of your property as a firing range, wouldn't you have kicked up a fuss about it? They were playing their own political games. If you want the masses with you, you will have to explain that lapse too."

Kwan stared at me for a while, and then said: "You're not making this easy for us, are you?"

I shrugged. "You and your friends want to make this a public issue, not I."

"I'll talk to the others and see what they think. If we arrive at something non-confrontational and legal, would you support our bid?"

I signified my assent. With that Kwan took his leave.

* * *

After each meeting, I reported in writing to Donald Luddington, recording the names of each interlocutor, the gist of our discussions, my assessment of him and likely future developments.

When May of 1972 came around, America handed the disputed islands to Japan, though retaining a large number of highly unpopular military bases on Okinawa. High-level homilies were naturally uttered about the need to settle international disputes in a peaceful manner.

Faced with a *fait accompli*, student activists in Hong Kong were left frustrated and helpless. Eventually, they decided to mount one big, final protest before ending public demonstrations. They decided to gather at Victoria Park, march from there to deliver letters of protest at the American Consulate General in Garden Road and at the Japanese Consulate General in Connaught Road Central, and then to disperse in an orderly manner.

The student leaders appraised me of their plans, stressing that they honestly wanted the entire show to be conducted legally and without violence and with a minimum of disruption to the general public. The purpose of the march was meant to arouse awareness to the issue. They needed active police assistance, to escort them along the route of the march, to direct motor traffic at road junctions, and to control possible disruptive elements. They also asked for my support in gaining the necessary authorisations.

I questioned them closely on their unity of purpose and their organisation of the event. I agreed with them about the possibility of criminal elements exploiting the occasion to create trouble, such as picking pockets of onlookers or breaking display windows to snatch valuables from shops along the way.

They said that was one of the reasons they were asking for a police escort throughout their journey. They had purposely chosen a Saturday morning, to minimise disruption to normal activities. They had also appointed a large number of security marshals to ensure that the marchers remained disciplined and to proceed at no more than four abreast. The marshals would be charged with overseeing the orderly dispersal of participants afterwards as well.

I asked their intentions should the government refuse their request. They replied they were determined to march regardless, in a peaceful and non-disruptive manner. Should the police refuse their applications or try to disperse them before the march, then the police would have to bear the consequences. None of the participants was out for a confrontation or for getting a criminal record.

When I was convinced of the earnestness and peaceful intentions of the student leaders, I advised them to provide as much detailed information as they could in making their applications, such as the expected number of participants, the routing and duration, the number of security marshals appointed, the likelihood of traffic disruptions and so forth. If they submitted applications in the terms they have described to me, then I would undertake to support them at best I could.

I told Luddington I believed in the stated intentions of the student leaders.

They were motivated largely by patriotic fervour over a matter they regarded as of national importance. Since they represented nothing less than the future leaders of Hong Kong, they ought to be given a chance for a peaceful protest. To deny them again would merely generate further resentments and more social alienation. I strongly recommended that the students be allowed to march legally and to deliver their letters of protest. The Secretary for Home Affairs was receptive to my proposals.

* * *

After the students had filed their applications, the situation was still viewed in some government quarters as being fraught with potential for unrest. That caused Sir Murray to convene a meeting at Government House to discuss the differences of opinion from different departments.

In attendance at the meeting were the Commissioner of Police, the Director of the Special Branch, the Director of Public Prosecutions, the Deputy Director of Urban Services, the Secretary for Home Affairs and myself. It went without saying that I was the only Chinese and also the most junior.

The Governor invited the Secretary for Home Affairs to present his recommendations. Luddington said that since I had been the one with the closest contacts with student leaders, he would like me to speak on behalf of Home Affairs. I assumed he must have already circulated my recommendations to the rest of the attendees.

I rehearsed my assessments and recommended that the students be granted permission to hold their march. For good measure, I suggested it might remove a bone for future contention if a part of Victoria Park could be designated permanently as a place where people could freely get on their soap boxes and express their opinions, along the lines of Speakers' Corner in Hyde Park. Hong Kong society was becoming more sophisticated, I added, and it would be a good move to give the public an outlet for airing different points of view.

"Hong Kong's not London," the Governor said evenly. His words fell like a guillotine, killing off further discussion on the subject.

Sir Murray was absolutely right, I immediately told myself. My proposal about a Speakers' Corner was completely unworkable. Wooden soap boxes would be virtually impossible to find in the colony.

The Governor then asked the Commissioner of Police to give his views. The Commissioner said he was opposed to allowing any march. The city was crowded enough already and it was difficult to keep things running smoothly. It would set a very bad precedent if people were allowed to disrupt normal life with marches whenever they chose.

I countered by saying that if the march turned out to be orderly and peaceful, then that might set a good precedent for allowing them.

The Director of the Special Branch said he had intelligence that agitators would be among the marchers, out to cause trouble.

I said if I could have the names of the potential troublemakers, I could get the student leaders to exclude them.

"The intelligence is secret; it cannot be divulged," the Director of the Special Branch replied.

The Commissioner of Police then set out his plans for handling the situation should the students persist with an illegal march. He would not attempt to stop it or to break it up at the assembly point. But the police, both in uniform and in plain clothes, would be in ample numbers every step along the way, to escort the marchers and to control them. Police cameramen, some posing as journalists, would film the participants, to gather evidence for any future prosecution. Traffic policemen would be posted at every road junction along the route, to direct or unsnarl vehicular traffic and separate marchers from road traffic. Riot police would be on hand to intervene at the first sign of disorder.

I pleaded once more that if the police were prepared to invest so much manpower in overseeing an illegal demonstration, why not improve the atmosphere by approving the march, while keeping all those security arrangement in place? It would ensure the same degree of order while at the same time not make law-breakers out of the students.

But the Commissioner of Police was adamant that public demonstrations had to be discouraged. The Governor endorsed that strategy without further elaboration.

* * *

I contacted the main student leaders immediately after the Government House meeting. I told them the police intended to deny their application for a march. They would be getting an official rejection shortly. I had spoken up for them but was unable to sway the government. As a civil servant, I had to advise them to abandon the march. But the decision on what to do next was solely theirs to make. They should also be aware that there might be troublemakers out to create disorder.

As I conveyed the news to the students, my heart was tormented by forebodings. The peremptory way the Governor had made his decision seemed a dismal augury for the rest of his tenure. It amounted to a negation in one fell swoop of what his predecessor, Sir David Trench, had visualised for the City District Officer scheme — a people-friendly method for tapping into grass root opinions and taking them into account. What was the point of gathering public sentiments if they were to be flicked off like so much dust from a riding jacket?

In the event, the students decided to stick to their plans. Thousands gathered at Victoria Park and marched four abreast with banners and shouted slogans to the two consulates general to deliver the letters of protest. But there was not the slightest disorder along the way, no traffic chaos and no agitators stirring up trouble or engaging in thievery. After delivering the letters of protest, the demonstrators dispersed quickly and peacefully, as their leaders had indicated they would.

Students march to the US and Japanese consulates. Photos: *South China Morning Post*

* * *

During the following week, a debriefing session involving the same cast of officials was called at Government House. Most of those present soon began patting themselves on the back, remarking on how smoothly and free of trouble the whole incident had been. The Commissioner of Police and the Director of the Special Branch seemed particularly pleased with themselves.

I could sense that the whole meeting was heading towards sweeping the illegal procession under the carpet. I therefore seized indiscretion by the throat and without any prior authorisation from Luddington tossed a stone into that developing pool of complacency.

"Sir," I said, addressing the Governor, "I am the most junior and least experienced officer here. I am not familiar with how things ought to proceed in a situation like the present one. But it seems to me that the law has been breached on a grand and blatant scale. The police have gone to a great deal of trouble to have witnesses in place throughout the march and to collect photographic evidence of the law-breakers in the act. Would it not now be the duty of the Director of Public Prosecutions to consider charges against the offenders? Otherwise, the rule of law would fall into disrepute. More importantly, the young and the immature might draw the wrong lesson from government's inaction. They might conclude that if they could muster the numbers, they could defy the government. This would be a very dangerous development. One day, it might become necessary for blood to be spilled to maintain public order."

A stunned silence enveloped those sitting around the gubernatorial conference table. It was as if I were a drunk who had somehow staggered into a meeting of the Ladies Temperance League. Nobody made a sound, not even Luddington.

After a pregnant moment, the Governor stood up and went back to his desk, signifying that the meeting had ended. As I watched all my seniors trooping out of the Governor's office, I could not unfrown my face. An inability to disguise my feelings has been one of my consistent shortcomings. I suppose that was one of the reasons why the hard-drinking Assistant Cultural Attache at the Soviet Embassy in London did not offer to put me on the KGB payroll as an informant or agent.

Of course I had tossed my stone deliberately, though not out of sheer mischief or because I did not get my way. I did so because I believed that public officials should be held accountable for their decisions, particularly when they impacted upon matters of public interest.

The march had been heavily covered by the media and watched by tens of thousands along the route. But with the heavy police presence, it was doubtful if very many knew whether it was a lawful or an unlawful event. The media never raised that matter as an issue nor did they probe into that point afterwards. The thousands of students who had participated, however, knew beyond the slightest shadow of a doubt that they had taken part in an illegal event and got away with it.

To my way of thinking, no impression should be left among them that, if they could muster sufficient numbers, the law could be broken with impunity. The law might be an ass but it was the law and it should be upheld till it was changed.

The government should have foreseen the possibility of thousands of students taking part, regardless of whether the procession was legal or illegal. It could have made a virtue of necessity by granting permission for it to be held, but with strict conditions attached. There was no realistic possibility of sentencing thousands of students to two years' gaol for illegal assembly, as happened during the 1967 riots, or of giving each of them a criminal record, as in the case of Mok Chiu-Yu. The government had chosen to ban the march. It should be made to justify its decision in public.

My intervention at Government House was intended to remind the government that it, too, had to abide by the law and to enforce it. My hope was that I could shame the government into mounting a few prosecutions against some of the student leaders. Should that happen, then I was sure I would end up in the witness box to give my account of the dialogues prior to the march.

I did not think it possible for a court to convict any student leader because each could show he had acted in good faith in exercising their right of free speech while avoiding any disturbance to the public order. They had followed all the rules, consulted with government officials beforehand and had sought permission appropriately. And whatever the judicial outcome, I felt sure that in the court of public opinion the government would be the one in the dock.

But the government decided not to prosecute, preferring to hide its decision away from public examination. Therefore I had failed twice to get the right of peaceful assembly and protest accepted as a normal for the colony.

I nonetheless gained an emerging insight into how Sir Murray intended to exercise his power as Governor after those two Government House meetings. He intended to be autocratic, to shoot from the hip, as one of my colleagues had described it.

During his years as a diplomat, he could not have imagined getting anything remotely resembling the kind of authority he could exercise as a Governor. It might have gone to his head. I have heard it said that power was something like measles. The later in life the disease caught a person, the more dangerous and itchy it became. The first inclination of someone affected would be to scratch, without realising that the more it was scratched the worse it would become. In my humble opinion, Sir Murray gave me every indication he was a scratcher.

In retrospect, it might also be said that Sir Murray had gathered around himself too many people who thought like him, that is, people who would rather swallow convenient half-truths than masticate slowly upon harder and more complicated truths. Such an attitude at the top was not a very happy augury for the colony.

* * *

Following the imbroglio of an illegal procession through the city without attracting due punishment, the students wound down in high spirits. They were delighted they had got the better of government. They soon went back to their studies.

I also returned to the more mundane duties of a City District Commissioner in my office at Hysan Avenue. With the end of the demonstrations over Diaoyu Tai, my proposals for a dedicated official to deal with student and youth affairs must have been quietly filed away in some dusty Secretariat pigeon-hole. Certainly no long-term plan for keeping tabs on the sentiments and aspirations of future generations of Hong Kong students emerged out of the McKinsey reorganisation.

One day, some months later, I was surprised when Donald Luddington turned up at my office without warning. After chatting with my staff and giving them a pep talk, he handed me a sheet of paper. He said it was a draft confidential assessment on me, the kind senior officers were required to make each year on those working directly under them. He said that before submitting his assessment, he wanted to know whether I considered his comments to be fair and balanced.

His approach was novel to me. During my 11 years in the civil service, none of my previous superiors had ever asked me to comment on their assessments. David Baron and David Alexander merely told me each year they had given me "a good report" and that was it. Mike Clinton and Sir John did not even go that far. They were both extremely shy and the prospect of telling someone to his face about his quirks and shortcomings must have been very off-putting for them. I could only surmise their reports had been fairly satisfactory because I got accelerated promotion to Staff Grade C.

After touching upon the standard bureaucratic qualities of diligence, initiative, analytical capabilities, clarity of submissions, leadership potential and so forth, Luddington's draft concluded as follows: "Wong sets very high standards but he often expects too much from his colleagues. In the area of policy formulation and execution, his solutions sometimes veered towards the radical and unconventional, perhaps suggestive of the outlook or temperament of a loner."

The draft brought into relief the differences between how a superior might see a subordinate and how a subordinate might see himself. I was not really trying to set particularly high standards; I was merely trying to put into practice some of the basic notions I had of how a public official ought to act.

I fully recognised that different people had different abilities which they could exercise at a higher or lower level. It was a matter for individual decision according to their own circumstances — except when they choose to work for the civil service.

Anyone making that particular choice ought to be committed to the public good. If his salary was inadequate or his treatment unfair, he had the choice of quitting or struggling for change within the system. Should he stay, then he had to work to the utmost within his assigned sphere of responsibility. He would not be entitled to use poor treatment as a justification for performing his duties half-heartedly. It was that simple.

Where I myself was concerned, I had not the slightest doubt my first loyalty belonged to the Hong Kong taxpayers who paid my salary. But I was also conscious I was a British Crown servant who had sworn allegiance to the Queen. How should I balance those two demands? What if some high British official required me to act against what I conceived to be the best interests of the people of Hong Kong? Should I obey?

My grandfather had also been a British Crown servant. But he had no such conflicts of loyalties. He was a medical doctor. His personal priority — apart from his medical work at a distant outpost of someone else's empire — was to raise funds among overseas Chinese to support a revolution in China itself.

I was not so lucky. The Chinese blood in me resented having to live under foreign occupation and letting outsiders decide on how Chinese people ought to live.

On the other hand, many Westerners had touched my life and most of them had been thoroughly likeable and decent — beginning with my English godfather right through to my secondary school English teacher Miss Fox, the Australians who had welcomed me as a refugee and my many American university classmates. Those experiences softened my distaste for foreign impositions, although the occasional white racist readily re-ignited my resentments.

A certain vague undercurrent of guilt nagged me as well. My paternal grandfather had committed himself to a cause and had stuck to it throughout his life. My maternal grandfather had found a religion and had given everything he had towards its furtherance. I had done neither; I had often teetered on the brink of indecision.

When Hon-Kit and Frances decided to return to China "to do some good" in 1949, I could have gone back with them but I vacillated instead and that crucial moment was lost.

Could there be something equivocal or questionable about my belated stance on patriotism? Was it intended to make amends, to soothe a guilty conscience or to improve my self-esteem in my own eyes? How could I explain such mixed and confusing feelings to Donald Luddington when I could not be clear about them myself? Admirable boss and decent man though he was, Luddington was also an instrument of the occupation.

In the end, I telephoned him and told him simply that I considered his assessments eminently fair and reasonable. The only suggestion I ventured was that he could save a few words in the final sentence by just describing me as a maverick. I never discovered whether he accepted my suggestion.

* * *

In the spring of 1973, the British Foreign Secretary, Sir Alec Douglas-Home, paid an official visit to Hong Kong. It coincided with the preparations for the Lunar New Year, during which Victoria Park was taken over for a week or so for holding a New Year fair. Sir Alec's programme included a visit to that fair. I was asked by the Governor to take Sir Alec around the stalls and explain the relevance of their offerings for the Chinese community during that festival.

It was an opportunity I greatly relished, for I had previously read an article about Sir Alec which left a considerable impression on me. The article stated that when Sir Alec became Prime Minister in October of 1963, he confessed to facing two sets of problems. The political ones, he reportedly declared, were insoluble while the economic ones were incomprehensible. What an extraordinarily frank thing to say for someone at the helm of a major Western government!

I was not entirely sure whether that account was accurate or whether it was just one of those urban myths put out to obscure the fact that his Prime-ministership was one of the shortest in modern British history. It lasted for just under one year. He nonetheless continued to serve as Foreign Secretary for a number of years thereafter, when the Conservatives held power. And by all accounts he served with great distinction.

Of course, back in 1963 politicians had not been so locked under the strangleholds of public relations minders as at present. They had not yet mastered the dark art of dissembling falsehoods and being economical with the truth.

Against such a background, I was naturally keen to discover for myself whether he had been really so refreshingly frank about his own limitations. If so, he would be a truly remarkable man for whom the ancient virtues of truth and humility still counted. I wanted to learn from so insightful a man.

Unfortunately, the time I had with Sir Alec was extremely limited, and there were too many photographers trailing after us. I was given little opportunity to ask him the questions I wanted to ask. All I could do was to explain why the Chinese were attached to certain colours, symbols and traditions during the spring festival.

Nonetheless, I came away with the impression — from the questions that *he* asked — that he was a gentleman of great civility, modesty and intelligence. What a great pity the modern-day electoral processes have failed so consistently to produce more office-bearers like him.

Sir Alec Douglas-Home examining a porcelain figurine at the Lunar New Year Fair in 1973.

* * *

Meanwhile, rumours began to circulate in the upper levels of the bureaucracy that Luddington had ran afoul of the Governor. I was too remote from the power plays in the Secretariat to know the specific details but there was talk of Luddington failing to carry out certain orders because he had considered them unrealistic. I could well imagine that some of the grass root opinions gathered by City District Officers and conveyed upwards might not be to Sir Murray's liking.

The upshot was that Luddington got "kicked upstairs". He vacated the post of Secretary for Home Affairs in May of 1973 to become the Governor of the Solomon Islands. His departure saddened many of his junior colleagues for he had been a thoroughly thoughtful and upright leader, providing a steadying influence not only within the Department of Home Affairs but also more generally within the top echelons of government. He was well-liked by many for being cheerful and cautious, always down-to-earth and approachable, and with an uncommon fund of common sense and humour. He never put on airs and attached no importance to the petty trappings of power.

He stayed in the Solomons till that territory gained independence in 1976. He received a knighthood for being the Governor there and afterwards returned to Hong Kong to head the Independent Commission Against Corruption in1978, bringing his own brand of moral purpose to the job.

He finally retired in 1980 and chose Easingwold in Yorkshire for his retirement. Some ten years or so later, I and another Administrative Officer who had previously served under him paid him a visit in Easingwold. We found him in fine fettle, still wearing his magnificent handlebar moustache. He passed away in 2009.

* * *

More than four decades have passed since the quarrel over Diaoyu Tai erupted. That problem remains festering today. Chinese and Japanese fishing boats and naval vessels have been regularly engaging in recklessly close encounters with one another. Political leaders of both claimants seemed blinded to the prospect of a miscalculation or a mishap in such cat-and-mouse activities igniting the fuse for another more deadly conflict.

It speaks volumes about the lack of wisdom in the governance of the world when two Asian neighbours, which had been fighting each other for decades, cannot resolve with fairness and honour the ownership of a few pieces of uninhabited rocks after more than four decades. Instead, jingoistic rhetoric has been on the increase in both the claimant countries.

The dispute has not been helped by outside powers and their complicit media fanning the embers of resentment between the two claimants. Whereas at the start of the quarrel America had declared itself neutral, it is now changing its tune to outright support for Japan's claim and has included the islands under the terms of defence agreements. It was like waving a red cape in the face of a bull and could only sour relationships between those nations for years to come.

The wild optimism of Prince Albert when he spoke of "the realisation of the unity of mankind" at the time of the Great Exhibition of 1851 must appear pretty hollow today. Mankind might have turned itself into some form of technological giant but its moral and ethical orientation remains back in the stone ages.

So far as Hong Kong is concerned, there has been one small consolation arising out of the illegal Diaoyu Tai protests. When David Alexander became the Director of Urban Services, he pursued the idea of a Speakers' Corner at Victoria Park. Today there is a spot where the ordinary person can go and publicly sound off his views, without having to get anyone's permission beforehand.

I imagine it could only be through such slow accumulation of small advances, patiently nursed along by dedicated public officials, that a society can acquire a measure of maturity.

And it is important for those who enjoy civil liberties to cherish and respect them and not to abuse them for trivial purposes.

CHAPTER 4

Friendships Through Mah-Jong

EVER SINCE COMING ACROSS the Chinese gambling game of *mah-jong* as a child of six or seven in Singapore, I have been fascinated by it. My paternal grandmother used to play it off and on at Blair Road, dextrously shuffling and stacking the hand-made bamboo-backed tiles fixed to carved ivory faces. I found that bewildering adult activity more absorbing than any game played by children. I was given few opportunities to watch proceedings, however, because my elders did not start playing until well after my siblings and I had been sent to bed.

The basic game involved four participants playing against one another, with a set of 136 tiles divided into three suits of nine, in multiples of four, plus four "winds" and three "honours", also in multiples of four. The three suits were commonly referred to as "circles", "bamboos" and "characters" respectively. Should there be general agreement, additional tiles known as "flowers" could be added to spice up the game. They made for bonus winnings if they happened to be drawn by a player. Such additions were much sought after by women players who considered the game to be one essentially governed by luck. Serious players eschewed playing with flowers.

Several myths attended the game's origins. One common account has it that Confucius had been its inventor. The basis for that theory was that its name, *mah-jong,* meant "sparrows". The ancient sage had been known to have had a great interest in birds. The red, green and white "honour" tiles were supposed to represent, respectively, the middle way, family prosperity, and benevolence and filial piety — all ideals which permeated the sage's teachings.

The truth, however, was probably more mundane. The game was more likely to have been invented much later, possibly around the early Ming Dynasty. It must have already taken on considerable popularity by the beginning of the seventeenth century, because the Portuguese Jesuits made references to it in their accounts of China.

The game suffered its only major setback when the Communists took over the country in 1949. It was then banned as part of an anti-gambling drive. The ban was not formally lifted till 1985. Today, the game has once again reclaimed its position as a much favoured Chinese pastime. It goes without saying that in countries with a large concentration of Chinese — as in Singapore and Malaysia — the game, with slight local variations, remains hugely popular. It has likewise established itself in countries neighbouring China, like Japan and Korea, again with local variations.

For some unclear reason, the game did not transfer well to the West. It had enjoyed a brief vogue in the United States in the 1920s but its appeal did not last.

In Hong Kong, it has become so popular that games would be laid on almost as a matter of course before banquets celebrating weddings, anniversaries or the birthdays of elders. Likewise, they would also be on offer at staff dinners held by Chinese enterprises to mark the commencement of a new Lunar New Year. Hence the ubiquitous clatter of tiles being shuffled and stacked was a sound seldom out of earshot in the territory. Indeed, hardly a local film or television drama about life in the city could be made without one or more scenes involving *mah-jong*.

Because the Chinese are inveterate gamblers and are firmly rooted to notions of karma and other cosmic unknowns, it is inevitable that an extraordinary number of superstitions should attend devotees to the game. Should a player draw a succession of bad hands, he is apt to take a toilet break to wash the ill luck from his palms. Or else he might light a match and wave it around like a joss stick to ward off anything jinxing his tiles. We are supposed to live in an age of science but there is no stopping those who believe that some things are beyond science.

When I first immersed myself in the game, I was a cub reporter in the *Morning Post,* at the tail end of the 1940s. I found its combination of skill, strategy, calculation, deception and yes, luck, thoroughly challenging. By then, the former hand-crafted tiles of my grandmother's era had been replaced by cheap mass-produced plastic ones.

I had begun by learning its simplest and most common form, known as "old style", a form stripped of flowers and extraneous bonuses. Its approach was essentially conservative and defensive, placing a premium on tactical skills. A winning hand had to be made up of four sets of either three-of-a-kind or consecutively running numbers in the same suit, such as two, three and four; or four, five and six; and so on, in a pattern similar to gin rummy. In addition, a pair known as "eyes" was needed to make game.

Each player would begin the game with 13 tiles. A winning hand consisted of 14 tiles and a player depended upon drawing that crucial 14th tile to complete his hand when his turn came to draw a tile or else when that tile was discarded by one of the other players.

A marker, rotating in an anti-clockwise direction among the players, denoted the banker for each hand. The marker would move only if the banker lost the hand. Sometime if the banker was on a winning streak, the marker would not move for several hands. The banker had the right to initiate a hand after stacking by throwing a set of dice. The number produced by the dice determined the starting point among the four stacks of tiles for drawing the initial hands.

The supreme winning hand yearned for under all styles of play would be a maximum hand known as "13 wonders". It was an occurrence infinitely rarer than a hole-in-one in golf. In over 50 years of playing *mah-jong*, I have seen it successfully completed only once. Under the "old style", the maximum winning hand would be limited to four or five *fans* or "doubles". Therefore there was no practical need for trying for anything so difficult and exotic as "13 wonders". A hand reaching the payout limit could be achieved through a number of other much easier combinations.

When I was still a neophyte, I asked my father if I could join him and my Eighth Granduncle in an occasional game, so as to gain some practical experience.

My father's answer was direct and unambiguous. "Do you have enough money to pay for your losses?" he enquired. "Once a person sits down at a *mah-jong* table, he should forget all about family relationships and ties of blood. No quarter or credit can be expected, even between father and son." I got that message loud and clear.

After I had started to earn a government salary sufficient to withstand minor losses, I became immediately hooked. I wasted no time to organise a weekly session with colleagues similarly keen on the game.

But all of us had modest means. So we held those games at the unpretentious premises of the Hong Kong University Alumni Club because that was the most economical and respectable venue we could find. We also agreed to tax each winning hand on a graduated scale to defray the cost of refreshments, snacks, meals and Club fees. The minimum winning hand was known as a "chicken". Since it came below a single *fan* or double, we decided that all winnings from such hands should go straight into the taxation kitty. As a result, winners seldom ended the night with anything very substantial. On rare occasions, all four players could end up losing!

Among friends, the enjoyment came as much from the good-natured bantering known as "the war of jaws" as from winning money. Putting down others for misfired techniques or crowing over a clever coup lent additional spice to the game.

Although all forms of *mah-jong* had fairly well-established rules, the game is also attended by an unspoken ethos about fair play. It has something akin to the spirit of bridge or of cricket when played at the village green level. Professional cricket matches, now attended by widespread bookie betting, ball tampering and match-fixing, were a different matter.

In *mah-jong*, the character and temperament of an individual could become readily apparent. Just as in poker, a great deal could be discerned from body language. It is permissible to make a pretence of wanting a tile thrown by the left-hand opponent — in the boxing ring it would be called a feint — but once the face of any tile is exposed, then the player exposing it must play it.

I have stuck exclusively with old style for many years before I got interested in the "new style" played by Ip Yeuk-Lam and his friends at the Hong Kong Chinese General Chamber of Commerce. Their system was decidedly more exciting, for it stretched potential winning hands to a maximum of 22 *fans*! And that was entirely without the addition of flowers, jokers or other easy multipliers.

The new style required a strategic approach entirely different from the one I had been accustomed to. The reason was that hands were much more fluid and mutable, enabling them to be easily transformed from a run-of-the-mill hand to one of multiple *fans*. Stakes could also mount rapidly and dramatically because of that. I hesitated for a good long while before trying my hand because I realised that a weak or inattentive player could easily be taken to the financial cleaners.

* * *

My 39 years of friendship with Ip Yeuk-Lam, the long-serving Vice-President of the Hong Kong Chinese General Chamber of Commerce, began in the latter part of 1968, when I accepted one of his invitations to a Sunday lunch with his family at the Chamber's club. The purpose was ostensibly to explain to me some of the intricacies of the new style he played, in order to persuade me to try my hand. But deeper and unavowed purposes were present at the back of both our minds.

Both of us knew times were unsettled following the deaths and upheavals caused the previous year by the spill-over of the Cultural Revolution from China. An undercurrent of suspicion and uncertainty swirled like undercurrents through various sectors of society. It appeared that both Peking and London had fumbled the strings to their respective marionettes, allowing them to behave in some demented and unpredictable ways. Yet neither side was prepared or able to reassert control for a time. Both resorted to trying to pin the blame on the other side.

An anti-colonialism demonstration in Hong Kong in 1967 during the spill-over of the Cultural Revolution. Photo: *South China Morning Post*

In that fraught atmosphere, any initiative by a Chinese civil servant to consort with a known left-wing stalwart was bound to come under scrutiny. For a colonial officer to enter a Chinese leftist bastion, even on a Sunday, would probably excite imputations of disloyalty, subversion or worse.

I was acutely aware that only a few years earlier, in 1961 to be exact, the most senior Chinese police officer in Hong Kong, an Assistant Superintendent by the name of Tsang Chao-Ko, was suddenly and summarily expelled at Lowu, for allegedly spying for the Communists. He was never charged or brought before a court. His British citizenship and his employment rights within the civil service counted for nothing. The Chinese response was to embrace the expellee and elevate him to membership in the National People's Congress.

When the Cultural Revolution spilled over, the Hong Kong authorities again attempted to expel people for alleged incitement. Quite apart from the real or fake blood being spilt on the streets, this brought personal hardships to two left-leaning motion picture personalities. One was the popular actress Shek Wai and the other her husband and film director Fu Chi.

The Chinese authorities, however, having learnt from the experience of Tsang, refused to accept their expulsions, insisting upon their right to remain in the colony. The unfortunate couple therefore became stuck for days in the no man's land of Lowu bridge, exposed to all the elements. Whether back-room deals had to be done to resolve the impasse were unknown to me. What eventually transpired was that China accepted their expulsions and, after some time, Shek Wai was also made a member of the National People's Congress.

Today, both Shek Wai and Fu Chi are honoured in Hong Kong, along with other local motion picture personalities, in the Avenue of Stars on the waterfront at Tsim Sha Tsui.

It was not difficult to see, therefore, that associating with the Chinese Left was attended by risks. I could be expelled too, notwithstanding that I was part of the civil service and a British subject by birth. Those qualifications did not do Tsang much good. Besides, my British citizenship had been turned progressively into a third grade one compared with the citizenship of those born into a white race.

Moreover, 15 years earlier, I had been summarily fired from the *Hong Kong Standard* because someone in the administration apparently did not like some of the articles I had written. My brother Francis had fared worse in a similar situation in Singapore. All kinds of pressure could be exerted behind the scenes. The Leviathan of the modern state knew no bounds. Those who objected to dastardly or underhanded deeds had little option except to resign, as some did during the Suez crisis and the Iraq invasion. Others took to blowing the whistle, as Chelsea Manning and Edward Snowden did more recently.

Against such realities, the prudent man had to hesitate. I doubted if I would be expelled; I was simply too insignificant. In addition, I had done nothing that the government could show to be disloyal. I might be asked to resign on the grounds I had turned into a security risk. That would mean losing my iron rice bowl and starting all over again, with three young children in tow. Not a pleasant prospect but one I could live with.

Yet, I could not in good conscience fold my arms and watch from the sidelines when I believed I could make a contribution towards a more harmonious Hong Kong. The British were certainly not about to help bring Chinese citizens of different political persuasions together. Rather the reverse. Since my wages were being paid by local taxpayers of all political persuasions, I felt it my duty to do what I could to foster reconciliation and social harmony.

At the same time, I could not be oblivious to the other side of the coin. Should I venture into the Chinese General Chamber, how would the other stalwarts react — apart from Yeuk-Lam? Would I be accepted or would I be shunned as an interloper, a colonial running-dog?

After all, one of their more distinguished members, Tong Ping-Tat, was serving a sentence in Stanley Prison because the British had considered him guilty of participating in an illegal assembly. Why should they want to have anything to do with me? What had I to offer? They had time on their side, safe in the knowledge that when the chips were down they had the kind of political and economic clout that counted. They could afford to wait and be indifferent to what the British might think.

Yeuk-Lam's companies, for instance, held the monopolies for the wholesale importation of both vegetables and eggs from China. Others had different monopolies and not a few occupied significant official positions in the mainland. Their connections would be invaluable for the well-being of the city. But they could hardly be reached by expatriate officials. Yet if I were to initiate contact under my own steam, there was no telling how my superiors would react.

After that muddled imitation of Hamlet, I decided to chance entering the left-wing bastion. Nothing ventured, nothing gained. I made for the sixth floor, which consisted of two small fixed private dining-rooms and a large hall. The latter could be segmented into smaller units through the use of moveable panels. A name plate on the door of one of the two fixed rooms indicated it had been reserved under the name of Ip Yeuk-Lam.

Upon entering, I was greeted heartily by a smiling host. His jet black hair, immaculately combed, gave him the appearance of a man far younger than his fifty-odd years. I was swiftly introduced to his wife, Suze, a matronly figure confident of the social position she had attained through long years of voluntary work in various women's organisations. One lazy eye required her to use a pair of glasses.

The youngest of their three sons, Ip Shing-Kwan, was also there with his charming and delightful wife, Maureen. Shing-Kwan was a gynaecologist, recently qualified, and his wife was a nurse. Maureen was to prove in later years to be one of the most consistently filial Chinese daughters-in-law I have ever met. Another two Chinese guests from overseas were present. I have forgotten their names, however, because our paths never crossed again.

* * *

"I hope you wouldn't mind an ordinary family lunch," Yeuk-Lam said as we took our seats around the table.

"Suits me down to the ground," I replied. "Have missed decent home cooking for a very long time. My servant is hopeless and my wife doesn't cook."

"Why haven't you brought your missus and your children?"

"They've committed themselves to another outing. Next time."

When the food came, I found it consisted of a congee accompanied by dishes of fried noodles, a seasoned chicken, a large helping of stir-fried seasonal vegetables and some Chinese doughnuts. Because of the great number of Sunday lunches I subsequently had with the Ip family, I cannot now remember the kind of congee served up on that particular day. It would have been one of the standard ones, made with salted pork and preserved eggs or with legs of frogs or perhaps with slices of fish or chicken or other ingredients.

The food tasted so delicious and well-prepared that I was reminded of the meals I had ages ago, served up by the amazing hunchbacked servant, Ah Sei. I could not help remarking that their quality reminded me of meals I had when I was a small boy in Singapore.

Yeuk-Lam chuckled. "Can you figure out why the dishes here taste so much like home-cooking?"

I shook my head. "All I can say is that they're superb. I love them."

"The kitchen here is forbidden to use monosodium glutamate. The natural flavours of food therefore come through better. There's too much eating in restaurants in this town. Taste buds get ruined as a result."

"How true!" I exclaimed.

At the same moment it occurred to me that the kitchen staff of the Chinese General Chamber Club must be security vetted too. After all, a great many mainland dignitaries and delegations ate there. I was reminded of the remark dropped by the Soviet Assistant Cultural Attache in London, about how much safer it was to eat among friends!

Over subsequent decades, I was to marvel over the consistently high standard of dishes the kitchen produced for our *mah-jong* dinners. The seasonal soups — be they sea turtle or snake, or herbal ones to cool the blood in summer or fortify the body in winter — would always be prepared to perfection. And the steamed whole fish, which was a standard dish, would always be done to a turn.

As I write today and think of the leftovers I now have to make do for dinner — with the aid of a microwave oven — I cannot help my mouth watering over the delightful repasts of yesteryears.

* * *

After lunch, and after the other partakers in the meal had dispersed, Yeuk-Lam handed me a sheet setting out all the possible permutations for gaining doubles in new style *mah-jong*. At first sight they appeared frightening, until I discovered it was not a case of progressive doubling for 22 times. Contrary to the old style, where a player could make game with a "chicken" hand, the way that Yeuk-Lam and his companions played with required a minimum of three *fans* to make a winning hand. The doubling started only after that point. Furthermore, there was a cut-off point after 10 *fans*. A hand worth 11 or 12 *fans* would still be paid out at the same level as for 10. Doubling the pay-out again would only occur when a hand reached 14 *fans*. There were similar cut off points at 18 *fans* and 22 *fans*.

Yeuk-Lam told me he had a game starting at 3.00 p.m. and I was welcome to stay and watch. I did so. It appeared the players also practised taxing each winning hand to pay for the food and the use of the premises, just as my Thursday group had done at the Hong Kong University Alumni Club. Although the stakes being played were reasonable, they still came to more than I could afford to lose, even with my acting pay as Assistant Economic Secretary. On the other occasions Yeuk-Lam had invited me to dine with the players, I merely confined myself to the meal and watching the game.

By being around, I got to meet a number of left-wing personalities and to develop some important friendships. Apart from Yeuk-Lam, I got along well with Wang Kuan-Cheng, who had been elected President of the Chinese General Chamber in 1968. He was not a *mah-jong* player, however. I also made friends with H.T. Liu, a shipping magnate who had learnt from the British the advantages of flying flags of convenience on his vessels.

Both men were from Shanghai, although Wang was a native of Jiangsu. He had arrived in the colony in the late 1940s and had bought a large granite quarry at what was then a quite underdeveloped North Point. When the granite was exhausted by the successive building booms, he was left with an invaluable stretch of prime real estate the size of a city block right smack along King's Road. He subsequently became an influential member of the Chinese People's Political Consultative Conference.

Liu was thick with an intimate circle around a then rising political star in the mainland called Jiang Zemin. Jiang subsequently rose to the Politburo in 1983, the Mayorship of Shanghai in 1985 and then, following the Tienanmen upheavals in 1989, the General Secretaryship of the Chinese Communist Party. He was President of the country from 1993 to 2003.

Liu was a short, impish and jolly fellow, standing a shade under five-foot-three. He knew no English and, apart from his native tongue and Mandarin, he could only manage a rather fractured kind of Cantonese. At the Chinese General Chamber Club he was generally referred to by the Cantonese version of his name. It was Lau Hao-Ching. Among the *mah-jong* fraternity, however, he was addressed simply as Uncle Lau.

He was a fiend when it came to *mah-jong*. He would happily play every night if given half a chance. After China had opened up in the 1980s, he renovated a mansion in the former French Concession in Shanghai and fitted it out with a *mah-jong* room. He kept inviting Yeuk-Lam and myself and another regular player to go as his guests to Shanghai, so that we could spend an entire week playing every day. None of us could take him up on it, however, because none could spare the time.

From left: Ip Yeuk-Lam, H.T. Liu and myself

Wang, Lau and Yeuk-Lam all turned out to be stout and steadfast friends. Fifteen years later, when I was forced to pick a fight with the Provincial Government of Jiangsu, and in particular with the apparatchiks in the city of Nantong, they all rallied to my support and carried the fight to Politburo members in Peking.

Surprisingly, I prevailed in the end, in a manner of speaking. It had been mainly due to their support and the support of their connections. But the latent humanity in the hearts of many of my countrymen — even when they describe themselves as members of the Communist Party — was also an important factor.

In achieving my objective in that row, I gained myself not only a beautiful woman as a wife but also an extremely likeable failed Communist as a father-in-law. He was an Assistant Manager in a local government organisation responsible for determining and allocating quotas for fuel oil to factories and industrial organisations. He had twice applied to join the Communist Party but he was rejected on both occasions because he was deemed not to be "red" enough.

Furthermore, in marrying his daughter in China, I acquired a slew of interesting, intelligent and genial card-carrying Communist relatives. But those would be stories to be recounted in the next volume of these memoirs.

* * *

Yeuk-Lam had been very frank and open in his dealings with me. He made no secret of the fact he found it difficult — quite apart from the impediments of language — to engage openly with responsible British colonial officials. There were simply too many suspicions and blind spots on both sides. I echoed his sentiments.

Because of our mutual openness, it did not take me long to gain an understanding of his character. He was basically an astute, dedicated and modest man who wanted to do his best for both his country and for the Hong Kong community. The city was his home, although he had been prudent enough to keep a bolt-hole in Vancouver, where his eldest son also had a home.

He was an able administrator and immensely popular with both the membership of the Chinese General Chamber and with mainland officialdom. Both had urged him repeatedly to run for the presidency of the Chamber but he had always declined. He did not relish the limelight, preferring to bear the political and administrative burdens of that organisation behind the scenes. Thus he remained its longest serving Vice-President. In that capacity, I found him a very reliable sounding-board on left-wing developments both locally and across the border.

He had an office at the Chamber which he attended religiously every day. The entire staff of the organisation looked to him for day-to-day directions. The New China News Agency, which served as the *de facto* Chinese government representative in Hong Kong, trusted him enough to brief him regularly on the evolving political lines. He supervised most of the arrangements for visiting mainland bigwigs to the Chamber. But he always left photo opportunities to others.

Early on in our relationship, he asked me for a minor favour. Apparently the then Director of Urban Services, an expatriate Administrative Officer, was due for retirement and Chinese etiquette required the monopoly importers of Chinese foodstuff using Urban Services facilities to host a farewell dinner for him.

"You know how it is," Yeuk-Lam said. "Most of us don't speak English and the few who do are very *luk-luk kuk-kuk*. I need someone to keep the chit-chat going. Otherwise there will be dreadful silences and the dinner will drag."

"I've not had much dealings with the Urban Services," I said. "I hardly know the departing Director. But if you think my presence will help, I'd gladly come."

The dinner was duly held at the Chinese General Chamber Club with a table for 12 people. The conversation was banal in the extreme. It consisted essentially of exchanges of courtesies, good wishes for a happy retirement and thanks for the courtesy of the farewell gesture.

The location of the Director's retirement home was touched upon but he said his wife had not yet decided whether it ought to be in Surrey or Devon. That led to some generalised talk about weather conditions in various parts of Britain, such as Cornwall and East Anglia, where other expatriates had retired. I acted as no more than an interpreter throughout.

When that meal was over, I thought that was the end of the matter. But about 10 days later, I received a telephone call from the Defence Secretary.

"Why haven't you filed your report on your meeting with a left-wing organisation?" the Defence Secretary demanded.

He was referring to some rules in Security Regulations which required any officer meeting with officials from a left-wing organisation to report on the names of all those attending and to detail who said what to whom.

I was baffled. "I can't recall any substantive meeting with a single left-wing organisation recently," I replied.

The Defence Secretary then cited the date of the dinner and the names of some of those present. He then cited the chapter and verse of Security Regulations. Apparently the departing Director of Urban Services, being an exemplary bureaucrat, had filed a report fingering me among the attendees.

"That wasn't a meeting," I protested. "It was just a social occasion, a farewell dinner. The people were essentially importers of Chinese foodstuff, a collection of ordinary businessmen and not officials or politicians. Most of the conversation was about the suitability of the weather in various parts of Britain for retirement. No information was ever passed which could not be readily found in any tourist brochure.

"If you're worried about Chinese Communists planting sleeper cells in Britain or myself becoming an oriental version of Burgess and Maclean, I can assure you that nothing was raised about the weather at GCHQ in Cheltenham or about the possible locations of MI-5 or 6 sub-stations. If you want me to confirm all this in writing, I'll do so."

"Oh, never mind," the Defence Secretary said, wanly. "Just remember for the future that regulations *are* regulations."

I supposed that must have been just another of the many black marks in my dossier. I could hardly imagine why such a senior and highly paid official should busy himself with such trivia.

* * *

I was promoted to Staff Grade C in the Administrative Service in March of 1971, although an announcement was not made till July, after I had assumed the post of City District Commissioner for Hong Kong Island. It implied that my cheeky exchange with the Defence Secretary had not done as much damage as I had feared. That eased my mind.

My promotion — which commanded the magnificent salary of $6,800 per month — left me with sufficient financial leeway to try my hand at new style *mah-jong*. This was especially so since I had separated from my wife and no longer had to provide her with pocket money. I kept up, nonetheless, the weekly old style game with my civil service colleagues.

Having observed the games at the Chinese General Chamber crowd since 1968, I had picked up some pretty shrewd ideas about how the game should be played. More importantly, I had sized up the strengths and weaknesses of most of the regulars. Some were long-time China traders, committed to the mainland because of business considerations rather than political ones. But there was also a number of young turks who smelt opportunities long before the country was ready to open up. They were seeking connections and intelligence on out-of-the-way localities where suitable factories could be built or joint ventures launched.

An occasional carpetbagger, after a quick kill, would also sometimes try to ingratiate himself into the *mah-jong* circle. The rascal's intention to exploit the lack of capitalist savvy among Communist cadres would soon be exposed and he would be given short shrift.

Among the regulars, Yeuk-Lam was, without doubt, the oldest and most expert player. He commanded an excellent defensive game, of the kind my cousin, Chau Yiu-Hung, had taught me when I first started.

Uncle Lau was a persistent risk-taker. He always fell for the excitement of building the biggest hand possible, regardless of the tempo of the play among other players. The game would often be over before he could get anywhere near success. But he had a happy-go-lucky way of treating success or failure with indifference. He was about three years younger than Yeuk-Lam.

Another regular player I developed a strong liking and affection for was a retired banker named Lo Yuk-Chuen. He was in fact an old friend of Yeuk-Lam's. They both lived in the same apartment block in Bowen Road and would take a taxi home together after a game, that being the simplest way since the nearest car park to the Chamber was a fair walk away.

Lo's family had owned one of the 101 licensed banks which existed in Hong Kong at the end of World War II. Lo Yuk-Chuen had worked for most of his life at the bank. He was the sixth child in his family. Although he was a year younger than Yeuk-Lam, all his friends followed his younger siblings by addressing him as "Sixth Eldest Brother".

He was a jolly and loquacious fellow, who dressed immaculately like an English country squire, in chequered fawn shirts with a jacket and tie. His shoes were custom made.

He had a weakness for branded antique timepieces, like those made by Patek Philippe, Constantine, Audemars Piguet, TAG Heuer and others. He apparently had an enormous collection, for he confessed to having to spend an hour each day winding them up and selecting one to wear for that day.

He would lose me, however, once he started explaining what a *Contrôle Officiel Suisse des Chronomètres* certification meant or how sapphire-on-steel had a lower coefficient of friction compared with steel-on-steel. I was glad I did not have to concern myself with such refinements; my inexpensive Japanese quartz told the time quite adequately.

Lo, like myself at that time, was a cigar smoker. At our *mah-jong* games, we would each normally light up a cigar after dinner. Yeuk-Lam used to smoke but had given it up years earlier. Uncle Lau did not smoke but he had an extraordinary fondness for the aroma of burning cigars. He would from time to time present both Sixth Eldest Brother and myself with fine Cuban cigars so that he could enjoy the smell while we smoked. The three of them became my favourite *mah-jong* partners.

Sixth Eldest Brother had another eccentricity. I discovered that every time he went out and about, his pockets would be stuffed with bank notes in 500 and 1,000 dollar denominations, amounting to as much as $200,000.

Some of us were naturally concerned over his being mugged. But he explained it was precisely for that reason that he carried so much cash. He did not care about money. He had a defective hip which impeded his movements and his main concern was that he should not be physically harmed. Should a mugger tackle him, he intended to toss those banknotes into the air as quickly as possible. The prospective robber would be so busy gathering them that he would have time to make his less than swift get-away, before any mugger could begin to think of harming him.

It followed that Sixth Eldest Brother was generous to a fault. The attendants at our meals and the night watchmen of the Chinese General Chamber building all loved it whenever he played *mah-jong*. They could always count on generous tips.

* * *

One night, when I went home after a game, I was surprised to find Ah Duen waiting up for me. Normally, she would have retired to her own quarters once the boys had gone to bed at 9.00 p.m. and after the dinner things had been tidied up.

She told me she had waited up to tell me that she had found my youngest son, Tien-Kit, crying by himself in a corner of the dining room that afternoon. She asked him why he was crying and he said because nobody loved him. He said that his mother loved his eldest brother and his father loved his second brother but no one loved him. She thought I should know that. She had waited up for me on that account.

I thanked her and sent her off to bed.

That night, as I lay wide-eyed in bed, I tried to figure out how to deal with the situation. What Tien-Kit believed was certainly not entirely true. But I did not know how to get that message across effectively. I had never been very good with children and my own upbringing had given me few examples to follow.

Both my father and my grandfather had never been very demonstrative with children. They had tended to regard rearing them as a province best left to womenfolk. I might have fallen a bit into that attitude myself. The trouble was that I had been separated from my mother at the age of five, so I did not have enough exposure to her. Such memory as I could retain of her till I was 18 centred upon her look of suppressed irritation because I was always asking too many foolish questions.

My father had been like a remote god, a deliverer of scoldings and punishments, but never of an encouraging word. Throughout my life, he had never so much as put an arm across my shoulders. I had noted that his charm and his witty remarks had all seemed reserved for other adults and not for children. Perhaps he had intended me to learn the harder lessons in life through such observations. I was never sure. In any case, it had been I, late in my teens, who had taken the initiative to put my arm around his shoulders. He had appeared pleased when I made that gesture.

It was against such an inadequate background that I tried the following day to reassure Tien-Kit. I took him aside after dinner and told him what Ah Duen had recounted to me.

I then said he had been completely mistaken in his perceptions. I could not speak for his mother, but so far as I was concerned, he was the son I loved most, although I readily admitted I had found it difficult to give voice to that fact or to demonstrate it. One should avoid taking overt acts or spoken words as expressions of genuine love.

It was true that his mother devoted a lot of attention to his eldest brother. But that was because his brother had suffered seriously from asthma since birth. He also had a recurring series of other health and dental problems. I had given more attention to his second brother because he was quick-tempered and bull-headed, frequently at loggerheads with his elder brother and getting into trouble in one way or another at school.

Tien-Kit himself, on the other hand, had always been sweet-natured and accommodating, giving me no cause for worry. He always fell in easily with whatever his brothers wanted to do. His school work had also been fairly passable. My lack of attention to him did not mean I did not care for him. Quite the contrary. Because he was turning out just the way I would like him to, I saw no need to be unduly concerned over him.

There were many things vital to an individual to which that individual paid scant attention, until something went wrong. For example, the heart, the lungs, the kidneys and the other internal organs were all vital. But, unless they acted up, everybody took their smooth functioning for granted. No one would tell his heart and his other organs every day how much he appreciated them. Their importance was a given.

Some of the deepest truths could often only be intuited and felt, without the use of words or gestures. The accumulated experiences of life would lead a person to discover eventually what was actually true or false.

I was uncertain how much of what I had been trying to convey had been taken in by my eight-year-old son and, if taken in, whether he believed any of it at all. He hardly said a word after I had finished. So I just patted him on the shoulder and gave his upper arm a squeeze. That was the best I could manage. And what I had said about my feelings towards him was the truth.

* * *

In October of 1973, the world was astounded by an oil embargo imposed by the Organisation of Arab Petroleum Exporting Countries on the United States, Britain, Canada, Japan and the Netherlands for their support of Israel in the six-day Yom Kippur War. The price of a barrel of crude oil jumped fourfold and the fallout reverberated around the world. In America petrol stations were told to stop selling petrol on weekends while in Britain the then Prime Minister, Ted Heath, urged families to heat only one room in their homes that winter.

Hong Kong was not spared. Being a relatively small consumer, it had no leverage with the oil companies, known collectively as the Seven Sisters, when they imposed quotas on all their customers.

Cutting usage was the only way to reduce consumption. But such a move was not easy to achieve and quite harmful for the colony's economy. The local power stations depended on oil and many factories needed electricity to operate around the clock. Neon signs were ordered to be switched off to save fuel and that in turn adversely affected bars, night clubs and other places for evening entertainment. Long-haul airlines started cutting back on services to the territory because there was no assurance their planes would be able to secure enough aviation fuel for their return journeys. That impacted upon trade and tourism.

Mike Clinton was swiftly appointed as Deputy Colonial Secretary (Special Duties) to tackle the crisis.

The city darkened noticeably by night. The unaccustomed gloom in which my *mah-jong* partners and I found ourselves when we made our way home depressed us. It had never occurred to us before that we would miss the garish neon lights touting the excesses of our consumerist society. Yet we did. The risk of being mugged loomed larger upon our collective consciousness, especially for the last one left waiting for a taxi in the ill-lit and near-deserted streets. Being the youngest, that last one was usually myself.

As City District Commissioner for Hong Kong, I had no direct responsibility for dealing with the crisis, apart from urging citizens to economise on lighting and electricity.

It occurred to me, however, that one of the people I had become acquainted with at the Chinese General Chamber had good connections with cadres in the Chinese oil and gas sector. It might be possible for me, as an individual, to probe for possible help from China in a way that the Hong Kong government could not — because of the considerations of political rectitude and face.

I reasoned that China was a country with enormous energy requirements. For that reason, it had to have considerable strategic fuel reserves. If a tiny fraction of that reserve could be diverted to Hong Kong, then the local shortage could be virtually solved.

In line with that thinking, I bounced the idea off the person I knew. If China could come to Hong Kong's assistance when the free market mechanism of neoliberal capitalism was failing, it would be a timely demonstration of the Motherland's concern for the well-being of its compatriots, I stressed. It could win hearts and minds.

My contact — who shall remain nameless — thought it a good idea and agreed to sound out his connections. The answer that came back two or three days later, however, was not what I had expected.

Mainland officials apparently took a dim view of the people of Hong Kong, regarding them as an ungrateful and unpatriotic lot. They accused locals of forever criticising Chinese policies, without ever expressing gratitude to the People's Liberation Army for preventing the territory from being swamped by illegal immigrants or to the Kwangtung provincial authorities for providing them with subsidised foodstuff and drinking water. If Hong Kong now wanted fuel supplies, then it would have to pay an appropriate price.

"Hong Kong would of course pay at the full prevailing market rates," I said. "No one is looking for a subsidy or handout."

"The mainlanders want something more than that," my contact said. "They have learnt some of the hard lessons of capitalism."

"What have they learnt? What do they want?"

My contact then explained that Chinese authorities had for some time been keen to gain a foothold in the local petroleum retail market. But each time a site for a petrol station came up for public tender, Western oil companies would out-bid Chinese corporations with grossly inflated bids. The Chinese kept doing the arithmetic but could not see how the Western companies could offer the prices they did and still turn in a profit. Then it gradually came to them that the oil giants, with an already established network of petrol stations, merely wanted to keep out competition. They did not seem to mind losing money on any one site so long as they achieved their wider goal to preserve a cosy cartel.

China could not afford to waste its resources in that way. Therefore, if China were to help with fuel during the present crisis, it would expect some petrol station sites to be granted at fair and equitable prices, not through any perverted public tendering system.

My immediate reaction was that I could not possibly get involved in that sort of negotiations. I had already overstepped my authority in floating the proposal. If it were a simple matter of a sale and purchase of petroleum products, I could possibly steer it through Mike Clinton. He would understand my motives. But if grants of land were to be involved, then that was an entirely different matter.

In the gossip-saturated environment of the colony, there was no telling what kind of allegations about my involvement might be bounced around. Some would suspect the worst of me, implying I might be getting some secret financial advantage under the counter.

"To get what the Chinese want, I'm afraid you'll have to deal directly with the official handling the oil crisis," I said. "It's too awkward for me to be involved."

"Why? You're a senior Chinese official."

"Not senior enough and not in the right sphere. An expatriate official has already been given the responsibility to tackle the crisis."

"Can he speak Chinese?" my contact asked.

"No, he's an Englishman."

"How can I deal with him? I don't speak English."

I thought for a moment. "Look," I said. "I'm not at all sure the British will go for the kind of arrangement being suggested. Let me sound things out first. If the government is interested in talking, I'll let you know. Then it will be up to you or the Chinese to appoint an English-speaker to deal with the government direct. I don't want to be further involved."

"Pity, but fair enough," my contact said.

On that basis, I telephoned Mike Clinton. I told him what I had done and apologised for sticking my nose where it did not belong. I then outlined the kind of proposal the Chinese were prepared to offer. It was one fraught with policy difficulties. If the government did not wish to consider it, I would send that message back and the matter would be closed.

Mike said the situation was so dire he had to explore all options.

I then said I had no wish to get involved in any shape or form. Some segments of the establishment already regarded me as a man who did not know his proper place. I did not want to make a worse reputation for myself. Should the government wish to take the matter further, I would like no mention at all to anyone about my involvement. I would arrange for an English speaker to give him a ring. They can then both make an appointment direct. I would appreciate it if Mike would just pass off the Chinese contact as one which he had made himself.

Mike agreed and I withdrew completely from the scene. I purposely kept myself in the dark on subsequent negotiations, on who would get what from whom and on what terms. I later learnt that Hong Kong got extra fuel supplies from China in return for three sites in the New Territories designated for petrol stations, all granted under private treaties made by the Governor in Council.

Presumably neither side wanted to publicise the arrangements, for fear of handing the other side some propaganda advantage. The local media, just as in the case of the illegal Diaoyu Tai procession through the city, failed to pick up the story. If anyone wanted confirmation of the grants, all he had to do would be do a search of Land Registry records.

* * *

The OPEC embargo of 1973 should have been a wake-up call to the world. It had created since the mid 19th century economic systems and lifestyles utterly dependent upon the use of fossil fuel and natural gas. Those bounties of Nature had to be created over eons of time though their temporary abundance and cheapness after uses had been found for them obscured that fact. That led mankind to assume they would be inexhaustible. But they were in fact quite finite and not at all renewable within any human timescale. When they were used up, that would be that. The whole human pattern of existence would have to change radically.

The economic and human chaos caused by that first OPEC disruption should have warned both governments and the consuming public that a crisis was coming. But the message did not sink in. It elicited no serious review of the world's dependency on those limited resources. Neither was any meaningful consideration given to finding alternatives.

When the disruption occurred, evidence had already been piling up that the use of fossil fuel and natural gas on such a vast scale was immensely damaging for the earth's environment and the living creatures inhabiting it. The progressive extinction of bird, animal and plant life, the pollution of air, river and sea, the acid rain, the changing weather patterns, the greenhouse gases damaging the ozone layer and global warming all signalled worrying developments.

But instead of facing up to the challenges, governments collectively buried their heads in the sand. They attributed the temporary disruption to obstreperous Arabs; they assured citizens that oil was in plentiful supply, that new sources were bound to be discovered and that science and technology would, in any eventuality, find suitable replacement fuels in the nick of time.

The big oil cartels, too, took to ramping up their estimates of oil reserves they had buried beneath the ground and seas, to reassure both their shareholders and their customers.

Other vested interests went on gaily making profits from the reckless consumption of oil and gas. Automobile manufacturers kept producing ever more powerful gas-guzzling machines and promoting them as essential status symbols. At the same time, the tourism industry and their handmaidens inundated the world with promotional material about visiting romantic and exotic places faraway.

The governments of developing countries added fuel to that travelling jamboree by establishing their own airlines, as if having a loss-making flag carrier was a hallmark of modernity.

Countless millions of ordinary Jills and Joes, lulled by those comforting narratives, responded by booking journeys to every conceivable corner of the globe, either singly or in motley groups. They descended upon historical towns and location of surpassing natural beauty like locusts and left them the worse for wear.

They journeyed not to engage with other cultures but too often merely for self-titillation and to globalise their superficial lifestyles, leaving trails of noise, litter, congestion and money-arrogance wherever they went. They might frivolously demand to be served hamburgers done just the way as back at Houston, Texas, or Yang Chow fried rice as dished up in Shanghai. Small wonder that many towns like Venice now want to limit the influx of tourists

The only major world leader who tried to warn of approaching dangers was President Jimmy Carter and he got promptly voted out of office. Thus the world rushed headlong towards an uncertain doom.

Now, four and a half decades after that first oil shock, the world is only beginning to glimpse the enormous problems left by the long and wasteful use of fossil fuel. A number of wars have been fought and millions have been killed in the struggle to secure fuel supplies. Many more wars are on the horizon as the hour of fuel depletion looms nearer.

Since the start of the Industrial Revolution the world's population had grown sevenfold from about one billion. This is one of the by-products of rampant oil usage. Fossil fuel provided the feedstock for fertilisers, which in turn permitted agriculture to be practised on a massive scale and food to be cheaply sent all over the world. The abundance of food up-ended some of the old constraints formulated by Malthus. One could only shudder to imagine what would happen to those poor hapless billions when the present form of agriculture and the ease of shipping produce half wasy round the world would no longer be economically practical. There would be a scramble for food as well as for oil.

It is now clear that all the known alternatives to conventional oil, such as, coal, tar sands, shale oil, solar, wind, tidal, water and nuclear power, all depend to some degree on an underlying fossil fuel supply and that all of them taken together would still not make up for the amount of oil currently being consumed. Some have other drawbacks. Something has to give.

While it is true that electric cars are making an appearance, no one has yet come up with an electric airplane. Commercial aircraft use prodigious amount of jet fuel and at current prices fuel comes to roughly a quarter of operating costs. When fuel prices go up, how many could keep jet-setting all over the place?

Meanwhile, cities around the world are busily adding to the sterile and ugly forests of skyscrapers with windowless curtain walls. One can only wonder who would be using them when there would be no longer enough power to operate their lifts and run their air-conditioning.

Roughly two-thirds of the known oil reserves are located in the Middle East, a notoriously unstable and restive area. Should some hardline fundamentalist cliques seize power, they might well decide spontaneously to cut off supplies to punish infidels. Nothing can be ruled out in our present cockeyed world. An oil crisis of that sort would be more extreme than any previously experienced.

Even without such provocations, the depletion of natural gas and fossil fuel is likely to occur some time during this century, sooner rather than later. The world had better start preparing for that event.

Yet, all the while, governments around the world seemed incapable of making common cause to tackle one of the most severe existential crisis facing mankind.

CHAPTER 5

No Sure Winners

MY INVOLVEMENT WITH HORSES started many years ago, in a quite roundabout way. My initial interest was fuelled by little more than wishful thinking. Soon after I had landed my first steady job as a cub reporter with the *South China Morning Post,* I discovered my pay was perilously close to starvation level, at HK$150 per month or five dollars per day. At the then prevailing exchange rate, that would come to around 80 American cents per day. Though I had only a secondary school education and no job experience to speak of other than washing dishes, I doubted if even proponents of a free labour market could argue that the sum amounted to a reasonable living wage. I could both hear and feel my stomach perpetually growling for food.

I therefore joined the countless thousands of indigent and desperate people by investing two dollars from time to time in one of those sweepstake tickets issued by the Hong Kong Jockey Club for one of its big races. A ticket holder was entitled — until the race in question has been run — to dream of untold riches coming his way. For the overwhelming number of ticket purchasers, however, the outcome had to be one of disappointment. The system, however, was a money-spinner for the Jockey Club, enabling it to finance its various charitable projects.

The system also provided an opportunity for some clever people to display their entrepreneurial flair. After the race, the number of the ticket linked to the winner horse would be announced together with the figure for the prize. The word soon got around that if someone was lucky enough to hold the winning ticket, all he had to do would be to let that fact be known. Soon he could become even luckier. A stranger could approach him and offer him a sum in ready cash significantly higher than the sum announced to purchase his winning ticket from him.

The rationale for such strange losing transactions was based on sound practical considerations. Anyone appearing at the Jockey Club with the winning ticket would be issued with a cheque in his name for the winning amount. That cheque would be irrefutable proof that that person has been lucky and had come by the money legitimately. It would not be a surprise, upon closer scrutiny, to discover how lucky some police officers and others with a need to explain their wealth could be! And who could argue against luck after it had been laundered and certified by the Jockey Club?

In my own case, upon learning of what went on, I soon decided to dream without a sweepstake ticket. Moreover, reality told me that for the two dollars required to dream I could have the sure thing of two large and steaming bowls of *wonton* noodles to fill my stomach.

The government was not slow to note how readily a gambling-obsessed population was prepared to part with money for any kind of punt. In conjunction with the Jockey Club, it inaugurated a government lottery in July of 1962 to replace sweepstake tickets. On that first try, 1,712,000 tickets were sold and the top prize came to a far greater sum than for a sweepstake — HK$684,800 to be exact.

* * *

My first brush with a living horse came about four years later, when I was studying at Stanford. I had a friend who ran a riding stable nearby and he offered me some riding lessons. The experience of galloping over open country at 20-odd-miles-an-hour was truly exhilarating. For a short while, I developed a different kind of illusion, no doubt one inspired in part by the Chinese comics I had read during boyhood and in part by the Hollywood cowboy films I had seen; I imagined it would be marvellous if I could spend my life riding around outlandish places on horseback, to right wrongs and to deliver justice with a fast gun.

On horseback in California in 1951.

That fantasy also evaporated the moment I returned to the urbanised setting of Hong Kong. My interest in horses remained, however, though along a more intellectual bent.

I gradually began to appreciate the symbolisms that the Chinese attached to that magnificent animal and then its representation in paintings. The Chinese way of painting seemed to bring out better the spirit of the animal than the verisimilitudes portrayed in Western art. The Chinese approach could be traced back to the eighth century rebellion in art, led by the painter Wu Tao-Tzu, against mere physical accuracy in reproducing reality. Wu's rebellion, carried on by his pupils, had far-reaching consequences and accounted for some of the unique characteristics in Chinese paintings still much appreciated today.

In respect of horses, those two traditions came together in a painting by the Jesuit missionary Giuseppe Castiglione. He depicted them in a hybrid style, combining Western realism with Chinese composition and brushwork. His celebrated painting, One Hundred Horses, was much admired by several Ching Emperors and hangs today in the National Palace Museum in Taipei.

* * *

My interest in horses continued because of my father-in-law. He punted regularly on Jockey Club races. In 1959, upon returning to Hong Kong after marrying in Singapore, I found I could not earn enough to set up a home on my own. The high rentals demanded by local landlords meant I had either to go for a sheer money-grubbing job or else fall back on accepting temporary support from my in-laws. A woolly mix of idealism and stubbornness caused me to choose the latter. But I was not to know that the "temporary" nature of that support ended up lasting nine years!

In sharing an apartment with my father-in-law, I noted his absorption with magazines and newspapers containing reports of training times of horses, their past performances in races over different distances and the selections made by various tipsters on each weekend's racing programmes. He apparently did not have any other form of diversion, like drinking, playing *mah-jong* or keeping mistresses.

I never discovered during those years living with him whether he came out ahead or otherwise on his bets. He was a man with quite impassive features and a wonderful trait of never saying more than absolutely necessary. I noticed, however, that he sometimes returned home from a race meeting with a brighter sparkle in his eyes. I could only surmise he might have had a few winning punts. But as a guest in his household and as a son-in-law, it would not have been seemly to be inquisitive about his triumphs or defeats.

It remained a guessing game.

In pondering his obsession, I wondered whether betting on horse races was a mug's game. It was a gamble over which the bettor had not the slightest control over any of the variables. Wagering on an outcome based largely upon the performances of two thoroughly unreliable creatures — the one doing the running and the other the riding — competing against a host of other equally unreliable creatures had to be risky beyond calculation. If I had to gamble on anything, I would much rather do it in a form over which I had some control, like in a game of *mah-jong* or bridge. Horse racing thus failed to spark any inordinate interest in me.

Two or three years later, however, I was nudged into taking a greater interest in horse racing in general and in the Hong Kong Jockey Club in particular.

By then, I had joined the colony's civil service and one of my first assignments had been to serve as the secretary of the Hong Kong War Memorial Fund, a statutory body responsible for the welfare of the families of members of the voluntary armed services killed during World War II. The chairman of the Fund was a local notable by the name of Sir Sik-Nin Chau. He was the head of a prosperous Chinese bank and a senior member of the colony's Executive Council. In addition, he was also the first Chinese to be made a steward in the expatriate-dominated Jockey Club.

I must have caught Sir Sik-Nin's eye in some way because one day, out of the blue, he asked if I would like to become a member of the Jockey Club. The proposition took me aback. It was notoriously difficult for a Chinese to gain admission. Thousands wanted to join because the club's amenities, apart from horse racing, included many excellent restaurants, a country club complex and various sporting, gym and horse-riding facilities. Its dues were also amazingly modest.

But the club's byzantine rules rendered it a devil of a job to gain admission. The club was dominated by an inner core of 200 members known as Voting Members, about two-thirds of whom were expatriates. For a person wishing to join, he must be proposed by a Voting Member and seconded by another. Each Voting Member was limited to putting forward only a single candidate per annum. Hence the maximum number of new members could only be 200 each year.

Because most of the Voting Members were expatriates, many of whom were either unknown or inaccessible to the Chinese making up 98% of the population, the local Voting Members were usually inundated with requests for sponsorship. The limitation to one nominee per annum made for long waiting lists, probably more indefinite than waiting for Godot.

Sir Sik-Nin's offer, therefore, was quite unexpected. I did not have the means, as a civil servant, to indulge in the sport of kings, but I was much attracted to its other facilities. Moreover, becoming a member meant I could get my father-in-law into the more comfortable members' stand as a guest on race days, instead of leaving him to be jostled in the overcrowded public stands. On that basis, I signified my keenness to become a member and I was duly made one by February of 1963.

Sir Sik-Nin went to the trouble of not only arranging for my membership; he went out of his way to invite me and Man-Ying regularly to lunch on race days in his Steward's Box. In that way I began rubbing shoulders with the rich and powerful. In due course, other Stewards invited us to their boxes as well and I got to meet many in that selected coterie of Voting Members and racehorse owners.

Though I enjoyed the sheer excitement of watching horses thundering towards the finishing line, what attracted me more were the sumptuous meals laid out at the various boxes. As for wagering on the outcome of races, I sometimes sought the fruits of my father-in-law's studies. But I never had the luxury of betting more than a few dollars and most of my selections were made like a blindfolded man sticking a pin into a random list of runners. Horse racing during those early years simply did not captivate me anywhere near the degree that *mah-jong* or bridge did. I mainly attended race meetings to get to know people on the upper crust and to enjoy their fine lunches. But could that be considered — for a civil servant — as accepting advantages in meals and entertainment? There was certainly no possibility of reciprocating on civil service pay. Or should such contacts be considered as part of his social duties? Or should there be no supping with the Devil even with a long spoon?

* * *

As the years trundled by, the number of children in my family multiplied. A routine gradually evolved whereby Man-Ying and I would take the kids for weekend outings, usually beginning with lunch. If the meal were to be in a restaurant in town, the family would walk down from Wise Mansion by way of some of the side streets I usually took to get to work at the Labour Department or the Colonial Secretariat. One of those routes went through a street-side wet market.

I soon noticed that my eldest son, Tien-Kuen, could get easily startled or frightened by fowls suddenly squawking or kicking up a ruckus in their rattan containers. That caused me to reflect on how little contact children had with birds, animals and even interesting insects in the concrete sprawl of Hong Kong. Only urban vermin and pests seemed to be left to multiply.

Most of the wildlife had been hunted to virtual extinction for food during the Japanese occupation. Farms in the New Territories were also steadily being converted to building land. My Eighth Granduncle's holiday bungalow, the Abode of Butterflies, abundant with bees, butterflies and ladybirds, had long since been flattened. Tsing Yee Island itself, where the bungalow had been located, had disappeared as well, to make way for yet more commercial or industrial development.

Hong Kong did not even have a zoo worthy of the name, only a small aviary and a few caged animals at the Botanical Gardens. Though the city is today among the wealthiest communities in the world and is a territory with no public debt and eye-watering amounts of money in reserves, no one had apparently given much thought to installing a genuine world-class zoo for the edification of its citizens.

How deprived and restricted today's children must be from any direct knowledge of other life forms. What chance had they in an urban environment to come into contact with animals of any size? What price must they pay in terms of a crimped and distorted upbringing, just so that society could go on making money?

Looking back to when I was my son's age, my siblings and I always had our grandfather's chicken in the rear courtyard of No. 10 Blair Road to rely on for eggs and random amusement. We also had grandfather's pet canary delighting us with its chirps and those occasional forays into tall tropical grass to hunt for grasshoppers to feed the bird. Outside the home, an Indian vendor used to come by regularly with a couple of she-goats. Anyone in need of milk could get it, freshly squeezed on the spot.

Even when we were refugees in Australia, I had Jackie Sue, my bosom pal, taking me out to the bush to catch snakes and insects and to trap small game for our meals. Kangaroos and dingoes had been common sights and flocks of sheep and herds of cows were everywhere. In the case of the latter, one could see them, smell them and touch them, as living adjuncts to normal life, before man-made structures in concrete and steel ousted them from our view. To add insult to injury, multiplying strips of car-choked macadam generating pollution and grime became the normality for our everyday lives.

Another aspect of that dismal fate was brought home to me a short while later by a 16-month-old girl. Her parents had invited me for a meal in their home and her mother was anxious to display how precocious her child had been in learning about the facts of life. One of the questions she asked of the child was: "Where does milk come from, darling?"

"The supermarket," the child replied brightly.

The mother was as pleased as punch. It struck me forcefully then that the child would probably grow up in Hong Kong without ever seeing a cow. At 16 months, she was already being conditioned to the artificiality of urban living. I longed to show my children a less restricted view of reality but I was stumped as to how to do so.

* * *

In the meantime, I chanced upon some of the novels by Dick Francis, a former British champion jockey. Francis had ridden for Queen Elizabeth, the Queen Mother, among others. After a nasty fall in a race in 1957, he decided to exchange his riding crop for a pen. His tales, woven around the shenanigans of horse owners, trainers, jockeys, stable boys, bookies, sport writers and others on the fringes of the horse racing industry, became immensely popular.

Notwithstanding the popularity of those books and the hundreds of winners he had ridden as a jockey, Dick Francis was likely to be best remembered among horse racing fanciers for a race he did not win. In 1956, he rode the Queen Mother's horse, Devon Loch, in the prestigious Grand National. Devon Loch cleared the last fence by several lengths and looked to the world like a certain winner. But 50 yards from the finish, the horse suddenly collapsed and could not continue the race. The reason for that failure had never been properly determined and that loss went down in racing history as a shocking surprise, especially for punters who had their money on it.

In Hong Kong, horse racing was big business. The amounts wagered on the Jockey Club tote set world records, not to mention the unquantifiable sums betted with illegal bookies. Although jockeys were sometimes suspended or disciplined for "riding an injudicious race" or for "excessive use of the whip", the local extent of some of the malpractices touched upon by Francis in his novels was by no means clear. At that point in time, the local jockeys were all supposed to be riding as amateurs; it was thus not always easy to nab anyone for throwing a race should he be slow out of the starting gates or if he dropped his whip early in a race. Or if a horse bored out and lost many lengths upon entering the straight.

As a member of the club, I became intrigued by how everything operated. I began gathering data on the economics of owning a horse. It appeared that stable charges ran to about HK$600 per month while the winning purse for a race stood at around HK$6,000. However, 10% of the prize money had to be given to the trainer and another 10% for the jockey. In addition, most owners also conventionally set aside another 10% as tips for the riding boy, the groom, the farrier and others associated with looking after the horse. Therefore, on a rough calculation, a horse had to win at least two races a year to pay its way.

Since I had a number of friends who were owners, I began culling information from their experiences. The first one I approached was Fung Hon-Chu, the Legislative Councillor and businessman I first met when he headed the Hong Kong delegation to the 1963 meeting of the United Nations Economic Commission for Asia and the Far East.

But H.C. was no help. Although he had previously owned a horse, he readily admitted he had little interest in it beyond it conferring upon him a bit of social cachet. His elder brother, Fung Mo-Ying, had been a keen racing man and he had left it to him to manage the animal. He simply paid whatever sum his brother asked him to pay for upkeep. When his brother passed away, he stopped keeping a horse.

My other friends with horses seemed as casual as H.C. over their animals. It was largely a symbol of social and financial arrival for them too, like travelling around in a Rolls Royce or having a pleasure boat bobbing about in the marina.

They no doubt relished having their pictures appearing in newspapers leading their horses into the winner's circle and receiving congratulations from their friends. But they were all busy people, with their own businesses or professions to run. They could not afford time to manage horses. Hence run-of-the-mill chores were left to trainers. As for betting on their own nags, they did so more or less in blind faith, according to the tips and advice of their trainers and jockeys.

Finding so many owners being so hands-off in overseeing their horses, it occurred to me that there must be plenty of scope for the unscrupulous to manipulate the outcome of races at the expense of the gambling-addicted public. The rules of the Jockey Club had been framed during an era when horse racing was supposed to be indulged in by gentlemen. In the modern era, when gentlemen were an endangered species, those rules would appear to be in drastic need for review.

But I had no direct experience upon which to base suggestions or conjectures. Underlying my thinking was also another group of nagging puzzles: Was it possible for an ordinary member, through prudent management, to maintain a horse on prize money alone? What if the horse acquired was not a sound racing proposition? Would the financial implications be too onerous to bear for a mere salary-earner like myself? I did not have the wherewithal to finance any experimentation on my own. The notion that the sport had to remain a preserve for the wealthy in a city where the gap between the haves and the have-nots had become so stark did not sit well with me.

* * *

In 1968, I was promoted to a level eligible for allocated government quarters. This advancement brought a significant change in my economic circumstances. All at once I became entitled to an apartment three times the size of the one I had been sharing with my in-laws at Wise Mansion. And instead of paying a commercial rental running into the thousands and subsidised by my father-in-law, I was only required to pay 12.5% of my new salary of HK$4,580 for rent.

The financial elbow room thus gained caused me to mull the possibility of purchasing a racehorse. Since a civil servant like Sir John Cowperthwaite had made a go of owning one, I did not see why I could not. After due consideration, I decided to chance my arm. But I was cautious. I did not want to shoulder the entire risk; I needed a partner.

The one who came immediately to mind was Fung Hon-Chu. He had previously owned a horse for social kudos, with little interest in horse racing itself. So I approached him. I told him that for my part, he could have all the kudos of ownership; I wanted only full control so that I could either verify or disprove certain theories I had about the viability of horse ownership as a paying proposition. He did not particularly interest on that score. So he readily agreed to share in the venture.

The Jockey Club arrangements for allowing horse ownership were at that time rather antiquated. The club usually bought about 100 yearlings of unknown pedigree from Australia each year — mainly geldings and a handful of mares. Private importation of racehorses was then not allowed.

When the geldings and mares had been passed as sound racing propositions, they would be shipped to Hong Kong and prepared for racing as two-year-olds. Since the number of club members wishing to become owners usually far exceeded the number of ponies available for allocation, a lottery had to be drawn to determine which applicants would get one.

After arrival in Hong Kong, each pony would be assigned a number and a further lottery would be held to match them with the successful winners in the first draw. Since horses had different racing potential, the law of chance determined what an owner might get.

* * *

At around that time, I was fortuitously "elected" to fill a vacancy within the elite group of 200 Voting Members. I did not know how the whole thing came about because I had not put my name forward. But having been chosen, I felt more duty-bound than ever to discover how things operated within the club.

H.C. and I therefore put in an application to become joint owners for the following year's draw. The cost of acquiring a racehorse was quite modest back then, at only a few thousand dollars. We were lucky enough to be selected in the first lottery and when the horses finally arrived we got assigned a lively-looking chestnut gelding. It turned out to be a very plucky and big-hearted animal.

The elaborate processes of naming our possession, designing our racing colours, engaging a trainer and overseeing its training were left largely to me. Each was a weighty matter. In naming our horse, both an English name and a Chinese name had to be found. In selecting each, the chief requirement was for the names to be capable of exploding easily from human throats, especially when the creature came thundering towards the finishing line. With a Chinese name, it also could not sound inauspicious.

For the English name, H.C. and I settled upon Free Town, as a nod to the free-wheeling business culture in Hong Kong. We wanted a Chinese name that was phonetically similar and eventually decided upon two characters which meant "flying steed", taken from an old quotation. For our colours, we chose a chocolate background with two bands in white and baby blue coming down the centre of the jockey's helmet, across the front of his jacket and down the sleeves. We figured those coloured bands would stand out enough for us to track the horse during a race.

H.C. had no interest in the rest of the arrangements and they were left entirely to me. I had a couple of friends with horses. They had stabled them with a trainer from Shanghai by the name of Cheung Hok-Man. They suggested I did the same with Free Town. They did not consider Cheung to be demonstrably better or more successful than other trainers. Their argument was that all trainers treated owners of a single pony with little consideration. But if a trainer knew that a group of owners were good friends, he would be more careful in not upsetting any of them, lest the whole lot moved their horses elsewhere. That sounded like practical advice, so I went along with it.

Cheung was a tallish and well-fleshed man of about my own age. He had mournful and slightly diffident eyes. His Cantonese was only fractionally better than that of my *mah-jong* playing friend, Uncle Lau, and his English was nothing to write home about. He was a jovial man, however, one quite anxious to be in the good books of all owners stabling with him. This proved a handicap, as things turned out, because he kept telling owners flattering things about the potential of their animals rather than home truths. Thus it required a fair bit of cross-examination to elicit a reliable assessment. His commentaries were often better after he had a couple of stiff drinks. He seemed to have an iron constitution though, which made light of everything from whisky to vodka and *slivovitz*.

I knew little about preparing a horse for racing but I did know enough to emphasise to Cheung that I did not want Free Town to be rushed. The general expectation was that a horse would not be fully matured till it was about four; therefore it should be allowed to mature at its own pace. Its training should be confined for the time being to conditioning it to jump smartly out of the starting gates — for I had witnessed many a race lost through a bad start — and to exert itself to the utmost once it entered the final stretch.

For a jockey, both Cheung and my friends recommended an amateur by the name of Shum Kam-Sheung. Shum had previously ridden some of the horses owned by H.C. and his elder brother, so I went along with the recommendation. Shum was not the most scintillating of riders but he was simple and guileless and an agreeable companion. In ordinary life he helped his family run a poultry business.

After he had given up riding, I roped him into an occasional *mah-jong* game. I also once went with him on a stag trip to Manila with a couple of other adventurous men and we all behaved with less than proper decorum at a variety of Filipino night spots.

One weekend, when a *mah-jong* game had been scheduled with Kam-Sheung in the afternoon, Mrs. Shum rang me in the morning to say that her husband was not feeling well and would be unable to play. I accordingly arranged for someone else to take his place. By the afternoon, he was already gone, from a heart attack. He was only in his 40s.

* * *

I soon settled down to studying the racing game. I acquired a pair of binoculars and a stopwatch before cultivating the trust and friendship of all those having anything to do with looking after Free Town. This included the riding boy, who galloped it in morning training sessions whenever the jockey was not available, and the stable groom or *mafoo*, who tended to its feeding and its walking exercises the rest of the time.

The riding boy was a particularly helpful character. He had a cleft lip and spoke with a slur. But he knew his horseflesh and could have made a decent living as a jockey except that he was too big and heavy-boned to make the weight required. Thus he was left to scrape a living as a riding boy. He had a sound feel for the potential of every horse he took out, however, and I could readily rely on his judgements.

The handicap system of racing operated by the Jockey Club divided horses into eight classes. The higher the class, the stiffer the competition and the riskier the betting propositions. Horses in Class Eight had to retire at the end of the racing season unless they could secure a win to get promoted to Class Seven. New arrivals, sometimes called griffins, would not be classified until after they had demonstrated their capabilities in a few races. There was a natural propensity for owners and trainers to try to hoodwink handicappers to gain a lower classification.

Handicapping was, as with most things in life, not an exact science. It was a combination of mathematical calculations and subjective judgements. The theory behind handicapping revolved around the supposition that the weight being carried by a horse affected its galloping speed. Past performances therefore mattered, though other factors were also taken into account, such as the length of a particular race, the pace of the race, the condition of the ground, the age of the animal and the finishing distances relative to other horses in the race. The aim of handicappers would be to assign weights which would — theoretically — give every horse in a race a more or less an equal chance at winning. That made for not only exciting racing but also exciting betting.

In a nutshell, if a horse won, that would be a *prima facie* indication it was superior to the company it had raced against. The handicappers would then either promote it to a higher class or else add a few pounds to the weight it would carry in its next outing. The amount of weight to be added depended on the distances separating the winner from the rest of the field and on the length of the race. The rule of thumb was that three pounds would be added for every length a horse had won by in a five-furlong race, two pounds per length for an eight-furlong race, and so on. By the same token, a horse which finished well back in a race might have its weight reduced.

A common but unauthorised practice followed by some jockeys would be to stop riding out a mount should he find his horse in a hopeless position to win. The hope was that the handicappers would then take the losing distance into account in reducing the weight to be carried in a subsequent race. But such a practice was an infringement of the rules and handicappers could not be so easily fooled. A jockey who did not ride out his horse could be penalised.

One of the assumptions behind the whole system was that every runner in the race would be doing its best to win. But, as the stories of Dick Francis showed, that assumption was not always sound. Whenever big money was involved, somebody was bound to seek opportunities to fiddle for an advantage.

Within racing circles, gossip and tall tales routinely circulated. Stories of betting syndicates planning coups and of illegal bookies trying to fix racing outcomes were often bandied about. Sometimes, one could see last-minute surges in betting on the tote on some less than fancied runner. Occasionally, simply following the betting on such splurges paid off; at other times it would just be rash money going down the drain. Those in the know often spoke of secret signals by jockeys as they left the saddling enclosure for the starting gate — in the form of a whip being held in the left or right hand or the way he would salute judges as he made his way out of the enclosure. But finding hard evidence to prove trickery or collusion was almost impossible.

* * *

The racecourse at Happy Valley had two tracks — a grass track and a sand track. The day racing would take place on the grass track whereas the evening racing would use the sand track. Some horses preferred the grass; others the sand. Racing on grass was more variable because the going could be anything from firm to good to yielding or to heavy, depending on the weather. The sand track was more consistent. All training took place on the sand track.

Sometimes I would go down to the Happy Valley at the crack of dawn to watch Free Town in training. I would clock its runs and ask the riding boy or the jockey to test its various capabilities, such as how long it could sustain a finishing rush. I would also discuss with the trainer whether the horse would run better with blinkers or whether it needed to be armoured by another horse during training. I would carefully record such bits of information. After watching the training, I would have breakfast in the club house before walking over to my office at Hysan Avenue to start my official duties.

By entering Free Town in races over varying distances I also tried, in conjunction with the jockey and trainer, to determine the most suitable distance and the most favoured going for the animal. Free Town turned out to be essentially a miler which preferred good going, although against a weak field it could also do well at six furlongs and nine furlongs.

During school holidays I would bring my sons down for the morning gallops, to enable them to feed Free Town with lumps of sugar or handfuls of grass. I warned them to keep their thumbs well tucked while feeding it, lest they be bitten off. They enjoyed those close contacts with a large animal. Later, I also took them to the stables at Shan Kwong Road where horses were kept.

To the best of my recollection, Free Town was initially classified into Class Six but it gradually won its way right up to Class One. It never managed to win a race in that top class, however, because it was by then ageing and had suffered a fetlock injury from which it never fully recovered.

* * *

Since my main purpose in owning a horse was to determine whether it could reasonably be maintained on prize money alone, I set about planning Free Town's racing career with that objective in mind, while taking cognisance of the rules of racing as well.

Straight away, I came face-to-face with a range of ethical tripwires. Without a doubt, I had amassed a considerable amount of private information about the capabilities of Free Town. But what moral obligation had I to share that information with the handicappers or with the general betting public?

That prompted me to make mental comparisons with the approaches of business corporations. Coca-Cola, for instance, spent vast sums in advertising to persuade consumers to buy the beverage. Yet the company had been under no moral or legal obligation to inform purchasers about its exact make-up and the quantum of ingredients used for manufacturing the drink. They were considered trade secrets. I, on the other hand, had never attempted to persuade the public to bet on Free Town. So why should I disclose what I knew?

Of course, that did not mean sports writers, racing tipsters and others had not recommended Free Town for a wager. Railbirds were a constant presence at morning gallops, each one assessing in his own way the potential of runners. They would naturally note Free Town's trials as well. But they would not have the detailed information I had. They would not know, for instance, my instructions to the riding boy or jockey to begin the training run at what point and over what distance. I would clock those runs myself.

The assessments and recommendations by railbirds would thus be no better than those touted by stockbrokers for companies listed on the stock exchanges — done on limited information and coloured by their own speculations, misconceptions or vested interests. Corporations were often in any case in cahoots with stockbrokers to get favourable write-ups but I wanted only a low profile for my horse. I saw no need to go out of my way to correct misconceptions circulated by others. Like all capitalists, my first responsibility must be to protect the capital investment of H.C. and myself. Indeed, could my private information not be regarded as a form of "intellectual property" to be protected by the law?

In any case, the handicappers were supposed to be there as impartial arbiters, to ensure through the weights they assigned to the whole field that each runner had an equal theoretical winning chance. If people wanted to wager on a horse based on dubious or unreliable opinions, then it was their own lookout.

* * *

During the first two years of Free Town's racing career, it did so well that H.C. and I made a yearly profit on the enterprise. I presented the accounts to H.C. at the end of each season, together with a cheque as dividend. As a consequence, I managed to persuade H. C. to be a partner for another horse.

We duly put in our application and were again lucky enough to draw another fine chestnut gelding. It had a distinctive white stripe right down the middle of its forehead. We decided to call it Free Lad. For the Chinese equivalent we chose two characters which meant "flying strength".

Free Lad happily followed Free Town's winning ways. Thus we demonstrated conclusively — at least to our own satisfaction — that an ordinary Jockey Club member with limited means could nonetheless afford to own a racehorse, provided he managed things patiently and systematically — and also enjoyed a modicum of luck.

Receiving a piece of silverware from the Stewards of the Jockey Club. The lady on my right is Grace Yam, wife of Yam Chi-Kwong, then a statistician in the Economic Services Branch of the Secretariat. Yam was to become the most highly paid central banker in the world when he was made Chief Executive of the Hong Kong Monetary Authority.

Free Town out-classing its opposition far more easily than I had calculated.

* * *

As time passed, the Jockey Club decided to upgrade the standard of jockeyship by inviting professional riders from Britain, Australia and other places to participate in Hong Kong racing. One of those jockeys was a Malaysian by the name of Peter Cheam. After a while, Cheung Hock-Man took Cheam on as his stable jockey and persuaded a number of owners to try him out. Many owners did so, including myself.

Cheam was a young, sturdy and good-looking lad in his late twenties. There was a definite likeableness about him. He demonstrated himself to be a competent and courageous horseman. In spite of his diminutive stature, it soon became evident that he cut quite a dash among young ladies who plied their company in some of the Tsim Sha Tsui nightclubs. He, in turn, had a weakness for their expensive company.

After Cheam had ridden both my horses a couple of times and I felt sufficiently comfortable with him, we settled on a briefing routine. Whenever he was down for riding either of my horses, we would meet up on the evening before, for a drink or a meal. We would then go through the records of the other mounts ranged against us and discuss tactics for the up-coming race.

On occasion, when we had no expectation of getting anywhere close to winning by virtue of the distance or the going or the strength of opposition, we nonetheless saw every race as an opportunity to test our horses. We might, for example, decide to test one of them on an untried type of surface or distance or to experiment with a short sprint to determine whether it could keep up with the early pace to attempt a win over a longer sprint later in the season.

After we had reached a degree of rapport with each other, I put a proposition to Cheam. I said neither Mr. Fung nor I was a big punter. We had little interest in the odds in any particular race. Our objective was to prove that a person of modest means could still own a racehorse in Hong Kong. That boiled down to the need for each horse to win at least two races per season to pay its way.

I was prepared to grant him the exclusive right to ride my ponies, I said, provided that we would plan their races together and that he would ride during each race according to our joint decision. Given the number of rumours doing the rounds about race-fixing by illegal bookies or betting syndicates, I wanted no surprises and certainly no scandals. I would expect him to be truthful about the capabilities and potential of my horses and to keep those assessments between ourselves. Cheam readily accepted my proposal.

Our arrangement worked well for a couple of seasons and Cheam was delivering the expected winners for the horses to pay for their keep. Cheung, the trainer, seemed happy with him too.

During a subsequent season, I began planning for a win by Free Lad by entering it for a mile race. The mile was its favourite distance; it had won easily over that course in previous outings. The week before, I had asked the trainer to seek the club vet's permission to give it a shot of vitamins as preparation. I had also gone down for one of the morning gallops to seek assurance from the cleft-lipped riding boy that the horse felt fit and strong under him. I had likewise gone to the stables to ask the *mafoo* whether Free Lad was eating normally and healthily. I saw for myself when I fed it carrots and bunches of fresh-cut grass that its coat was lustrous and glowing with rude health.

After the field had been declared, everything else seemed favourable. Free Lad had drawn a good position at the starting gates and the going was expected to be firm, It was a surface it relished. It had also slipped under the radar of the handicappers, for I figured that, on the weights, it must have at least a class in hand over most of the competition. Therefore its chances ought to be very good. In the overnight betting, it was the third favourite.

It was under those circumstances that I met Cheam for dinner on the evening before the race. He was also to ride another horse in a later race which had already become the raging favourite on the overnight betting.

After we had assessed the rest of the field and agreed the riding tactics for Free Lad, I said: "It looks as if you might be having two winners tomorrow."

"There's no such thing as a sure winner in racing," Cheam replied, in a somewhat more lacklustre manner than usual. "On any given day, a horse or a rider can go off form. Lots of unexpected things can happen in a race."

I felt slightly apprehensive. "You're not trying to tell me that Free Lad's chances are not as sure as we had concluded, are you? I've told Mr. Fung the horse had a good chance and Mrs. Fung's looking to come down to help me lead it into the winner's circle."

"No, I'm confident on Free Lad," he said. "But I'm not so sure on my other mount."

A portentous silence hung between us for a moment, like a doom. I could sense he wanted to tell me something but could not quite get it off his chest. The silence stretched.

Then Cheam said: "Look, you're a man who's knocked around the world.

Do you think people like me are in this racket for our health? We have to get up at the crack of dawn for morning gallops; we starve ourselves silly to make the weights; we work like the devil in the gym to keep fit. And what do we get in return? A lousy contract as a stable jockey, a riding fee for every ride we take, and 10% of a measly purse — if we win, that is. Don't people realise that every time a jockey goes into a race he's risking his neck? Something clips the hoof of his horse and he goes flying over its neck at 35 miles an hour. The second he hits the ground, half a ton of horse flesh might land right on top of him. He could easily get killed or maimed for life. And for what?"

I felt stunned for a moment by his outburst. I was not sure what he was leading up to. Perhaps it was a request for me to lay a bet for him, something some owners have been known to do for jockeys. I had never done so, however, not only because it was contrary to the rules but also because I never had the means to splash money around like that.

Before I could work out a response, Cheam spoke again. His tone sounded more resigned. His momentary agitation had passed.

"You know, the only way a jockey can make any real money in this game is to betray everybody — the trainers, the owners, the stable boys, everybody. Sometimes it's easier to make money by losing than by winning. You've been warned; be smart, be on the lookout for betrayal by anybody who works with your horses."

"Look, you'd better ride a good race on Free Lad tomorrow," I said, sternly. "Otherwise you'd have me to answer to."

Cheam offered a half-smile and a shrug.

The air became heavy with sentiments which could not be expressed. In order to lighten it, I deliberately put on a more jocular tone. "When you run short of money, why don't you simply charm it out of those ladies you're always hanging around with at night spots at Tsim Sha Tsui?"

"What? You expect me to live off the immoral earnings of women?"

"What's the difference — you living off their immoral earnings or they living off yours?"

Cheam half-opened his mouth for a retort but he would not find the words. Instead, he stared at me and wagged an angry index finger in my direction.

On that note, we called it a night.

* * *

After I had got home, the conversation still weighed on me. Was Cheam trying to warn me that he was going to lose the race on Free Lad the following day? I had known the man for more than two years; yet I knew so little about him and his inner configuration. I had taken him mainly as an extension or adjunct to my part-ownership of horses, as a source of information and an executor of my ambitions. Though I had shared drinks and meals with him, I had not taken him as a fellow human being, with everyday joys and sorrows and dilemmas. It had been the same with the trainer, the riding boy and the *mafoos*.

All of a sudden I felt thoroughly ashamed. How could I have gone so insensitive to the fate of others? I was supposed to be one of the elite 200 Voting Members overseeing the affairs of the club. Yet, like so many others of that group, I had merely voted for the stewards and left it to them to run things. To concentrate on making my horses pay their way had shrunk my angle of vision and caused me to slip unnoticed into an elitist attitude. That awareness troubled my sleep that night.

As things turned out, Cheam did not betray me. Free Lad won handily, as he had said it would, but the raging favourite he was on in the other race only managed to come fourth.

* * *

It was to be more than a year later, after our uneasy conversation had slipped from memory, that Cheam blind-sided everybody by unexpectedly winning a mile and a half race at long odds on Free Lad.

It happened towards the end of the season, after both my horses had won sufficient in prize money for their keep. I then decided to enter Free Lad for a mile and a half race, not expecting it to get anywhere but in the hope of persuading the handicappers to cut a few pounds from its back for the following season. The horse had by then won so many races over a mile that the public perception was that it was an ideal miler but nothing more.

That had become my impression too. Cheam and I had previously tried the horse out over a mile and a quarter and it had faded badly towards the end. So Cheam, the trainer and everybody else agreed that it could not last out for a mile and a half. So no special effort had been made to prepare it for the race. Moreover, the going was predicted to be good to yielding, which was not best suited for Free Lad. It preferred firm ground.

The evening before the race, Cheam and I met briefly and agreed we would let Free Lad set the early pace so that after the first mile it would be well exhausted. I then went out for dinner with a friend who was also a horse owner and a Voting Member. He held the sole agency for importing a wide range of Italian household appliances.

During the course of dinner, my friend told me he would not be able to attend the races the following day because he had to fly off to Italy in the morning. But he wanted me to bet HK$100 on both win and place on Free Lad and another HK$100 on a quinella bet, which would link Free Lad with the rest of the field. That meant Free Lad had to come either first or second for the bet to win.

I told him to save his money because there was no chance of Free Lad being in the frame. I went into all the detailed reasoning for that conclusion, much as Cheam had set out for me, and pointed out in addition that the overnight odds were being quoted at 80 to one.

But my friend could not be persuaded.

"My dear chap, you're talking about horse racing," he said. "There are no sure winners or losers in that game. Anything can happen. It has been my lifelong habit to bet always that same amount whenever a friend of mine has a horse running, regardless of what he might tell me. Overall, my system hasn't done too badly. So don't jinx my system." So saying, he handed me HK$300.

Rather than arguing further with him, I accepted the money. My intention was not to place his bets but to return the money to him after his trip, telling him he should really have had more faith in my assessment.

As the race was being run, Cheam appeared to be riding to plan. He opened up a big early lead and eased Free Lad after about a mile. But as the rest of the field began catching up, Free Lad somehow found a second wind and finished strongly enough to win the race.

I watched dumbfounded. The winning odds had shortened before the off but they were still more than 60 to one. The eventual quinella payout came to a couple of thousand. On the basis of the bets I had failed to place for my friend, I owed him in excess of HK$10,000, almost twice the net amount of prize money coming to the partnership.

I realised that Cheam must have been secretly testing out the capabilities of Free Lad over the years but had kept his findings to himself. I remembered then that the riding boy had once remarked that he felt Free Lad might do well over nine furlongs. But since the horse was such a consistent miler and had failed over a mile and a quarter, I had carelessly given no further thought to that opinion.

By the time I had recovered from my shock sufficiently to want to give Cheam a piece of my mind, the man had disappeared. The race had been towards the end of the season and he had gone back to ride in Malaysia. That was the last I saw of him.

A few years later, news came from Malaysia that Cheam had fallen off a horse during a race and had been instantly killed. I felt a great sadness upon hearing the report. It struck me that he might somehow have foreseen his own demise. Although he had made a thorough fool out of me, he had remained a quite likeable man. In a way, I suppose he had also been as honest with me as anyone could have expected from a jockey.

* * *

After Free Town and Free Lad, Fung Hon-Chu and I went on to co-own two more horses before our partnership ended. Neither was as magnificent or as consistent a racehorse as either Free Town or Free Lad. But overall our partnership had been profitable enough to substantiate our point about the viability of horse ownership on slender means.

Over the years, our horses amassed collectively quite a number of silver cups and trophies. Whenever it happened, I would go to the same silversmith as the Jockey Club and have a duplicate made, so that each of the partners could have his own trophy. The cost was met out of our common kitty.

The trouble with silverware was that it tarnished quite quickly. When I was living in Hong Kong, the polishing was done by Ah Duen or some other servant. I was not terribly bothered by that chore when someone else had to do it. But after I had migrated to London and had to do the polishing myself, I soon grew weary of the task.

One day, I took the cups and trophies to a precious-metal scrap dealer in Hatton Garden and sold the lot. They fetched a handy sum of over £1,000.

CHAPTER 6

The Lottery of Recruitment

THE ROOTS OF THE ADMINISTRATIVE SERVICE in Hong Kong can be traced back to September of 1862, when three Cambridge graduates arrived as "cadets" during the governorship of Sir Hercules Robinson. Their arrival signalled a departure from the previous practice of making official appointments as "offices of profit under the Crown." That practice had led to a number of very troubling scandals in the early days of the colony.

The three new cadets had secured their posts through passing competitive examinations. That innovation began in the early part of the 19th century, after inadequacies in governance throughout the British Empire had become more apparent. British public opinion thus gradually turned in favour of a civil service based on merit rather than patronage.

It was doubtful whether in bringing that change to Hong Kong the British authorities had been mindful at all of the examination system already in place in China for over 2,000 years. The Chinese system, instituted by Emperor Wu of the Han Dynasty in 141 BC, came about after he had elevated Confucian teachings into a form of state education, forcing those seeking official positions to first master the Confucian classics. Examinations were held periodically, at different levels, for selecting district, provincial and national officials. By allowing anyone with the appropriate knowledge to sit for them, the system brought a democratising effect, since noble births, family connections or the sheer power of wealth could no longer be the determining factors in securing preferment.

Unfortunately, while the more merit-based system was being introduced into Hong Kong, a more retrogressive development was also taking place in China. The Ching Dynasty, under Western attack and desperate for additional sources of finances, began openly selling public offices. That merely hastened the collapse of the nation by encouraging more corruption.

The new Hong Kong system differed in several respects from the ancient Chinese system. First of all, it was not based upon mastery of any Confucian or Western classics. Rather a First Class Honours degree in any subject — or at least a Second Class Upper — from a recognised university would be enough. Whether a degree from a university outside the British Commonwealth would be recognised or not remained a matter of some uncertainty.

Because World War II had interrupted the university education of some British students, the British government decided after the war to admit into the colonial service those who had distinguished themselves in the armed forces or emergency services, notwithstanding that they were without a university degree. Among those who found their way to Hong Kong that way were Mike Clinton and Jack Cater. Both of them subsequently reached the top of the hierarchy.

The second difference between the Chinese examinations and the Hong Kong system was that the Chinese system was open to all, whereas the examinations for Hong Kong posts were restricted to only graduates of European stock. Both the examinations and the interviews were conducted by the Colonial Office in Britain. Such an arrangement entailed an inevitable European bias. It was possible that a belief in the superiority of Europeans was too ingrained in the white psyche to shift. Or it might have been that Whitehall had real or perceived reservations over the loyalty of all non-white subjects.

That racial restriction was not lifted until after World War II, after

Japan had demonstrated amply that an Asian country could give Western nations a run for their money. But even then, despite pious Colonial Office declarations to the effect that Hong Kong candidates would henceforth be given preference in appointments, a quota system heavily coloured by race was still surreptitiously employed. The number of Chinese officers to be admitted was limited to only one each year, regardless of the number of vacancies and regardless of the number of suitable Chinese candidates coming forward.

Local candidates also had to surmount a few other impediments. They had to be British subjects to begin with. Then, even with a recognised university degree, they still had to pass both a written English test and an aptitude test before qualifying for an interview by the selection board. Many local candidates fell well before that point. The selection boards throughout the 1960s and the early 1970s was made up largely of expatriates. All proceedings naturally had been conducted in English.

After being selected, a successful candidate still had to serve on probation for three years and to pass a further examination in English criminal law before being confirmed to the pensionable establishment.

That unpublicised quota system enabled many vacancies to be filled by expatriates from Britain and other white commonwealth countries, often through transfers of serving officers from those places. For that reason, many exceptional Chinese candidates — like Eric Peter Ho and Lai Ka-Wah — failed to gain admission on their first attempt. Lai Ka-Wah was eventually admitted in early 1961, at the same time as myself, after the restriction on a single Chinese admission per annum was lifted.

Others who had been rejected became generally lost to the public service because they would then naturally go off to seek careers in other callings.

* * *

Before I returned to Hong Kong in 1953 with two Stanford degrees, I — like many young Chinese who had grown up in British colonies and subjected to a largely colonial education — had gone through an identity crisis and a great deal of soul-searching. I had gone to study in America just prior to Chairman Mao proclaiming at Tiananmen on October 1, 1949, the establishment of a Chinese Communist government. That event took me and many Americans by surprise. Fellow students asked me whether America ought to recognise the new regime or stick with the old one, with its remnants holed up in Taiwan under the protection of the American Seventh Fleet.

I could only hum and haw in response. I had no political affiliations to speak of. Nor had I any in-depth understanding of the complicated situation in China. My natural instincts, after witnessing hyper-inflation and rampant corruption in 1947, while staying with my mother in Canton, were to follow those of my revolutionary grandfather. He had throughout his life wanted his country to be at peace, prosperous and united.

There had to be a losing side in any civil war, I reasoned. And the losing side should accept defeat with grace. Otherwise fighting would never cease. Outside powers had been interfering in Chinese affairs long enough and they ought to stop too. Yet I realised most Americans tended to be instinctively against anything associated with Communism. So I merely waffled, to get out of providing an opinion which I could not fully explain. But the pressure kept mounting, particularly after the outbreak of the Korean War.

On the other side of the Pacific, Chinese and Americans began killing each other, along with their Korean allies. A wider conflict might well be ignited, given the loose talk about American armies marching all the way up to the Yalu and beyond. If a wider conflict erupted, how would that affect people inside China? Those in Hong Kong and Macau were bound to become involved too. In a time of national peril, the Chinese people would surely defy the United Nations embargo on China and smuggle needed vital supplies to help their homeland.

How could I remain a bystander with folded arms, enjoying the comfort and security of California, while my country was once again forced to defend its national integrity? I felt compelled to explain to my American friends and classmates the Chinese perspectives. Yet I found I did not know enough about China's history and politics to give convincing explanations.

It came upon me forcefully then that all I knew about my own nation and its culture were the tiny bits of unconnected flotsam and jetsam I had picked up during my childhood, from Miss Nice and Tutor Tam and from eavesdropping upon conversations between my elders and their friends. I was in fact a cultural freak. Thanks to my early education in Singapore and Australia, I knew more about Western history, literature and values than I did those of China and the East!

I resolved immediately to rectify that situation. I signed up for courses in Chinese history and philosophy and devoted every spare moment I had outside my degree requirements to reading up on different aspects of Chinese culture. The more I read, however, the more I realised how inadequate my knowledge was. It was in fact a curse to be a Chinese. It was infinitely better to belong to a newly developed nation; there would then be no need to get acquainted with such a lengthy history and so many philosophies and traditions. I could see that no matter how much I read, I would never catch up with Western Sinologues like Thomas Wade, Robert Hart or Joseph Needham.

* * *

My promiscuous reading nonetheless gave me a heightened consciousness of my own Chinese-ness. That fed a sharper resentment over having to return to a corner of China under foreign rule. But I had little choice. I did not want to remain in America, for I did not feel I belonged there.

My great-grandfather had chosen Hong Kong as the family home shortly after the start of the British occupation and my father was still living there, as a guest in the home of my Eighth Granduncle. My mother had gone off to the Philippines, with her new family. I could have chanced heading for the mainland to assist in its national reconstruction, like many other Chinese did during that time. The new Chinese government in fact had a special programme to lure overseas Chinese to return, with promises of good jobs and special treatment, because it need professional people in all spheres were needed to support the country's development. But I hesitated again, for fear I would not be accepted because of both my questioning attitude and my lack of specialised skills.

So it had to be Hong Kong, till the place was reclaimed by the motherland. But that eventuality had been pushed back into an indefinite future after the Chinese Premier, Chou En-Lai, declared that the status of the colony was a problem left over by history and that the two countries involved would deal with it "when the time was ripe".

That statement sent a message not only to the British but also to the Chinese living in the territory. It implied there should be no premature effort to stir up a patriotic opposition to foreign occupation. The motherland would deal with matters at its own pace. Hence the ordinary citizen could only wait in limbo — either in hope or in trepidation, depending to his own political inclinations.

* * *

Meanwhile, there was the mundane business of finding gainful employment to attend to. I was averse to entering the money-grubbing world of commerce, with its pervasive slipperiness and its dog-eat-dog ethos. My choice was either to try teaching or to return to journalism.

I began by seeking registration as a teacher but struck a snag immediately. The expatriate official in charge of teacher registration refused to register me. He said he had never heard of Stanford. There were a lot of "funny little colleges in America with dodgy degrees," he added. My registration would have to wait till he had established the bona fides of Stanford degrees.

Stymied, I turned to sounding out possibilities in journalism. At the same time, I chanced upon an advertisement inviting applications for posts in the Administrative Service. The starting pay was in line with what I could expect in journalism. But the administrative posts came with a salary scale providing for annual increments. In my experience, pay rises in journalism often depended on the health of the publication's bottom line and on the whim of the editor-in-chief. Security in pay progression within the civil service seemed an attractive proposition. So I applied.

Working for the British, of course, risked being branded as a collaborator by the more nationalistic Chinese. But, historically, accommodating conquerors had been quite common. When China was a collection of warring kingdoms, people whose king had been defeated had to submit to a new ruler. After the unification of the country under the First Emperor of Ch'in, there had been long periods when foreigners like the Mongols and the Manchus ruled. Any Chinese wanting to throw off a foreign yoke would still have to eat while formulating plans for rebellion.

Collaboration was nothing new for members of my own family either. My grandfather had done so in the Straits Settlements for 20 years, when he put his medical skills at the disposal of the British Crown in order to facilitate raising funds among overseas Chinese to finance uprisings against the Manchus. Those uprisings had been led by his friend, Dr. Sun Yat-Sen.

Anna, the mother of my siblings, and Wong Hok-Keung, her cousin, had both collaborated more directly, working for the British Special Branch in Singapore before World War II. My father, too, could not help accommodating the Japanese during their occupation of Singapore. He had to ensure that 10 members of our family would not starve to death.

There had also been a more subtle kind of collaboration on the part of my maternal grandfather, Mok Shao-Tsang, when he spent much of his life promoting a foreign religion. He was a true believer in Christianity. During the two years I had spent with him as a small boy in Canton, he had filled my head with the alarming notion that I had been born bad, loaded with original sin. I could only escape damnation, he said, by gaining the grace of his alien God.

He himself had been utterly convinced that he carried his own original sin, though he was a very sincere and kind-hearted man. He spent most of his life caring for the poor, the sick, the hungry and the dispossessed. Whether his deeds gained him salvation in heaven could not be discovered. But at least on earth, when the ecclesiastic office of Anglican Bishop of Canton was created, he became the first person to fill it.

My maternal grandfather's teachings had left me with a nagging residue of guilt. I began to rationalise that by doing some public service I might make up for whatever sins I might have committed too. That was part of the reason I applied to become an Administrative Officer. But I got nowhere; I failed the selection.

I did not discover till long afterwards about the unannounced quota of only one Chinese Administrative Officer to be admitted each year. Moreover, if several candidates were considered to be of equal ability, then preference would be given to one already in the civil service.

* * *

Following my failure, I got a job as a sub-editor and feature writer with the *Hong Kong Standard,* then under the editorship of Leslie Sung, a Eurasian graduate of Hong Kong University. Leslie and I got along extremely well and we became fast friends until well after we had both retired and had migrated to different parts of the world.

I had been working happily at the *Standard* for less than a year before I was summarily sacked. Leslie told me that some people in the government had taken a dislike to the tone of some of my articles and had applied pressure on the management to get rid of me. Leslie told me he had objected to my dismissal on grounds of freedom of speech and freedom of the press. But to no avail. He wanted to resign in protest, as a matter of principle, but I deterred him.

"Be pragmatic," I said. "It's better for men with principles to be working inside a newspaper than left on the outside. Besides, you're married and have a family to support."

On that basis, Leslie stayed. But he began studying law in his spare time to prepare for a career outside of journalism and later became a senior partner in a leading law firm.

* * *

By then I had acquired registration as a teacher, so I set about teaching secondary school for a couple of years. It proved a dispiriting experience, teaching European history to young people who really had little interest in a foreign civilisation. In despair, I decided to end the farce and to leave for Europe, to resume work as a journalist or to engage in some other form of writing.

During the next few years of an itinerant life, I found I had enough leisure to delve deeper into the Chinese philosophies I had begun studying at Stanford, particularly the ideas of Mencius. Confucianism had attracted me enormously once I got a taste of it. The emphasis of its sages upon the importance of basic human relationships, as between king and citizen, father and son, husband and wife, got me thinking about the progressive disintegration of the old extended family. And of the different degrees and gradings of each relationship also.

It had been Mencius who had first tried more than 2,000 years ago to offer the theoretical justifications for many Confucian beliefs. He held that human nature was fundamentally good. If it were allowed to develop unimpeded, then "human-heartedness" and a sense of righteousness would take hold. But man's nature also contained other elements which had to be controlled. Otherwise they could lead to evil.

In the Confucian scheme of things, man was also a political animal, which meant that human relationships had to develop within a state or a society. The state therefore had to be a moral institution and the head of it a moral leader. In short, a real king was also required to be a real sage, someone who could place the welfare of the "old hundred surnames" before other considerations. I suppose that over the centuries the concept developed of selecting public officials from those who were steeped in the classics. Such officials could then serve as both the father and the mother of the people.

The government of a sage king would in practice be carried out through moral instructions and education. When a ruler lacked the ethical qualities to be a good leader, then the people had a right to rebel and kill him as a "mere fellow". Such ideas exerted tremendous influence throughout Chinese history. They struck me as much more realistic and attractive than my maternal grandfather's theory of original sin and the need for a god to intervene to attain salvation.

As a counterpoint to Confucianism, I also delved into Taoism and found in it much food for introspection and speculation.

* * *

When I got back in Hong Kong in 1959, I was no longer alone. I had recklessly acquired a wife. I got a job as a night sub-editor with the *South China Morning Post*. But it soon became apparent that nocturnal work was not very conducive to family life, especially after a son in poor health came quickly upon the scene in 1960.

When I saw another advertisement about openings for Administrative Officers, I reflected upon it. The notion of working for a colonial government overseen by a distantly appointed foreign autocrat was still not an agreeable one. My experiences with governments had been largely unsatisfactory.

But, now that I was saddled with a family, a civil service job did offer a measure of security. A regime with fixed yearly salary increments was also not available in the media or in the private sector. Moreover, the government would provide free medical attention for dependants of civil servants. That was an enormous plus, given the sickliness of my son. On that basis, I decided to give it another try, at least as a stepping stone. I had no great expectation of being successful.

* * *

Going through the recruitment process for a second time, I was surprised to find that candidates still only had to be tested on English and not on their ability to communicate in Chinese. Before the war, expatriate officers had to spend two years learning Chinese before taking up their posts. Could the waiving of the need for fluency in Chinese be an attempt to send candidates a subliminal message that so long as they knew how to take orders in English, there was no need to pay heed to views expressed in other languages?

The obsession with facility in English was sometimes carried to absurd levels. Labour Inspectors, for instance, whose jobs required them to deal almost exclusively with factory workers, and Housing Officers, who dealt mainly with working class tenants in government housing estates, had often been selected or rejected on the basis of their command of English. It must have been due to some grace from heaven that no such requirement had been imposed upon rubbish collectors and manual labourers as well!

That bizarre and unenlightened state of affairs must have been due to the Establishment Branch having been as fast asleep as Rip Van Winkle for most of the last century and a half. It later morphed into a bloated Civil Service Branch under the McKinsey reorganisation.

The civil service, then as now, was the largest single employer in the colony. Whatever it did, for good or ill, inevitably set the tone for the rest of the community. And yet, for much of the colonial period that tone had been set mainly by expatriates whose contacts with the masses were minimal. Their forebears in the former foreign concessions in China had set the pattern, restricting communications with Chinese to the staff in their offices, their sedan chair carriers and their domestic servants at home. It was only after World War II that that situation slowly began to change.

That cocooned mode of existence was by no means unique to British colonial masters. It was quite common among well-meaning people committed to bringing civilisation to those described as "lesser breeds without the law." Comintern agents sent to China, for instance, also appeared to be locked into a similar mindset.

Otto Braun was a prime example. He was known as Li De or Li the German after he had been sent by the Soviet Union in 1932 as military advisor to the so-called "Red bandits" in their struggle against the Kuomintang. Braun had studied at the Frunze Military Academy where German strategic thinking prevailed. He could quote from Caesar or Napoleon, or from Tacitus or von Moltke at the drop of a hat. But China and its people had remained blank pages for him. He knew no Chinese, made no attempt to learn it, and after two years in the country still preferred eating bread to rice, even if he had to bake the bread himself.

Of course, Braun also treated with disdain the guerrilla tactics advocated by Mao, labelling them as *passé*. How wrong he had been did not become clear until much later, until after Mao had secured control of the Red Army by out-manoeuvring Chang Kuo-Tao and proceeded to beat the armies of the Kuomintang hands down.

In fairness, I should perhaps not criticise the likes of Braun when I myself, in spite of having spent more than 30 years in the West, still preferred eating rice to bread — even if I had to cook the rice myself!

If the British elite in Hong Kong shared the mindset of a Braun, that should be quite understandable. After all, the *raison d'être* for the colony was initially to facilitate that morally equivocal business of peddling opium. Ingenious and amoral ways of making money were thus at the forefront of thinking among the top wheelers and dealers. I doubted if any colonial administration would wish to disturb such a cosy status quo.

* * *

Unbeknownst to me, the previous annual quota on admitting only one Chinese into the Administrative Service per annum had been lifted around the same time as my application. To my surprise, therefore, I found I was offered an appointment at the start of 1961.

That offer forced me to re-evaluate the hitherto rudderless mode of my life. It appeared a very important decision, with many ramifications. The financial impact was not the least among them. It would mean an immediate cut in income, for the starting point of the Administrative Service scale was below what I was earning. It would require a couple of annual increments to get back to my existing level.

But even a return to that level still meant not earning enough to support my family. I had been relying on a substantial subsidy from my in-laws ever since my marriage to make ends meet. Living at the economic margins was one of the causes for my shaky marriage. How could that inadequate level be further lowered for an indefinite period of years? How furious would my wife get?

The counter argument was that there was no future in journalism in Hong Kong. I was stuck on an income plateau, if not actually slipping into a rut. Pay increases were at the discretion of the employer and subject to the profitability of his publishing enterprise. At least government service had an established system for salary increases and also more sociable working hours. To cap that off, there would be considerable savings on my son's medical bills.

But it was other imponderables that worried me most. Although the Administrative Service had been touted as an elite service, made up of the best brains in the administration, how would that brainpower be deployed — for the benefit of the local population or to maintain an imperial agenda at all cost? The British record was not reassuring. Messes had been left behind at almost every place where the Union Jack had once fluttered. Would I be called upon to be complicit in sustaining a similar mess in Hong Kong?

Confucian sages had envisaged the art of governance — at its highest — to be a noble and ethical enterprise. Should I not try my hand at it, even under a foreign ruler? It had to be a challenging quest to identify that shifting centre ground upon which individual citizens could maximise their freedoms consistent with a state's overriding requirements for order and security. There would also be the task of mediating between local attitudes and foreign impositions.

I was not without certain notions about the rightness of things. There were principles from which I was not prepared to depart. If called upon to do the unacceptable, I could follow the example of Tao Yuan-Ming, that Six Dynasties poet and official, by refusing "to bow like a servant in return for five bushels of grain." If pressed, I might even be able to throw a spanner or two into an infernal foreign machine.

After a couple of weeks of debating with myself and consulting with my in-laws, I decided to take the plunge to work for the government.

* * *

After joining, I had the extreme good fortunate of being assigned to work for David Baron, the then Director of Social Welfare. He turned out to be one of the most kind, fair, principled and compassionate colleagues I have ever worked for. We became life-long friends and we kept in touch for decades after our respective retirements.

My next expatriate boss was Alistair Todd in the Government Secretariat. He was equally principled and intelligent and was straight as a die. I thus had two wonderful introductions to civil service life.

In later years, my good fortune continued, for I was assigned to superiors like David Alexander, John Cowperthwaite and Donald Luddington.

Those I have named were all in their different ways exceptional colleagues. They went out of their way to mentor juniors and to inspire them to adhere to integrity, dedication and openness. They contributed mightily to the excellence and *esprit de corps* associated with the Administrative Service and offered friendships which transcended racial divides to become enduring and treasured.

But like most professional organisations, the service also had its fair share of duds, gasbags, time-servers, chancers and unreconstructed racists. In my own view, the service was probably at its best during the early 1970s, before the steadying influence of many old-timers was lost through retirements. The top levels then became more flamboyant and more given to public relations gimmicks.

At the same time, cliques started to develop around personalities or mutual interests. For example, it was an open secret that a handful of local Administrative Officers had been meeting regularly since the early 1960s for the purpose of pushing the government to grant them equal treatment as expatriates. Expatriate officers too had their own lobbying groups. Some of the idealism, sense of service and unity of purpose began to fade as a result.

I have not been in the picture on how the service had evolved after the sovereignty over Hong Kong had been returned to China. Someone else would have to take up that story.

Three Administrative Officers, all Chinese, had to the best of my knowledge been sent to prison over the last 30 years for corruption of one kind or another. Two of them had been sentenced after the sovereignty of Hong Kong had been returned to China. Perhaps more, both Chinese and expatriates, should have been imprisoned. There certainly had been cases of blatant intellectual dishonesty which went unpublicised and unpunished though they bordered on criminality.

* * *

Soon after I had been confirmed into the permanent and pensionable establishment in 1964, I was asked to serve on a recruitment board for Administrative Officers. I reacted with some ambivalence, for I was not sure whether the invitation was on the up and up. Had I really gained sufficient experience in three short years to pass judgement on the suitability of others? Or was it a baited trap, to serve as a figleaf to obscure racial discrimination and to test my reliability in serving the British Crown? How far should I allow myself to be compromised or bent? After all, it was not for nothing that the Marquis de Ximénèz had described the British as "*la perfide Albion*."

But the invitation to participate appeared pretty much like the ones issued by the Mafia — impossible to refuse. So I duly turned up at the board to do my duty. The board consisted of four other serving officers, all expatriates, with a Staff Grade B officer as chairman. I was the only Chinese and also the most junior member. The chairman of the Public Services Commission, another expatriate, sometimes sat in as an observer.

I had expected to be given instructions on the kind of candidates the board should be looking for before proceedings commenced. But no instruction was forthcoming. Since I was unsure whether only pliable types or those unlikely to rock the boat were being sought, I asked the chairman what qualities we wanted in candidates.

"The same as our own, of course," the chairman replied chirpily.

I was not prepared to rest on his evasion. I persisted. "Would that not be rather difficult, seeing that almost half the candidates to be interviewed are women?

I doubt if we would find very many with masculine characteristics."

"You know what I mean," the chairman snapped testily.

Since the chairman appeared disinclined to explain, I did not attempt to tell him what was on my mind. I was keen to recruit candidates with qualities of heart and mind capable of developing human-heartedness and a sense of righteousness. I did not want to be responsible for selecting some flunkey who could turn readily into a Quisling or a Wang Ching-Wai. But I kept that thought to myself.

On that slightly ruffled note, I began my duties.

* * *

The recruitment interviews turned out to be fairly unstructured, with no agreement beforehand as to who would ask what type of questions. It was pretty much catch-as-catch-can, according to the personal inclinations of individual board members. Each candidate was scheduled for at least half an hour's grilling. More, if thought necessary.

The use of English favoured female candidates, for they had studied the humanities or English literature for the most part. Thus they had greater facility with the language. The men tended towards more scientific degrees.

To put candidates at their ease, someone might begin by asking questions falling well within a candidate's field of study or interest. For a woman, she might be asked her views on equal pay for women or abortion laws or the adequacy or otherwise of statutory provisions for maternity leave. For a male physics graduate, he might be asked to explain the Copenhagen interpretation of quantum theory or Planck's Constant.

I myself preferred questions entailing moral dilemmas. For instance, I might say: "In ancient times, there used to be a Chinese saying that if the emperor asked a minister to die and the minister failed to die, he would be considered disloyal; and if a father asked a son to perish and the son did not perish, the son would be considered unfilial. Do you think such dicta still relevant in our modern age?"

There would, of course, be no correct or incorrect answer. The candidate had to stake his or her ground and defend it. After an answer I would pass the candidate to another board member. But I would have laid the groundwork for later questions. For instance, I might return later as follows:

"As you may know, the government has enforced, following a big influx of illegal immigrants from Kwangtung Province in 1962, a policy known as the 'touch base' policy. It is predicated upon illegals being able to outwit both the Chinese and our own border controls.

"An additional security cordon has therefore been set up in the New Territories, to prevent any illegal from reaching any urban centre. The teams manning that inner cordon are required to arrest all illegals they can find, for quick repatriation to China. If an illegal manages to reach an urban area, however, he is considered to have 'touched base' and allowed to remain. The assumption behind the policy is purely pragmatic. First, it would require too much manpower to track down anyone who has reached a built-up area. Secondly, a person's ability to do so would suggest some sort of local assistance, which might also be deployed to help him hide.

"Now imagine that you have been successful in this interview and, as a fresh Administrative Officer, you have been assigned to lead one of the teams manning the inner cordon.

"One night, you receive a telephone call from a stranger, a trafficker, if you like. He tells you your father — or maybe your brother — has got himself out of China to Hong Kong. Assume for the time being that you do have a father or brother who might want to come here. The trafficker continues by telling you that your kinsman is hiding in a chicken coop at a certain location in the New Territories. He requires you to help your kinsman to 'touch base' before he is picked up and sent back. What would you do under such circumstances?"

Some of the human faces in the 1962 influx. Photo: *South China Morning Post*

The earlier questions about loyalty and filial piety had already nailed the candidate down to certain doctrinal positions. He would now have to defend those positions. In practice, the answers offered ranged from the sublime to the ridiculous.

Half an hour of interviewing was of course far from foolproof in determining whether a young person could fulfil the requirements of becoming a good public official. But it was often sufficient time to reveal whether he lacked the makings of a good public official.

* * *

Subsequent to that initial recruitment board, I was asked to serve on two more boards during the next few years. The subsequent boards had been constituted in much the same way as the first. I had remained the sole Chinese member and I had chosen to continue the line of questioning I had adopted for the first board.

The greatest difficulty I encountered during the subsequent exercises concerned two exceptionally gifted candidates who appeared in the same year. Their names were Wong Sing-Wah and Chan Cho-Chak. Both had gone through the process with flying colours, fending off successfully some of the toughest questions thrown at them. Both displayed fine potential for the service.

However, after their interviews, I argued strongly against giving either of them an immediate appointment. I felt unable to explain some of my reasons before an expatriate-dominated board.

First of all, both candidates were short, standing at only about five-foot-three. Both of them had fresh, boyish faces which belied their status as university graduates. Their eyes shone with eagerness and intelligence. But I noticed that one of them — after more than 50 years, I cannot now be sure which one — betrayed evidence of biting his finger nails. Still high-strung, I thought, feeling the need to shield him from more insensitive colleagues to give him time to mature.

Secondly, I felt the potential of the two was too precious to be exposed to the vagaries of an unimaginative Establishment Branch. One or the other of them might be thoughtlessly sent to a frontline department responsible for, say, squatter clearances from Crown land. Such duties might demoralise a raw and untried officer before he could find his feet.

Squatter clearances were sometimes met by fierce resistance from those about to be displaced. Should that happen, would a fresh recruit know how to handle the situation? Would the tough and seasoned clearance teams under him obey his orders? He might in their eyes appear younger than their own sons or grandsons. Would either of them panic in the face of bloodshed? I wanted to protect both of them from such an early ordeal.

I had gone through a similar conflict during my first assignment at the Social Welfare Department. I fortunately had the advantage of being much older and more experienced. Nonetheless, it had rattled me and caused me to wonder if I was really suited to be in foreign administration.

My test had occurred soon after I had been made head of the Relief Section. It came in the form of an agitated telephone call from a redoubtable lady named Mrs. Elsie Elliott. I had never met the lady but she had already made a fearsome name for herself as the bane of the colonial bureaucracy. She had a penchant for involving herself as a champion of underdogs in all sorts of social disputes.

She had asserted over the telephone that some unfortunates were being tossed off Crown land in Kowloon and that their huts were being demolished by squatter control teams. Why was I, as the head of the Relief Section, not out there to stop the demolition, she asked.

I explained that land clearances were not my responsibility. If people were illegally occupying Crown land and that land was required for some public purpose, then the illegal occupants had to be cleared.

"You're the head of the Relief Section, aren't you?" Mrs. Elliott retorted. "Innocent people, women and children, are having their homes destroyed. Shouldn't you be out there offering them relief? Otherwise what kind of relief are you supposed to offer?"

"If they should be in need of food, they can register at a Social Welfare Department centre and I will see to their being processed for dry rations," I replied. "I am sure the people undertaking the clearance have made provision for temporary shelter. I have no control over clearances. They are not my responsibility."

"Not your responsibility!" Mrs. Elliott echoed. "What kind of man are you, to have no responsibility for the suffering of your fellow human beings? How would you like it if someone tore down your home and tossed your family and their belongings out on the street?"

"I'm sorry, Mrs. Elliott, but I cannot help you in this matter."

"You just have no heart," she said. "You should be ashamed of yourself." She then rang off.

A surge of hopeless impotence had gripped me as I replaced the telephone in its cradle. What *was* I in the public service for, I asked myself, if I could not help the needy navigate through the thickets of public regulations and private needs? It was as if I were back at the Central Magistracy ages ago, watching bewildered defendants being sent to gaol for offences they could not apprehend. I could hardly fall back on the bland excuse I was not my brother's keeper.

And yet, I suppose I was trying to act as my brother's keeper in respect of Wong and Chan. The salary they would earn upon acceptance would be meagre enough but I wanted to give them the chance of finding their feet first, by inducting them into the civil service but at a lower level. I feared they might become disheartened by facing insoluble dilemmas too early. I was convinced they had potential; I did not want to risk losing either of them because of unsound initial postings.

It was because of such a tangle of considerations that I argued they both looked far too school-boyish to be Administrative Officers tasked with decisions beyond their experience. It would be safer to appoint them initially as Executive or Trade Officers. In order to encourage them to try again for the Administrative Service, they could be invited to apply next year. That would also test their determination to serve.

I must have cast sufficient doubt among other members of the board for it to decide as I had recommended. Both joined at a lower grade but were admitted into the Administrative Service the following year.

After their admission, I told them both I had been responsible for delaying their admission as Administrative Officers. I got the impression that neither held anything against me.

* * *

Some years later, Wong Sing-Wah was posted to the Economic Services

Branch to work under me. I found him to be a meticulous and dedicated officer. His recommendations were always sober and thorough. After I had left the civil service and migrated to Britain, we maintained contact for many years. I had, unfortunately, no opportunity to work directly with Chan Cho-Chak. But such comments as I had received from his superiors suggested that he too had been doing splendidly.

Both of them in due course reached the highest grade of Policy Secretary and retired with distinction.

In 1993, when the British authorities could no longer resist the pressure to have a Chinese in the post of Chief Secretary before the return of sovereignty to China, I heard gossip in London that Chan Cho-Chak had been offered the post but he had declined it. No specific reason came to my ears. The appointment subsequently went to Mrs. Anson Chan, née Fang, another officer with whose appointment as an Administrative Officer I had been marginally involved in.

After Chan Cho-Chak retired from the civil service, he took on a number of important positions in community organisations, including the much prized chairmanship of the Hong Kong Jockey Club.

* * *

Some time in 1973, I received a telephone call from the Deputy Secretary for the Civil Service. He said he would like to sound me out on a couple of ideas. Although he was a Chinese colleague, I was immediately put on guard. I had long ago arrived at the conclusion that senior Secretariat officers usually found my opinions inimical to the enjoyment of their quiet cups of morning or afternoon tea. For one to seek my views suggested there had to be a catch.

The Deputy Secretary indicated in a leisurely way that orders had come down from Government House for a rapid increase in the intake of

Administrative Officers. The Governor wanted to expand public services, which meant finding more bodies to man new posts. One way of achieving that result would be to reduce the rigour of recruitment interviews.

That would not necessarily mean any lowering of standards, the Deputy Secretary was quick to add. It merely meant that the weeding out process would be deferred to the time of confirmation, after three years of probation. The advantages to such a proposal would be a more thorough assessment of the abilities of the officers concerned, apart from the immediate availability of more hands.

I saw through the stratagem right away and replied that I disagreed wth that approach and wanted no part of it. I had no access to recruitment statistics but, impressionistically, I think the recruitment boards I had served on had, on the whole, produced far lower intakes than the ones I had been absent from. I suspected the Establishment Branch of thinking of putting me on yet another board but wanted to be sure beforehand that I would not queer the Governor's pitch.

I told the Deputy Secretary frankly that I did not think the Government House proposal would work at all. Over the years, I said, I have had a fair number of probationary Administrative Officers placed under my charge. In four cases — involving both locals and expatriates, male and female — I had recommended after several months of supervision that their probations be terminated. It would have been a kindness to the probationers as well as to the bureaucracy because, whatever talents they might have, were clearly not the ones suitable for public service. They ought to seek careers elsewhere.

But in each and every instance my recommendation had been ignored. All those probationers went on to be confirmed. Fortunately for the public, three of them soon reached their own conclusions they could not cope as Administrative Officers and resigned. The fourth soldiered on till retirement but ended up in a very middling position. Those developments indicated to me that the people responsible for managing the civil service had fallen into the bad habit of evading hard decisions.

"Those cases happened before my time," the Deputy Secretary injected.

"I'm sorry," I said. "I didn't mean to imply you were personally responsible. I was criticising the system which allowed such nonsensical things to happen."

I then went on to recall for the Deputy Secretary a specific event which happened some years back when both he and I had been present. The event had been a dinner held by local Administrative Officers to which the Governor of the time, Sir David Trench, and his wife had been invited. The number of local Administrative Officers was then quite small and the most senior one had reached no higher than the dizzying height of Staff Grade C. But we all had gripes.

The dinner was held at the Hong Kong University Alumni Association and consisted of two tables. As was normal for such occasions, the two most junior officers were selected to escort the Governor and his lady respectively, at the two different tables. I had been at the table with the Governor. The officer assigned to Lady Trench at the next table was a relatively fresh recruit. I could see him engaging in animated conversation with the Governor's wife.

At the end of the meal, when the party was about to break up, one of the more senior officers said to Lady Trench — by way of small talk — that he hoped young So-and-So had been taking good care of her during the meal.

To the amazement of everyone present, Lady Trench declared in a loud voice: "That lad's still wet behind the ears."

I had no idea what the young man had been holding forth on. Perhaps he just wanted to impress the Governor's wife with his cleverness. Whatever that was, it misfired badly. It must have taken some time for that young man to live down that public rebuke.

Some years later, he committed suicide in his bathroom, though it was doubtful whether the two events had been in any way connected.

I also drew the Deputy Secretary's attention to another recent incident at

Government House. As had been customary for a long time, every Governor would invite one or two new Administrative Service recruits to dinner at Government House, both to give them a taste of life in high society and to bolster the illusion they had become part of an enviable elite. It had been a black tie affair.

Everybody was taken aback when a fresh recruit from the Chinese University of Hong Kong turned up in an ordinary suit wearing the kind of black tie meant for funerals. Of course, being well-bred, none of the guests betrayed anything more than they would if someone had broken wind loudly at a vicar's tea party.

The poor man should never have been admitted to the Administrative Service. Even if he had got in by fluke, his inadequacies should have been apparent to his supervisors during his probation. But somehow he got confirmed into the pensionable establishment.

That man's lack of common sense and the administration's bungling over his career were almost beyond belief. He could easily have consulted his seniors if he did not know what "black tie" on an invitation card meant. His lack of initiative reflected poorly on both his selection process and on his fellow Administrative Officers.

It was only after more than 20 years that the Civil Service Branch finally woke up to the fact he was incapable of discharging any of the normal duties of an Administrative Officer. It then resorted to a bureaucratic device known in the jargon as MIR or "management initiated retirement" to remove him.

After citing those two instances, I argued that recruitment procedures should be toughened rather than relaxed. Mentoring a fresh recruit demanded a great deal of time from seasoned officers. If they did not display the right potential to begin with, time spent in mentoring would be a waste.

Furthermore, I added, a measure of good governance depended upon the quality of officials undertaking the tasks required to be done and not merely on the number of people assigned to them. More fundamental matters ought to be tackled first, before searching for extra bodies.

If the problem to be tackled concerned education, for instance, the entire system should first be systematically re-examined. If we were producing poorly educated citizens, the first investigations should be into what was being taught to them, how and by whom. Bad curricula and bad teachers could not produce good citizens. Associated issues like affordability, school meals, colleges for training teachers, recreational facilities and so on also had to be looked at. None of those related problems would disappear simply by building more schools and offering more school places.

The Deputy Secretary listened to my lengthy exposition in relative silence. I could sense his discomfiture; but I was enjoying myself too much delivering an earful to the Civil Service Branch. In his heart, I imagined the Deputy Secretary probably agreed with at least some of my points but he could not find it in himself to speak against the instructions from Government House. In the end, he just thanked me for my views and rang off.

In the normal course of events, the Deputy Secretary would probably note in a Secretariat file somewhere my utter unsuitability for service on future Administrative Officer recruitment boards. Whether he did or not I could not say. But after that exchange I was never again asked to serve on another recruitment board for the rest of my career.

* * *

Of course, I only had the Deputy Secretary's account of the Governor's demand for a speedy increase in the number of Administrative Officers. If Sir Murray MacLehose had indeed sanctioned a watering down of standards to achieve that end, then he has done both Hong Kong and the Administrative Service a great disservice.

Administrative Officers, for good or ill, formed — and continue to form — the backbone of the Hong Kong civil service. The aim, therefore, should be to inspire and attract the ablest and the most idealistic of each generation. The civil service could not — and should not — stoop to competing with the private sector in seeking talent on the basis of material rewards alone. It should instead project public service as a vocation calling for plain living, integrity, dedication, vision and anonymity, rather than as just another cushy job.

If enough serious effort were made, such people could be found in every age. Chinese history has been filled with examples. Take at random Chancellor Fan Chung-Yen of the Sung Dynasty. He worked himself to the bone for the public good and enjoined other public officials to be "the first to bear the world's hardships and the last to enjoy its comforts."

Another worthy coming readily to mind was Chang Chu-Tseng, a statesman of the Ming Dynasty. When he was in power he placed himself completely above personal success or failure and the praise of men. He instilled discipline into officialdom and insisted that officials fulfilled their duties with faith, determination and courage.

Unfortunately, colonial education largely avoided teaching students about such ancient personalities from Chinese culture. The newer generations of local Administrative Officers had probably never even heard of them. Besides, how many bright youngsters would rush to become an underpaid civil servant when business corporations were offering big bucks for the ability to draw up flattering corporate accounts or for stripping assets after a leveraged buy-out?

And even with 1997 fast approaching, the MacLehose governorship made little effort to prepare the young for significant change. Local community leaders had to bear some of the blame too, for they failed to put sufficient pressure on the administration to prepare for the future.

* * *

I lost touch with the pattern for recruiting Administrative Officers after my conversation with the Deputy Secretary. What I can confirm, however, was that a couple of positive changes occurred in 1974.

By that year, Eric Ho had become senior enough to be asked to chair a recruitment board for Administrative Officers. He immediately allowed, for the first time, candidates to answer all questions in the language of their choice.

His approach was entirely logical because in 1972 Chinese had been made — with much public fanfare and after a wait of some 130 years — into a second official language. Eric's move no doubt put the noses of some non-Chinese-speaking expatriate board members out of joint.

Eric also made another startling innovation — he demanded to see all the written English examination papers of candidates who had failed to qualify for an interview. When he found that some with good scores on the intelligence test had failed over English, he invited them for interviews nonetheless.

His argument was that if candidates had good brains, then language could be improved through usage. Because of his approach, a small number of extra Chinese officers with potential got appointed. If not for him, those officers would have fallen by the wayside.

* * *

To run a little ahead of myself in chronology, it might be worth recording as a footnote that Sir Murray MacLehose began to recognise in 1981, towards the end of his stint as Governor, the dearth of top flight talent within his administration. He could not find among his coterie of blue-eyed boys anyone to fill the important post of Financial Secretary.

My own belief was that suitable Chinese talent existed both within the civil service and outside to fill that and a number of other posts. Many personages in the private sector had served with distinction and without remuneration as members of the Legislative and Executive Councils, for instance. Their expertise and local experiences would have been invaluable in formulating polices in fields like education, medical and health, and engineering and public works.

But it was possible that neither the Governor nor Whitehall felt trustful enough of the loyalty of any Chinese at that stage to risk appointing them to high office.

In any event, the person ultimately chosen to fill the post of Financial Secretary was a very able British businessman named John Bremridge. He was a former Chairman of the Swire Group who had also served on the Legislative and Executive Councils. He was eminently suited both by experience and by temperament. He took a very significant cut in income to assume public office and his appointment turned out to be one of the most astute decisions taken by Sir Murray during his entire tenure.

CHAPTER 7

Bureaucratic Run-Ins

WHEN I WAS APPOINTED City District Commissioner for Hong Kong in 1971, I was simultaneously appointed a Justice of the Peace. Justices of the Peace came in two categories — official and unofficial. The official ones were essentially senior government officials accepting the appointment as part of their duties; the unofficial ones were made up of solid citizens in business or in the professions, selected for appointment because of their interest in unpaid voluntary work. To become an unofficial one, a person would normally be recommended by either the Secretariat for Home Affairs or the New Territories Administration. Those found to be even mildly anti-colonial in sentiment would be naturally weeded out.

All appointees would be entitled to put the initials JP after their names on calling cards. The public at large often mistook the suffix as some kind of honour. Appointees from the private sector were naturally in no hurry to disabuse anyone of that misconception.

In reality, a JP enjoyed no free ride for that title. He or she had to assume a range of judicial duties. Among the most frequent was the inspection of public institutions like hospitals, orphanages, prisons and the like, to see that they were being properly run. This was to cultivate in the public a perception that impartial community oversight was in place to identify defects and mismanagement.

Inspections were always carried out in pairs, with one official JP accompanying an unofficial one. Although visits were theoretically supposed to be spontaneous and unannounced, they were in fact arranged according to a schedule overseen by the Councils Branch of the Secretariat. The bureaucratic penchant for regularity and system made it easy for most institutions to figure out roughly when a visit might be due. They would then spruce up their institutions in anticipation.

A JP also had a range of other duties, most of which would devolve upon official JPs rather than on the unofficial ones. For instance, during long holiday weekends, when the courts were closed, a police inspector might well turn up at the home of an official JP to request a warrant to confine someone to a mental institution for observation, pending the re-opening of the courts. The JP would need to be fully satisfied that the behaviour of the person in question was such as to merit detention, because the liberty of a citizen was at stake. I had signed such warrants on more than one occasion.

One of my earliest JP visits was to the maximum security prison at Stanley. The regulations of the prison had a provision whereby inmates could demand an audience with visiting JPs for the purpose of lodging complaints. Any prisoner wishing to complain about treatment would then be brought before visiting JPs.

It so happened that an inmate did want to lodge a complaint during my visit. The complainant alleged an unreasonable denial of reading material. In order to remain unbiased, my fellow JP and I deliberately refrained from asking about the crime for which the complainant had been convicted and the length of his sentence.

According to the prisoner, he should have reasonable access to reading material. His choice of reading was a Chinese daily newspaper of leftist inclinations brought to him by his family. However, the authorities had refused to pass him that publication.

I cannot now remember whether the newspaper had been the *Ta Kung*

Pao or the *People's Daily*. It had been one or the other. My JP colleague and I both thought a British prison was a place for punishment and reform, not for altering political inclinations. The newspaper concerned was freely available at street corner news kiosks throughout the colony. So we recommended that, on the face of things, the prisoner ought to be entitled to his newspapers. We recorded our recommendation in a visitors' book set aside for that purpose.

A week or so later, a letter addressed to both visiting JPs was received from the Commissioner for Prisons. He thanked us for visiting Stanley Prison but said it was his policy not to allow subversive literature to be circulated within prisons. Therefore he regretted that our recommendation could not be acted upon.

My immediate reaction was that the Commissioner for Prisons had exceeded his authority. It was for the government to determine whether any publication was subversive or not. Since the newspaper in question was being openly sold throughout the colony, it could not *ipso facto* be considered subversive. The Commissioner might not like its politics but he could not unilaterally deem it subversive. Neither was he entitled to deprive any prisoner of the right to read it.

Under British law, a man did not lose all his civic rights upon conviction. Neither was he required to abandon his political preferences. If the prisoner had asked for some books on how to break out of maximum security prisons, then the Commissioner for Prisons might have some grounds for denying him the material.

I telephoned my unofficial JP colleague to enquire if he had received an identical letter from the Commissioner for Prisons. When he confirmed that he had, I asked for his reactions.

"Well," he said, "seems a bid hard. But I suppose if the Commissioner considers the newspaper subversive, then that is that."

I replied that I did not think that needed to be "that" at all. I explained my own feelings and said I intended to challenge the Commissioner because

I considered it better to make a stand now rather than wait till circumstances forced me to adopt one in public.

"What do you mean?" he asked.

"Well, we can never tell how things might develop," I replied. "Suppose the family of the prisoner wrote to newspapers about his being denied the reading material of his choice. The issue could become public and political. We might be forced to explain why we had made our original decision as judicial officers and what we thought of being overruled by the Commissioner. So it is better to object to the Commissioner's ruling now rather than later."

"But won't that upset the administration?"

"Our duty as JPs *is* to upset the administration, especially if we feel it is not following the rules or abusing them. I will naturally first attempt to sort things out informally and diplomatically, through the Secretary for Security. He has policy oversight over the prison service. No need to put anybody in a huff or make him lose face. You don't have to go along with me, you know, if you're comfortable with the Commissioner's decision. I can pursue the challenge on my own."

My statement placed my fellow JP squarely between Scylla and Charybdis, between either going back on the recommendation he had attached his name to in the prison visitor's book or else taking on an administration which had conferred a JP-ship upon him. He was anxious to remain in the government's good books.

After a moment's hesitation he said: "Of course, you are perfectly right. It is wrong not to allow a fellow to read whatever he likes, unless there is a good reason to do otherwise. 'Subversive' is pretty vague, isn't it? If you think you can get the ruling changed without upsetting anybody, I would certainly go along."

"Leave it with me then. I'll keep you posted."

Armed with that lukewarm support, I rang my old sparring partner, the Secretary for Security. I outlined the facts of the case and said that both my unofficial colleague and I considered the Commissioner's decision to be flawed. We did not want to put in a formal written objection if we could help it, hoping matters might be resolved more quietly. Should news of the Commissioner's decision leak, or appear in the press at the instigation of the prisoner's family, both the Commissioner and the government might have difficulty defending the decision in public.

The Commissioner was a European, with scant knowledge of Chinese. His interpretation of what was subversive might be hotly contested and the government would have to either support him or overrule him. A humiliating prospect in either case, leading perhaps even to questions before the British Parliament. In the circumstances, it might be better if the Secretary could have a word with the Commissioner, drawing his attention to the potential political ramifications of his decision.

The Secretary for Security grasped the implications very quickly. He asked me to leave the matter with him for a few days.

In due time, another letter from the Commissioner for Prisons arrived for myself and my unofficial JP partner. The Commissioner said that after further consultation with his staff, he had discovered that the fear of the newspaper's ability to subvert had been somewhat overstated. Hence he had re-considered his earlier decision and would now accept our recommendation about allowing the prisoner access to the newspapers supplied by his family.

Thus honour was preserved on all sides. A tiny victory perhaps, but I doubted if I had endeared myself to the Secretary for Security any more than on the previous occasion we had crossed swords.

* * *

Some time in 1972, I received a letter from my father, then aged 71. He indicated an intention to visit Hong Kong "for one last time". He knew I was in an unsatisfactory marriage and that I had been living with my in-laws. In order not to cause me inconvenience, he said, he intended to accept the hospitality offered by a long-standing university friend of his surnamed Tseng.

I replied immediately, informing him for the first time of my separation with Man-Ying and the migration of her parents to America. I was now in government quarters and it would be presentationally bad if he were to stay in Hong Kong with a friend instead of with his own son. People might think there had been some fracture in the family.

He could stay with me for as long as he wished, I said, though I was in the midst of calming agitated students and my time was not my own. The children were too young to offer him much help. All I had to keep the household ticking over was a semi-illiterate one-foot-kick providing unexciting meals. It would mean he would have to rely largely on his own devices during his stay.

The last occasion I had seen my father was in 1970, when I went to Singapore for some civil aviation negotiations. He had by then grown as lean as my grandfather had been at his age. That well-fleshed man-about-town image of his middle years had vanished; he was now as lean and spritely as my grandfather had been at that same age. His movements had slowed, however, to the leisurely tempo of one ambling through a traditional Chinese garden, complete with moon-gates and meandering paths. I doubted whether the hectic noon-day pace which had taken over in Hong Kong would suit him.

He must be feeling more lonely and out of sorts, I surmised, after the death of Anna in 1971. It came to me then that the Chinese extended family structure which had been available to him — and also to myself during my boyhood — had collapsed following the demise of my grandfather in 1961, marking a decisive end of that form of living for my family. My aunts had all gone their separate ways and so had my siblings and myself. The only unmarried one of my generation then was Tzi-Seng, still at university in England.

My understanding was that the bungalow at Berwick Drive had been sold some time after my grandfather's passing, with the proceeds divided between my father and my uncle Yan-Wing. My uncle married and eventually set up home in another part of the Serangoon Gardens Estate.

I have no clear recollection of where my father and Anna had gone after the sale of the bungalow at Berwick Drive, probably with one of their children. Losing the roof over their heads and the recurrent subsidy from my grandfather's pension would have placed them under too much financial pressure to acquire a home of their own. In addition, Anna had to pay off the considerable debts she had incurred to finance Tzi-Seng's education abroad.

Tzi-Seng had returned to Singapore and got married in 1964. When he started to work for Shell at Pulau Bukom in 1965, my father and Anna did move in with the young couple and stayed till Anna's death.

Apart from Anna's death, the misfortune of my brother, Francis, with the *Singapore Herald,* which I had detailed in Volume 2 of these memoirs, must have been a disappointment for my father too. Francis was his favourite son. A visit to Hong Kong, therefore, would be sure to lift his spirits, although many of the relatives he was most familiar with, like my Eighth Granduncle and my Ninth Grandaunt, had already passed away.

I cannot now remember exactly when he came, but it would have been when the climate was at its most pleasant, either November and early December in 1972 or March and early April in 1973. I found him little changed from our last meeting, except perhaps with a little more abstracted air than before. His six-week stay had been during the racing season, for I took him for lunch at the Owners' Box once. He was quite taken when I introduced him to other horse owners as my father and they all treated him with elaborate courtesy.

But he almost got me into serious trouble by upsetting the tenuous domestic equilibrium I had managed to establish. It happened one evening during the second week of his stay. I had gone into the kitchen to get a drink of water and found Ah Duen doing cleaning. She immediately turned and said: "Master, you must find someone else to take my place. I do not know how to take care of *lo-yeh*. I think I have offended him."

I was surprised because I did not think my father required much taking care of. When I asked what had happened, Ah Duen said that before she set out for the market each morning, she always asked my father what he would like to eat that day, so that she could buy the right food for him. But he always replied "*sze-tan*" which in Cantonese meant "whatever" or "as you like".

However, at meal times, my father would sometimes leave the table without touching a single dish. Therefore she felt she must have displeased him in not preparing food to his taste, making him go hungry.

Ah Duen's threat to leave really worried me. Although I realised there had to be some misunderstanding somewhere, I could only think of the mess I would be in without Ah Duen. I went straight to my father and confronted him with what the old servant had told me. My father readily confirmed as correct what had been reported.

I blurted out: "Father, why not help the poor woman by telling her each morning what you would like to eat that day? She is a simple country woman, not too bright. Why make life difficult for her by saying *sze-tan*?"

"I was making life easier for her," my father replied, in the tone of one aggrieved. "When I said *sze-tan* I really meant *sze-tan*."

"But you don't always eat what she has made," I said. "I know you like fish and almost every form of steamed eggs, whether cooked with minced pork or with preserved eggs and the yolks of salted eggs. Why not just tell her that?"

"Do you tell the servant every day what you would like to eat?"

"No, but I do eat whatever she produces."

"Ah, that is where the difference in our ages comes in. You are still at an age when you eat only to fill your belly, like any other dumb creature. Have you ever considered how tedious it can be to have to specify each morning what one would like to eat for the rest of the day? I have better things to occupy my mind than food.

"Besides, I have learnt how beneficial for the human system a fast can be once in a while. If Ah Duen produces food that does not suit me, I simply fast and go without. That's not meant as a rebuke or a show of displeasure. Neither do I want her to adjust her cooking for my sake. I wanted to see how my grandsons take to her food, whether they liked it, and how they normally ate at the table. You can always read something of a person's breeding from the way he eats."

I felt both chastened and humbled by my father's remarks. I suddenly realised how seldom I ate with my sons. They had lunch by themselves each day after returning from school. I only had dinners with them when I did not have to go out. Hardly enough opportunity to instil good table manners into them, I reflected. I recalled how my grandparents used to oversee how I and my siblings ate as children. I had acted altogether too abruptly in remonstrating with my father over Ah Duen. I had failed to take his considerations into account.

His words brought back to me an episode more than two decades earlier, when both of us had been guests of my Eighth Granduncle and Aunt at No. 33 Leighton Hill Road.

We had a difference of opinion on some philosophical point. After a few inconclusive exchanges, he had cut me short by saying: "Every boy at 19 thinks his father is a bloody fool. By the time he is 29, he begins to think his father might have a valid point or two. But usually he has to be 39 before he thinks his father has been pretty smart after all. So come back to me on this point when you're 39."

And it had turned out very much as my father had predicted. At the age of 43, I was still learning lessons from him. Small wonder some of China's ancient sages considered a man could not reach full maturity before the age of 40.

At the same time, I recognised afresh that after my rupture with Man-Ying I really needed a woman around the house. But what sensible woman would want a relationship with a man saddled with three fractious sons?

So far as Ah Duen was concerned, I smoothed things over by saying that my father would be returning to Singapore soon. In the meantime, she should not ask my father for his food preferences each morning. Instead she should simply buy whatever was appropriate and ensure that each meal included either a fish or some form of steamed eggs. I also explained that when my father did not touch food, it merely meant he had decided to fast.

* * *

The rest of my father's stay was largely uneventful. He spent most of his time in his room, engaged in the type of *zazen* meditation favoured by followers of Ch'an or Zen Buddhism. That had been slightly puzzling for me because my sister Helen had told me that when he lived with her he was quite active in a Christian church near them.

I could not help wondering if my father was trying to come to terms with his own life through meditation. It could be that he was after self-knowledge, for it was during that stay that he passed me a number of his personal seals. Perhaps he had already reached the stage when he could fully grasp the meaning of the four characters — cold, hot, self and know — that had been carved on one of the *tien wong* seals he had given me. The four words formed part of a Buddhist quotation. My grandfather, too, had turned religious late in life, after being an agnostic for most of it. I wondered whether I might go the same way in old age.

My father remained true to his old form where communications with children were concerned. During my boyhood and adolescence, he had reserved his charm and wit for grown-ups. In his scheme of things, children should be seen but not heard and should learn the lessons of life through their own observations. He thus remained distant and aloof towards my sons; they in turn held him in considerable awe.

The only one of them he made some lasting connection with during his remaining years was my second son. They had exchanged a few letters when my son was at university in North America. Before he passed away in 1994, he left my son a small collection of his Chinese poems. A relative had deposited a few of them at the University of Hong Kong archives together with those written by other members of the family.

* * *

Meanwhile, bureaucratic life continued in an erratic course.

In spite of the heretical views I had expressed throughout the student demonstrations over Diaoyu Tai, Sir Murray MacLehose invited me several times during the first two years of his governorship to have meals at either Government House or at his box at the Jockey Club. Being at times rather simple-minded, I had taken those invitations to mean he was a big enough man to overlook my unhelpful or inconvenient opinions.

He did sound me out during those meals on subjects outside my area of responsibility. For example, he asked me how the wider public regarded corruption within the government and whether I thought corruption was as widespread as generally believed.

Those were tough questions to answer. I had insufficient direct experiences to fall back on. Certainly there had been numerous stories about ambulance crews refusing to pick up the sick unless they first received "tea money" and about firefighters called to fires declining to turn on their water hoses until they had received payments. Given the Chinese penchant for puns, the firefighters' demands came in the form of an innocent-sounding slogan — "No water, no water." The first "water" was the local slang for money.

The Preventive Service was supposed to guard the territory against smuggling of dutiable goods. But, if the right palms had been greased, almost anything could be smuggled in or out. The ineffectiveness of enforcing the

United Nations embargo against China during the Korean War and the continuing successes of "snakeheads" in smuggling illegal immigrants into the colony proved the point.

The police force, of course, was the most notorious for exacting squeeze and it was the target for much public ire. Payments for "protection" from gambling dens, drug dealers, establishments of ill fame and others were taken as read by everyone. Rumours circulated that some desk sergeants, controlling the rank and file at police stations, had personal fortunes running into millions.

At another level, there was also the increasing risk of intellectual corruption among top civil servants. Revealing secret government plans to outsiders could be a form of corruption. If an officer did not challenge dubious proposals for the sake of gaining promotion, that too in my book constituted a form of corruption. So was being intellectually lazy, turning into time-servers, precedent-followers and clock-watchers.

In earlier life, I myself had not been without sin. When I was a cub reporter at the *South China Morning Post*, I used to treat court clerks at the Central Magistracy to the odd cigarette or cup of coffee, in return for getting a peek at the day's court docket. I had also accepted a free annual bus pass from the China Motor Bus Company, albeit indirectly through my City Editor. Did that compromise my integrity and objectivity as a journalist? Did it amount to accepting a bribe? Against what standards should such deeds be measured?

Fearful I might be stumbling onto treacherous terrain, I was reluctant to cast the first stone. I prevaricated. I asked the Governor which aspects of corruption he was most interested in.

"Well, you know, public officers like policemen taking squeeze or cumshaw to overlook infringements of the law," the Governor replied.

"I am not sure I'm the right person to address your concerns, Sir," I said. "My knowledge and experience are limited. It would be far better for you to talk to some of the Administrative Officers in the Defence Branch or those who had previously supervised the government's uniformed forces.

"As to public sentiments, the perception is certainly that corruption is widespread. There is plenty of talk about syndicated corruption but no one knows exactly how far up the chain of command that rot has gone. That leaves plenty of scope for rumour-mongering. Systemic issues are also involved. For example, anti-corruption activities are currently being dealt with by a branch within the police. That seems to many as on a par with asking a motorist to enforce the Highway Code against himself.

"There is, at the same time, the far wider issues of fairness, equity and justice in society. If one section of the government gets significantly better treatment than another, disaffection is bound to arise. If a man in public service cannot earn enough to support his family, the temptation to make a little on the side will be hard to resist. Taking bribes may be just a symptom, not the real disease."

I was trying gingerly to indicate to Sir Murray that the colonial system he oversaw could be at the root of many corrupt practices. I had no way of knowing whether he took my comments to heart. He said neither yea nor nay.

Not long after those conversations, however, the Godber scandal erupted and it turned into the focal point for all round condemnations and displays of public anger.

Peter Godber was a Chief Superintendent in the police. He was on the point of retirement in 1973 when it was discovered he had several millions in his bank account. Government gave him a week to explain how he could have accumulated so much on a policeman's salary. But instead of explaining, he did a quick bunk back to Britain, by apparently slipping out without going through immigration.

The public reaction to his escape was virulently negative. The government was forced to hold a public enquiry. The Governor also announced in a speech before the Legislative Council in October of 1973 his intention to set up an independent body to tackle the problem of corruption. That gave rise to the establishment of the Independent Commission Against Corruption the following year.

The upshot of all that turmoil and anger was that Godber was arrested in Britain in 1974, extradited back to Hong Kong in 1975 and, after a six-day trial, sentenced to four years for corruption.

Godber's was by no means the only case uncovered of police misdeeds. Dozens of other policemen fled elsewhere, mostly to Taiwan, since the territory had no extradition arrangements with Britain.

The worst cases concerned four Chinese police sergeants, the most notorious of whom was named Lui Lok. He fled to Taiwan with an accumulated HK$500 million and subsequently managed somehow to migrate to Vancouver to become a prominent businessman. He died at the age of 90, without ever being called to account.

* * *

Over time, it slowly dawned on me that the Governor might have been inviting me for meals not because he liked the sound of my voice or the scintillating nature of my conversation. The possibility came to me that he might be making use of some of my other attributes.

I was, after all, a single man of a supposedly sober and matured age. I also had a smidgen of standing in the community. Therefore I might have appeared to him as a relatively safe choice for making up a table at Government House, should some lady without an available spouse be invited. In short, he might have considered me a kind of suitably house-broken "wog", who had mastered a few niceties of English etiquette, like the correct way of passing the port after dinner. He might have also thought me dependable enough to offer a few mildly amusing tales of Oriental obscurities to keep conversation moving.

I did not know whether such considerations had played a part in my being designated to escort Princess Alexandra when she came to Hong Kong on a Royal Visit. I was asked to take her on a walk-about through some of the more huddled side streets with market stalls.

Princess Alexandra was a tall and gracious lady. She asked a lot of pertinent questions on what she saw, such as the various types of Chinese preserved eggs and how they were made and commonly consumed. She asked a hawker woman selling eggs what her turnover was and the prices for the different kinds of eggs.

Explaining to Princess Alexandra how the Chinese preserved different kinds of eggs.

Sir Murray was among the scrum following the footsteps of Her Royal Highness like a pack of tamed poodles. Why had the Governor asked a local nobody like myself to handle such an assignment? After all, a Governor who could splash out HK$4.7 million for a McKinsey report ought to know something about the prices of food and the various types of eggs. Or at least one of his expatriate policy secretaries he had positioned around himself like an obedient phalanx should know.

Or had our latter-day colonial rulers followed the silly examples of their predecessors, living in a bubble and losing touch with the everyday lives of ordinary people? Decisions based on fanciful or wildly unreliable reports could hardly produce good governance.

* * *

But I seriously let Sir Murray down on another occasion when another titled lady — a dowager of some kind — visited. He wanted to take her to the races, so I was called into service at the Governor's Box at Happy Valley.

In passing her over into my care, he told her reassuringly: "Mr. Wong here is very knowledgeable about horse racing. He owns a number of horses and is one of the 200 select Voting Members of this club. He won't let you go wrong."

The dowager was a kindly soul, made-up elegantly, though perhaps a trifle overweight and over-powdered for her twilight years. She had been provided with a Jockey Club racing programme, so I went through the races with her, marking out two or three possible selections for each race. Most of my suggestions were for safe but unexciting favourites or near favourites. I had no horse running that day.

When we came to the start of betting on one of the races — the ultimate source of the disgrace which subsequently was etched forever into my memory — the dowager got slightly excited.

"Oh, I love the name of that horse," she cried, pointing to her programme. "Vanity Fair! How marvellous a name! I'm going to put my money on its nose."

Vanity Fair was an ageing grey. Its odds on the tote were about 60 to one. For the distance of the race it had been entered for, it had chalked up a dismal record. It had come home trailing the field over its last three outings on similar going and distance.

At that stage, I had not yet been taught my lesson by Peter Cheam. So I stuck my neck out and advised strongly against her inclination. Instead of a Jockey Club programme, I was in the habit of using a programme commercially printed by a Chinese outfit. It featured photographs of previous races run by each of the horses in the field. I showed the lady the pictures of the grey's past performances. She reluctantly accepted my advice and betted on one of the horses I had recommended.

As fate would have it, Vanity Fair came romping home to win handily, with a couple of lengths to spare. I could hardly believe my eyes.

The dowager rushed towards the Governor in a state of well-mannered excitement. "Murray!" I overheard her crying. "Vanity Fair has won at 60 to one! I wanted so much to bet on it. Such a sweet name, you know. But Mr. Wong convinced me it could never win."

It was one of those moments in life when I wished the ground I was standing on would open up and swallow me whole.

I have never discovered the kind of personal relationship which was then existing between the titled lady and the Governor. But my disastrous advice about a horse must have caused Sir Murray to be wary about my judgement on weightier matters, for I was never again invited for another meal with Sir Murray during the rest of his governorship.

* * *

When Donald Luddington was "kicked upstairs" to become the Governor of the Solomon Islands in May of 1973, he was succeeded as Secretary for Home Affairs by another expatriate Administrative Officer, but one not half as thoughtful as he. Luddington's successor simply left my recommendation for a senior Chinese officer to be appointed to keep tabs on student and youth groups to gather dust in some Secretariat pigeon-hole.

In October of 1973, the vacancy for the newly created post of Director for Home Affairs at the Staff Grade A level had also to be filled. A Eurasian Administrative Officer by the name of Eric Peter Ho was picked. It was his first shot at heading of a major government department. He was from a well-to-do and prodigiously large family. Its roots, like that of my own family, had been planted in Hong Kong for several generations.

Eric Ho was on that account admirably suited for tapping those sectors of public opinion the Home Affairs Department had been hitherto committed to. His partially Dutch ancestry provided him with easy access to the tightly-knitted local Eurasian community. Being locally educated as well, he could rely on the friendships, respect and contacts he had built up with former classmates during his secondary education and at the University of Hong Kong.

He was further aided in his career by being married to a talented and charming wife in the person of Grace Young, who was for many years the executive head of the Hong Kong and Yaumati Ferry Company and a long-serving Urban Councillor. During his civil service career, he had ended up occupying a far greater variety of top posts than any other Administrative Officer before him or since.

Eric was a tall man with an erect carriage and a nose a little too prominent to be taken as belonging to a pure Han Chinese. He was very popular with local Administrative Officers because of his straight-talking ways, especially when points of principle were involved. He had a very caring attitude towards subordinates. He was the only local Administrative Officer senior to myself who had made the extra effort to nurture juniors in the byways and pitfalls in the careers before them. He regularly invited them for dinners at his home in Kowloon Tong.

He was so well liked that when he decided to retire to Britain in 1991, a group of local women Administrative Officers adopted him and Grace as their godparents.

* * *

Although I had previously worked with Eric as a fellow trade unionist in the Senior Non-Expatriate Officers Association, fighting for parity of treatment between local and expatriate officers, we had never worked together in a government department. Our career paths had gone in different directions. One of the common threads that bound us was that we had both been rejected on the first occasion we applied to become Administrative Officers. We had both been considered unsuitable material by expatriate recruitment boards.

Following Donald Luddington being "kicked upstairs" to become the Governor of the Solomon Islands, I was also "kicked upstairs" at the beginning of 1974, to work as Deputy Director to Eric.

That elevation expanded my responsibilities over the entire range of duties in the department, instead of just for the City District Offices on Hong Kong Island. It meant a temporary additin of income in the form of acting pay but that was soon overtaken by events. In April of 1974, I was promoted to Administrative Officer, Staff Grade B.

Eric Ho and myself at a Home Affairs departmental sports day.

My new post meant moving from my small and cosy office at Hysan Avenue to the department's headquarters at International Building in Connaught Road Central. One advantage in the move was that I could walk in almost a straight line from Palm Court down to my office in the morning, without having to take a bus to get to Hysan Avenue.

In some ways, I regretted the move. During almost three years as City District Commissioner, I had developed the habit of mixing work with play with some of the staff in City District Offices.

I saw such interaction as necessary, for they were my eyes and ears in a fragmented and many-levelled Hong Kong. They belonged to certain economic, provincial, clan and family circles I was unlikely to be able to penetrate. Hence they could see or hear things I would not. Through knowing their individual characters, their strengths and weaknesses, and interacting with their families, I could weigh how much reliance I could place on their reports. Moreover, I wanted them to feel comfortable with me, more as an equal and a friend rather than as a superior. In that way I was hoping they would not hold back from telling me unpalatable truths or even vague rumours which might illuminate shifting sentiments in society.

To that end, I would gather a few of them and their families together on weekends to go on outings. Sometimes it would be a picnic or a hike. At other times, it might be a trip to Macau to sample Portuguese cuisine or else an overnight stay at a Buddhist temple in the New Territories to try out vegetarian meals. For myself, the latter might be driven by a subconscious attempt to recapture some of that vanished sense of tranquillity I had experienced when staying with my Eighth Grandaunt at The Abode of Butterflies on Tsing Yee, now mutilated and reduced to just another chunk of linked-up real estate.

For a selected two or three who had displayed skill and keenness for *mah-jong*, I brought them into my regular weekly games. The proof of the endurance of some of the relationships forged more than 40 years ago is that I still get occasional greeting cards from some of them on festive and other occasions.

After being saddled with a much broader range of responsibilities and very many more staff, I could no longer maintain that same degree of closeness and intimacy with everybody. Information had to reach me through an added layer of bureaucracy.

So far as my official relationship with Eric Ho was concerned, our interfaces remained quite limited in spite of remaining in the Home Affairs Department for another year or so. The reasons were two.

On a weekend outing with staff from the City District Offices and their families. Standing beginning from the third on the right were my three sons.

First, shortly after I had assumed the position as Deputy Director, I was asked by the Secretariat to lead a group of Administrative Officers and Senior Executive Officers on a Southeast Asia study tour. The purpose was to investigate how comparable government organisations in Thailand, Malaysia and Singapore worked and to compare notes with civil servants in those places on their approaches in discharging similar duties.

Since the tour ended in Singapore, I also took some leave there to spend time with my father and my siblings.

The second reason for a limited interface was due to Eric Ho having accumulated overflowing leave entitlements from his previous post in the Commerce and Industry Department. The exigencies of international trade negotiations on which he had been engaged meant he could not take the leave he was due. Therefore he now had either to take the leave or have any excess above six months forfeited.

He chose the former; and that choice led to my acting as Director for Home Affairs for a few months. That necessitated the appointment of another Deputy Director to replace me. Thus during my final year in the department, I only had limited interaction with Eric. Nor did I work with him again thereafter, for our careers continued to take us to different parts of the bureaucracy.

After Eric and Grace retired to Britain in 1991, they set up home at Sunningdale, near Ascot. I myself had already migrated to London in 1989. It was only then that our friendship and interactions became closer and more frequent. We often met for *dim sum* lunches in London's Chinatown whenever they visited London. Or when former colleagues happened to be passing through. They regularly hosted each year a Lunar New Year meal for friends and relatives, either at their home at Sunningdale or at a Chinese restaurant in London.

* * *

In *Animal Farm*, George Orwell made an observation that all animals were equal but some were more equal than others. In my own meandering life, I had arrived at a similar kind of observation. I have concluded that all factual statements contained facts, but some facts were more factual than others.

Let me illustrate what I am driving at. If someone were to state that the velocity of light in empty space was 186,000 miles per second, that is a statement of fact, pure and simple. Anyone with the right knowledge and right equipment could test every element of that fact at any time. It would always remain true.

But if someone were to state that a certain person had been found guilty of armed robbery and had been sentenced by a court to five years in prison, that collection of facts would give rise to imputations and subjective judgements. Did the person get a fair trial? Did he have a defence counsel? Was the trial conducted in a language he could understand? Who convicted him? A single judge or a jury? If by a jury, what was the vote? Unanimous, 11-to-one or seven-to-five? What kind of weapon had been used? A sub-machine gun or a pair of scissors? Were there eyewitnesses or was the evidence completely circumstantial? Would he have to serve the full sentence or would there be scope for remission? Had he previous convictions? Could the conviction be based on mistaken identity? And so on and so forth. Questions and doubts would swirl around that sort of factual statement.

So it turned out to be the case with not a few of the factual statements associated with the governorship of Sir Murray MacLehose. They might appear impressive when listed in biographies or history books but they seldom could stand up to close examination. Such statements are known in political jargon as "spin".

Take the following statement often appearing in accounts about Sir Murray's accomplishments: "Chinese was introduced as a second official language in Hong Kong in 1972, during the governorship of Sir Murray MacLehose." The facts are, on the face of it, all perfectly correct. Being put together that way, they conveyed favourable imputations of laudable intentions. They implied that the Governor had been in some way progressive and enlightened, setting aright an unfortunate imposition of an alien language — together with its associated values and humbug — upon an occupied people for the past century and a quarter. Those imputations could be quite false. People should be assessed by their deeds and not by what their publicity machines handed out.

In terms of actual history, the most recent demands for Chinese to be made a second official language arose out of a motion moved in the Urban Council by a member named Brook Bernacchi in 1964. But the administration nonetheless tried to pooh-pooh that demand as unnecessary, as just an intellectual indulgence. To brush it off, the administration deployed the most senior Chinese member in the Administrative Service to voice dismissive remarks. That attempt backfired more than badly.

The standard tactic by governments to delay inconvenient demands was then employed. It took the setting up of a Chinese Language Committee to study the issue. By the time the Committee reported in 1972, affirming the need for Chinese to be made a second official language, all the excuses for further delay had been exhausted.

Bearing in mind that Sir Murray only assumed the governorship of Hong Kong in November of 1971, the question that begs to be asked is: What positive contribution did Sir Murray make towards making Chinese a second official language?

If a deeper look were to be taken into the matter, a host of other questions could be asked. For instance, during Sir Murray's 11-year tenure as Governor did he attempt to make a single speech in Chinese to promote the spirit of Chinese being an official language? Did he enjoin any of his policy secretaries to attempt a single public speeches in Chinese? Did he instruct the Secretary for the Civil Service to do away with the absurdity of conducting recruitment interviews in English for posts interfacing with only a Chinese public? Did he issue instructions that henceforth all appointees to senior positions had to be competent in both official languages? And so on. Or was all the hoo-ha just empty political lip-service rather than a sincere attempt to change an unsatisfactory situation?

I have raised such questions because the Home Affairs Department had been designated as the government's Chinese Language Authority, responsible for oversight of all interpreters and translators serving in government.

During my years as a newspaper reporter, I had witnessed day after day people before magistrate courts being sent to prison who might have been set free if only they had a good lawyer or were better served by court interpretations of the charges levelled against them. On the other hand, their insouciance over going to gaol could fit well with an alarming hypothesis — that life in prison was preferable to the misery of impoverished living outside!

Their dull, indifferent eyes said it all.

So the issue of sound interpretation and translation was no minor bureaucratic slip-up. Yet there remained a breathtaking reluctance in the Secretariat to deal with the special impediments standing in the way of recruiting competent interpreters and translators. Anyone who has had any dealings with United Nations organisations could vouch for the difficulty in securing the services of competent translators or interpreters. It seemed that the already moribund hands of bureaucracy were still clutching desperately onto the breaks to progress at the tail end of the 20th century.

* * *

During my brief tenure as Director for Home Affairs, I went through two of the more trifling but nonetheless revealing experiences in my career as a bureaucrat. The first involved a "barred" file and the second a contretemps with Donald Luddington's replacement as Secretary for Home Affairs.

A "barred" file was any file with two black diagonal lines printed across its cover. It meant that the file could not be accessed by any officer other than ones specifically authorised to see it. The file in question contained correspondence pertaining to the posting of Administrative Officers to the department and the only two persons authorised to see it were the Director and the Deputy Director for Home Affairs.

The reason for "barring" a file was fairly understandable. Administrative Officers considered themselves the cocks of the civil service roost. It would simply not do for the lower orders to gain access to what Administrative Officers thought of each other — all spelt out in imperishable black and white.

The file came to me because I had to consider a candidate for Deputy Director to fill my post during Eric Ho's leave. That matter was easily disposed of. But my inborn curiosity always spurred me into reading any unfamiliar file from the beginning. In the case of the "barred" file, I was astonished to discover that there had been an exchange of correspondence concerning myself some ten years earlier, between the Establishment Officer in the Colonial Secretariat and the then Deputy Secretary for Chinese Affairs. It concerned an offer by the Establishment Officer to post me to the department.

The timing of the exchange was around the middle of 1963, after I had completed two years at the Social Welfare Department. It was customary to try an officer on probation out in two jobs before confirmation. Hence the offer to post me to Chinese Affairs.

But what astonished me were the terms of the then expatriate Deputy Secretary's reply. He rejected me, stating that he considered me "temperamentally unsuited" for work in the department.

That was surprising because at that point I had never met the said Deputy Secretary, had not spoken to him on the telephone or even exchanged any memo with anyone in the department. On what basis could he have arrived at the conclusion that I was temperamentally unsuitable? He had impugned upon my character before everyone with access to that correspondence, yet without a shred of knowledge or evidence to back up his opinion. It certainly called into question the fairness and integrity of that particular member of that so-called elite corps. I was in a way thankful for the rejection because as a consequence I got posted to the General Branch to work for Alistair Todd.

I did not meet the writer of that rejection letter till some years later. I found him to be a chubby, friendly and personable individual. I never challenged him on his assessment nor did I ask him for his reasons. I took malicious delight in thinking that, temperamentally suited or not, I was now sitting as head of that entire department and that must somehow contradict his judgement.

* * *

The contretemps with Donald Luddington's replacement occurred towards the end of 1974.

Previously, when the Secretary for Chinese Affairs operated as head of an independent secretariat charged with taking the pulse of the community, he hosted a reception for community leaders each year around the Lunar New Year, to which the Governor would lend his grace. After the reorganisation, he was effectively downgraded. He had previously been — along with the Colonial Secretary and the Financial Secretary — part of a triumvirate at the top of government. He had special responsibilities for the welfare of the Chinese population. But he had now been reduced to just another of a proliferating group of policy secretaries. All his line functions would be taken over by someone in a newly created post of Director for Home Affairs.

How the Chinese population would interpret such a disguised yet noticeable shift in the power structure was not immediately apparent. Part of the reason was because the change had been obscured by Donald Luddington continuing to discharge the line functions of the department, pending the appointment of a Director for Home Affairs. But once the appointment of Eric Ho as Director had been made, the jockeying for status and position began.

I was caught unaware and largely unprepared by virtue of becoming the Director during Eric's absence. I was asked to attend a meeting at the Secretariat with Donald Luddington's replacement. Upon arrival, I learnt that one of the topics to be discussed was the arrangement for the spring reception the following year.

The previous year, the arrangement had been settled upon before the appointment of a Director of Home Affairs. Hence the invitations went out in the name of the Secretary for Home Affairs. The line of least resistance would be to continue issuing the invitations in the name of the Secretary. But with his removal from line functions in the reorganisation and with a Director now appointed, it would not appear entirely appropriate for the

Secretary to remain as host. In any case, if the Director was to remain the main official channel of communication for 98% of the community, then the status of the Director had to be built up.

I spotted immediately a number of tricky political and presentational bear traps lying in wait. The Secretary had already been downgraded in the reorganisation. His frontline responsibilities now devolved upon the new Director. The general public should get used to the notion that the Director and his staff remained the main government sounding board for local opinion. To continue to issue invitations in the name of the Secretary would therefore be misleading and confusing.

And yet, to issue invitations in the name of the Director would make obvious too abruptly the reduced importance the government was attaching to Chinese opinion. Within the bureaucracy there was also an unspoken consideration: Eric Ho was a local and too junior to take centre stage. He was only a Staff Grade B acting in a Staff Grade A post. He might not have sufficient gravitas to play host to Executive Councillors, the kingpins of commercial hongs and banking, the captains of industry, *et al.* Hence it would be safer to have the invitations go out, as usual, under the name of the expatriate Secretary.

I could sense some such calculations floating in the air before the Secretary asked me to arrange for the invitations to be printed and issued as before. He caught me on the hop.

My personal view was that the new organisation called for the new Director to be built up as the natural person for the Chinese community to go to with their opinions and dissatisfactions. But I had little idea of what Eric's position might be since I had no opportunity to discuss the issue with him. I was only temporarily keeping his seat warm; I did not want to agree anything which would sell the toss during his absence. I wanted him to be free to make his own pitch when he returned.

So thinking, I suggested that in the light to the reorganisation and the changed responsibilities, it might be better to issue the invitations in the joint names of both the Secretary and the Director.

"No," the Secretary said. "Just stick to the old format and get the cards printed." He was a man with a temperament not unlike Sir Murray's, fond of shooting from the hip and dishing out *obiter dicta* without thinking too deeply about them.

"I'm afraid, Sir, I don't quite agree with that," I replied.

"Just do it."

"Are you going to provide me with the funds, Sir?"

"Funds? You have plenty of money in your departmental budget."

"Yes, but those funds have been voted for departmental use by the Legislative Council and I, as the current Director, am accountable to the legislature and to the public for their use. I cannot authorise an expenditure I believe to be improper and incorrect."

The Secretary was by now not exactly frothing at the mouth but his face was growing as dark as thunder. "Just do it! That's an order!"

"I'm sorry, Sir, but with great respect, I do not think you can order me to spend money from a vote I am personally responsible for when I do not agree with the purpose. I have a legal duty as a trustee. You can arrange for my removal as Director. But so long as I am the Director, I am obliged by law to control all expenditures. I am willing to authorise the printing of the cards if they are to be printed in the joint names of the Secretary and the Director. Forgive me, Sir, I am not trying to make trouble. But I am duty-bound to safeguard the flexibility of the substantive occupier of my office while he is away."

There were a few moments of heavy breathing by the Secretary but he soon saw both the legal and the moral validity in my position. "All right," he said. "Have it your way."

Upon my return to the office, I wrote a long letter to Eric about the incident and explained I had taken the position I had because I did not know what his own preferences were.

* * *

Morals can be drawn from such an incident. The first one is that splashing out HK$4.7 million of taxpayer money for a consultancy report by outsiders does not assure that all loose ends and contingencies would be covered, even the most basic and obvious ones concerning legal obligations under the new hierarchical arrangements.

The second is that the most finely drawn charts illustrating chains of command and institutional structures would count for next to nothing unless the dynamics of interpersonal relationships had been factored in. And no matter how many diplomas are handed out at business schools and military academies, when the moment for a crucial decision arrives, it will be determined by the informal practices and relationships between the individuals involved. Only then would it become apparent who would be the mover and who the moved. Anyone relying solely on his position in some hierarchy diagram to get subordinates to do his bidding might find himself already a failure as a leader.

Sir John Cowperthwaite was able to set the pace and direction of much of the Hong Kong government because of the sheer power of his intellect and the understanding he possessed of how the community functioned. He was a hefty man who spoke with a very soft voice. But he got things going his way even though the Governors who sat above him and his more remote masters in Whitehall all preferred proceeding along distinctly different lines. Sir John's successes in getting his way were what I longed to emulate, though I possessed nowhere near his intelligence and his intellectual capabilities.

If anyone doubts my proposition about the importance of personality rather than rank, just think of some of the many instances in history. Say, King Henry the Second's *cri de coeur*: "Will no one rid me of this turbulent priest!" Henry was the king yet he could not get Thomas Becket, Archbishop of Canterbury, to see things his way. Legend has it that someone had to murder Becket in his cathedral to get the result the king wanted.

Or think of how much President Harry Truman had to bend and swallow his pride as Commander-in-Chief to accommodate a wayward but popular general like Douglas MacArthur.

I rest my case.

CHAPTER 8

Of Love and Lust (Part I)

NO READER SHOULD GET EXCITED by the title of this chapter and that of the next. Very little in the way of sexual titillation will be in them. If anyone expects a confession *à la* Rousseau or Tolstoy, his hopes will be dashed. Neither will the chapters contain naughty bits like those in Chinese erotic classics like *Chin Ping Mei* or *Before Midnight Scholar*.

Indeed, they will not even get anything as saucy as H. G. Wells' *Postscript to an Experiment in Autobiography*. Wells detailed an account of a country walk with Elizabeth von Arnim, during which they took their clothes off under some pine trees, opened up a copy of the *Times* at a page featuring a woman's complaint about the immoral tone in the works of young writers, and then proceeded — in his words — to "made love all over Mrs. Humphry Ward."

In my chapters, no lady outside my own family need ever fear her real name being revealed in any sexual indiscretion. If they had been at the centre of escapades I am writing about, then they can rest assured their identities and the circumstances of their indiscretions will be suitably disguised.

I have to acknowledge, however, that the title of the chapters has been cribbed from a book of the same name written by the Viennese psychiatrist Theodor Reik. He had defined love as an attempt to change a piece of a dream world into reality and had advanced the proposition that a man would probably never be wise in love if he had never made a fool of himself in love. Those were judgements I could subscribe to.

Something similar had been said by Samuel Johnson, who deemed love to be the wisdom of the fool and the folly of the wise. Having received such warnings from various notables, I should perhaps have refrained from venturing into a realm where angels have generally feared to tread. But nature has, incongruously, given me a reckless and iconoclastic disposition. So I simply had to rise to the challenge.

Hence the deliberate choice of title for these chapters. So many books have been written about these two human emotions that I might as well add my take to the collection. Few of the books written, however, have been enlightening. They have in the main been unrealistic or unauthentic, filled with psycho-babble. The problem has often stemmed from their loose usage of the words "love" and "lust".

Such words are by their very nature quite greasy have been used to refer to a multiplicity of conditions in a variety of situations. For instance, a person can talk in one breath about loving his parents or siblings and in the next about loving freedom, justice or peace. Another person might use that same word to express his fondness for *dim sum* or bird-watching or designer shoes or ice cream cones. And what child would not love an ice cream cone on a hot summer's day? Possibly that might even be his or her first awakening of lust!

The religiously inclined, like my maternal grandparents, might employ the word "love" to project their feelings towards a God nobody has ever seen. My grandparents must have been truly blessed, for they had not seen and yet believed. Indeed, they had spent most of their lives trying to persuade countless others to believe.

Romantic poets and writers harness the same word for their own purposes, often without distinguishing it from the far baser instinct of lust. Quotations from St. Augustine's *Confessions* illustrate the problem. "I loved not yet, yet I loved to love . . . I sought what I might love, loving to love," the saint had written. A trifle confusing, no doubt. His plea to God was also telling. "Give me chastity and continence — but not yet!" If a saint had trouble coming to terms with his baser feelings, what chance has a poor ordinary sod of understanding those apocalyptic moments when they strike and overwhelm?

It goes without saying that "lust" is equally unreliable. It requires little imagination to visualise a person lusting after money, power, dominance, fame or glory, quite apart from that for the flesh. Different societies simply have to decide for themselves which form of lust might be more unsavoury.

The books I have read have contributed little to my understanding of messy events within my own family or, later on, within my own life. Take, for instance, the relationships between my parents and the tantalisingly beautiful and languid Anna, my mother's erstwhile bridesmaid and best friend. To complicate matters further, Anna also happened to be a member of our extended Wong clan.

Chinese tradition, Christian morality and the obligations of friendship would have rendered unthinkable any sexual relationship between my father and Anna. It had been on that basis, so far as I had been able to make out, that my mother had entrusted my father to Anna's care, while she herself went off to take gainful employment in Canton. And yet, somehow, my father had ended up siring four children by Anna, before finally marrying her a few decades later!

When news of that love triangle first emerged, my father's explanation had been he loved both my mother and Anna. As simple as that. A council of family elders was convened to consider that awkward situation. It ruled against the liaison of the two offenders; our clan had a strongly-held taboo on sex between those tied by blood in the same clan.

My grandfather, however, suggested that since the matter had reached such a pass, an alternative solution might be possible. My father could marry both of them. Polygamy was quite proper, legal and socially acceptable back then. My grandfather himself was reputed to have had nine wives.

My maternal grandparents, on the other hand, having been converted to Christianity, objected to such a solution. Notwithstanding their mindfulness of original sin and their supposed Christian capacity for forgiveness, they argued for monogamy. The elders, after much to-ing and fro-ing, eventually came down against continuing that unacceptable relationship. They required my father to apologise to my mother and to seek forgiveness. He did so on bended knees.

My father's inner feelings, then or later, have remained unknown to me. To this day, I have no idea whether he ever broached the double marriage solution to either my mother or to his paramour. He was then only a university student, entirely dependent upon my grandfather. I can only surmise that the prospect of continuing his studies lumbered with two wives — and an uncertain number of dependent children — must have terrified him more than a little.

On my mother's part, she apparently accepted my father's apology and resumed conjugal relations. My younger brother, Tzi-Choy, stands as testimony of those activities having taken place.

In spite of the ruling of the elders, however, my father and Anna soon resumed their affair. Was that due to the power of love or of lust? A very open question.

In the case of my father, it could have been either or both. When the chips were down and a choice had to be made, he chose Anna. Why? Was Anna temperamentally a more equitable person to cohabit with or merely more sexually exciting? Was love, in all its tempestuous glory, the victor? My father never let on and neither had anyone else.

If it had been love, his subsequent actions contradicted it — unless one accepted the notion that love was merely a transitory intoxication. He was separated from Anna for the duration of the Japanese occupation of Singapore. After they had been reunited, he stayed with her for barely a year before decamping for Hong Kong. There he remained for another ten years.

Again why? Hardly the behaviour of a man genuinely in love with a devoted woman.

My mother was understandably incensed by what went on between her husband and her best friend. The Christian marriage vows of cherishing each other unto death, sanctified in a house of God, had to be undone. And so it was, by some more mundane temporal authority.

When I was a child, some of those puzzling events frequently crossed and re-crossed my mind. But the most nagging one was where exactly did children like myself and my siblings fit in. That lack of clarity left me with a sense of something missing from my life, though I could not at the time quite pin down what it was.

As I grew older, I tried to gain greater clarity. It was not so much a lack of security, a want of attention or an absence of affection that affected me most. My grandparents, my Aunt Soo-Leung and Aunt Kwei, and Ah Sei, that marvellous hunchbacked servant, provided an abundance of all that. Perhaps it was just my abnormal desire to know my rightful place within an extended family, whether it was conditional upon good behaviour or whether there was a shade of differentiation between being the firstborn and the rest. Both my parents had been as uncommunicative as a sphinx. Other elders had not been very forthcoming either.

As for Anna's attitude in that mêlée of love, I suspected she might have been simply infatuated with my father or overwhelmed by him. I had seen during my boyhood and later how his smooth-talking ways could exert a remarkable effect upon many women.

Anna's own temperament over the subsequent decades added a further element to the puzzle. She betrayed not the slightest suggestion of a voracious sexual appetite, for she had endured years of abstinence and loneliness during the war. Later, she again waited patiently for ten years for my father to return to marry her. Was she another Penelope capable of so cruel an amputation by both time and space?

And what of her friendship with — and commitment to — my mother, a woman who had entrusted her husband to her, because she had been her bridesmaid and best friend? Wittingly or unwittingly she had stolen that husband. How much guilt or regret did she feel?

On all those issues, Anna had also remained like a sphinx. Over the many years I had lived with her under the same roof, both in Singapore and in Perth, she had never uttered a word about her feelings towards my father. The only impression I got was that she did not relish the sight of *me*. This she conveyed through a coldness, which was strangely without either anger or hatred. Could I be merely reminding her of phantoms she would rather forget? Did I stand out too much, like an accusing finger pointing towards an immoral crime?

When that ancient family kerfuffle first started, I had been only an infant, without any awareness of what was actually taking place. A glimmer of awareness only emerged much later.

What I have recorded here represents only a few scattered fragments of what I could piece together from overheard conversations among elders, plus a few judicious speculations of my own. It is far from a complete picture of the tangle my parents and Anna had left behind.

Now that all the main players have departed the scene, it can only forever remain an incomplete jigsaw, with too many crucial pieces still missing.

* * *

What lessons about love or lust can be learnt from such a tangled history? Probably not very many. Times and social fetishes always change faster than social institutions. Scientists may throw a little more light on this or that, on subconscious drives towards pullulation, genetic instincts and predispositions, human vulnerability to conditioning, like Pavlov's dogs and Skinner's rats, and so forth.

But in reality, the human personality is still as little known and understood as the black holes in outer space. People are being subjected to conditioning every day, subliminally and without fully realising it, by advertising, government propaganda and peer pressure, among others. If a person ever examines the norms he has accepted as part of his culture, he might be in for a nasty surprise or two.

Go back, for instance, to the early days of the Soviet Union. It was then thought quite normal for adults, married or unmarried, to engage in sexual activities. Any children resulting therefrom could be brought up scientifically by the state, to form the nucleus of a more perfect and enlightened socialist society. Romantic and emotional attachments, however, were deemed to be as anti-social as the plague, because they would amount to a return to decadent bourgeois behaviour, if not a type of mental disorder.

Half a century on and the Soviet model was out. Fashion moved towards conspicuous consumption, keeping up with the Joneses, the lifestyles of movie actors and pelvic-gyrating rock stars, GDP growth and economic statistics endlessly misinterpreted by politicians and media gurus. The ubiquitous pornography now on the internet was still then in the future. Against that, the shock once expressed over *Lady Chatterley's Lover* or *The Tropic of Cancer* would appear utterly trivial! But modern communications did open up a means for lonely hearts to find love or lust, though seldom without danger or a considerable degree of risk of personal exposure.

* * *

In reaching back through my own memories, I can only recall decades of stumbling around, trying to catalogue the varying shades of emotions I had gone through in connection with love or lust. It had been an altogether unrewarding exercise, worse than trying to find my way home at night through a London pea-souper while slightly inebriated.

I had sensed vaguely from an early age that my paternal grandmother loved me more than she did my siblings. But she never said so in as many words. That silence, in my child's mind, invited doubt. If a thing was true, why should an adult not declare it to be so? What was the catch? There had to be one.

Another event soon added to that doubt. My grandmother had enrolled me in a Chinese pre-primary school with a reputation for sternness and discipline. I quickly got into trouble for an infraction of its rules. Caning on the calves before the entire school was the established way of delivering punishment. My grandmother could have prevented my punishment but she did not. If she truly loved me, why did she not intervene to spare me the humiliation and pain of being caned? And why remove me from the school after my caning, instead of before it had been inflicted? There appeared no rhyme or reason to the adult world.

Such inexplicable happenings called into question the quality of her love. It seemed so ambiguous that I held it against her for not declaring it. That uncertainty hampered my developing a warmer feeling towards her.

Years later, as she lay sick and dying in an alien land, my concern for her was still insufficient to overcome my paralysing fear of her clinging to me during her death throes. I therefore hid myself away from her to avoid that possibility. Yet it had been precisely at that moment that she needed me most. It was a most unkind and cowardly thing to have done to someone who had taken care of me throughout my boyhood. That failure in human decency left a scar on my conscience which has never quite healed.

* * *

The start of what might be described as lust has been equally well etched upon my memory. It happened towards the end of 1939, when I was about ten and a half. My youngest brother, Tzi-Seng, had been born in October and a village woman by the name of Ah Yee had been employed to be his wet nurse because Anna wanted to return to work.

One afternoon, I saw Ah Yee breast-feeding my brother. The sight stirred a strange, indefinable sensation in me. After she had finished with the baby, I asked if she could feed me too. She laughingly agreed. As I sucked upon one of her breasts and fondled the firmness of the other, I felt a delicious thrill of excitement and pleasure. At the same time, however, I could sense I was doing something wrong and shameful. Yet I had enjoyed the experience so thoroughly that I kept longing to repeat it.

Ah Yee must have reported the incident to my Aunt Soo-Leung because a few days later my aunt took me aside and told me in the gentlest way possible that I should "not disturb Ah Yee" when she was carrying out her duties. That put an abrupt stop to my lusting.

* * *

Love, if it were to be defined as an overwhelming attachment to another person, came about three years later, in Australia. I met an older boy living next door by the name of Jackie Wong Sue. Jackie was about four years older than myself but he had a wealth of knowledge and an amazing range of talents.

He taught me a plethora of things, from building a crystal set to trapping small animals, from catching poisonous snakes to capturing beautiful butterflies. He acquainted me with the names of an amazing number of creatures. It was an unalloyed joy to go running alongside him with a home-made butterfly net, trying to capture an iridescent blue-green Blue Mountain Swallowtail or some other butterfly without damaging its wings.

At the beginning, I could not figure out why Jackie should devote so much time to me. I had seen myself as an unattractive lad with little to commend to anyone. I had an over-large head stuck on top of a skinny and ungainly body. I had been a total failure in every sporting activity that schoolboys found glory in. I could not dribble a football or kick one with accuracy; I had difficulty batting even a single run at cricket, against the easy fours and sixes delivered by others; I could not win a race over any distance on the flat or over hurdles. I was just as incompetent at the net games of tennis and badminton. What I did enjoy enormously was reading. But that soon got me labelled as a bookworm.

Perhaps Jackie took pity on my failing to find favour with my peers. He certainly took greater pains with me than he did with his own younger siblings, though his brothers and sisters might not have been as enthusiastic as I had been over the things he could teach.

It was Jackie who taught me the difference between theoretical knowledge and actual experience. One might learn the differences between the scales of a Mulga and a Crowned Snake from a book. Or one might learn how snakes used their flickering forked tongues to "taste" the air for scent particles. But unless a person had actually controlled a live black adder or black tiger snake with his bare hands and had stared into its cold and murderous eyes, he could not be said to have mastered the fear of poisonous snakes. Jackie showed me how to overcome that fear at a formative stage of my life. In return, I hero-worshipped him shamelessly.

It was completely consistent with Jackie's character that he should eventually serve out the war in the Indonesian jungles behind enemy lines. He was decorated more than once for his daring.

After the war ended, I left Australia to return to Singapore. My associations with Jackie thus came to an abrupt end in 1946. Because of the nomadic life imposed on me afterwards, even our correspondence petered out.

* * *

The next person I developed a strong attachment to came two years later, when I was 18. It was towards my Eighth Grandaunt who, from the moment I turned up at her home at Leighton Hill Road, offered me both hospitality and kindness.

I must have had sight of my Eighth Grandaunt when I was an infant, when I was under the care of my grandmother, who was her eldest sister-in-law. But I had no memory of her till I saw her at the age of 18. She came over as a benign lady with the beatified face of a Goddess of Mercy. From time to time, an enigmatic smile would play upon her lips, as if she were enjoying a secret and unshared amusement.

If there was any truth to the saying that the easiest way into a man's heart was through his stomach, then my Eighth Grandaunt personified it for me. When she clapped eyes on me at her Leighton Hill Road home, some maternal instinct must have told her I was underfed and craving for food. She immediately ordered a servant to bring me some dessert, which I wolfed down more quickly than I should have done. From that moment on, she took to mothering me more than anybody else I could remember.

My Eighth Grandaunt Kwok Yee-Hing, taken in 1948.

Over the following two years as a guest in her home, she saw to my being not only adequately fed but also properly attired. The few items of tropical clothes I had brought from Singapore were not only unfashionable but unsuited to the Hong Kong winter. She must have read my unspoken yearning for some of the smart items in department stores which my meagre pay as a reporter would not allow. She set about quietly fulfilling my dreams, even though some of the items I had hankered after had turned out, in retrospect, to have been rather silly ones.

One of the most pleasurable experiences I had during that period was to spend the odd weekend with her and her children on Tsing Yee Island, at her country bungalow aptly named The Abode of Butterflies. Many types of butterflies flourished there, together with a host of other friendly insects like ladybirds, dragonflies, honey bees, crickets, fireflies and cicadas. One of the most commonly seen butterfly there was the bright orange-coloured Monarch, with the telling white spots and black veins on its wings.

Sadly, all the insects which used to flourish there have since been virtually wiped out by urbanisation. In the process, Tsing Yee Island itself disappeared too, to become by way of reclamations and bridges just another part of the mainland.

The most precious gift that my Eighth Grandaunt arranged for me was my university education. She knew of my fervent desire for further studies and concluded at once that no matter how hard I might try to save I would never make it. She therefore spontaneously suggested one day that I approach my Eighth Granduncle for a loan. I hesitated, for I could not visualise how I could ever repay it unless I took up one of those money-grubbing commercial callings my instincts deeply deplored.

But she urged me on, in spite of my hesitancy. I never knew whether she had smoothed the way with her husband beforehand. In any case, when I did ask for a loan, my Eighth Granduncle readily granted it.

Sadly, my Eighth Grandaunt passed away prematurely in 1952, while I was still studying at Stanford. I was thus deprived of even a chance to bid her an appropriate goodbye as she departed the world.

* * *

Once I got to Stanford, the pea-souper obscuring the two overlapping realms of romantic love and naked lust grew immeasurably thicker. I was for the first time alone in a foreign land and in an unstable emotional and financial state, beyond the help of any family member. A man in my circumstances, I told myself, simply could not afford to get involved with either love or lust. He had to keep his nose clean and concentrate on his studies. But the openness of American girls and their penchant for showing off their physical assets posed constant temptations.

Although I made many long-lasting friendships with women during my four years at Stanford, I only once came close to metaphorically losing my head over a girl. She was a svelte and dreamy girl from Southern California who had entered Stanford a year or two after myself.

We had met quite by chance, perhaps a year after her arrival. I was then working for my meals as a counter waiter in a campus cafeteria called The Cellar. She came by one day for a late lunch. Her arrestingly beautiful face was aglow with rude health, after an obvious engagement in the sun. Her eyes were soft and misty, suggesting a reserve of mischief and happiness. She appeared the very embodiment of immaculate youth, suffused with the joys of being alive.

She happened to sit at my section of the counter, so I served her. Since the lunch-hour rush was already tapering off, we got into a conversation. It flowed easily from one topic to another. It soon became apparent she had just returned from a weekend of skiing.

That was how our friendship started. I became attracted to her almost immediately, as if drawn into a magnetic field. But I cautioned myself I should not be deflected by a skirt since so many large question marks still hung over my future. I was debt-ridden and had no idea when funding for my annual scholarship might come to an end.

Shortly afterwards, that beautiful girl fortuitously came into The Cellar again for a cup of coffee. Her loveliness got the better of my prudence. I felt again that unaccountable tingling in the blood I had felt over Lai-See at St. Matthew's Church at the age of ten. That had been puppy-love. Why was the sensation revisiting me at the age of 22? Was it because I was still a virgin?

The girl and I talked some more and we exchanged names. She asked if

I was the David Wong who was writing for the *Stanford Daily*. I had to plead guilty. I had gained a little notoriety on campus because I had once publicly challenged a Marine colonel to a duel — chopsticks at six paces — for insulting the Boy Scouts.

"I've enjoyed your pieces," she said.

The conversation soon touched upon existentialism. It was a big thing back in those days; it permeated several spheres of cultural activities. It proved easy for us to toss around some of its core beliefs.

Existentialism, as a philosophy, emphasised the individual's capacity to act as a free agent, to determine his own development through acts of the will. I had my reservations, however. I could not visualise how any act by me could possibly free me from debt, let alone offer me a sporting stab at romantic love. But I kept this to myself.

Thereafter, as each of us followed our individual routines around the more than 8,000-acre campus, I bumped into the girl a couple of times more. She was apparently popular, for each time she was attended by classmates or roommates. She readily introduced me to them and I thereby gained some new friends. Her enchantment over me grew with each meeting.

Curiously, I subsequently found it much easier to ask one of her friends or companions out for a cup of coffee or beer than I could the girl herself. There must have been a subconscious awareness that I had no real romantic designs on her associates, whereas a date with her might unleash an avalanche of false hopes and wild imaginings. Perhaps I had subconsciously asked her friends out simply as a roundabout way of gathering personal information about her.

Sometimes I would gain a snippet of information which gave me pause. For example, I learnt from one of her friends that she had been going skiing with a somewhat boorish male student. What was the point of intruding? I had no time, no money and no skill in skiing.

Though Existentialism asserted that a man could define himself through his actions, I tried to define myself through inaction. I made no attempt to contact the girl, either at her dormitory or on the telephone. I simply left it to chance to decide whether I would ever see her again.

Chance was not unkind, however. Our paths did continue to cross. Whenever they did, I felt as if butterflies were doing a vigorous dance inside my chest. Our conversations, however, remained impersonal or academic, about student life, courses being pursued and opinions on the writings of Dostoevsky and other existentialists.

One day, upon another chance meeting, she produced a book which she said she had been carrying around to give to me. It contained two plays by Sartre — *No Exit* and *The Flies*.

I felt utterly overwhelmed; my spirits soared. Our chats must have held some meaning for her. I wanted to give her a present in return. But I had no money to buy anything remotely appropriate or meaningful. I decided eventually to write her a poem. My effort was obviously miles away from anything done by Donne or Shelley. It was in fact rather schoolboyish. Yet I wanted to express a little of what I felt about her. The last stanza of the poem read as follows:

> "She touched my heart, this Nature's Child,
> So free and unrestrained.
> She conquered with her simple charm
> And like a sovereign reigned."

After it had been written, it became my turn to carry it around in an envelope, tucked between the pages of a textbook. I remained on tenterhooks, not knowing when I might meet her again. The opportunity came about a week later, when I caught her walking with a classmate. I rushed up and handed her the envelope, saying: "I've written you a poem. A most inadequate gift, I know, in return for yours."

"Oh! How sweet of you!" she replied. "Nobody has ever written me a poem before."

"Just a poor chap's way of saving money." But before she could take the poem out of the envelope, I quickly added: "I'm sorry; got to run. Late for work."

I was simply too bashful and frightened to see how she might react to the poem. The humiliation I had suffered after passing Lai-See a silly note years earlier resurfaced in my mind.

* * *

During my final year at Stanford, as I was finishing a master's degree, a mutual female friend invited me to spend a few days at her home in Los Angeles, during the break between the winter and spring quarters. She said she wanted me to meet her folks.

There was no significance to that invitation beyond friendship. I had previously received several similar invitations. Fellow students must have regarded me as a curiosity, a strange Anglo-Chinese hybrid who spoke like an Englishman even when talking about Confucian "rectification of names" or Taoist obscurities. Apart from wishing to acquaint their families with such a specimen, they were merely displaying that open and disarming hospitality common among Americans.

When the girl I had referred to as "Nature's Child" heard of my going to Los Angeles, she invited me to stay at her home as well. By then she was in her third year and had shed her associations with that boorish young man. I quickly accepted and agreed to spend at least a day with her.

She lived in an exclusive area known as Palos Verdes Estate. That area had once been run on the same basis that the British did the Peak area of Hong Kong before World War II, that is, barring non-whites from owning property and taking up residence there.

I discovered for the first time the girl came from a fractured family like my own. She was living with one of her parents. That revelation underlined how few personal details we had exchanged during the two years we had known each other.

We spent much of our time just talking, in rather abstract and philosophical terms, about the human condition and the discords affecting mankind. It was as if we did not dare to touch upon our individual feelings and predicaments. Our silences, too, seemed loaded with unuttered sentiments, like the empty spaces in Chinese landscape paintings, leaving the unexpressed to the imagination of the beholder.

In the evening, we had a glass of wine with dinner. Afterwards, we sat out in her open patio. There was a small bar, with a gramophone. Under a star-spangled sky, we listened to some of the popular ballads of that era. One of them was of Nat King Cole's "Autumn Leaves". When it was being played, I asked if she cared to dance. She stood up and we came together naturally, cheek to cheek. Apart from the odd handshake, it was the first physical contact we ever had in two years.

My head swam with intoxication as we danced. She was supple; her movements graceful. The subtle fragrance of her person washed over me like a perfume. I could not inhale it fast enough. My blood stirred and my heart began pounding like a bongo drum. Strange sensations possessed me. What were they? Was I falling in love? If so, they were certainly not unmixed with baser instincts.

As our dancing continued, the smooth baritone of Nat King Cole and his lyrics of separation and loss seemed to underscore the ephemeral nature of my current state. I tightened my arms around her, wanting the dance to last for all eternity.

But the music had to come to an end. The record had to be flipped. That interruption enabled me to regain a degree of composure. I had to stop my craziness, my sacrilegious fantasising, I told myself. There was not the slightest evidence the girl felt for me in any way other than as a friend. What right had I to toy with notions of love? I was a man burdened by debt, without a future, with nothing to offer. Even to imply a viable future would be to behave like a cad. I sat down on a patio bench, breaking out in a cold sweat, as she turned over the record.

After that had been done, she stood indecisively in front of me, majestic in the undiluted splendour of the night. Was she expecting us to dance again? I did not dare to move. If I held her in my arms again, I was bound to lose control and to say something or do something utterly stupid and irretrievable. I froze.

She then sat down beside me on the bench, a little apart. I could hardly find a word to say, let alone to touch her. Thus we spent the rest of that unforgiving night not saying much, just listening to sentimental music, and hoping that thoughts and feelings could somehow be conveyed without words, through the thickening shadows of the night.

* * *

The final quarter of my stay at Stanford was a period of unmitigated misery. I had to complete my thesis for a Master's degree but my heart was not in it. I could not stop cursing myself for failing to express what I had felt for the most enchanting girl I had ever met. There would be no second chance. Soon, we would be physically separated, as effectively as the Cowherd from the Weaving Maiden in the Chinese fairytale. The difference was that I, unlike the Cowherd, would have no prospect of seeing my beloved again after a year. We would have to part for good, with neither knowing what each might have meant for the other.

Desperate stratagems ran amok inside my head. I toyed with applying for a doctorate fellowship to prolong my stay. But then, what? I would be back in the same position a year or two hence, with no more to offer than at present.

Ahead of me, Hong Kong loomed like a frightening form of financial servitude, filled with emptiness and oppression. My Eighth Grandaunt, the only person there I had cared for and from whom I could count on for help, was already dead. My father could offer no comfort. He was living like a fugitive himself, trying to resolve his own relationship with Anna.

The only initiative I took while the clock ticked relentlessly away was to ask the girl for a photograph to take home. She readily supplied me with a portrait of herself, measuring eight by ten inches, duly inscribed "with love".

After I got back to Hong Kong, we exchanged a couple of letters. But mine were written under false pretences, loaded with fake optimism. I did not have the courage to tell her of my being summarily sacked from the *Hong Kong Standard,* at the instigation of some faceless colonial bureaucrat, or how the loss of a job had reduced me to sharing a room with a friend at a cheap workingmen's hostel.

That friend, Auyang Ming, noting my misery, took me to a Kowloon whorehouse in an attempt to cheer me. There I managed to lose my virginity to a Hakka girl. But it had been a joyless, mechanical and diminishing experience, more like an execution, exploiting another human being as a substitute for love. It became quite impossible for me to continue a correspondence with the Californian girl after that.

* * *

Oh, with what flimsy and insubstantial materials we construct our grand romances! I must have tried to relive a thousand times that single night of dancing to the crooning of Nat King Cole. But my memory could not summon forth again that same old feeling of physical closeness and of the musk of her person.

I have since travelled the world, carrying a portrait of a girl, immaculate and unattainable, and two plays by Sartre. As I moved from continent to continent, I dreamt of missed opportunities and alternative outcomes. Sometimes I asked myself whether I had truly fallen in love on that Californian night. The answer remained ambiguous, like the one that teased the Taoist philosopher, Cheung Tzu, after his celebrated dream.

According to legend, the ancient sage went to sleep and dreamt he was a butterfly, happily fluttering hither and yon. When he woke up the next morning, he became unsure whether he was a man who had dreamt he was a butterfly or whether he was now actually a butterfly dreaming of being a man!

A similar conundrum, filled with the shifting overtones and undercurrents of love and lust, had confounded me for years. Had I been genuinely smitten on a Californian night or had I only imagined it all? If I had been smitten, how could I have allowed love to slip away without a fight? Did it mean I had loved without the kind of commitment and daring suitable for a man? Or had I been as faint-hearted and timid as a butterfly, disguising my cowardice and hesitations as prudence and pragmatism? Could my want of experience and maturity be only an excuse?

Each time I reminisced, I felt as if I had got onto one of those London Underground trains at Stanford, to head for a destination incongruously called Love. A couple of complicated interchanges were required to get there, so I got off at an intermediate station to check if the first interchange had to be made there. By the time I had established it was not due till another couple more stations down the line, the train door had slammed shut and I was left on the platform. Nothing to be done except to wait for the next train.

However, the next train did not come along for a dozen years. When I got on, I found another American girl already in the compartment. Her name was Sharlee and she was heading for Holland. We travelled together for a spell and got involved with each other. Then she too got off, leaving me to continue that uncharted journey alone.

Today, after another failed marriage and many inconclusive affairs, I am not sure whether I am still on that journey or whether I had ended up at an entirely different destination!

* * *

I envy people who could separate out love from lust, as easily as they could extract a peanut from its shell. That ability is all the more extraordinary when they can readily pronounce on the emotional state of any third party and prescribe a sure-fire remedy.

After my separation from Man-Ying, some friends and relatives quickly took out their big palm-leaved fans — that standard symbol of the professional Chinese matchmaker — and advanced a remedy for my situation. A speedy re-marriage. Both I and my three sons required womanly care, they pronounced.

While I never doubted that need for my sons, I had grave reservations for myself. Having had one marital misadventure, I was not about to embark upon another. No sensible woman, I figured, would want to tie the knot with a poorly-paid civil servant lumbered with three sons.

Nonetheless, against my better judgement, I accepted some of the invitations to tea or dinner, for the purpose of meeting unwed relatives, spinster classmates, recently divorced colleagues, widowed friends and an assortment of career women who had discovered — as they skidded rapidly down the wrong side of 35 — that professional accolades and fat bonuses were all right so far as they went, but they did not keep them warm at night. The suppression of their maternal instincts was also turning them grumpy and short-tempered.

There is probably some basis for saying that all satisfactory matches can only be made in heaven. The precise temperaments, psyches, expectations and prospects of those heading into a union often elude earthly matchmakers. Different people want different things, certainly in their imaginations, and they are possessed by vastly different fantasies.

In addition, my entry into the marital market was not without complications, for I had a misleading media presence. Having been photographed in walkabouts with the Governor and other notables, and having been repeatedly shown leading racehorses into the Winner's Circle, I might have created a mistaken impression of both my financial and social circumstances. The fact I had three sons hanging around my neck like albatrosses was conveniently obscured.

The net result for all concerned was a farrago of wasted time and effort. Most meetings were hail-and-farewell affairs. Few produced spontaneous attraction or sexual buzz. An occasional merry widow or a liberated divorcee, however, did lead to an enjoyable dalliance or two.

Such dalliances, taken together with my being seen with a succession of beautiful women, soon saddled me with a reputation for being a Don Juan, a libertine trifling with the affections of unsuspecting women. Such a reputation was actually not entirely fair. I had honestly been searching for a wife with an equitable temperament, who could be a mother for my sons as well as a soulmate and bedmate for myself. My failure to find one could hardly be blamed on me alone.

My reputation suffered the greatest damage from my associations with two of the most superbly attractive non-lovers I have ever escorted. Although I had plied them with displays of amorous intentions in public, neither romantic love nor lowly lust was involved in either case. My behaviour had been pure play-acting, carried out for what I had deemed to be worthy purposes.

But because my motives were unknown except to those directly involved, my deeds were taken at face value by others not in the know. They soon caused ill-founded rumours and gossip to spread like wildfire. The ill repute I earned thereby became something I could neither live down nor live up to! It was a most frustrating state of affairs.

I am therefore now using these memoirs to set the record straight. Before I do so, however, I would like to briefly recapitulate the social milieu prevailing in Hong Kong at the time.

CHAPTER 9

Of Love and Lust (Part II)

HONG KONG, EVER SINCE it became a British Crown Colony, has always been receptive to outsiders and to external influences and ideas. The initial waves of outsiders who came were naturally people from the neighbouring Kwangtung Province of China, compelled to move either by harsh living conditions or dreams of a better future. Among those early arrivals was my great-grandfather, a school teacher. He decided to make the then malaria-ridden place as his home. He raised six children, three boys and three girls, the youngest of the boys being my grandfather.

My great-grandfather's three sons all attended the then Hong Kong Medical College, with two of them qualifying as doctors and the third a dentist. All three migrated. My grandfather took an appointment with the British Colonial Service as a medical officer in Singapore. His eldest brother, also a doctor, migrated to San Francisco, while his dentist brother set up a practice in Ipoh in Malaya. Unfortunately, family oral history left no mention of what happened to the three sisters.

My father, born in Singapore, returned to Hong Kong for his university education and while studying there married my mother and produced me, thereby giving me my connection with Hong Kong.

Over time, for those undergoing hard economic times in their native places, the colony functioned as both a haven of hope and refuge and an enclave offering business opportunities. During the 1960s, for example, the Vietnam War brought boatloads of Vietnamese refugees as well as vast numbers of Western servicemen on"rest and recreation" to sample the fleshpots of Wanchai and Tsim Sha Tsui.

Inside the United States, however, the Vietnam conflict gave rise to social divisions. The deployment of chemical weapons like Agent Orange and napalm (which had been secretly developed at Harvard) against civilian populations alarmed the more idealistic Americans students. In 1966, they began demonstrating against the war at Berkeley in California and at Wayne State in Michigan.

They sought a more harmonious and humane way of settling disputes. Under the influence of rock music and psychedelic drugs, they coined the slogan of making love instead of war. Small groups began gathering in San Francisco, with headbands, beads, tattoos and outlandish clothes. It culminated in 1967 in over 100,000 spermatozoid-fuelled and drug-enhanced people participating in a "Summer of Love".

That mood found further expression at Woodstock in August of 1969, when a crowd of some 400,000 gathered at a 600-acre farm in the Catskills for three days of music, peace and youthful exuberance. Although the weather turned the gathering into three days of rain, mud and promiscuous sex, the participants nonetheless enjoyed themselves.

The song of sexual liberation, thus given voice, was not lost upon Hong Kong. But it was picked up in the colony initially by only middle-aged fuddy-duddies in the elites rather than by the young. The latter were probably too crushed by financial hardships and an educational system fixated upon examinations to give much thought to the great issues of war and peace or about sexual liberation. It was left to the better-off academic crowd, the legal professionals and the Administrative Officers in the government to make the running.

I only had limited knowledge of what went on in the universities and in the legal profession. It was among Administrative Officers that my knowledge was far more extensive and direct.

* * *

Ever since I joined the Administrative Service, I had detected a covert struggle between the prudes and the sexual libertarians. The hanky-panky that went on ranged from the then Colonial Secretary all the way down to the lowest ranks. There was possibly something in Henry Kissinger's remark about power being a very potent aphrodisiac.

Upon my return from Oxford in the second half of 1971, I discovered already in existence a coven of three married expatriate Administrative Officers engaged in a lively wife-swapping arrangement. Unsurprisingly, their marriages did not survive their sexual experiments.

As for the rest of the service, adulteries and infidelities were far from uncommon at all levels. Today, more than 45 years after that period, I can still reel off from the top of my head the names of at least a dozen local and expatriate Administrative Officers, evenly split between males and females, who had engaged in out-of-marriage sex. And I do not even have to include myself in that number!

It was during such a morally equivocal period in 1971 that the Hong Kong government chose to propose outlawing the long established Chinese institution of polygamy. Up till then, both monogamy and polygamy were legally recognised, with the latter being dealt with under customary law of the Ching Dynasty.

What had possessed the government to take such an initiative has remained unclear. There had been in 1957 a petition signed by 100,000 women calling for the prohibition of concubinage. Thereafter the issue simmered, notably among feminists, church groups and expatriates who felt that their matrimonial arrangements were far superior to the Chinese ones and hence should be adopted.

No one appeared to have bothered to organise a counter-petition to demand that the existing freedom to choose between monogamy and polygamy be retained. If one had been organised, I think a far greater number of people — including many concubines and their offspring — might have signed it. In any event, the absence of any vigorous opposition allowed the colonial administration to pretend it was following the general will towards monogamy.

The Chinese Communists had abolished polygamy when they took power in 1949. Earlier, both the Taiping rebels the Kuomintang had adopted a similar approach. The Taiping rebels had announced their position a century earlier, when they set up the Kingdom of Heavenly Peace. But under both instances, the leaders calling for change still managed to enjoy multiple spouses or mistresses.

Singapore banned polygamy in 1961. Agitation in Hong Kong for a ban had waxed and waned over time but I cannot recall demand being significantly greater during 1971. Perhaps it came from the bogus puritanism rampant at Westminster, itself an institution riddled with members selling honours, fiddling expense accounts and engaging in peccadilloes of one kind or another.

For the Chinese, the change proposed met with little enthusiasm. The status quo seemed sensible and acceptable. I might perhaps have been slightly biased because I had been brought up in a polygamous extended family with lots of aunts and step-siblings around.

The majority in Hong Kong seemed rather indifferent, due to some extent by the uncomfortable reality of many Chinese bigwigs having one or more concubines. In addition, many others had themselves been the offspring of concubines. The proposed change would impact upon their social standing, their legitimacy and their financial positions.

In China, the institution of concubinage was as old as marriage itself.

Chinese culture emphasised the importance of perpetuating the family and honouring ancestors. Male descendants were therefore required to give substance to that custom. To leave no male progeny was deemed the worst of all filial failings. Concubinage thus arose as a sort of insurance policy, to guard against such an unhappy eventuality.

Indeed, during the Ming Dynasty, married men were sanctioned to take concubines should they fail to produce a son upon reaching the age of 40. When the Ching Dynasty followed, inheritance laws were put in place to protect the status and financial entitlements of concubines and their offspring.

As I have said, I had been brought up in a polygamous family, with my grandfather maintaining a succession of nine wives. My father's mother only had two children — my father and an older sister. By the time I arrived on the scene, the older sister had already moved out upon marriage. Both I and my siblings would have had no aunt to interact with if our grandfather had not practised polygamy. I therefore gain the impression that polygamy offered a better environment for children. At least the number of adults around the home ensured children got plenty of attention.

Polygamy under the extended family system might possibly be beneficial for adults as well, given the growing number of cases involving domestic violence and even incest. Such crimes had to be more difficult to carry out with the larger number of adults around in an extended household.

There had been, of course, other grounds for recognising polygamy. Ancient civilisations had recognised the diversity in human needs and wants. The Hindus thought nothing of having a spouse to bear children, another to discourse on the Upanishads and a third to provide the delights of zither, flute or song. The prophet Hosea had recorded polygamy among Jews in the eighth century B.C. The Muslims had been accustomed to multiple wives. There appeared to be no compellingly practical or moral objection for disallowing people to choose freely the form of marital arrangement they wished, so long as they accepted full responsibility for the children they might bring into the world.

Lest anyone should think that I am cooking the case for polygamy from a selfish male point of view, let me hasten to state that I am equally supportive of women having as many husbands as they might wish. For example, I have no difficulty whatsoever in accepting the matriarchal and matrilineal customs of the Mosuo or Na people. Nor of other tribes like them.

The Mosuos live around the Lugu Lake in Yunnan Province. They follow an agrarian form of life, cultivating crops and keeping livestock. Today they number around 40,000. Their religion is essentially animistic, mixed with elements of Tibetan Buddhism. Women head their households and inheritances flow only through the female line. They maintain extended families, with several generations sharing a communal life. When girls reach puberty and are capable of sexual intercourse, they are each given a room of their own.

That is because they practise a form of marriage known as "walking marriages" where all initiatives for having sex rested with the female. If she finds a man attractive, she indicates to him he would be free to visit her after dark. But he has to vacate her room at sunrise. If she still likes him, he could be invited to come again. Otherwise she would look for another man. There is no question of divorce in such "walking marriages" and there is no word for "jealousy" in the Mosuo language.

Such liaisons are kept secret from the rest of the community. When a woman dies, however, the men who had enjoyed her favours are supposed to attend and hold up a banner. It would only be then that her community becomes aware of how many lovers she had entertained. It has been suggested that 50 partners are not uncommon. If a hundred men turn up holding banners at a woman's funeral, then that woman would automatically be remembered as a great beauty.

When Marco Polo wrote about the promiscuous sexual behaviour in the kingdom of Caindu in Yunnan, he was probably referring to a tribal community similar to the Mosuos.

Any child born out of "walking marriages" belongs absolutely to the mother. It would be brought up by her family, with the males in her family playing a fatherly role. It is not easy to tell the biological father of a child under such practices. If one could be identified, and if he wishes to maintain a relationship with the child, he is free to call from time to time on the girl's family and to bring along presents. No custody battle ever arises.

For years Communist cadres have been trying to persuade the Mosuos to convert to "normal" marriages, whatever that might mean. But the Mosuos have clung steadfastly to their traditional ways.

Puritans and pseudo-moralists need not lose sleep over the rest of the "civilised" world being contaminated by Mosuo ways. Entrepreneurs are rushing to destroy that culture. Fleets of buses head towards Lugu Lake every day, filled with tourists eager for a chance to sample a "walking marriage". Another version of sex tourism, I suppose. The tourists would no doubt pollute both the lake and its environment as well as the culture the Mosuos in no time. It would be the loss of another very sensible way of human existence.

What I find puzzling is why feminists around the world have not rallied to defend or even to demand some of the elements of the Mosuos' way of life. They obviously hold out advantages for women. I can well imagine the world being a better place if some of their customs were extended and accepted.

At the moment, polygamy or polyandry still co-exists with monogamy in more than 80% of human societies. There seems no good reason why that freedom to co-exist should not be further encouraged rather than rolled back. In the animal world, very few species are monogamous.

Mounting evidence suggests that the legal imposition on monogamy is not working. Divorce rates are rising in advanced countries, in some instances reaching 50% or more.

In Hong Kong in 2016, the rate was estimated at roughly one in three.

That ratio is likely to grow. More and more people appeared to be opting to live outside of wedlock as well, spearheaded by revolutionary writers and artists who, as a matter of principle, wanted to defy bourgeois marital ties. When they do get married, they not infrequently indulged in wife-swapping, "free marriages", or other types of conjugal arrangements.

The number of children born to unwedded couples is also increasing, and likewise the number of single parents. The proper care for children is becoming a very serious social problem, hardly capable of being solved by institutions like the Po Leung Kuk. The problem is being compounded by some misguided Western countries simply lavishing welfare benefits on unmarried mothers at levels beyond what girls could normally earn by engaging in full-time employment.

* * *

The considerations I have touched upon have never been given a fair or proper airing in Hong Kong before the law on monogamy was passed. It was remiss of Administrative Officers, the supposed shapers of government policies, not to have initiated a more comprehensive public debate on the whole issue.

In addition, the problem of decriminalising homosexuality might also have been dealt with. It had been an issue upon which a blind eye had been turned for decades, because Hong Kong laws still proscribed homosexual sex although such private activities had been decriminalised in Britain in 1967. The administration, probably fearing that the bulk of the local population would be against liberalisation, chose to sweep the matter under the carpet.

Since a small number of expatriate Administrative Officers were practising homosexuals, I should have thought they would have come out in favour of more sexual freedom. But they remained silent. Another case of the abdication of leadership.

A few years later, the administration found itself in an uncomfortable position. The police arrested two men *in flagrante delicto*, one of whom was an expatriate Administrative Officer. As the law stood, they should have been charged with a crime. But as the Administrative Officer held a senior post in the Finance Branch of the Secretariat, a prosecution would have been very embarrassing for both the government and the officer concerned. The law was somehow sidestepped, with both being released without a charge. The expatriate officer remained in his post till the end of his career.

To the best of my recollection, the short, rotund and plain-speaking Executive Councillor, Sir C.Y. Kwan, was the only community leader to speak out against the proposed ban on polygamy. He was the senior partner in a firm of solicitors and had headed the Hong Kong delegation to two plenary sessions of the United Nations Economic Commission for Asia and the Far East — in Australia and Singapore respectively. I had been on both those delegations and hence got to know and respect him as a sober and serious man. But his efforts failed and the ban on polygamy went into effect.

* * *

In the aftermath of that change in the law, I found myself inexorably drawn into a complicated triangular love and marital affair involving an old friend, his jolly and agreeable wife and his good-looking and street-smart mistress. In the end, two of the parties asked me to mediate a satisfactory way out of the tangle. I could hardly refuse because of my past associations with all three parties.

I shall begin the story by introducing my friend, whom I shall refer to as Y, and his wife, Mrs. Y. I first met them in the early 1960s, soon after I had joined the Administrative Service and posted to the Social Welfare Department. It had been at one of those race-day luncheons given by one of the stewards of the Jockey Club. Both had been around my own age but, because they had married much earlier than myself, they already had three children — two daughters and a son.

Both had come from wealthy business families and both had graduated from one of the lesser known American universities. Y was the only child of a principal wife. His father's concubine managed to produce only two daughters. Mrs. Y was herself a daughter of a concubine. In religion, they were fairly eclectic, with perhaps an inclination towards everyday Buddhist practices. Intellectually, they were low-brows. Their reading materials amounted to little more than a local broadsheet, two tabloids and a scattering of gossip magazines. They followed the comfortable routines of the financially well-to-do — ballet and piano lessons for the children; golf, charity balls and some voluntary work for the adults; and a pleasure boat for family weekends.

On the face of it, there was little about Y to attract anyone's attention. He was a quiet man of medium height, without charisma and without that dynamic spirit frequently claimed for Hong Kong business types. His facial features were nondescript, conveying an impression of a dull and unimaginative salaryman. His clothing was unostentatious; a well-made bespoke suit, which somehow appeared off-the-peg on him, and a tie that did not let out a murmur. Neither an excessively expensive watch nor any diamond-studded cuff links appeared as accoutrements. If I were a stranger passing him in the street, I would not give him a second glance. I doubted if very many women would have noticed him either.

The main impression Y left with me after our initial meeting was one of incongruity. His father had considerable standing in the community. Yet he had given his only son the prosaic and unchallenging business of heading a small motor and fire insurance company within his empire, while assigning his two sons-in-law the much more substantial import and export and warehousing subsidiaries.

Insurance was the kind of activity which could produce a steady living without much effort. The law required all motorists to have third party insurance as a matter of course and fire insurance was a staple, though one had to keep an eye out for arson. A couple of cheerful and diligent after-sales staff handling claims would have been enough to keep customers coming back year after year.

Those judgements by the father must imply something about either the father or the son. It never occurred to me to chase that line of speculation, however, because I had taken Y as a passing acquaintance I was unlikely to have dealings with afterwards.

Events turned out otherwise. When Y discovered I was in the Social Welfare Department, he invited me and Man-Ying to a fund-raising ball that he and his wife had helped to organise for a children's charity. Since the charity was one of those bodies subvented by the government, I felt it both polite and politic to accept.

At the ball, I met a number of Y's closest friends. They appeared to have been mainly his former secondary school classmates, now comfortably established in various professions. They included a solicitor, a stockbroker, a dentist, a chartered accountant and an interior decorator.

During that evening, Y intimated that he and his wife were keen on charitable projects. If government knew of voluntary groups in need of finance for starting a playroom for infants, a children's library or the like in a deprived area, he said, I should feel free to send them his way.

I followed up on Y's offer and referred one or two charities to him. He never let them down. He also invited my family once or twice to join him and his family for weekend outings on his pleasure craft. I noticed how attentive he was to the needs of his wife and children and I envied him his rapport with them. Perhaps having daughters made a difference. In any case, that was how our relationship began.

* * *

My relationship with Mrs. Y took a little longer to develop. It came about in a roundabout way. Once I had got to know some of the friends of the couple, I learnt that the men occasionally went on a "boys' night out". I could well visualise their petty bourgeois notions of fun — a Tsim Sha Tsui topless bar, a bit of taxi dancing at a nightclub or, at worst, some underground live sex show. They had invited me to join in but I declined. Not only had I no interest in such diversions, I also had no money to waste so frivolously.

It was obvious that the men in the group had become fairly well-tamed husbands, from the way they saw to the entertainment of their *tai-tai*s before they stepped out. Due to that consideration, Y suddenly called me one morning to ask if Man-Ying might be free that evening for a game of *mah-jong* with the wives. One of the men going out had a sick wife, so an extra lady was needed to take her place at the table. I said my wife did not know the game but I would be glad to make up the table.

In that way, I got involved with the *tai-tai*s. They were, to a woman, the most awful and careless *mah-jong* players I have ever had a game with. The game was merely an excuse for them to natter about their children, their Filipino maids, the recommendations of their hairdressers, the dresses they had on order, and the latest scandals uncovered by gossip magazines. I did not mind their excruciating plays, since they worked to my advantage, even though the stakes were derisory. So I got quickly bored with being completely left out of their conversations.

After a while, I hit upon an idea. I had a fund of literary and bohemian anecdotes; so I tried a couple. I first told a story of the over-sexed writer, Anaïs Nin seducing the psychiatrist engaged to cure her of her affliction, and then another about the French poet, Gérard de Nerval, tying a pet lobster to a blue ribbon to lead it for walks along the boulevards of Paris.

Those stories apparently amused the ladies, for they had never heard their likes before. Thereafter, whenever they were short of a player, they never hesitated to ask me to make up the table. How could I refuse? Such stories became my staple — Dostoevsky's roulette obsession; Li Po's deftness with his sword as well as his versifying brush; Baudelaire's drug habits; and so forth.

The *tai-tai* I got to like most was Mrs. Y. She was plump, jolly, wifely and hospitable to a fault. She was sensible, home-efficient and without airs. Her soft spot for the less fortunate in society went beyond the conventional Buddhist desire to store up merit for the next existence. She genuinely wanted to do some good.

* * *

When a marriage begins to disintegrate, certain phenomena become quickly observable. First, friends start to drop the warring duo from invitation lists. Then, when the fracture becomes patently irreparable, an irrational choosing of sides, without carefully weighing the facts. Indeed, the full facts might never be known, even to the quarrelling spouses themselves, for such is the state of modern-day matrimony. Therefore rumours, innuendoes, personal chemistry, half-truths, plain lies and perceived professional advantages came into choosing one way or the other for third parties.

When Man-Ying and I decided to go our separate ways, Y and his wife decided in my favour. They therefore did their match-making best to see me re-married. But to no avail.

One day, Y invited me to have tea with him after work. He said he was sorry that none of the ladies whom he and his wife had introduced me to had clicked and asked, with considerable diffidence and circumspection, whether my interest might rest with younger candidates.

I replied I was already 43 and could hardly be looking for a teenaged Miss Hong Kong. The most important requirement was someone to help bring up my children. My job — and its social and official obligations — did not leave me much time to be an adequate single father. Of course, I would want a practical and level-headed woman whose psychological outlook and temperament meshed with my own. But I was past the stage of grand passions. The prognosis for landing the right kind of wife thus appeared quite grim. Some women who might otherwise be suitable also had children of their own. I could certainly not contemplate taking on both the emotional stress and the financial responsibilities for a marriage involving seven or eight people.

Y thought for a moment. "A new sub-stratum of womanhood is developing these days, you know," he said. "They used to be concubine fodder — young, pretty, under-educated, unambitious as to careers and looking only for a steady meal ticket and some home comforts. Perhaps a child or two, as bargaining chips.

"They're mainly daughters from less well-to-do urban families, either with no inclination towards higher studies or else without funds to undertake them. They get launched into working life after middle school, at 18 or 19, as receptionists in multi-national corporations, merchandisers, air hostesses, secretaries, office assistants or whatever. Unlike peasant girls, they're urbanites who consider factory work beneath them."

"Where did you pick all this up?" I asked, surprised by Y's exposition on the subject. "Surely not on the nights out with the boys?"

Y chuckled. "Let's just say I've done a bit of research. They all dream of some rich Prince Charming on a white charger coming to carry them off. Of course no Prince Charming is going to show and their jobs are dreary beyond belief. In former times they would hope for some moneybag to take them as a concubine. But that avenue is now no more, with the change in the law. They have to settle for being a mistress, at the mercy of whichever feckless man they happen to find. Or else, as age creeps up on them and their looks start to wane, they lower their sights by marrying some middle-management type.

"They're not unintelligent, these young women; they've got street-smarts. They're broad-minded, they've been around, they don't mind offering a nibble before a sale, if you know what I mean. Being a virgin at marriage is going out of fashion here, though as a father of girls I dread to consider the implications. Virgins or not, I suppose they can still be bed-worthy and make good housekeepers, if that's what one's looking for. You feel like giving them a try?"

"I fear I've had no contact with the type of women you've been talking about," I said. "They sound like a cold-blooded lot."

"That just goes to show how out of touch some of you government officials are," Y said. "Aren't you supposed to be keeping your fingers on the public pulse? No good just looking after the destitute at one end and hobnobbing with the rich and titled at the other. It's the great silent majority that governments have to keep tabs on. Their sweat keeps this place ticking over. Why did government take notice of students only after they had rioted over Diaoyu Tai? Why did nurses have to march on Government House to demand equal pay? It's the total ignorance of what people really want that has caused the government to mess around with local marriage laws."

"Okay. Points taken. I'm culpable in failing the students. The nurses are a cock-up by the Civil Service Branch. But I'm in the dark on what led to the banning on polygamy. That doesn't affect you, does it?"

Y lowered his eyes for a moment, as if considering an awkward answer. Then, looking up again, he said: "Swear you'll never reveal what I'm about to tell you. Not to *anyone*."

I nodded, assuming it was one of those run-of-the-mill secrets doing the rounds in the gossip mill that was hardly worth keeping.

"I've had a mistress for more than half a year," he blurted out. For the first time in ten years I saw his normally bland and emotionless features take on a degree of animation.

"What!" I was almost shocked out of words. How could so uncharismatic a man, overtly devoted to his wife and family, pull off so great a deception on me? There must be some truth to the old saw about still waters running deep! On reflection, I realised I had been at Oxford when the liaison started and, since my return, I had my hands full with the Diaoyu Tai demonstrators.

Then Y unfolded his story. The girl worked in the customer service department of a leading hotel. He and his wife had booked the hotel's ballroom for one of their charity dances. The girl had been assigned to note down their requirements — the positioning of the top table, the kind of fresh flowers needed, the availability of a drum for drawing raffle tickets and so forth. After the event, Mrs. Y asked him to arrange a small thank-you present for the girl. One thing led to another, even though the girl was only five years older than his eldest daughter.

The girl was now installed in a Causeway Bay flat, presumably at Y's expense. Since she worked shifts at the hotel, she was often available during the day. Y would then meet her for a couple of hours, disappearing on the pretence of visiting an important customer.

"She's fantastic," Y enthused, in a voice that was half an octave higher than usual. "She makes me feel young and reckless again."

"Reckless, all right," I said. "You're sure it's not just a mid-life crisis? You've a perfectly fine wife and family, you know."

"When you meet her, you'll understand. She makes me feel alive! She's part of a sisterhood, all looking for husbands. You should meet some of them. You may get lucky."

"Thanks for the thought," I said, without much enthusiasm. "Have you really thought this thing through? The women are looking for *husbands*, remember? Have you considered consequences? Don't forget it's now no longer legal for you to follow in your father's footsteps."

My friend sighed. "I know, worse luck," he said. "That's why I want you to meet the girl and advise me. You're the only one I can trust to understand my situation. She has an effect on me I can't resist. It's as if a new adventure was awaiting me every day. I cannot give her up. Yet I can't see a satisfactory solution either. Why did the Brits have to mess things up by changing the law? I'll arrange for you to meet her. Then you can advise me."

* * *

The suggestion from Y filled me with apprehension. I was very leery of getting involved in other people's private affairs. The more I knew, the more complicit I would be in a betrayal of his wife. Besides, I doubted if any girl in her 20s would ever make a surrogate mother for my boys. On the other hand, I wanted to satisfy myself that my friend was not being taken for a ride by a pretty gold-digger.

Those considerations caused me to agree to having tea with Y and the girl one day after work. The girl appeared in her hotel uniform, an outfit designed to emphasise efficiency in greeting customers rather than feminine pulchritude. But there was no denying she was pleasing to the eye. She was bright, cheerful and slender, bringing with her a streak of youthful and unpractised sensuality. She had arranged her hair in a casual style resembling Brigitte Bardot's. Her figure might be as agreeable too, except it was difficult to tell beneath the conservative cut of her uniform.

She evoked an image of what an older generation of Chinese would call a *fa ping* or flower vessel, that is, of someone outwardly decorative but might not contain very much inside. For simplicity, I shall refer to her as Ping.

"I've heard so much about you," Ping gushed merrily, upon being introduced. "You must be someone special because you're the first friend of Y's I'm being introduced to."

"Nothing special about me," I replied. "Just happened to be an old family friend."

"He's a big shot in the Home Affairs Department, looking for a wife," Y interjected. "He'd be a spectacular catch for one of your friends."

"Don't be misled," I supplemented quickly. "I *am* looking for a wife but I also come with many negatives. I'm not from a rich family like Y and my salary is my only income. I have three kids from a previous marriage as well. Not anybody's idea of a prize catch."

"When a woman goes fishing, she can never be sure what she might hook," Ping said, cheerfully. "Plenty of girls are only interested in a good and steady man. I'll see what I can arrange."

And so it was that a week later I had dinner with Y and Ping for the purpose of meeting one of Ping's friends. That proved to be the start of my deepening entanglement in their relationships. I eventually ended up with three brief liaisons but, as I had anticipated from the very start, all of them proved too young and inexperienced to play mother to my children. Their bed-worthiness was a separate matter.

* * *

Meanwhile, I had begun a warm and intellectually satisfying relationship with a very attractive Canadian woman in her late 20s. I first encountered her at one of those National Day receptions peppering the colony's social calendar. Such festivities, as usual, would be held in one of those characterless hotel banqueting halls. An abundance of buntings and replicas of that country's flag made brave attempts to enliven the atmosphere. Snacks and drinks proffered by roving waiters were plentiful, however, and more than enough to cater to hard-drinking guests as well as to those who made a profession of gatecrashing.

Small collections of guests would form momentarily on such occasions, before dissolving to circulate and to re-form again elsewhere, engaging the while in exchanges of anodyne greetings, stale platitudes and ritualised toasts to mutual happiness and success.

I noticed, however, a cluster of buttoned-down middle-aged men in buttoned-down suits gathered rather more statically than usual in a corner of the room. The object of their interest soon became apparent. It took the form of a startlingly beautiful young lady of European extraction, dressed in a smart, form-enhancing business suit.

There was a certain gravity in her brown eyes, an assured confidence in the way her head tilted and a sardonic cast in her faintly lipsticked mouth. She stood no more than about five-foot-three. But there was grandeur in her carriage; her clothes also showed to advantage her magnificently proportioned figure. She appeared almost as enticing as if she were standing naked like Bouguereau's Venus. Small wonder so many men hovered around her, with their tongues metaphorically hanging out.

I discovered her name was Barbara, a foreign service officer assigned to the Canadian High Commission in Hong Kong. I concluded quickly that such a woman, if wrongly handled, could well become a weapon for masculine destruction. But such women intrigued me. They posed a challenge, as Everest or the North Pole might for other men. I therefore worked myself into the circle around her and introduced myself.

As an opening gambit, I went for the unconventional. I asked for her assessment of current separatist sentiments in Quebec, following the 1970 kidnapping of a British diplomat and a provincial cabinet minister by supporters of Quebec independence.

Barbara did not look the least put off by so provocative a question. She could easily have parroted the safe official line. Instead, she opined that the situation was fluid and unpredictable. Her voice was soft, melodious and slightly smoky. It was one suggestive of a capacity for whispered intimacies.

A ripple of chemistry flowed between us and a sort of mutual understanding and respect took root. By the time I left the reception, she had accepted an invitation to go night racing with me at Happy Valley the following Wednesday evening, those evening races having been introduced in 1973.

* * *

It did not take me long to discover two other very agreeable circumstances about Barbara. First, she shared with me a number of intellectual interests in current affairs, international relations, history and philosophy. To come across a truly beautiful woman was an occurrence rare enough; to find one with that sort of intellectual interests had to be something of a miracle.

Secondly, she turned out to be a very close neighbour. She lived in Conduit Road, on the side of Victoria Peak just one street above Robinson Road. Palm Court was located on an elevated terrace and her flat was almost directly on top of Palm Court. Being such close neighbours, I fell quickly into the habit of inviting her down for a few fingers of cognac or armagnac.

She would come just a touch after nine. I had told her my children retired to their rooms by nine because they had to get up early for school. We could then chat without distraction.

There was a public path a short distance from Palm Court, connecting Conduit Road to Robinson Road. But Barbara soon found a more convenient short cut. Another building on the terrace a couple of buildings removed from Palm Court had a flight of back stairs with open access to Conduit Road, intended no doubt as a fire escape. Those back stairs were cleaner and better lit than the public path, so Barbara used them to get to my home. I would also escort her home the same way around midnight.

* * *

Every man harbours within himself multiple selves, each with different potentials for doing both good and evil. Ancient Chinese philosophers tried to explain this through the *Book of Changes* and the cosmic elements of the *yin* and the *yang* inherent in each individual. How a balance worked out between the two elements was largely a function of chance, circumstances and evolving relationships.

At the more mundane personal level, for instance, I had an interest in horses. I enjoyed riding them, feeding them, racing them, clocking them and calculating their likely performances against one another. The company of trainers, jockeys and riding boys and their tales of racing coups were highly agreeable, as were generally the sounds and smells of horses and stables. Under those different circumstances, the *yin* and *yang* elements in me would not be balanced in quite the same way. As one waxed the other would waned.

The necessity of making a living and discharging other obligations, however, limited the time I could devote to horses. Otherwise, the imbalance in the *yin* and the *yang* might have tipped me into an obsession as insane as Caligula's. Likewise, if Hitler had been given the opportunity to develop his talent in painting, perhaps the world might have been saved a whole lot of agony by his imbalance.

My association with Barbara revolved around a shared but seldom fulfilled need — the one for tossing around ideas which few others would find interesting. We would delve into them repeatedly, sitting in armchairs set at an angle to each other and separated by a small round table upon which rested bottles of the alcohols of our choice.

This is not to say that while we talked I was oblivious to Barbara being a very attractive and desirable woman. I was as red-blooded as the next man and as open to the temptations of a truly sensual woman. But the self in me craving for intellectual and metaphysical excitement trumped the self seeking carnal gratification. Our exchanges thus remained philosophical and abstract, ranging wherever the news of the day took us. The trigger was often some dispute or proposal connected with changes in the European Union.

I often advanced the view that the European project had been started far too early. It had begun with the coal and steel industrialists trying to create an oligopoly. They sold the war-weary continent the idea that such a move would promote peace, in that no nation could re-arm in secret without coal and steel. The ruling elites then jumped on the bandwagon, seeing the possibility of more lucrative jobs for the boys in following suit in other spheres of social and economic activities. The project then grew like topsy, before the nations involved were ready for it.

The unity of the Chinese nation, in contrast, had been bruited about for at least 3,000 years. Yet, in spite of similar racial stocks and common values, identical customs, compatible religious beliefs and the same written language, the goal of unity was still far from accomplished. The Chinese had been too slow to learn the bitter lessons that whenever the country was disunited, outsiders would usually come and take advantage.

How much more difficult it must be for Europe to learn its own hard lessons, to find the right elements for unifying different races, speaking different languages, and following different religions and traditions. At the same time, they had long histories of conflicts, enmities and subjugations of each other. It would make more sense for Europeans to practise living together harmoniously first, before aiming for closer union.

Suitably lubricated by vintage brandy, we ranged over such conundrums, each with its own shifting kernel of truth. We might talk about national identity and internationalism one evening and about an individual citizen's rights versus his obligations to the state the next. Then whether the individual or the family should form the basic unit in society or the unending hypocrisies of politicians.

The self-immolation of a Buddhist monk somewhere might lead to a discussion about that religion's tenet of cycles of causes and effects and hence to the old metaphysical chestnut of whether ends, however nobly conceived, could ever justify means that were obviously obnoxious. Some harangue by a politician over the failure of immigrants to integrate might cause us to examine the trouble-free assimilation of Jews at Kaifeng, the former capital of the Northern Sung Dynasty. The only snag was that the integration process at Kaifeng took about 800 years.

"You Chinese do take your time, don't you?" Barbara remarked, when I mentioned that timeframe.

"Well, civilisation can only advance at a very slow pace and we humans do our damnedest to trip it up and knock it backwards," I replied. "People did not used to be in such a hurry as nowadays. Don't forget it took more than 1,100 years before St. Bede got declared a saint back in 1899."

Over the many months of sipping drinks and engaging in high-brow talk, both Barbara and I had stayed studiously away from personal matters. I was contented to be completely ignorant of what she did the rest of the time. She could be gathering Hong Kong statistics, penning reports on market potential in the colony for Canadian exports or bestowing her favours upon half a dozen suitors. I simply did not want to know. Neither did I share with her what I was up to with Ping's sisterhood.

Once we started to ransack each other's personal affairs, we might find it too difficult not to slip into emotional entanglements. That would be disastrous. No workable future existed for either of us. She was a bird of passage; her career and life were destined to be elsewhere; whereas I was rooted in Hong Kong, at least so long as I had responsibility for my children. It was wiser for us to remain as if we were on an intellectual archaeological dig, to be jubilant or amused by an as yet undiscovered philosophical layer buried in each of us.

Emotional involvement was a road I had travelled down before under unfavourable circumstances; I was not about to venture that way again. It had led only to separation and heartache. Besides, how could I expect someone like Barbara to bring up my sons in a Chinese fashion? For that reason, I had not even bothered to introduce them to her.

The only occasion we edged towards something personal was when she told me one evening that the first book she ever read about China was during her teens. It had been a novel, in French, by André Malraux called *The Conquerors*.

"Yes, I know that book," I said. "It came out just before I was born, I think. Set in Canton in 1925, after the slaughter by British and French troops of Chinese protesters at Shakee. A road near the spot was named to commemorate the date of the massacres — Six Two Three Road. My mother used to live there."

"No kidding! Must have been very evocative. Like living at Peterloo where agitators for political reform had been cut down by the British cavalry. Or living near where the Battle of Waterloo had been fought. Do you remember Garine, one of the Comintern agents in Malraux's book?"

"Yes, an intellectual throwing his life away for a hopeless ideal. He was trying to help an unstable Chinese government in the south fend off warlords and at the same time get back at the British, by fermenting a general strike in Hong Kong."

"He wasn't much of a Communist in my book," Barbara said. "He had such contempt for women. He took two Chinese girls to bed at the same time and when he was done, he told a newly arrived comrade the best way to deal with Chinese women was to sleep with them and then forget them. That was back in 1925.

"Since arriving here, I've discovered that the same attitude still prevailing among expats in the commercial and financial houses. Their careers are finished once they marry a local woman. How can that remain the norm in this day and age? And your Chinese girls are so gorgeously slim and slender, not heavy and clumsy like me."

"No, no, my dear girl. You're absolutely gorgeous in more ways than one. But entertaining though such a topic may be, we must stick with discussing the racism inherent in colonial societies. It's not restricted to the commercial sectors, you know. All sorts of differentials in pay, perks and entitlements have been institutionalised within the government as well. Expats usually feel the sting of that discrimination only when they fall for a local woman. I know of two cases of European officers suffering for that."

"Really?"

"Yes. The first one was a quite intelligent chap, who got interned during the Japanese occupation. During his captivity, his Chinese girlfriend smuggled him what small comforts she could. After the war, he married her. For that, the administration banished him to the bureaucratic backwaters, in a post much beneath his natural talents. He was left there till he retired.

"The second case occurred more recently. A promising young officer fell in love with a local girl. She was actually a star pupil of the English poet and war hero Edmund Blunden, when he was teaching English literature at the University of Hong Kong.

"When the young officer's head of department heard about his liaison with a local girl, he sent for the lad and warned him, perfectly well-intentionally I imagined, that his career would be seriously compromised if he married her. The officer duly resigned, married the girl and pursued a career in academia instead." *

"Good heavens! How racist!" Barbara cried. Then, after a moment's reflection, she asked: "Would the reverse also be true?"

"What do you mean?"

"Well, if a Chinese officer like you, for example, were to carry on with a European woman, would you be warned that your career was being compromised?"

"Don't know. That situation hasn't arisen, so far as I know."

"Want to find out?"

"What are you suggesting? I think my career has been compromised enough already."

"Look, speculative tales of all kinds go through this place like a dose of salts," Barbara said, with her smoky voice taking on a conspiratorial tone. Her grave brown eyes, too, sparkled with the sunny echoes of a mischief more befitting a younger age.

"Your staff at Hysan Avenue have seen me coming to your office more than once, to go racing with you," she continued. "Your friends in the Voting Members' Box at the Jockey Club have witnessed our dining together, and no

* The two cases have also been mentioned in a memoir entitled *Good Second Class* written by Trevor Clark, a fellow retired Administrative Officer, and published in 2004.

doubt your night watchman here must have already told all his cronies along the terrace of a European woman going in and out of your home at all hours of the night. A judicious display of mutual infatuation before an expatriate audience and a tale of a Chinese City District Commissioner being lured into sin and treason by a white Mata Hari will spread like a house on fire. We can then sit back and enjoy watching your bosses' reactions."

"Capital!" I cried, laughing uproariously. "If you're game, so am I. Come to think of it, the Administrative Officers Association will be holding a ball in two weeks' time. All the bigwigs will be there. It might shock many of them. Most of my fellow officers, however, are decent and hard-working chaps, though there remains still too many displaying their layered snobberies and Blimp-like prejudices. An Oscar-winning performance would be just the thing to put their noses out of joint."

"The sight of an Asian man blatantly enjoying the favours of a white woman would give some of the sahibs and memsahibs kittens," Barbara declared. "Let's do it!"

* * *

A fortnight later, I put on my tuxedo of midnight blue and my silk cummerbund of muted crimson to escort Barbara to the ball of the Administrative Officers Association at a leading hotel. Barbara had decked herself out in a taffeta ball-gown of powder blue with a *décolletage* so devastating that many males had their breaths taken away.

We fortified ourselves suitably with alcohol during dinner and when the music for dancing started we stepped out for our command performance.

During the slow foxtrots, we delivered to the tuneful orgasms of clarinets and saxophones all the stunts Hollywood had rendered commonplace. We displayed the gazing into the eyes, the tight clasping of body to body, and all those little gestures of obvious enchantment. Barbara caressed the back of my crew cut head with her playful fingers and I planted the odd conspicuous kiss upon her swan-like neck. We were at our best — or possibly our worst! — during the tangos. We executed their sharp turns and sometime languishing steps of synchronised passion as if making public declarations of love.

What did we achieve through all that contrived effort? A total flop!

We created a spectacle all right. But it laid only the foundations for my reputation as a roué and caused a few British eyebrows to be raised over the unladylike dancing of women from the Dominions. Certainly no senior officer took enough notice to warn me my career had reached a dead end.

It slowly dawned on us later that we had perhaps started out on a wrong premise. We had assumed I had some kind of career left, whereas I had none! Long before our performance, I had probably already been marked out as too much of a maverick to deserve any higher responsibility. I had already adopted too many positions inimical to the bureaucratic culture; the system's usual response was a one-way ticket to the outer darkness. Although I was appointed Deputy Director for Home Affairs shortly afterwards, my fate had already been more or less sealed.

But I did gain one insight after that evening's performance. I began to understand why movie actors playing romantic roles opposite one another sometimes allowed their screen lives to intrude into their private lives. After that night of close physical contact in pretended love, the detached and metaphysical distance which had hitherto separated Barbara and myself began to shrink dangerously.

Prior to that, the only physical contact between us had been those conventional pecks on the cheek on meeting and upon parting. The intimacy of the dancing had broken an unspoken taboo. I think both of us recognised it. In my case, when I thought about Barbara, my thoughts strayed from platonic realms towards areas far less chaste.

It was just as well that soon after the ball, Barbara's tour of duty in Hong Kong came to an end. She returned to Canada to await reassignment. We refrained from maintaining contact because we each knew we had different destinies in store.

In parting, she left me with a wistful memory of a spectacularly beautiful girl, who had spent many evenings sipping drinks and exchanging musings with me. But she also left an awkward and unanswerable question. If it had not been for the vagaries of a diplomatic posting system, would I have fallen for her and made a fool of myself again?

* * *

No sooner had Barbara departed, I received an SOS from Y. Apparently the Love Boat on which he had been sailing with Ping had hit a submerged reef, holing the vessel below the waterline. He pleaded for an emergency salvage operation.

"Ping has gone completely out of her mind," Y complained, when I met up with him. "She wants me to divorce my wife and marry her. How can I do that? I love my wife; I love my children. I can't get her to listen to reason. She's threatened to complain to my father, to expose our relationship in the media. It's insane. Please make her see sense."

"Not sure what I can do," I said. "Let's get a few facts straight first. Is there any basis for her demand? Did you promise to marry her?"

"No, no, never! I only said I would look after her, give her whatever she wanted. And I've made good on that. Fixed her up with an apartment, bought her clothes, shoes, handbags, jewellery, French perfumes, whatever. What she's demanding now isn't fair."

"Seems getting your name on a marriage certificate has been what she had been wanting all along. You went into this with your eyes wide open, my friend. Presumably, you had intended only a fling, but you should have known beforehand what Ping and her friends had on their minds. Now things are going awry. Have you told your wife about Ping?"

"Oh, no! Of course not. I've kept everything tight as a drum. You're the only one who knows. No friend or office staff suspects a thing."

"Well, I wouldn't be too complacent about that in a place so notorious for insider trading. Best to think carefully where you wish to go before taking another step. You own the apartment where Ping's living now?"

"Technically. The place belongs to a Virgin Islands corporation on lease to my father's insurance company on rather outrageous terms. An entirely legal state of affairs, mind you. If people were to dig under the Virgin Islands shell — and a couple more shelf companies in other jurisdictions — they would probably discover I'm its owner."

"Not very clever, putting a mistress in a flat owned by you and leased to your father's company. Suppose your wife starts asking questions about why an insurance company should lease an apartment in Causeway Bay?"

"My wife's the perfect Chinese wife. So long as the family is well-provided for, she has no curiosity about how business is conducted. Besides, everything's on the level and above board. A little tax avoidance, that's all. The flat I live in, as well as the homes of other members of my family, are all leased from a Panama corporation."

"A Panama corporation? Why so many complications?"

"In my case, I am entitled to quarters as head of the insurance company; part of my terms of employment as chief executive. The Panama outfit issues bearer bonds. No names of its real owners appear anywhere. I and other family members all have some of the bonds, given by my father.

"So long as we hold those bonds, we're all part owners of the properties concerned. In a roundabout way, we're paying ourselves for living in our own properties. Another beautiful aspect of the scheme is that real estate can change hands through the bearer bonds, without having to pay stamp duty. If someone looks into the accounts of my insurance company, all rental payments are covered by a global sum listed under a heading of: 'Office, Quarters and Other Rentals'."

"What a corporate wizard your father must be! The West has been steadily elevating corporate rights above the rights of individuals and of society in general for over a century. I see that your father has not been slow in picking up the tricks of the trade. Can't you just get him to corporatise matrimony into some form of bearer bond as well? That might be sufficient to get you out of your pickle. You wouldn't need me to talk to Ping then."

"Be serious, David. I need you because she has refused to talk about anything except marriage. I still love her, however, and I don't want to lose her. You have to talk some sense into her, to stop this silly business and get back to where we were before."

I shook my head. "I'm sorry, Y, I can't do that."

"Why not?"

"You're my friend; but your wife's also my friend. To an extent, so is Ping. I can't help any one friend by betraying another. It's one thing to pretend I don't know anything about what's going on; quite another to actively smooth out and cover up an affair you're having behind your wife's back. There's also Ping to consider. I have no idea what her views might be. Surely you do not expect her to remain your mistress for the rest of her life. That would be most unfair.

"Even if both of you can patch up your quarrel, how long do you think it will be before it blows up again? Times have changed, my friend. Polygamy has been banned. You cannot follow in your father's footsteps, having your cake and keep eating it — even if you can afford it. You've had your fun. Isn't it time to end it?"

Y kept shaking his head dispiritedly. "I don't want to. I still love her," he declared.

"A moment ago you said you loved your wife and your children. Ping's a young, pretty and sexy woman, one capable of making men drool with desire. Are you really in love with her or is it just a temporary fascination? If it's love, you must be prepared to pay the price, not just in monetary terms, but also emotional and social terms. And those closest to you are likely to be very deeply hurt by whatever decision you make. Are you prepared for all of that?"

Y continued to shake his head. "What am I to do?" he cried. "I want her but I can't marry her. She knows that. Yet she's threatening to cause trouble for my family. I can't allow that either. What to do? You've got to help me."

"I would like to," I said, soothingly. "But I don't want to be caught in conflicting cross-currents. If you want me to negotiate a decent and reasonable end to the relationship, that's a different matter, though I'm not sure I can bring it off. For sure I'm willing to try. To do that — and assuming money's not an important consideration — I will require *carte blanche* from you."

Y remained silent for a long moment. "There's no other way?" he asked, in a pained voice.

"Not for me," I replied.

After another long moment of silence, Y said: "All right. My head tells me that's the sane and sensible thing to do. But my heart's rebelling like hell against the whole idea."

* * *

Opening a dialogue with Ping was the easy part. We met in a quiet coffee shop. It appeared she wanted my help too — to persuade Y to marry her! But it took several meetings to get across to her that love conferred not only entitlements but also demanded sacrifices.

Her side of the story went roughly as follows:

It had all started out as a bit of a lark. She was tired of having to keep putting on a smiling face for hotel patrons, always saying "Yes, Sir." or "Yes, Ma'am." She wanted to demonstrate that though moneyless, she had another form of power. So when Y — whom she knew as the only son of a wealthy family — asked her out, she accepted.

She had not meant to get so deeply involved. However, when she saw how kind and generous Y was and how ardent his declarations of love, she began falling for him. The way he got an apartment for her to avoid prying eyes showed his consideration for both their reputations. It came across as part of a more enduring plan.

As he showered her with gifts, he kept saying how much he loved her. The gifts were the kind she never dreamt she would ever receive. Designer clothes and French negligées, for example. The latter appeared completely pointless because whenever he visited her, he wanted to see her wearing only French perfume!

She realised that sex could not be the be-all-and-end-all in their relationship. As the months rolled by, she began feeling like a bird in a gilded cage. Y seldom took her out and when he did it was usually to some out-of-the-way restaurant where he was unlikely to run into people he knew. Needless to say, going dancing or to a movie together was out of the question. She began to wonder if he was ashamed of her.

He gave her money for whatever she wanted but she had no opportunity to wear the clothes she had acquired or to display her expensive accessories while going to work. What was the use of possessing nice things when one could not show them off?

She had thought of quitting work but Y was against it. He said she would become bored with too much time on her hands. He persuaded her that her existing shift pattern would enable them to fit in assignations two or three times a week. He telephoned her every day but forbade her ever to call him. He was ever so careful, refusing even to have a duplicate set of keys for the apartment lest he had to explain what the keys were.

Over the period of 15 months, they never spent a single night together, however. On the rare occasions Y could come during the evening, he would always disappear before midnight, like Cinderella before bewitching hour. She could not bear the thought of him spending the night with his wife, while she herself had to sleep alone.

As the first anniversary of their affair rolled around, she began to fear there might be no more progress to their relationship. Although Y kept constantly declaring his love, he made no move to give it substance and permanence. She wanted to secure a position within his family, a social status of her own, so that she could start having children. She hinted strongly her desire for marriage but he only prevaricated. The harder he tried to shelve the issue, the harder she pressed. It led ultimately to her threatening to approach Y's father or to go public with their relationship.

* * *

At our second meeting in the same coffee shop, Ping urged me to help her persuade Y to marry her.

"You must have realised from the very beginning that Y was a married man," I said, tentatively. "Did you really expect him to leave his family to marry you? Surely you're not asking me to become complicit in being a home-wrecker?"

"No, but am I not entitled to a life and a family of my own?" Ping replied. "When a man keeps telling a woman how much he loves her and how his wife did not understand him, you'd expect him to do something about it, wouldn't you?"

"Did Y promise to marry you? Was that the basis upon which you began the relationship with him?"

"Not in so many words. But when a man keeps saying he would look after you and give you whatever you wanted, wouldn't that include marriage as well?"

"Not necessarily. Don't be misled by the old rhyme about love and marriage going together like horse and carriage. Royal families used to marry their children off to foster better inter-state relations. I'm offering to marry a companionable woman now, mainly to gain help in bringing up my sons. Love doesn't figure much in that sort of deal — at least not initially."

Ping gave me a wickedly amused look. "But you did have fun with the girls I introduced to you, didn't you?" she said. "They told me all about it. To your credit you were up-front with them. If Y had been up-front with me, that would have made a difference. Instead, he wormed his way into my affections with his lovey-dovey whispers and flashy presents. Now he wouldn't give me the one thing I want. That makes me mad."

"Look, Ping, you're still young; you've got a lot going for you. Love is still love even if it does not end in marriage. Why not just write off this episode as life experience and let it go. I know Y loves you a great deal; he told me so. In his heart, he doesn't really want to give you up. But he absolutely cannot give you the future you want and deserve. He cannot just give up his wife and family. He doesn't want trouble for his parents either. It's really in your own interest to terminate your relationship with him. Please try and understand."

"What does he see in that wife of his? She's old and fat."

"Please don't be mean, Ping. It's not like you. Y's wife is a very pleasant and kind-hearted lady. She's the mother of his three children. She may be a little on the plump side, but you'd look pretty much the same 16 or 17 years down the road, after you've had three children."

"What about me then?" Ping cried, with her voice breaking with barely suppressed agitation. "Am I not as good as she, just because I don't come from a wealthy family? Don't I have feelings? What am I left with after having given him my heart for 15 months? Am I to be tossed away like an old shoe?"

"Y wants you to be well taken care of; he told me so. He is concerned about you and is sorry things have to end this way. It's not what he really wants. Tell me what *you* want; I'll get a good settlement for you."

"I don't want any damn settlement! I want him to marry me! Does he think he can just pay me off like some common whore? He can go to hell!"

A flood of tears began rolling down Ping's cheeks. It was just as well that the coffee shop was fairly poorly patronised at that hour.

"Please, Ping! Don't cry," I whispered, offering her my handkerchief. "I didn't mean my remark to be taken in that way. I'm sorry. I'm just trying to help both of you."

Ping ignored my offer and pulled out her own from her handbag. As she dabbed her tears, I continued: "Y and I want to do what's best for you. He's heartbroken and I'm troubled too, because you are both my friends. Otherwise I wouldn't have got involved in your private affairs. Nobody benefits from a public row."

Ping took a few moments to compose herself. Then she said: "I don't want a single damn thing from that phoney, cowardly liar. He does not even appreciate my true worth."

I shook my head slowly and sighed. "Ah, it seems Aristotle has got it right all along," I said.

"Aristotle? Who's Aristotle?"

"A Greek philosopher."

"What has he got to do with me? Why are you trying to confuse me by talking about a Greek philosopher?"

"I'm sorry. Bad habit. But he's worth listening to. He said the young always overdo things, loving too much and hating too much. He put it down to their being insufficiently humbled by experience to accept life's limitations. I, on the other hand, have been repeatedly and roundly humbled and humiliated, so I know whereof I speak. I had no choice but to become philosophical. The only other option would be to go insane with frustration. You're too young to turn defeatist or to go insane. Make the most of the opportunities that are coming your way. Do not reject them too hastily. Think each one over carefully. Let me take you to dinner a couple of days hence. I'll call you. We can talk at greater length then."

* * *

I duly took Ping out to dinner. She had appeared more reconciled to disengaging with Y by then. We went to Jimmy's Kitchen on Wyndham Street, my favourite European restaurant. I had first patronised it right after the war, when it was just a hole in the wall at Theatre Lane. In 30 years it had morphed into an up-market eatery, with branches popular with both well-heeled locals and tourists. I had often taken my sons there on special occasions. There they all acquired their taste for escargots, prepared with lots of garlic.

At the restaurant I bumped into a couple of acquaintances already having their meals. I introduced Ping to them as we made our way to our table.

After we had been seated, Ping said wistfully: "Why couldn't Y have brought me here and introduced me to his friends, instead of hiding me away all the time?"

"Because he's a married man and you're not his wife," I replied. "If anyone he knew saw you two dining together, tongues would wag. I'm different. I'm a bachelor. It's expected that I should be escorting young ladies around. In fact, I had brought one of the girls you've introduced me to here."

As our meals proceeded, I gradually got down to brass tacks. "Are you okay by yourself at the Causeway Bay apartment?" I asked. "Is there anything I can help you with?"

"You mean moving my stuff out and handing back the keys?" Ping responded. "It'll take a little more time to find a suitable housemate, to get back to sharing a place like before. Space more of an issue now, since I've got more stuff than before."

"Look, there's no need for you to move out if you like the place. Y's adamant you should be properly provided for and he's authorised me to say he would buy the apartment for you, as a parting gift, if you wanted it. That way you would have a roof over your head for life, without the need for bank loans, mortgages, rents and so forth. It's a very generous offer, given the way property prices are in Hong Kong. I would advise you to take it. I have a good lawyer friend who can act on your behalf. Y would pick up that legal tab too. What do you say?"

The offer seemed to have taken Ping entirely by surprise. She looked down ruminatively at her plate, poking her food around with a fork. Then she said: "How can I afford to pay the service charges and rates for an apartment like that on my salary?"

"Good point," I said. "I'm fairly confident something extra can be worked into a disengagement agreement. Both parties would, of course, have to refrain from disclosing all past and pending arrangements."

"What does that mean?"

"Not telling anyone what went on between the two of you and not revealing the terms of any final settlement."

"You mean I will return to being a non-person again, a nobody in the hotel's customer relations department? I can't buy that."

"I wouldn't put it like that. It simply means neither you nor Y would tell anyone about your relationship."

"He's been a part of my life for 15 months. He's been the centre of my everyday existence. Now he wants that period to be blotted out, to become a total blank? No, I can't buy that. I want some public recognition, some record of what had once existed and had been shared between us. Otherwise, it would be as if I had never existed for 15 months."

"You've lost me, Ping," I said. "What do you mean by public recognition? I thought I was supposed to help both of you wind things up quietly and privately, without recriminations and without public commotion. That's why Y's agreed to a very generous offer."

"I know you mean to be helpful, David," Ping said, "but I can't revert to being a nobody again. I need some memento to keep, to prove I could be as good as any other woman in high society. I want Y to take me to one of his charity balls, to dance with me in front of all his friends, and for us to have photographs taken. I need him to show me he's not ashamed to be seen with me in public. Otherwise, no deal."

"But how can Y take you to a ball? He's got a wife. What's he going to say to her?"

"That's his problem. I've got photos of us fooling around in the apartment. Does he prefer for those to be shown around?"

* * *

"I told you she's gone crazy," Y said, when I conveyed Ping's demands. "She's already turned my life upside down. How can I take her to a ball? That would create precisely the kind of scandal I want to avoid."

"We've come quite a long way towards an agreement," I said. "It would be worth humouring Ping a bit more. You could invite her to a ball without actually 'taking' her, couldn't you? After I broke up with Man-Ying you've invited me to a couple of balls and I brought a different partner each time. All your intimates know I've been scouting for another wife. Ping could be passed off as one of my current candidates. Besides, your wife already knows her."

"That's just the problem. I'm not sure I can hide my feelings for her. My wife might suspect something. Or else Ping might make a scene at the table or while dancing with me."

"Well, that simply means you'll have to maintain control. Don't play the excitable lover. Just be your usual deadpan self. If you can do that, most things can be plausibly explained. You normally invite four or five couples as guests. As host, you would normally dance with the wives. So you do a couple of turns with Ping. So what? Society photographers can snap all they want and probably will. What does that matter if you're not caught in any compromising light? Of course, I will try to make sure beforehand that Ping agrees to behave appropriately. A friendly word with her should do it. I think her word can be trusted."

"I don't know," Y said dubiously, shaking his head. "I still miss her, you know. It all sounds rather risky."

"You have a better idea to make this whole thing go away?"

Y sighed. "Okay. I guess there's no other way out. I don't know why love has tied me into such a knot. But I'm counting on you to save my bacon."

"Perhaps it's only infatuation. In any case, I'm counting on *you* not to lose your head again on the night."

* * *

I carefully explained to Ping I had been able to get Y to agree to inviting her to a grand charity ball, but as my pretended girlfriend. So she would have to behave with dignity and show the world what a fine and gracious lady she was. I intimated that film producers and talent scouts would be present at the ball and if she played her cards right, she might well be offered screen tests and openings in other careers. After my briefing, she seemed quite enthusiastic about participating in the masquerade before society's upper crust.

When I turned up at Ping's door about three weeks later to escort her to the event, I was met by an entirely different woman than the one I had expected. If Y was adept in working commercial angles, Ping was superb at working the womanly curves. The image before me was one sheathed in a form-hugging turquoise ball gown displaying a physical configuration which left little to the imagination. Now rid of her usual staid hotel uniform, her hourglass figure and provocative haunches were revealed to the full. Y could hardly be blamed for going overboard.

Ping had also done her hair up differently. She must have gone to a professional hairdresser to create a stunningly fashionable pile on top of her head. Her eyes, too, had been enhanced by mascara and eyeshadow while her cheeks had been pollened and lightly rouged. She had been transformed into one very sophisticated and desirable lady.

Around her throat she had on an elaborate but tasteful choker, with just enough sparklers to avoid being considered ostentatious.

"Wow!" I cried. "If I had known you were wearing such a bejewelled item I would have engaged a couple of armed escorts."

"Stop poking fun at me," Ping countered. "You know very well the jewels are just paste."

"Could have fooled me. Paste or not, the settings have been masterfully done. Must have cost a pretty penny."

"Yes, Y gave it to me. He explained that all the rich *tai-tai*s in town only ever wear paste. The real McCoys are kept in bank vaults for fear of being stolen or misplaced. We girls are such suckers. We work ourselves to the bone to save enough for a genuine designer handbag. But when we carry it around, everybody takes it as a fake because we're just ordinary working girls. The rich can wear fakes and yet everybody assumes they are real. It's so unfair."

"I'm afraid that's just the way the world is."

* * *

The evening went as anticipated. Ping stunned everybody with her grace and beauty. Dancing with her was a dream. Without any coaxing, she played the role of girlfriend as enthusiastically as Barbara had done, only this time it was before a local well-heeled crowd instead of largely expatriate bureaucrats. She gave an altogether convincing performance of a woman besotted with a man. When she danced with Y, on the other hand, she did it with the utmost rectitude, keeping a small air cushion between them to prevent bodily contact. If she were trying to make Y jump out of his skin with jealousy, she succeeded mightily. I was left slightly embarrassed by the play-acting, however.

By the end of the evening, Ping was in high spirits. It was as if she had finished a début performance to endless encores. She had got everything she wanted. A public coming-out before moneyed society, dancing tantalisingly with Y and getting photographed more than enough for her to choose whatever prints she needed.

When taking her home, I said: "You were a complete knockout tonight. You got everybody's attention, including Mrs. Y's. She complimented you during my dance with her, you know, even asked how seriously we were getting along. She didn't suspect a thing about you and Y. I'll introduce you to my lawyer friend tomorrow to begin the legal process of transfer. You can tell him yourself how you want things done."

At the entrance to her apartment, Ping thanked me for facilitating a smooth settlement. Then she added teasingly: "Do you think I'd be any good in bringing up your boys?"

"You're lucky you've never met them," I said. "They're sure to drive you crazy. Thanks for the tempting offer. But I think I had better say goodnight."

* * *

As a consequence of Ping's performance at the charity ball, coming hard on the heels of the escapade with Barbara, rumours began to circulate of a serious romance between me and a staggeringly beautiful girl only half my age. It so happened that my father was also in Hong Kong at that time. Before long, even relatives were ringing up to ask if a wedding banquet was in the offing.

There was, of course, no substance to the gossip. When no matrimony materialised, the two episodes with Ping and Barbara sealed my reputation as a philanderer, trifling with the affections of women who had lost their heads. That impression was deepened by my continuing to be seen with a string of other ladies as part of my search for a suitable wife.

So far as Ping was concerned, in less than six months after the charity ball, her marriage to a Chinese rubber and industrial tycoon from Southeast Asia was announced. The tycoon was a widower, about ten years older than Y. I got an invitation to the wedding. But since it was being held in a remote and romantic part of the Italian Riviera, I could not afford to attend.

To the best of my knowledge, Y had not been invited. His nights out with his friends also subsequently tapered off and ceased.

After the wedding, Ping took up residence in Southeast Asia, where her husband had his business interests. I never saw or heard from her again.

CHAPTER 10

A Square Peg

WHEN ERIC HO RETURNED from long leave in 1975 to resume his appointment as Director of Home Affairs, it became time for me to move on. I had been in the department for four eventful years and, with my former slot as Deputy Director already filled by another Chinese Administrative Officer during Eric's absence, it made management sense for me to go elsewhere.

One of the grand traditions of the Administrative Service, in common with that of the ancient Chinese mandarinate, was not leaving an officer in any particular area of activity for too long. Over-familiarity with a specific sector, it was felt, might breed contempt, intellectual laziness, compartmentalised thinking and even corrupt practices. Rotation was therefore deemed suitable for keeping alive the tradition for nurturing generalists with a range of skills, perspectives and experiences. Such skills, painfully accumulated, would then stimulate visions of social possibilities when eventually assigned to positions of command. When such experiences were pooled, they should provide enough creativity to tackle the most complex micro and macro social and economic problems in society.

Having such officials was an imperative frequently under-appreciated in an age of smug specialisations. The system for developing such officials naturally had drawbacks as well. For a start, garnering broad experiences over many fields might deny an officer a leadership role till it was too late in his career, after age had turned him less dynamic and innovative or more inclined to be lulled by thoughts of retirement.

A substantive Staff Grade B Administrative Officer would in the normal scheme of things be holding a position as Deputy Director of a major government department or else one as Deputy Secretary in one of the branches in the Secretariat. If the gods were to smile on him, he might be rewarded with an acting post above his own substantive grade — and pocketing some acting pay to boot.

I myself had no expectation of good fortune for I had too often displayed insufficient sensitivity towards the feelings and proclivities of my superiors. Since the Secretariat was the home of the largest collection of senior posts, especially after the dubious expansion following the McKinsey report, it required no mathematical genius to figure the odds for being sent there.

Assigning an officer to a post had very little to do with his personal preferences. He was essentially a pawn in an unseemly game of chance played out among the top mandarins. Unforeseen events or a roll of some celestial dice often dictated where he would end up. A sudden need might arise due to a natural disaster or else the personal tragedy for an incumbent might strike. That happened to Lai Ka-Wah, a close and contemporaneous colleague, when he unexpectedly died from cirrhosis of the liver. Ordinarily, someone being promoted or going on long leave might open up an acting opportunity. In those circumstances, the hole had to be plugged even if only a square peg was to hand.

This is not to say that an individual officer would never get a post of his choice. The chances, however, must be roughly of the same order as his getting an accurate prediction of his future from a fortune stick or *chim* at the Wong Tai Sin Temple. There used to be a perverse tradition in the bureaucracy to the effect that keeping mum about one's preferences somehow increased the likelihood of getting what one desired. I imagine it might have originated from the fear of a vengeful god or a spiteful senior seeing to it that keenness showed bad taste and hence should never be rewarded. I do not know whether that superstition has survived to our agnostic present.

The prospect of returning to the Secretariat filled me with both misgivings and anticipation. More than 11 years had passed since I first entered the Secretariat as a wide-eyed probationer. A great deal had changed. Back then, I had consorted with other fresh-faced juniors from Berkshire, Kent or elsewhere and I had been delighted with their wonderful British sense of resourcefulness, mischief and perversity.

No British colleague would mind, for example, being given a nickname like Five o'clock Bob for leaving the office on the dot. After all, the 1950s world of Suzie Wong still beckoned and had remained not fully explored. If an expatriate had reservations over his mission as a colonial servant during the death throes of empire, the requisition of a portrait of a still youthful Queen from the Government Stores for his office wall would soon stiffen his resolve to carry on regardless.

During those bygone days, juniors used to stroll into each other's offices and, over cups of tea, discuss with far greater earnestness the runs the Australians had piled up in the first innings of a Test match than with the more trifling matter of the proliferation of intercontinental ballistic missiles. They might also assess with sanguine eyes how each had bulked up "In" trays with moribund files to give the impression of being overwhelmed with work.

That had also been a time when, if a dull minute on a boring topic could not be avoided, one would liven up the piece by disinterring some dimly remembered quote from Horace or Pliny the Younger. A more harried age had since conspired with declining educational standards to bring an end to such displays of erudition. Education authorities, in fits of democratic enthusiasm, had succeeded in levelling the playing fields. Knowledge of Latin had been reduced strictly to a par with Sanskrit.

My second stint in the Secretariat a few years later had been more sobering and humbling. Under the tutelage of Mike Clinton, with his bomb-ravaged face, and John Cowperthwaite, with his shyly hidden intellect, I had begun to realise that colonial bureaucrats with no democratic mandate to rule and yet had to make decisions impacting profoundly upon society as a whole. That placed them quite close to the old Chinese concept of an official acting like the father and mother of the people. The weight of such responsibility pressed uncomfortably upon my awareness. I feared I might not be up to discharging such a task.

After Oxford, as I moved slowly up the hierarchy, I was increasingly thrown into closer contact with expatriate power-wielders. Those experiences were not reassuring. Virtually all the top posts were still occupied by expatriates. Somehow I gained the impression that the integrity, the ethos and the *esprit de corps* in the Administrative Service, built up painfully over more than a century by a number of decent men, were slowly being dissipated by their lesser successors. The spirit of a corps was like a pool of savings. One could not draw indefinitely upon it without replenishing it from time to time. I gained the uncomfortable impression that more and more decisions were being taken off the cuff rather than through careful deliberation of the holistic whole.

Sir Murray MacLehose had arrived too late as Governor to have heeded Sir John Cowperthwaite's oft-repeated warning about the dearth of intellectual resources to proceed at faster than a certain pace. Mesmerised by the bulging public coffers Sir John had left, Sir Murray went for a populist spending spree on social services, little appreciating that it could turn into a slow poison, eating into the self-reliance of a sturdy people. Sir Murray's motives for so doing were uncertain. He might have had good intentions. His governorship was to be the last public office he would ever hold and the unkind had ascribed to him the vanity of wanting to leave to posterity a name to be reckoned with.

I supposed that becoming the absolute ruler of one of the most commercially-savvy cities on earth could go to one's head. Given the ethos of the place, he might have calculated he could buy whatever talent he needed. If he had so calculated, then he had been mistaken.

The people available to him were confined largely to blinkered technicians, skilled in manipulating messages and numbers and putting a gloss on the workaday realities. Good governance needed people with moral and ethical commitments and philosophising capabilities towards wider visions. That type of people had to be nurtured over time, through dedicated mentoring.

What profit was there for anyone in simply boasting of an increase in the number of schools or school places if what was being taught were the wrong lessons? What was the point of brainwashing another generation with the economic shibboleth of rational free markets when they were patently rigged by big fund managers and money speculators? Or the trickle down effects of wealth when the invisible hand of corporate racketeers picked the pockets of ordinary citizens and caused wealth to flow upwards to the wealthy few instead?

The political responses and catchphrases were even worse. The lessons of the riots of the late 1960s and the student demonstrations over Diaoyu Tai in the early 1970s had not been learnt.

There appeared to be influential "China experts" in Whitehall who believed the Chinese could remain an easy touch for latter-day neo-imperialists. After all, the British had been bamboozling them into signing unequal treaties for 130 years and there was no reason why that could not continue for another 130 years. They even managed to convince a few Hong Kong moneybags of the absurd notion that China could be amenable to reviving its former tributary system. In other words, if Hong Kong could pay China a substantial annual sum, China might be amenable to letting the colony continue its wheeler-dealer ways under extended British management.

It was not very clear whether Sir Murray personally subscribed to that "expert" view. In any event, he had spent much of his career in diplomacy, a calling where smooth-talking and perceptions mattered more than actually delivering results. That might have driven him to make a splash over expanding social services.

But to expand any activity, more skilled managers were needed. In order to get that extra talent quickly, he resorted to watering down recruitment standards. That erosion in standards gradually picked up pace and instead of a system which promoted merit it turned slowly into one which made for mediocrity. It resulted in the uncalled-for advancement of a fair number of third-raters, intellectual midgets, paper-shufflers, buck-passers, back-stabbers, time-servers, pension-calculators, opportunists and the like.

Nonetheless, in spite of that qualitative decline, the Secretariat remained the only real and tangible centre of power, the place where policies were being formulated for good or ill and where decisions, however imperfectly arrived at, had to be made. Any officer wishing to exercise the slightest influence had to find a place in that semi-ivory tower.

* * *

There had been quite a number of Secretariat positions in which I would have loved to try my hand. The Security Branch was one of them. I wanted to learn the true extent of its knowledge about syndicated police corruption and the range of dirty deeds being committed in the name of national security. There had been rumours of the British allowing American Central Intelligence agents to interrogate illegal Chinese immigrants in Hong Kong, to identify the size and composition of People's Liberation Army units located in their home districts. It would have been illuminating to know whether there was substance to those rumours.

But the pigmentation of my skin barred me from the Security Branch. Apparently, there were too many communications marked "For British Eyes Only" and my eyes were considered not British enough.

The Secretary for Security, I supposed, had valid and adequate grounds for excluding Chinese officers like myself. After all, he had caught me red-handed violating Security Regulations, by failing to report conversations with people in left-wing organisations at a farewell dinner for the Director for Urban Services. On top of that, I had exploited my position as a Justice of the Peace to challenge the interpretation of the Commissioner for Prisons on what might be deemed subversive literature in prisons. An unflattering security profile about me no doubt already existed somewhere. Governments always preferred to be safe rather than sorry.

Having engaged the administration with very limited success in the past — when I had been an office bearer in the Senior Non-Expatriate Officers Association — I was naturally keen to enter the Civil Service Branch also to understand the full rationale for the better salary levels and perks granted to expatriate officers.

Historically, when the number of civil servants was relatively small, their management was left in the hands of an Establishment Officer. He was the custodian of a thick, red-covered tome setting out all the procedures from advertising a civil service vacancy to the proper disposal of bureaucratic zombies. Those regulations released such an air of nit-picking and ennui that the job of Establishment Officer sounded about as exciting as being a custodian of government furniture. Hence it was not a particularly sought-after post by the ambitious. Holders of that post tended to be mediocrities. On the rare occasions a top flight officer found himself in the post, he could rest assured he would not be there for long. His talents would always be more sorely needed elsewhere.

After World War II, the civil service became much more complex. At the same time it became the largest single employer in the colony. Thus the role of Establishment Officer assumed growing importance. The title was changed to Secretary for the Civil Service and it became still more powerful and sought-after. But elevating the grade of the post, however, did not necessarily mean an improvement in the management of the civil service.

At the time I was due for re-assignment from the Home Affairs Department, the post of Secretary for the Civil Service was occupied by a highly ambitious expatriate officer who had been transferred to Hong Kong from another colony which had gained independence. Although he was only a Staff Grade B Officer like myself — and indeed he was ranked beneath me in seniority — he got the appointment on an acting basis because he was the new governor's blue-eyed boy. Since he was responsible for proposing senior postings for the decision of higher authorities, the chance of my being assigned a post in the Civil Service Branch was nil, for he would have taken my presence in the branch as a direct threat to his own position.

Naturally, beyond the common desire for career advancement, personal antipathies and philosophical differences also came into play at every level of the posting process. For example, given the way I had ruffled the feathers of the Secretary for Home Affairs when I was Director of Home Affairs, there was hardly any chance of his ever accepting me as his deputy. Because of such extraneous considerations, I could only wait to be told where my next job was going to be.

* * *

In due time, I was informed I would be the next Deputy Secretary in the Economic Services Branch. It was a satisfactory appointment so far as I was concerned. I had served in the branch previously as Assistant Economic Secretary and was familiar with many of its responsibilities. But there was a hitch. The expatriate occupying the post at that moment was not due for leave for another four months or so, which meant I had to wait until his departure before taking up that position.

In the interim, it was decided that I should perform special duties under the Secretary for Housing. I would not be a formal member of the Housing

Branch but would work *ad personam* to the Secretary, doing whatever chores he might assign to me. My title would be an equally unspecific one — Deputy Secretary (Special Duties).

I felt slightly apprehensive over that *ad hoc* arrangement. Providing decent public housing in Hong Kong had been — and still continues to be today — a veritable Pandora's box of conflicting and tangled issues.

Affordable housing was a basic human need, similar to food and clothing. Providing it posed a serious challenge for cities everywhere because of uncontrolled and haphazard urbanisation. To my mind, it was an issue incapable of being satisfactorily tackled in isolation, without all the associated problems generated by urbanisation being taken into account, like traffic congestion, pollution, corruption, crime, fragmentation of the traditional family structure and human exploitation of various kinds. But that called for the long-term dedication of a highly skilled team embracing many disciplines and not of a single officer.

After World War II, the necessity of providing affordable housing was a matter left largely to market forces and the will of Heaven, except for some rent control legislation for pre-war buildings. That gave rise to the demand for "tea money" by those who possessed rent-controlled premises from those who wanted to live in them.

Meanwhile, as former residents who had fled to escape the Japanese occupation returned, and as refugees poured in to flee from the escalating civil conflicts in China, the housing situation became increasingly acute. Those with financial resources bought homes or paid "tea money". Those without means fell back initially on sponging off relatives, which was what I had to do.

Those sound of limb might find work as coolies or rickshaw pullers. But they would only earn enough to pay for cubicles or bed spaces in dank and airless tenements. Those without brawn, money or relatives found shelter wherever they could. With each passing day, legions were reduced to huddling beneath pieces of cardboard, sheets of corrugated metal or structures of salvaged plywood. Makeshift homes popped up everywhere, on hillsides and rooftops, in alleyways and every other conceivable nook of unoccupied land. Flimsy dwellings quickly turned into encampments, spreading omnifariously across the face of the colony like some unsightly and contaminating disease.

Still the government dithered. It had too many urgent problems on its hands. High among them was the anxiety over its own survival, whether it might itself be swept into oblivion by the on-rushing tides of Chinese nationalism and history. Somehow, fate turned out to be kinder than anticipated and crisis after crisis passed. That "invisible hand" of the free market somehow generated just enough wealth at the lower levels of society to justify non-intervention on providing housing.

In 1953, however, the government's *laissez-faire* approach was challenged by a horrendous Christmas Day fire at the Shek Kip Mei. The fire raged through an entire squatter encampment, killing two squatters and rendering roughly 53,000 homeless. Those who had used their huts and hovels to engage in handicraft or other forms of making a living lost their livelihoods as well.

A veteran Administrative Officer by the name of Ronald Holmes, who had joined the service in 1938, was given the task of tackling that human disaster. Holmes, incidentally, had been a war hero. After Hong Kong fell to the Japanese, he operated in a South China army unit tasked with helping Allied prisoners of war to escape from Japanese camps. For that dangerous work he was awarded a Military Cross. He was also to receive a knighthood in 1973 for his administrative accomplishments.

Holmes and his team performed a herculean feat in rehousing all the fire victims in an estate within approximately one year. It demonstrated what dedicated civil servants could do, once there was political will and the availability of the right human and economic resources.

The accommodation provided for the displaced squatters consisted of eight six-storeyed blocks built in the shape of an H. Small box-like units lined both sides of the long corridors to make up the two parallel lines of the H. The structures bore no resemblance to any architectural design in vogue in China during the last five thousand years. Space was allocated on the basis of 24 square feet for an adult and a fraction thereof for each child.

Another development impacted on the design of the resettlement blocks. Before the war, the building regulations required the ceiling heights in domestic dwellings to be between 16 and 18 feet. After the war, the ceiling heights were progressively reduced, so that by the mid-1950s they had dropped to a mere 10 feet.

It was nonetheless something of a marvel that 53,000 people — far more than the population of many European towns — could be fitted into just eight six-storeyed blocks. Of course, the allocation of the block and the floor where a family might go was largely a matter of chance. If a family wished to be accommodated next to another family it had developed a friendship with in the squatter encampment, that was not the sort of customer-oriented allocation any bureaucracy could cater for.

Facilities at the eight blocks were necessarily rudimentary. Only communal bathrooms and latrines were provided on each floor. They were located in that architectural hyphen linking the two arms of the H.

The need for creating a coherent community within the estate fell beneath the radar of officials tasked with setting up that first resettlement estate. Given the urgency for re-housing the fire victims, that was perhaps forgivable. Drawing an analogy from Dante's *Divine Comedy*, however, to move from a squatter area into that first estate was probably like moving from one level of purgatory to a slightly less awful level.

No sooner had Holmes completed the first phase of his mission, he was diverted to tackling exigencies in other spheres. Perhaps those who picked up the reins from him had other preoccupations; or else they had assumed the prototype Holmes had created was meant to be the one to be followed henceforth.

It was unlikely that an experienced officer like Holmes would have thought that the rules of thumb he had put in place needed no further refinements. The adoption, for example, of the 24 square feet per adult standard for allocating space simply had to be considered further.

Holmes could hardly have been ignorant of the attachments Chinese placed upon family bonds. Allocating that level of space per adult hardly provided enough room for hanging up laundry to dry, let alone for erecting an altar for ancestral tablets for prayers and offerings to ancestors. The fraction used to calculate entitlements for children also needed reconsideration. When should a child be considered an adult? At 16, 18 or what? It was not uncommon for girls to be married well before 18. Would it be fair to penalise them for housing purposes?

To complicate matters further, China did not issue birth certificates. Any child would merely be registered with the housing unit to which the family belonged. Most homeless people were immigrants from China; how could their ages be authenticated for allocating space?

Looming in the background was also the uncomfortable knowledge that contemporary British prison regulations specified that a prisoner in single confinement was entitled to a minimum of 48 square feet of space. Furthermore, one did not have to study the experiments of behavioural scientists to guess the adverse psychological effects upon small animals kept for any length of time in confined space. Similar effects on human beings could be easily imagined. So how could the 24 square feet rule be maintained, let alone publicly justified?

And what of preserving even a shadow of the Chinese concept of a multi-generational extended family? That had to go for a burton.

The provision of communal bathrooms and toilets soon gave rise to complaints of Peeping Toms and of women being sexually molested. At the same time, triad societies quickly made their presence felt. The grim and vulnerable corridors in each block were like enclosed streets.

No doubt complaints could be referred to the police. But the short-handed force, saddled with its own internal problems, could hardly be expected to patrol those forbidding corridors on a regular basis. A story of uncertain authenticity got circulated at one time, to the effect that two policemen patrolling a corridor in a housing estate in response to some alarm got waylaid by a triad gang and their service revolvers unceremoniously taken from them. Regardless of whether the story was true or not, residents drew their own conclusions. Steel gates became steadily installed outside the front doors of most resettlement units.

Today, seven of the original eight H-blocks at Shek Kip Mei have been demolished but one block has been retained. It has been made into a listed building for heritage purposes. I am not sure why. Should some structure built in Gin Lane at the time of Hogarth have been retained as a monument to the meanness of those times? I wonder.

* * *

Following the completion of the Shek Kip Mei Estate, the logical next step appeared the construction of more estates. But it was a hopeless game of catch-up even without the other needs for job opportunities, schools, hospitals, shopping, infrastructure, entertainment, parks and so forth. And also the important missing intangibles like social cohesion, a pleasing environment and a comforting sense of peace and security.

Some of the subsequent estates which went up were in the vicinity of the old Kai Tak International Airport. After the new passenger terminal had been completed there in 1962, it quickly became apparent that space in the Arrivals Lounge was often occupied by students from nearby estates doing their homework. Although the air conditioning in the lounge must have been an attraction, their presence suggested that their homes did not provide sufficient space for them to pursue their studies in comfort.

Planes landing at Kai Tak Airport — photos courtesy of *South China Morning Post*

It also suggested a recurring failure of government to be joined-up and creative in making strategic decisions.

Kai Tak International Airport, because of its location in the midst of a heavily built-up area, had long been known in aviation circles as one of the ten most dangerous airports in the world. If my memory is correct, it had at various times been ranked at about the fifth or sixth most dangerous. For that reason international airlines took pains to use their most experienced pilots for flights into and out of the city.

Millions of passengers must have dined out on hair-raising tales of flying in or out over Kowloon City. It must often have seemed that the plane was about to pick up somebody's laundry from a rooftop — if not actually landing on top of it!

Kai Tak airport had only a single runway. The flight path for take-offs or landings had to be either over the sea or over Kowloon City. Take-offs and landings were the most dangerous parts of any air journey. For that reason, airlines always required passengers to buckle up on such occasions. Prevailing winds dictated that more in-coming and out-going flights went over Kowloon City rather than over the sea.

In 1970, when the Boeing 747 came into commercial use, the Civil Aviation Department commissioned a secret assessment by aviation experts on the likelihood of a major air disaster striking, the worst case scenario and the colony's readiness to cope. Such an assessment was duly produced based on world-wide statistics. It indicated that — on average — every major international airport suffered from at least one serious disaster once every 25 years.

Hong Kong's deadliest air accident occurred in August of 1965, when a United States Marines Lockheed Hercules plunged into the harbour shortly after take-off. A total of 59 out of the 71 marines on board were killed. Less than two years later, in June of 1967, a Thai Airways plane also crashed into the harbour, while it was trying to land during a rainstorm. Twenty-four passengers were killed.

The experts concluded that the previous mishaps had involved smaller planes. The worst scenario facing Kai Tak now would be a fully-fuelled Boeing 747 crashing into Kowloon City during take-off. Because of the population density of the area, the number of deaths and injuries would probably number around 50,000, a scale far beyond the existing capacity of the emergency services to cope.

* * *

I had no knowledge of that alarming report till many years after the event. It came to light when a secret file crossed my desk as Secretary for Economic Services on some completely unrelated matter. Presumably, the Civil Aviation Department must have submitted the original report to the Secretariat for guidance or follow-up directions.

Upon discovering the report, I naturally read it and flipped through the file. The first thing that struck me was that I had no recollection of the crash of the Lockheed Hercules, although it had been represented as the worst air disaster in Hong Kong. As I pondered that fact, I slowly realised that I had not been in the colony when the tragedy occurred, on a cheerless European holiday with my wife, after I had completed my studies at the Institute of Social Studies at The Hague. I had also just said farewell to Sharlee. The European media did not give Hong Kong developments much attention. Therefore I was virtually unaware of what had happened. Since it had also been a tragedy with no Hong Kong victims, the subject scarcely came up in local conversation.

How easily the deaths of strangers disappeared from our collective consciousness! I suppose that is why it is easy for deaths in wars and revolutions in far-off places to be regarded as mere abstractions. Philosophers and men of letters might keep reminding us that no man was an island. But how can any sensitive soul survive in the present world of daily abominations without going insane? Nature must have provided us with some means of shutting tragedies befalling others from our consciousness.

The Thai Airways crash had occurred while I had been engaged in manning the midnight shift at the Emergency Control Centre during the spillover into the colony of the Cultural Revolution chaos from China.

Reading through the secret file, I gained an eerie feeling the Secretariat subject officer of the time might have merely filed the report away after receipt, without analysing it for upward submission. I could find no record of any senior official having seen it or considered its implications or given instructions for dealing with its contents.

It was as if some bright young spark had noted that Kai Tak had had more than its fair share of aviation disasters in 1965 and 1967 and that, on the basis of statistical averages, a further major mishap would be unlikely for at least another 30 years. By then, it would be another millennium and, predictably and perhaps almost thankfully, it would be somebody else's palaver!

On the other hand, it could have been just one of those periodic bureaucratic cock-ups, of a subject officer about to be transferred passing over an awkward problem for his successor to pursue. And somehow, that report simply slipped between the cracks.

My inability to pin down who had done what about it, caused a flurry of questions to flit through my mind. They rose like slumbering ghosts suddenly agitated by someone disturbing their burial sites. If there was a potential for a catastrophic disaster, then all top officials, including the Governor, should have been appraised of it.

At the same time, I tried to think of reasons why the administration might wish to suppress or take no action on the report. News of a potential disaster of that magnitude could cause panic and initiate a collapse in property prices around Kowloon City. It could trigger demand for a safer and alternative airport. Yet the idea of building one at Chek Lap Kok did not gain traction till the late 1980s. Why such a delay, if the risks were already assessed in the early 1970s? Had the risks of such a horrific disaster been taken into account before deciding to build housing estates in Kowloon City? Had a conscious decision been taken that putting the lives of so many at risk was a price worth paying in economic terms? Very awkward questions to answer.

And why had there been no public discussion about such a real and present danger? The colony had a free media. Where had their investigative reporters and commentators been over the years? Had they no nose for such a major public interest story?

After I had disposed of the separate matter requiring my attention, I asked my deputy to run down what actually happened to that report and whether its contents had been dealt with in some other file. Unfortunately, I never got answers because I was transferred to other duties before my deputy could get back to me.

* * *

Meanwhile, tracking backwards, Sir Murray MacLehose had assumed the governorship of Hong Kong in November of 1971. The following year he announced a grandiose ten-year plan for meeting public demand for affordable housing.

It seemed to me strange that in the middle of 1975 — three years after announcing an ambitious housing programme — the Secretary for Housing should be asking for an extra pair of hands to help over housing problems. He had a branch fully staffed with Administrative Officers. If they had not be able to deal with snags which might have surfaced, how could I? That question made me worried I might be heading into a no-win assignment.

The Secretary for Housing was known to be one of the longest serving Administrative Officers, though not generally regarded as being among the brightest. He was short for a European, not even as tall as myself. He appeared affable and in rude health when I reported for duty. A vague smile played upon his lips when he saw me. It was a disconcerting smile for it appeared mechanical, as if operated by clockwork and without roots in genuine pleasure or happiness.

I had never worked with the man before. I only knew him from two or three social encounters, plus some stories picked up from the rumour mills. He had a reputation for passing off Polonian platitudes like newly-minted profundities. Hardly an ideal type of superior to work for, I thought. But I consoled myself with the thought that my stint would be only for a very limited duration.

The Secretary began by telling me that he had arranged an office, a telephone and a stenographer for me. Those facilities, however, were to be located in a different part of the extended Secretariat building, on another floor and a considerable distance from the Housing Branch. I got the impression he was not very keen to integrate me into his team, preferring to keep me as a temporary outside helper. He accordingly did not invite me to participate in his branch meetings. I took that decision with indifference.

The Secretary told me that my job would be to make contact with major local property developers and find out how each could contribute more to meeting the colony's housing needs. I should also try to elicit from them, he said, what they thought of existing government rules and building regulations. Its systems could be adjusted if that would assist them in providing more affordable housing.

I was slightly surprised by the implications of the assignment. In the first place, the Housing Branch should have been in regular contact with local property developers all along. Secondly, such developers were primarily in the business of maximising profits and not in assisting the administration to solve problems over supplying affordable housing. Since more money could be made from commercial developments and luxury apartments, where a turn could be made in approximately four years, it was unlikely any developer would wish to divert resources into low-cost housing with its meagre margins.

In addition, should the likelihood or otherwise of developers entering this sector of the market not have been already factored into the equation before the Governor launched his ten-year programme?

Upon reflecting further, I realised that both the Secretary and his Deputy were expatriates, whereas most of the top property developers were Chinese. Many of the latter's grasp of the English language could at best be considered shaky. There could therefore have been a real communications gap between them.

So I drew up a programme for individual interviews with the chief executives of every major property corporation. Since I was acquainted with two or three of them, I got them to spread the word about my mission. After meeting each of them, I reported to the Secretary in writing. This worked out at a steady two or three reports a week. After the first few reports had been submitted, the Secretary asked me to copy my reports to the Secretary for the Environment since the developers were raising issues concerning the availability of land, whether the government intended altering the existing system of public land auctions, and so forth. So I did as I had been asked.

Generally speaking, the attitude of property developers was much as I had anticipated. They were in the business of maximising profits and it was in their interest to concentrate on what they did best. They had all acquired land banks through open land auctions. Though there had been recurrent rumours of bidding rings, nothing could be definitely proved. Since land was a finite resource and population growth an established phenomenon, land and property prices could only go up, to the benefit of developers.

Government intentions were of crucial importance to them. If they knew where the next new town or big infrastructure project was to be developed, then they could buy up parcels of agricultural land in the vicinity and simply wait for development to come their way. It required no great insight to know that if an alternative airport were to be built to replace Kai Tak, then it would have to be on Lantau Island. But where in Lantau and how would the infrastructure connections run? To know in advance meant money in the bank.

The government itself was an accomplice in the process by rationing land. It depended on land sales or the issue of leases for a significant part of its revenue. Thus it had an interest in keeping prices buoyant. The rate of release of land was crucial, as was the method of bidding — by open tender or sealed bids. I was unable to respond to many of the queries developers had on official intentions because I was largely in the dark myself. I could only suggest a range of possibilities and promise to pass on their queries.

* * *

During the months I was on secondment, the Secretary for Housing hardly responded to the issues posed in my reports. He rarely even telephoned me. During that entire period, he asked me to see him on no more than five or six occasions. Each time our discussion turned on some rather peripheral matter. He never once asked me to look into any particular shortcoming in the ten-year housing programme.

And I studiously avoided volunteering to do so. Since I had not been given access to Housing Branch files, I had no idea of who had contributed what to which component of the project announced by the Governor. To be critical of any part without establishing who had been the originator could be asking for trouble. It was a matter of self-preservation.

There was also a more fundamental reason for my reticence. I feared that if my criticisms hit home, the Secretary might ask for my secondment to be extended to fix whatever defect I had identified. Our personalities and our working styles did not mesh and I was keen to get back to economic matters.

Therefore I stuck to doing what I had been asked to do. The Secretary did not react to my reports on conversations with developers nor to the points raised by them. So I occupied myself by making observations on peripheral issues.

Public housing posed real challenges, even for very advanced countries. One look at one of the "sink estates" around London or at a graffiti-splattered Parisian *banlieue* would illustrate the extent of some of the challenges. If I am not mistaken, I think one of those suburbs holds the world record for the number of motor vehicles torched on a single night of rioting. Burning cars has now somehow become a tradition for expressing dissatisfaction in the suburbs of Paris.

Public housing did not become a feature in Hong Kong till about the beginning of 1955, after the first resettlement blocks at Shek Kip Mei had been completed and occupied. So there was scope for experimentation, for learning from the experiences of others.

To that end, I suggested to the Secretary that some of the windowless end walls of resettlement blocks might be decorated with large murals for a more inhabitant-friendly environment, to soften the oppression of too much concrete. There could be murals of misty mountains or singing waterfalls, like Chinese landscapes, or of activities associated with the celebration of one of the many traditional festivals. Or even simply splashes of colours like modern art to take away some of the drabness and the resemblance of a German *stalag*.

The Secretary replied that murals cost money. I pointed out that since the end walls of some blocks faced busy roads and highways, advertising companies might be interested in such wall space for advertisements for watches, cameras, soft drinks, shampoos and other consumer products. They paid handsomely for such space on private properties and it would not be a compromise too far to allow a few advertisements if that would generate sufficient funds to pay for some cheerful murals elsewhere in an estate.

The Secretary said he would have someone look into the possibility but I heard nothing further. That suggestion could well have foundered upon the normally sound bureaucratic doctrine of not allowing any particular source of revenue to be tied specifically to a certain type of expenditure.

* * *

In another memo to the Secretary, I suggested initiating a resettlement housing lottery. The thinking behind it was simple. Producing subsidised housing for the masses was bound to be a long-term challenge. There were just too many squatters and others living under unsatisfactory conditions. Squatters tended to be cleared only when the land they were on was required for some public purpose. But neither they nor the government really had much inkling of when that might be. They could be waiting in their unsatisfactory shelters for years.

Meanwhile, new resettlement estates would be continually coming on stream. It would be natural for the government to first re-house those who had been on the waiting list longest or for people who had been displaced from the very site used for building the new estate. But what about setting aside a small part of every newly built estate for winners of a lottery? The people eligible to take part would be people in need of subsidised accommodation or those already in the queue.

The idea of a lottery would prey upon certain human weaknesses. The Chinese were a gambling race, believing in the element of chance or providence in life. If they bought a housing lottery ticket for a small sum, it might just give them sufficient hope of jumping the queue to keep their impatience at bay. I thought back to the days in 1947 when I had returned to Hong Kong at the age of 18, jobless and with no more than two banknotes to rub my fingers against. I had nonetheless spent some of my precious dollars on tickets for the Jockey Club sweepstakes. The possession of a ticket at least gave me the licence to dream of untold riches for a while. The inadequately housed might likewise be soothed by a dream of suddenly being allocated a home in a lottery.

There was another consideration. The Chinese are also an enterprising and practical race. Having witnessed how the Shek Kip Mei fire victims had been rehoused within roughly a year, desperate souls might collude in a bit of arson to hurry their time along. Small fires of dubious origins had indeed occurred in a couple of squatter areas. It seemed better to offer people hope rather than to drive them into despondency and desperation.

I was conscious that my proposal went against one of my own principles. I have never much liked the idea of lotteries, especially when governments resorted to them to raise public revenue, because lotteries always hit hardest those who could least afford to part with their money. Millionaires were unlikely to buy lottery tickets. Under my proposal, the prize would not actually be a monetary prize but merely an earlier award of an entitlement to subsidised housing.

In spite of its shortcomings, I forwarded my suggestion to the Secretary. It met with no response.

A few weeks later, I was surprised to read in the newspapers a speech by a Legislative Councillor named Roger Lobo in the council chamber, urging government to institute a housing lottery for long-suffering squatters and others in need of subsidised housing.

I happened to bump into Roger Lobo in the streets a couple of days later and I congratulated him on his speech. I then asked him how he came by the idea for a housing lottery. Lobo replied that the idea had been suggested to him by the Secretary for Housing. The Secretary indicated that if he would make a speech about it, the Secretary would respond by saying that the government would give every consideration to such a scheme.

"I'm glad you've pursued his idea," I said. "The Secretary is a very creative fellow."

* * *

Soon after I had completed my secondment to the Housing Branch and had been installed as the Deputy Secretary for Economic Services, I heard rumours that the Secretary for Housing had been putting it about at senior levels that my assignment to his Branch had been a failure. He was reported to have said that I had made not a single contribution towards improving or accelerating the Governor's ten-year housing plan.

What the Secretary was reported to have said was undeniably true. But somehow I had a funny feeling that in making his comments he had omitted to mention he had not asked me to examine any component in the ten-year plan. That oversight would not have been surprising to me, for he was clearly not a colleague of the same calibre as either David Baron or Donald Luddington.

I have lost count of the number of ten-year housing plans announced since Sir Murray's in 1972. Neither have I tried to follow the aspirations set out in any of them. All I know is that, four and a half decades later, many citizens of the Special Administrative Region of China are still much exercised by their inability to secure affordable housing.

CHAPTER 11

Political Poker Games

WHEN THE RECONSTRUCTION of the Central Government Office complex at Lower Albert Road was completed in 1959, it consisted of two buildings. One ran from Lower Albert Road to Ice House Street and was referred to as the West Wing. It housed a number of government departments, including the Urban Services Department, the Registrar General's Department and the Civil Aviation Department.

The Government Secretariat itself, however, was located in an adjacent structure built in the shape of the letter T. The shorter section, representing the bar at the top of the T, faced the West Wing and was separated from it by a large courtyard with a venerable old tree and a couple of flagpoles. It was known as the Centre Block. Apart from housing top bureaucrats, it also included the chambers for the Legislative and Executive Councils, with the offices of the Colonial Secretary and Financial Secretary on the fifth floor.

The longer tail of the T-shaped building stretched as far as Garden Road. It was known as the East Wing. It also provided accommodation for some key departments, like the Attorney General's.

Incongruously, the Centre Block was built to a height of six storeys while the East Wing stopped at five. It was unclear whether architectural aesthetics had anything to do with it. In any case, the planners were aware of the unalterable law of bureaucratic expansion, so they left room for adding an extra floor to the wing.

Battalions of civil servants soon filled the two new buildings. But before anyone could do what the Chinese vernacular called "two somersaults", a go-ahead was given for an additional floor to be constructed on the East Wing. And thereby hangs a spooky tale.

The story centred upon an inauspicious office on the sixth floor, located right at the junction where the Centre Block connected the additional floor of the East Wing. I was scheduled to occupy that ill-famed office, for it had by then been designated for the Deputy Secretary for Economic Services.

I should explain that Secretariat branches tended to be moved around the different floors in the building, depending on their rates of expansion. To illustrate: When I was Assistant Economic Secretary towards the end of 1970, my office was on the fifth floor of the Centre Block, at the other end of the same corridor as the Colonial Secretary and Financial Secretary. By the time of I returned as Deputy Secretary for Economic Services in 1975, the branch had moved to the sixth floor of the East Wing. The room which I was to occupy had previously been used by senior officers in the General Branch and the Establishment Branch.

The offices throughout the sixth floor extension were divided up by partitions of wood and glass, materials calculated to provide maximum flexibility in dismantling and re-configuring room sizes. Because of the extension, one side of my designated office was in fact the original outer granite wall of the Centre Block. In order to give the room a less inhibiting feel, an enormous map of Hong Kong had been put up by one of the previous occupants to hide the grey granite wall.

The individual histories of previous occupants were as follows: The first three occupants had all been expatriate officers. The first suffered two heart attacks and had to be invalided out of the service. The second sustained a serious back injury from which he never fully recovered. The third, a man in his 40s, got an attack of mumps and went deaf in one ear.

The next occupant was a Chinese, none other than Lai Ka-Wah. He died in his prime of cirrhosis of the liver. The occupant after that had been my immediate predecessor, another expatriate. Prior to his going on home leave he was found to be suffering from pulmonary tuberculosis, something almost unheard of in the mid-1970s, especially for an expatriate. The pity was that no minutes by him could be found in the Secretariat written with a poetic eloquence to match that of a consumptive Keats. So instead of going on home leave, my predecessor went on medical leave.

The bad reputation of the room thus intensified exponentially. Civil servants high and low considered the string of ailments visited upon its previous occupants to be too consistent to be put down to sheer coincidence. Therefore, when it became generally known that I would be occupying that room, my Chinese friends and colleagues became worried. They suggested a range of protective measures.

One friend brought Mr. Choy Park-Lai, the foremost geomancer in Hong Kong at the time, to make an assessment of the *fung shui* of the room. Mr. Choy concluded there was indeed a dark and uncongenial atmosphere there. Although the granite wall had been hidden, Mr. Choy thought the *fung shui* still suggested the presence of a gigantic tombstone. He urged me to move to another room. When I explained that was not possible, he said the only advice he could then give was for me to change the position of my desk, to avoid as much as possible the bad influences coming from the wall. I did as he had advised, though I remained unsure whether it made any difference.

Another friend, a Buddhist, offered to arrange for Buddhist priests to perform purification rites. I politely demurred, fearful that such an exercise might reflect poorly on the reputation of my maternal grandfather. After all, he had been the first Anglican Bishop of Canton and, if I were to believe in evil spirits, I should at least humour his memory by going for a full-blooded Christian exorcism. But that sounded equally ridiculous.

Yet another friend wanted me to install a tank of goldfish in the room, as an early warning system, in much the same way as canaries were put in coal mines. He assured me that if there was something malevolent in the room, the fish would feel the effects and die first. I declined his suggestion, on the grounds that goldfish needed to be fed too regularly and changing the water in their tank would be too much trouble.

A lady colleague did present me a plant from the Philippines, however, which she vouchsafed would be effective in warding off evil spirits. She warned, nonetheless, that should the plant begin to die, I had to get out of the room posthaste. I accepted the plant and thanked her for her concern.

Nonetheless, other friends still remained apprehensive. Among them were the Legislative Councillor Lee Quo-Wei and his wife. Mr. Lee, known to his many friends simply as Q.W., was one of those remarkably fine and public-spirited gentlemen that Hong Kong used to produce in abundance back in those days. He had started his working life in 1946, as a junior clerk at the Hang Seng Bank. He rose inexorably and by 1983 had become the bank's Executive Chairman.

I first met Q.W. around 1968, after he had been appointed a member of the Legislative Council. This had been in the aftermath of the Star Ferry riots in 1966 and the upheavals of the Cultural Revolution riots the following year.

Q.W. was a quiet, humble and engaging man, keen to do whatever he could to benefit the wider society, while recognising the political realities that existed in the colony. His public speeches were always measured and courteous, not filled with bombast and the theatrical gimmicks common nowadays. His aim was neither to garner public recognition nor to stroke his own ego. He confined himself to working quietly and constructively behind the scenes. A pity that breed appears to be dying out in Hong Kong nowadays.

In order to discharge his responsibilities to the community, Q.W. reached out to whomever he thought could be helpful. To that end, he invited a small group of Chinese Administrative Officers to dine at his home once every two or three months, to engage in frank and open exchanges of views. I was privileged to be part of that group, which also included Eric Ho, Lai Ka-Wah and two or three others.

At those gatherings, all public issues were robustly discussed. Q.W. knew that Eric Ho and I had both been active in union activities in the civil service, fighting for equal treatment for locals as against the treatment accorded expatriates. He wanted to be briefed on our discussions, lest the government kept some things from Legislative Councillors. He himself was particularly interested in education, having been active in setting up the Chinese University of Hong Kong and later serving as the Chairman of the Board of Education. He had also served for a total of seven years on the Executive Council and was knighted in 1988 for his various public services.

When news of my fated occupation of that notorious room in the Secretariat reached Q.W. and his wife, they became alarmed.

"We cannot allow that appalling room to take two Davids from us," Mrs. Lee declared. She was referring to the recent demise of Lai Ka-Wah, who had also used the Christian name of David.

So declaring, she disappeared into a private part of her apartment and returned with a jade replica of a Chinese sword, measuring about an inch and a half long. She handed it to me and said: "You must wear this at all times. Do it before going into that room. It should offer you some protection."

I accepted the gift and had a gold chain made for it the following day. That event had taken place more than 42 years ago; today I am still wearing that jade sword around my neck!

I cannot say with any confidence whether the things done for me by friends had helped me to survive in that room for four and a half years without any major health disaster. Possibly my frequent absences from it due to overseas negotiations had helped.

But some strange things did happen during my tenure. I did undergo three minor operations — one for removing some gallstones and two others to excise tumour-like but non-cancerous growths on different parts of my body. Before each operation, the leaves of the Philippines plant would start turning yellow but would quickly recover once the operations had been completed. What could be the explanation for such unusual behaviour by the plant ? Had there really been something at work in that room?

To round off the story, I should record that shortly after I had been transferred from the Secretariat, there had been another reallocation of office accommodation. That room was expanded and turned into space for a Secretariat typing pool. So far as anyone has been able to ascertain, no succession of typists suffered from unusual maladies thereafter.

* * *

Because of the unexpected ailment of my predecessor, I had to jump into the job of Deputy Secretary without the benefit of a proper handover. One of my earliest surprises was to find myself appointed as a director on the boards of both the Kowloon Motor Bus Company and the China Motor Bus Company.

The two companies provided bus services for Kowloon and the New Territories and for Hong Kong Island respectively, both operating on government franchises which had been more or less rolled over since 1933. Franchises back then were simple and unsophisticated affairs, casually phrased and sparsely detailed. There was no specific provision in either for any director representing the government. But then, there was nothing to say one could not be appointed either. If anyone were minded to litigate on that or any other issue, it would probably be donkey's years before a court could come up with a definitive ruling.

A provision existed in the franchises, however, for the government to revoke a franchise for unsatisfactory services. That clause hung like a sword of

Damocles over both companies. But who was to define what "unsatisfactory" meant and who was to decide when that state had been reached?

My own surmise was that some sort of back-room deal had been stitched up between the administration and the two bus companies, with each party playing its own game of blind man's bluff. After the Star Ferry riots in 1966, triggered by a mere five-cent increase in ferry fares, a similar increase in bus fares would be much more provocative for the travelling public. The administration must have thought it prudent to have someone on the inside, primarily to demonstrate that an official was there to look after the public interest and secondarily to provide some early warning before things got seriously out of hand.

The two companies must have had their own calculations. Franchises had to be extended from time to time and with the Cross-Harbour Tunnel completed in 1972, turf wars over cross-harbour bus services were already arising. Furthermore, approval for the construction of an underground mass transit system had already been given. It would do no harm to get into the good books of the administration by accepting someone of its choice on the boards of bus companies.

The government's astigmatic oversight of the rapidly expanding internal transportation systems in the city was gloriously tangled. It rested upon a benign *ad hoc*-ery laced by a few dubious free market assumptions. The result was one which few geniuses could replicate at the present time. Yet, somehow, it worked — in spite of an occasional hiccup.

Under such a makeshift regime, the police was in charge of controlling road traffic and licensing most types of motor vehicles. The Public Works Department had responsibility for building and maintaining roads and for the erection of street furniture, although the Urban Services Department also had a say when it came to the location of kerbside hawker stalls and the erection of commercial neon signs overhanging thoroughfares.

To the frustration of both motorists and pedestrians, roads had the infuriating habit of being dug up half the time, to allow ducts, pipes or cables to be laid by franchised companies supplying gas, electricity and telephonic services. Needless to say, the government's own water works and sewage works did their fair share of digging as well.

The narrow streets in the older parts of town further tested human patience and ingenuity. The antiquated trams running on Hong Kong Island, on tracks first laid in 1903, provided a further complication. Tram rides were often a cheap, pleasant and sedate experience and many citizens had developed a sentimental attachment to those throwbacks to a more indolent age. But their fixed tracks did not make for the most efficient use of limited road space. Agitators for modernity had been clamouring for the upgrading of the trams or their downright removal for some time. The tram operators' efforts to move with the times, by abolishing first and third class compartments on trams in 1972, did not entirely appease their critics.

The funicular railway going to the top of the Peak, which was first opened in 1888, was another pleasant reminder of former times. That, however, had largely avoided the ire of modernisers.

To still complicate matters further, the part of the Kowloon-Canton Railway owned by the public had a separate department of its own, while the hotchpotch of marine traffic in the harbour for handling goods, tourists and pleasure seekers fell to the lot of the Marine Department.

And all the while, different sections of society kept agitating for more of everything — more private cars, parking spaces, taxis, tourist buses, school buses, roads, zebra crossings, ferries, seafront berths for pleasure craft and so forth. Naturally, everybody wanted less noise, less pollution, less road accidents, less traffic jams and a much more pleasant and less jangled way of living as well.

As befitting a city growing by leaps and bounds, thousands of non-franchised minibus services began operating to meet unsatisfied local or specialised needs, like taking workers to jobs at designated factories or children to schools. Such demands also spurred enterprising individuals to provide illegal taxi services known as *pak pais* for school runs. They proved immensely popular.

The beauty of the entire system, with its need to balance conflicting demands and tardy supplies, was that it left the long-suffering public too confused to know which government department to blame for any affliction it wanted to complain about. No Transport Department even existed till 1972.

It quickly became evident, even to superficial observers, that the supply and demand equation for internal transportation was out of whack. A study had been initiated in the 1960s to consider a mass transit system. The proposal for such a system duly went through legislative scrutiny and was authorised to proceed in 1972. Actual construction, however, did not begin till the end of 1975.

* * *

The policy responsibilities for that farrago of transportation arrangements naturally rested somewhere within the Secretariat. But the Secretariat had many branches and each branch was like a gigantic amoeba, constantly changing size, shape and authority.

The Economic Services Branch, in the latter part of 1975, was probably tasked with dealing with a little more than about a third of the issues touched upon above. The rest went to other branches. The boundaries between branches were sometimes ill-defined and nebulous and sometimes overlapping. The arrangement provided just enough scope for plausible alibis and buck-passing should things get sticky.

Being made a director on the boards of two publicly listed companies entailed a range of unclear and perhaps conflicting legal, political and ethical responsibilities. The unspoken imputation was that I was there to attend to the public interest. But what was the public interest? To have safe, reliable, comfortable and affordable bus services, I supposed. But what about the service conditions of those employed by the company? From my Labour Department days, I knew that the administration had been promoting the formation of trade unions though — as demonstrated during the Cultural Revolution riots — it seemed to have lost track of the political colouration of unions formed. What was going on in the unions within the bus companies? No one seemed to know. Obviously something was amiss; otherwise a public servant would not be inserted into two privately-operated franchised businesses.

In a Panglossian world, everything was supposed to turn out for the best that was possible. In the cut-throat world of laissez-faire capitalism, things were likely to produce different results. To have a safe bus service might mean more modern buses and more safety checks, which in turn would increase costs. To have contented workers meant they had to be given a fair share of the profits generated by the enterprise. Was I expected to see to some form of ideal balance?

Under corporate law, a director was supposed to look after the interests of shareholders, to reduce their risks and maximise their rewards. What if that legal requirement conflicted with the public interest in having a safer bus service? I could hardly be expected to resolve such conflicts without clear instructions. Yet none of that had been spelt out.

I was not so *gauche* and tiresome as to ask for clarifications. I had already been marked as a maverick and classified as "not a good team player". To seek instructions over shadowy situations would merely damn me further, as one lacking both initiative and willingness to play the game.

On the other hand, inside the boardrooms of the two companies, I would be expected to speak authoritatively on behalf of government. How could I even pretend to do so? There were bound to be conflicts between what was desirable in the public interest and what would benefit private capital.

Yet the authority of the Economic Services Branch remained vague and circumscribed.

The only clear instruction handed me was that all director's fees payable to me by the two companies should go straight to the public exchequer and not into my own pocket! No wonder I felt increasingly like a coconut — being set up for a coconut shy.

* * *

For the sake of brevity, I will restrict myself to an account of my dealings as a director with only one of the two companies — the China Motor Bus Company. It would be illustrative of the kind of issues affecting both organisations.

The chairman of the China Motor Bus Company was a doughty Chiu Chow gentleman by the name of Ngan Shing-Kwan. He was born in Hong Kong in 1900 and had a remarkable history. He began his working life as a rickshaw puller along Nathan Road in the early 1920s. He soon joined with another rickshaw puller to form a "transportation company" to ply their trade.

In 1933, when the government got around to recognising both the need for, and the viability of, scheduled bus services, it decided to offer two exclusive franchises for tender, one for Hong Kong Island and another for Kowloon and the New Territories.

Ngan won the Hong Kong Island franchise and another group got the other. Through sheer hard work and determination, Ngan created a very effective company. I first met him when I was a junior reporter with the *South China Morning Post* back in 1947, when he was trying to restore normal bus services after the ravages of the Japanese occupation.

By 1976, he had the company operating on 140 routes, providing work for over 2,000 employees and earning $20 million in annual profit. The company had also acquired a number of strategic properties, including four as bus depots at North Point, Chai Wan, Wong Chuk Hang and Kennedy Town. I quite admired the man for what he had achieved from his modest beginnings.

Ngan's personal standing in the community had risen in line with the fortunes of his company. He was appointed an unofficial member of the Legislative Council in 1951 and served till 1961, spending the last two years as a member of the Executive Council as well. He became active in charitable organisations, particularly in the Tung Wah Hospitals Group and in the Po Leung Kuk, a refuge for girls and young women in moral danger, that is, those who had been sold off as children to brothels or had been otherwise lured into the trade.

Ngan was made a Commander of the Most Excellent Order of the British Empire in 1961. He had three children, a daughter, Irene, and two sons, Horace and Henry. He lived to the grand age of 100.

So far as the bus operations were concerned, he had a reputation of being very hands-on in the company's day-to-day activities and being conscious of every penny spent. But he did introduce the double-decker bus to Hong Kong. Overall, therefore, he was a man to be reckoned with, a formidable opponent should I ever need to play any kind of political poker game with him.

* * *

My first attendance at a board meeting was a revelation. The number of directors was small but Ngan's daughter and one of his sons — Henry it was, I think — were among them. They did most of the talking.

Appointing kinfolk to management positions was quite a common practice among Chinese family-run companies. They had learnt very quickly the advantages under Anglo-Saxon corporate law of getting listed on stock exchanges to risk other people's money to run an enterprise where they previously had to risk their own.

I had prepared a few questions for my own edification at that first board meeting. I wanted to know the average age of the buses in the fleet, how regularly their engines were overhauled, what mechanism was in place for regular exchanges of dialogue between management and staff, the extent of cross-subsidisation — if any — on routes to new but as yet sparsely populated areas and so forth. The impression I got was that the board preferred to discuss broader matters rather than details.

From the tenor of those discussions, I concluded that board meetings were perhaps unnecessary in that company. The three Ngans could well have settled most company business at breakfast each morning — assuming they ate that meal together.

Life's ironies soon played upon my imagination. I surmised that I was in all likelihood the only one around the directorate table who relied on bus services on a regular basis. I frequently used the No. 23A bus, particularly on muggy days when I did not fancy walking uphill back to Palm Court after a long day's work.

How strange it was that by the time a person got to be a director of a bus company he would have little further use for buses. I recalled fondly what a delight it had been when I was given a complimentary bus pass as a reporter for the *Morning Post.* Now that I was a director of the company, I could not use one of its buses without paying my own way!

But by travelling on them I at least acquired some first-hand knowledge of how the buses sounded when they climbed uphill, the kind of passengers they picked up along the way and how effectively or otherwise their drivers carried out their duties.

* * *

In another of the early board meetings, I was myself caught flat-footed on the question as to whether the company ought to engage an international firm of accountants to revalue the assets of the company. I had not thought about that possibility although I knew that local companies had been undergoing similar exercises for various purposes.

All kinds of alarm bells started to ring inside my head. In respect of some franchises, like those for the bus companies, the government had attempted to limit a return on capital employed to approximately 15% or 16%. It was a modest amount by mid-1970s private business standards, especially when compared with what gorging property developers could make.

The bus companies, unlike the ferry companies, were land rich because they had long ago acquired space for parking their buses. Land prices had soared exponentially since they gained their franchises in 1933. On the existing regimes, shareholders could not be rewarded unduly. Excess profits would have to be ploughed back into the business for upgrading and improvements, to buy better and more comfortable buses and — heaven forbid! — to reward salaried staff for their contribution to the profits.

With a vastly revalued capital base, a bus company could well make out a case for increasing bus fares, in order to produce a reasonable return on capital. It was a move fraught with unpredictable consequences.

Caught out as I was, I could only resort to playing the slow-witted civil servant. I said I was no accountant and I was extremely bad with numbers. Before any decision was taken, it would be best if I were to get hold of one of the government's Treasury Accountants who could then go over with the bus company's accountant the details of what would be involved. They could then produce a joint paper for the board to consider.

Accountancy rules were a nightmare for me, I added. I had no idea what would be allowed and what would not. For example, over the last 40-odd years, the company must have written off some of its assets. But some of those physical assets were still there. Could written-off assets be turned back into real assets without giving rise to tax and franchise implications? I had no idea. Perhaps the Inland Revenue boys should be brought into the picture as well. I would find it impossible to give an opinion until a joint paper had been produced and studied by the board.

In that way I managed to fend off temporarily the ploy for a re-assessment.

* * *

The various elites in Hong Kong moved in fairly narrow and overlapping circles. Their members therefore tended to keep bumping into one another at the same social functions. I did not consider myself a member of the elite but sometimes, by fluke or through the kindness of others, I received invitations to functions. Since I had been given face, the least I could do would be to turn up to acknowledge their courtesies.

Thus it was that, soon after the board meeting concerning the re-valuation of assets, I came across the bespectacled Ngan Shing-Kwan at one of the perennial cocktail parties punctuating the colony's social calendar. At the age of 75, Ngan still cut an impressively erect and dignified figure. After exchanging a few civilities, we sipped drinks and engaged in desultory conversation. Neither of us was much inclined to adhere to the protocols of the cocktail cult by circulating and making our presence known.

After a while, surrounded by the low-toned murmur of cocktail chatter, I sensed the venerable notable falling into a mellow mood. Apropos nothing at all, he suddenly allowed: "You know, David, I'm getting on. Not so young any more. Don't know why I should continue to deal with the headaches of running a bus company. Could just give up the franchise; let somebody else take it on."

"Oh, you're still in fine fettle, Mr. Ngan, and performing a very vital public service," I replied. "So much more remains to be done and a man of your energy and experience is exactly the one to carry it forward. You've already dedicated your entire life to buses, to serve the public. It's not like you to throw in the towel at this stage."

"What is the point of carrying on? Shareholders are not satisfied, drivers are not satisfied, commuters are not satisfied and you — speaking with the voice of government — are also not satisfied."

"I've only ever spoken on my own behalf, to suggest improvements here and there, not voicing any official attitude."

Ngan looked for a long moment into my eyes through his dark-framed glasses. Then he said: "I've known you since you were a young reporter, just out of school. I saw your good work as secretary of the War Memorial Fund. You used to be a straight talker, David. Now your words appear hedged around with hidden meanings. You're beginning to sound like a Brit."

"I am indebted to the venerable Elder Ngan for pointing out the failings of a junior," I quickly replied, making a half-bow. "My shortcomings are indeed many. But, as the ancients have said, it is difficult to move in close proximity to ink without risking being stained."

Ngan looked at me closely again. "Yes, in life a man must exist on several levels; it's not getting any easier. But just between you and I, David, give me an honest opinion. Should I give up the franchise and all its associated headaches? I could just sit back and develop the company's properties. Make a bomb."

I suddenly realised that I had got myself sucked into a poker game holding the weakest of hands. Nonetheless, I had to make a play or withdraw. A bluff was possible; in desperation I took it.

"Providing the public with transportation has been your whole life, Mr. Ngan," I ventured. "You have earned social appreciation and respect through such work. Your children are now following in your footsteps. What do a few dollars one way or the other matter to a man like you? You're not aiming to become one of those for whom Horace coined the phrase *virtus post nummos*."

"What! My son said that? What did he mean?"

"Oh, I'm sorry for confusing you. I was not referring to your son; rather to the Roman satirist from 2,000 years ago. He mocked his fellow citizens for putting cash before conscience."

Ngan gave a humph. "Seems like nothing much has changed in 2,000 years," he observed dryly.

"But they have, Mr. Ngan! You've set a superb example; your long years in public service, in government and in various charities, with nary a thought for personal enrichment. If money had been your main concern, you would have given up buses long ago. Yours is an example worthy for the young to follow."

"You haven't been sipping the oil of flattery in that glass of yours, have you?"

"You asked for my opinion; I've given it. What satisfaction can a few more dollars bring? Why jeopardise the good name you've built up over decades?"

"How so?"

"Well, you know how things work. You've served on the Legislative and Executive Councils. For the sake of argument, let's assume you give up the franchise. Now, I'm not sure of the status of the land you're using for depots. If they've been designated as such, what good would they be to you if you were no longer running bus services? You could sell them to a successor company, I suppose, probably at knocked-down prices. Unless, of course, the situation has already been resolved while you are still holding a strong hand.

"You can, of course, apply to have the land use reclassified, in the way agricultural land in the New Territories have been changed to building land. But that could be a tedious process, involving a number of different departments and the Town Planning Board.

"Frankly, I have heard rumours from my old Department for Home Affairs. A number of district leaders have apparently been making representations over the lack of parks and playgrounds in their districts. Should the question of converting bus depots to other uses come up, the public pressure might escalate to such a degree that the government would feel obliged to resume the depots to meet popular demand.

"How would it look to the public if you were then to oppose the government's proposal, to request that the land be converted for building luxury condominiums or shopping malls or whatever else you might have in mind? I have no idea what the government might or might not do, mind you. I'm only speculating on possibilities."

I paused briefly to let my words sink in before continuing: "The internal transport situation is changing very rapidly. New towns are being built and new bus routes will be required. The Cross-Harbour Tunnel has opened up new patterns for cross-harbour traffic. The mass transit system being built will never obviate the need for buses. It is a period of massive challenges. Hong Kong needs people like you to meet them. Can you really duck out and say it has nothing more to do with you?"

The chairman of the China Motor Bus Company frowned and looked down into the half-filled glass he was holding. "This is not the place for this conversation," he said, eventually. "It is too noisy, too many people wandering around. Why don't we have a quiet meal together next week? We can talk further then."

"By all means," I said. "I'm always at your disposal."

* * *

After attending a couple more board meetings and having some conversations with old-timers like Ngan, I gradually came to the view that a key to reducing urban degradation had to lie in curbing the rampant passion for private car ownership, stoked regularly by the slick advertisements paid by car manufacturers and dealers.

But before the middle-class passion for car-ownership could be discouraged,

With Ngan Shing-Kwan at a cocktail party.

a cheap, efficient and comfortable system of public transportation had to be in place. That in turn meant the administration had to get more involved to bring it about, rather than leaving things to the vagaries of profit-driven private enterprises.

It must necessarily involve more governmental intervention beyond the window dressing of having a Secretariat officer on the Boards of Directors of private bus companies. A single officer, even if highly committed, could do little without appropriate supporting staff. He would have little feel for day-to-day bus operations, little hope of getting behind the algebra obscuring the reams of accounting figures presented to the public, and little opportunity of gauging the true sentiments of the travelling public.

More governmental involvement would also go against the touted economic ethos in the colony, not to mention the trend towards privatising public services being pursued in many countries in the neo-liberal world. Such a trend struck me as misguided, because profitability should not be the sole or even the main determinant in certain crucial public services. Other less tangible factors like public trust, reliability and satisfaction also needed to be taken into account.

But the key stumbling block lay in what Sir John Cowperthwaite had long drawn attention to — the dearth of sufficient intellectual resources within the bureaucracy. That demand for fine and innovative brains would always outstrip supply in every society, particularly in frequently underpaid civil services.

Nonetheless, I decided to launch a trial balloon along the lines of my thinking. I suggested it might be more effective if liaison with the bus companies were taken out of the hands of the Secretariat and transferred to a line officer like the Commissioner for Transport, since he had an entire department to do investigative work should such be required.

That suggestion contained an obvious snag. The Commissioner of the time was an expatriate. How would he handle a couple of all-Chinese boards without a working knowledge of Chinese? For that, among other reasons, I did not expect my suggestion to be met with any degree of enthusiasm. But it seemed worthy of a try, as a prelude to getting the services of a Treasury Accountant to do a forensic examination of the bus company accounts.

Another thought came to me during my reflections. I could not shake the idea that, in spite of old Ngan's set ways, there was something quite admirable about him. He shared the same pedigree as other community leaders like Q.W. Lee and Ip Yeuk-Lam. They were all native sons of Hong Kong, who had risen from lowly beginnings to reach the top of their chosen callings.

In reaching the top, they must have been seasoned and humbled by life's limitations, for they had all apparently paid only passing attention to material rewards and other forms of personal enrichment. None of the three had attempted to rush down what Tao Yuan-Ming, had described as "the dusty road to empty fame". Instead, each had tried, without fanfare, to give back to society whatever was in his power to give. Truly admirable.

Why was the number of that kind of people progressively diminishing? Had society itself turned more shallow, more materialistic and more meretricious? That baffling conundrum lingered in my mind.

* * *

My trial balloon on tackling liaison with bus companies had hardly got off the ground before my attention had to be switched to another vexing problem. A sudden development in the international civil aviation sphere required my immediate attention.

In July of 1976, Britain renounced the Bermuda civil aviation agreement with the United States. That decision triggered fresh negotiations between the two countries. Since nobody in the Economic Services Branch at that time had any experience in civil aviation negotiations except myself, the responsibility for tackling that issue landed squarely on my lap. It meant brushing up once again the text of Professor Bin Cheng's 726-page tome — *The Law of International Air Transport.*

The original agreement, made in Bermuda back in 1946, provided the first blueprint for civil aviation services in the world, because at that time Britain and the United States were the two dominant aviation powers. Its provisions were highly restrictive at the insistence of Britain, because it feared American financial dominance and the superiority of American commercial planes. Britain had concentrated on building fighter aircraft during the war. But it did have one important advantage — a far-flung colonial empire over which it could control landing rights.

The Bermuda agreement covered such matters as precise routes, capacity, load factors, frequency of flights and level of fares. In theory, it was supposed to provide fair and equal opportunities for both parties. In reality, deep pockets mattered. Equality of opportunity did not necessarily lead to equality in outcomes. It nonetheless set the pattern for some 4,000 subsequent bilateral aviation agreements between states, all registered with International

Civil Aviation Organisation.

In practice, BOAC, the British state-owned airline, could not compete with the privately-owned American airlines and hence could not gain an equitable share of the lucrative trans-Atlantic traffic. Indeed, it kept losing market share, falling steadily to only 30.9%.

Another reason for denouncing the existing agreement was because it had no provision for British Caledonian Airways, a private company founded at the end of 1970, to begin services from Gatwick to Houston and Atlanta. Those cities had not been nominated as "gateway cities" under the agreement. Therefore the British sought to secure a more beneficial regime through re-negotiations.

* * *

When the original Bermuda agreement was negotiated, Hong Kong had no airline of its own. So it fell upon Britain to call all the shots on landing rights in the colony. But over the years, Cathay Pacific had arrived on the scene and had developed a thriving regional aviation network. It harboured ambitions to go farther afield — across the Pacific in one direction and towards Europe in the other. Its interests, together with Hong Kong's wider interests, therefore had to be catered for.

The government's approach to civil aviation had been established by Sir John Cowperthwaite when he was the Deputy Economic Secretary. Whereas Whitehall saw the colony as a bargaining chip to gain commercial advantages for BOAC, Sir John saw the importance of developing Hong Kong as a hub for international air services, both to support the colony's trading activities and to provide local employment in the airlines industry and in the ancillary aircraft maintenance sector.

The government, at the behest of Sir John, was therefore prepared to fight Whitehall robustly to defend the interests of both the colony and of Cathay

Pacific, but not to the extent of restricting foreign carriers flying to Hong Kong simply to protect Cathay Pacific's bottom line. Otherwise, it was pretty much an "open skies" approach. Thus civil aviation negotiations with foreign powers involving Hong Kong landing rights tended to be three-cornered quasi-political affairs, with a strong local dimension.

* * *

Cathay Pacific was founded in Shanghai in 1946 by two pilots who had been flying supplies to Chinese forces over the Himalayan hump during World War II. One was Australian and the other an American. They began by using a Douglas DC3 to fly passenger services to Manila, Bangkok and Singapore.

In 1948, Butterfield and Swire bought a big chunk of the company and it became registered as a Hong Kong firm. Since becoming part of the Swire Group, it has seldom looked back — until quite recently. Today it remains one of the leading airlines in the world.

After I had become the Assistant Economic Secretary and given responsibility for civil aviation matters, I got acquainted with many of the top brass in the Swire Group. The one relationship I enjoyed best was the one with John Bremridge, especially after he had taken over as Chairman of both Swire Pacific and Cathay Pacific in 1973.

John was a buff, hearty, down-to-earth and straight-talking gentleman. He had joined the Swire Group in 1949, after reading law at Oxford. He was no stickler for rituals nor was he given to putting on airs. What endeared him to me most were the forthrightness of his opinions and his concern for improving the quality of life in the community. His refreshing approach on social issues soon earned him a seat on the Legislative Council in 1974, to be followed by one on the Executive Council in 1977.

The first time he invited me for dinner at his home on the Peak was an occasion I shall never forget. Once the meal was over, the ladies retreated customarily for powdering of their noses.

After their disappearance, John said: "Gentlemen, shall we go and water the garden?"

I was unsure what he had in mind but I followed him and the three other male guests out of the dining room and into his front lawn. He then led the party to a low hedge at the far end of the lawn. Above the hedge — of hibiscus, if memory serves — stretched a delightful panoramic view of the harbour and the lights of Kowloon, tremulously disguising both the wealth and the tawdriness of the city alike. Yet, somehow, those lights seemed to merge and complement the scattering of stars in the heavens.

John then unzipped his fly and without further ado began urinating on the lawn close to the hedge. His guests and I — with considerably greater hesitancy — followed suit. Apparently the other male guests had been accustomed to his routine. I surmised that with the limited bathroom facilities in his home taken over by lady guests, John had hit upon using the garden to cater for the needs of the men.

Some years later, John was knighted. Presumably not for his innovative way of watering his garden!

* * *

The British denunciation of the Bermuda accord necessitated a fresh aviation agreement between the two countries. The common aim was to conclude it within a year. The leader of the British delegation was Patrick Shovelton, the Deputy Undersecretary of State in the Department of Trade and Industry, a very experienced Whitehall mandarin who had been on the team negotiating Britain's entry into the European Union. He was supported not only by officials from his department and from the Civil Aviation Authority but also by industry representatives from BOAC, British Caledonian Airways and Laker Airways.

Since Hong Kong had become an important aviation hub in Asia after the first Bermuda agreement, it now had to be included in the talks on any new regime. It was decided that I should lead a small sub-group within the British delegation. I would be supported by the Hong Kong Deputy Director for Civil Aviation and a senior representative of Cathay Pacific.

By then Cathay Pacific had already indicated it had ambitions to fly across the Pacific and share in the Hong Kong to London cabotage route, particularly in the light of the unsatisfactory service being offered by BOAC. Local complaints about BOAC services had been loud and frequent.

Civil aviation negotiations were much like other types of commercial negotiations. Parties sought the most beneficial deal they could get, within the accepted rules of the game, or else they would have to walk away without a deal. The problem was that so much money, national prestige and consumer demands were involved that neither side could really walk away. The possibility existed that the British, in sealing a deal, might seek to benefit United Kingdom companies to the detriment of Hong Kong interests. It was my task to ensure that did not happen and, at the same time, to avoid any open ruckus with Whitehall.

Before negotiations began, Sir Murray summoned me to Government House to brief him on how I saw things developing.

I said that Cathay Pacific had legitimate ambitions for a trans-Pacific route and that ambition ought to be supported. But such a route would not be economically viable unless it included a "beyond point" like Vancouver, where a large number of Hong Kong people had migrated to find boltholes out of fear of the colony being returned to China. However, the Americans were unlikely to grant such a concession because of technical arguments over comparative catchment areas. In other words, territories did not normally simply exchange one route for another. Account had to be taken of the potential markets, based on the respective populations and the projected number of flyers in each territory.

In theory, if an American airline were granted the right to fly to Hong Kong, all the customers it could tap in the colony would be the few million people living there, most of whom would in any case be too poor to afford foreign travel. To grant Cathay Pacific access to, say, San Francisco, would in theory give it the entire population of America as potential customers. In practice, it would be economically quite difficult for Cathay Pacific to build up the kind of domestic connections and feeder services an American airline could rely on.

The likely outcome would be that a Hong Kong airline would be granted a route to San Francisco — the best gateway option among West Coast cities because of a sizeable Chinatown there — though it would be unable to operate it profitably without any "beyond point". In the civil aviation jargon that would be described as Fifth Freedom rights. In exchange, the Americans would want a route to Hong Kong with beyond points to compensate for the smallness of the Hong Kong catchment area.

Such a deal would have a slightly detrimental effect on Cathay Pacific's regional services, in that it would face more localised competition on the routes that the American carrier might elect to operate as Asian beyond points. But in the wider interests of Hong Kong, enjoying another aviation connection to its biggest market in North America would not be too excessive a price for Cathay Pacific to pay.

I could not foresee any real possibility of the Americans giving Vancouver as a beyond point for a Hong Kong airline, unless Britain were willing to compensate the Americans elsewhere. But given the unsatisfactory state of the trans-Atlantic traffic, Britain would certainly not be willing to make such a sacrifice. In my judgement, the greater danger lay in Britain sacrificing Cathay Pacific's interests to gain advantages for the United Kingdom-based airlines elsewhere.

After my grim prognosis, the Governor ordered that I make a presentation to the Executive Council, so that it could approve my negotiating brief. I duly did so and secured my mandate.

* * *

Once negotiations were joined, the entire process came to be known at the Bermuda II, although not a single meeting was ever held in Bermuda. The schedule settled upon was for a week's discussion every month, to be held alternatively in London and in Washington D.C. The thinking behind this arrangement was that neither of the teams would need to be out of its home base more than once in every two months.

What the scheme overlooked was the travelling required of the three members of the Hong Kong sub-group based in the colony. It meant each of the three had to travel half way round the world every month. If journey times and internal delegation briefings were taken into account, each would be away from his home for around two weeks each month. Moreover, since both the Deputy Director for Civil Aviation and myself were at the substantive Staff Grade B level, we were only entitled to travel tourist class.

Whoever assigned me to lead the sub-group apparently took no cognisance of the fact I was also a single parent, responsible for the welfare of three young boys. In the event, the negotiations lasted a full year, with a fresh agreement not formally signed till July of 1977 and with its provisions not to come into effect till the following year.

Fortunately for me, friends and colleagues rallied to my support, particularly colleagues from my former Home Affairs Department. One of them took the boys fishing while another taught them *tai chi*. A number of others took them out for meals together with their own children. My private secretary at the Secretariat performed the yeoman task of getting them to a doctor or dentist whenever it proved necessary. Ah Duen kept an eye on them at home after school. I would never be able to thank any of them enough for their many kindnesses towards my children.

* * *

Once the Bermuda II rounds began, it became clear the positions of the two sides would develop along the lines I had anticipated. The American side was led by a courtly politician who had once been a cabinet member, though not with a previous brief in either transport or civil aviation. He was supported by a strong but youngish government team plus a number of representatives from American airlines.

I very much regret that the name of the American leader has slipped my mind, so that I am unable to record it here. The reason I want to mention him is because, at a time when the talks had already gone well past the eleventh hour, he did Hong Kong an immense favour.

The contrast between the two sides could not have been more striking. From the start it was patent who held the stronger cards. Shovelton, although he was speaking on behalf of a socialist Labour government, delivered the British position with all the polish, courteousness and grace of his English upper class breeding. The American leader set out his position in the home-spun style of an experienced politician of his nation, leaving technical details to members of his team.

Both touched upon the long and fruitful relationships between their nations and expressed the goodwill and determination to reach a fair and equitable agreement, taking into account the need for reasonable competition, orderly markets and greater consumer choice.

Yet, if two close friends or siblings were to share a meal or a bottle of wine, would either make an issue out of how much the other had eaten or drunk? If issue were taken, then the inference must be that the relationship between the two was not that close or, if close, the spoils of the free market took on a greater significance for each than personal sentiments or friendship.

A completely free market in civil aviation, therefore, would appear to be little short of a tooth and nail free-for-all for profits, for dominance, for eliminating competition and for the eventual triumph of cartels or monopolies. Such developments were patently taking place in sector after sector of the economy, in oil, pharmaceuticals, food production, banking, mass media, service industries and so forth. Supermarket chains were using their buying clout to squeeze lower prices from small producers. That was the reason why governments had sometimes to intervene with anti-trust laws to abate the economic savagery.

American airlines, too, were caught up in that system. They had to secure anti-trust immunities from government to form alliances and share codes with one another. Yet governments and politicians seemed to have a way of pretending that none of that was really happening.

Most members of the British team were middle-aged or beyond. They behaved with the legendary reserve and *sang-froid* expected of them. Most on the American side, apart from its leader, were in their thirties, outgoing, lively and oozing with self-confidence.

It was perhaps a reflection of the times that I happened to be the only non-white among both delegations. That fact must have stood out like a sore thumb among them, although I myself had learnt, ever since my boyhood in Australia, not to be self-conscious among foreigners.

As my crew cut hairstyle hinted at an American influence, some members of the American team were curious enough to engage me in conversation during coffee breaks. One of them asked if the crew cut was popular in Hong Kong. I told him it was not popular at all but I had taken to it while studying at Stanford.

That revelation broke the ice and they quickly, with their usual American openness, overwhelmed me with their *bonhomie*. We chatted easily thereafter about the likeliest teams to be paired in the next Rose Bowl, the batting records of that celebrated New York Yankees slugger, Babe Ruth — some of whose records still stood — and the odd witticism coined by Mark Twain or Groucho Marx. One day, one of them ventured to ask me how I liked working for the British.

I replied mischievously. "What do you think it could be like to be a hewer of wood and drawer of water within a shrinking British Empire? Don't forget you chaps jumped ship in 1776. We're still stuck."

My statement must have resonated with some historical chord in his psyche, for he replied: "Yes, life's a bitch sometimes, isn't it? We spend years polishing the illusion we are completely free, bound only by our principles and our ideals. Once we start making a living, we find we're bound mainly by the orders of our bosses."

Another idealist biting the dust of reality, I thought. "Well," I said, "if you and I were to negotiate solely on the basis of our principles and ideals, I'm sure we'd end up with an agreement neither of our governments would ratify."

"Without a doubt. And we'd both be banished to our respective Bureaux for Paper Clips!"

We shared a good laugh over this.

I, of course, had a sneaky ulterior motive for cultivating relationships with the American team. I was not much concerned about the trans-Atlantic bunfight, where each side was trying to nullify the natural advantages of the other. The Americans were pushing for open skies whereas the British, under the cloak of orderly markets, were trying to introduce restrictions more severe than had previously existed under the original Bermuda agreement.

My focus was on teasing out the American attitude on granting Vancouver as a Fifth Freedom point on a trans-Pacific route and in making them more kindly disposed towards such a request, even though it could not strictly be justified under established rules. I was trying to plant the notion of it being a generous gift on their part, to an underdog haplessly caught up in a fight between Rottweilers.

Naturally most of the negotiations had to be concentrated upon the trans-

Atlantic routes, on what routes ought to run from London's Heathrow or Gatwick or Stansted, and to which United States gateway city. New private British airlines like British Caledonian and Laker had come onto the scene since the original agreement in 1946 and their ambitions now had to be taken into account.

American airlines all preferred operating out of Heathrow but there was simply not enough physical slots there to accommodate all of them. Provision to allow respective civil aviation authorities to designate particular carriers on particular routes had to be agreed upon, as had provisions against predatory pricing, capacity dumping and other competitive sharp practices.

During those trans-Atlantic talks I insinuated to the American team members over coffee breaks that Hong Kong's attitude towards international flights was much closer to theirs than to London's. Hong Kong was not the least afraid of competition, I declared. We were used to it and we would welcome more American airlines mounting services to our city. But, as a colony, we had to follow instructions from London. I had ventured those views in the expectation that they would be noted to generate more sympathy towards Hong Kong's position.

When it came to discussions on the trans-Pacific route, the Americans fought for beyond rights to Tokyo, Seoul and Bangkok, to counterbalance the differences between the sizes of the two catchment areas. The British side asked for Vancouver, but the Americans were not disposed to grant it and the British side was not inclined to press very hard. At the end of those sessions, the British team had to settle for just a route to San Francisco for a Hong Kong airline, without a beyond point.

* * *

Prior to the final plenary session for both sides to summarise and agree the terms of the accord, I had asked Shovelton for permission to say a few words on behalf of Hong Kong. He readily agreed. Thus I took the floor after Shovelton had concluded the summary of the positions agreed by the British side.

I began by thanking both teams for the fair and professional way they had dealt with Hong Kong's requirements. I then went on to express my own deep personal disappointment over the failure to secure Vancouver as a Fifth Freedom point for a Hong Kong airline.

"I blame this failure on no one except my mother," I continued, to the bafflement to everyone present. "My mother has made Vancouver her home for a great number of years; and I have visited her there a number of times. Each time I had dreamt of one day making a direct flight from Hong Kong on a Hong Kong airline to visit her.

"But during all my visits, she never told me once how valuable Vancouver was in civil aviation terms. It was only during the present negotiations that I realised Vancouver was more valuable than Tokyo, Seoul and Bangkok combined. Hong Kong has granted all those three cities for an American route but we have been denied the single point of Vancouver in return. If I had known earlier how valuable Vancouver was, I might have approached these talks differently. But now it is too late. My mother is in her mid-70s and it seems my dream of visiting her on a Hong Kong airline must — sadly — remain a dream."

It was then the turn of the American leader to summarise his agreed positions. At the end of his summary, he added the following final sentence: "Because of David's personal requirements, I grant Vancouver."

The entire British team was taken completely by surprise. For a short while after the signing of Bermuda II, Vancouver became known among a small coterie of civil aviation negotiators as "David's mother's point".

After returning to Hong Kong, I judged it prudent not to go into any of the subterfuges I had engaged in. I merely reported the success of the British team in securing a route to America which included Vancouver as a

Fifth Freedom point.

After further negotiations with the Canadians, Cathay Pacific began flying across the Pacific in 1983. And I did manage to fulfil my dream of flying direct to Vancouver on a Hong Kong airline to visit my mother.

CHAPTER 12

The Loves That Failed

WELL BEFORE I LEFT the Home Affairs Department in 1975, I had already failed miserably to find a replacement wife. The nubile females introduced by friends and relatives had proved unsuitable, much as I had anticipated.

The reasons were not difficult to see. My negatives were too patent — a middle-aged man, with a philandering reputation and lumbered with three young sons. As if that was not unappetising enough, I was also a civil servant with no hope of inheriting a family fortune nor of securing any spectacular official advancement. A future with me had to be one of austerity, deprived of the usual luxuries women longed for. Even the word "marriage" was plainly a euphemism. It was in essence a job as glorified housekeeper and substitute mother for three growing boys.

I saw little in myself that could weigh in my favour. I might have a modicum of charm and a gift of the gab. But, given my reputation, who could guarantee that the charm and the sweet-talking would not be dispensed outside the home rather than within? Marriage to a colonial bureaucrat might provide a little access to the fringes of high society but it could also spell recurring losses of face if funds were unavailable for fashionable garments and matching accessories. Too risky a pill for most self-respecting girls to swallow.

As for the ladies themselves, none came over as a suitable surrogate mother. Few had the right kind of experience or temperament. Most had been too young and many had too obvious a desire for a luxurious life or for children of their own.

That was not to say that none of them possessed potential in other spheres of human relationships. Two or three of them appeared to be — in the lexicon of my friend Y — eminently bed-worthy. But none had that tantalising *je ne sais quoi* possessed by Barbara or Sharlee. Besides, without any display of that mothering potential I wanted for my children, there was little point giving chase. Hence a project lasting many long months ended up as a complete waste of time.

Those repeated failures depressed me also. Time was marching on. When Man-Ying and I separated in 1971, our eldest son was 11. He was now in his teens and his two brothers were now rapidly approaching that awkward period in their lives as well. I felt increasingly that I was letting them down.

I remembered the loneliness and bewilderment I had experienced during my own boyhood, after my mother had chosen to keep my younger brother but surrendered me to my grandmother. I was five years old and quite lost when I was taken to a distant and unknown place called Singapore. Throughout the subsequent years, I began nursing a strange and acute resentment against my mother for abandoning me. I had felt it sharpest whenever I witnessed Anna lavishing her attentions upon my siblings.

I could not figure out why I should have been singled out for deprivation. Had I been too disobedient during my boyhood, or too ugly and unlovable to keep? The inexplicability of the situation troubled me more constantly than an itch. It was not until I had been reunited with my mother in Canton, after a separation of 13 years, that I began to understand the imperatives behind her original decision.

The possibility of my sons developing a similar resentment against their mother or against myself was troubling. At least I grew up in the company of grandparents and many aunts. My boys had only the ministrations of an old and uneducated domestic servant named Ah Duen.

Their deprivation forced me to pursue a course of action I had earlier sworn I would never take, namely, to seek a potential wife from among divorcees who had children of their own. I feared jumping from a frying pan into the fire in bringing additional children into the family. It involved too many imponderables.

But needs must when the devil drove. So I embarked upon three successive relationships with divorcees with children. It so happened that all three had been around their mid-30s and each had two children younger than mine. Two of those ventures ended fairly quickly, before I had even left the Home Affairs Department. I had judged that neither of the two, nor their children, could interact satisfactorily with my own.

The third divorcee offered some hope. She was an executive in a quasi-official community organisation. We hit it off easily. She was intelligent, pleasant-looking, fashion-conscious and loquacious, though a trifle possessive. As to sex, she was voracious and uninhibited, leaving me with no reservations. I therefore began arranging opportunities for our two families to mix. After a few outings, it became evident that relationships among all parties were developing quite naturally and harmoniously.

Having once been badly bitten by marriage, however, I hesitated over any deeper involvement before a fuller assessment of the lie of the land. Few marriages could be sustained on good sex alone. Otherwise there would not be so many divorces.

I wanted to ascertain whether that prospective partner intended to continue with her own career after marriage and whether her divorce arrangements had adequate provisions for the upkeep and education of her own children. Each could throw up unsurmountable obstacles. Yet a man could hardly probe such delicate matters without first declaring his intentions. I was, however, unable to form any real intention until I knew what I might be letting myself and my sons in for. It was that old chicken and egg problem.

Equally importantly, I needed to know more about the lady's temperament and intellectual inclinations. Up till that point, such time as we have had alone together, after her children had gone to sleep, had been consumed by the urgencies of animal desires. Little time had been devoted to talking. I did not want a woman who, before or after love-making, could only respond to a quotation from Li Po or Omar Khayyam like a cow chewing cud. A person's intellectual and other inclinations were bound to reveal themselves over time. But I could not afford to wait. A quick decision was necessary; my sons were growing up too quickly.

At the same time, I was concerned that both our reputations should not be damaged by too protracted a courtship. Where gossip was concerned, Hong Kong was akin to a small English village, overflowing with wagging tongues. Given my notoriety, however undeserved, word would soon do the rounds of my making sport with another woman. Her reputation as a marriageable proposition might be sullied should our relationship fizzle out. That argued for a swift conclusion.

But try as I might, I could not think of an appropriate way of raising the many delicate questions without first committing myself. But an idea struck me when I happened to have a meal with a friend who had strong business connections with Taiwan.

During the course of the meal I asked him how his business was doing. He said it was thriving and asked in turn when I might be visiting Taiwan again. He knew that some years earlier I had gone there with friends to view the countless bronzes, vases, jade carvings, lacquerware, paintings and other treasures at the National Palace Museum. He went on to say that he had acquired an apartment in Taipei, which he and his wife used no more than five or six times a year. The rest of the time the premises stood empty; I would be most welcome to use it should I pay Taiwan another visit.

It then occurred to me that if I took the divorcee there for a holiday, away from the gossiping hot house of Hong Kong, we could explore at leisure the various issues to be settled. Not staying at a hotel, where we risked bumping into Hong Kong people we knew, would also reduce the fear of being spotted staying together in a hotel.

There would be a further advantage. After visiting the National Palace Museum, we could spend a couple of days at Sun Moon Lake. That would give me further indications whether we had similar cultural interests.

On the spur of the moment, I thanked my friend for his offer and confided in him I was romancing a lady as a possible wife. The use of his Taipei apartment for a week would be just the ticket. However, I had a condition. I had to pay rental for its use.

My friend reacted with friendly outrage. "What's happening to you, David?" he exclaimed. "Have we become barbarians to talk about money when exchanging hospitality between friends? That's not Chinese culture. You must be my guest. My housekeeper's an excellent cook. Just tell her the kind of food you and your lady companion would like and she'll take good care of both of you."

"I really am enormously grateful, my good fellow," I said, "but I'm a public servant, working for a foreign occupying power. Accepting hospitality to the extent you're offering might appear to some of my superiors suspiciously like accepting some kind of advantage."

"Stuff and nonsense! I've not asked you to bend any rule or to grant me some improper benefit in return. You mean a public servant cannot have friends? Or exchange hospitality with them? We've had many meals together, sometimes you pay, sometimes I pay. That's normal in human relationships. What's wrong with that?"

"What's wrong is that I have no apartment anywhere to return a similar hospitality. We're living under laws framed by foreigners. Laws are at best blunt instruments, quite incapable of distinguishing between the varying gradations in human relationships. There is also an anti-corruption mania running riot at the moment, after the Godber scandal. An Independent Commission Against Corruption has been formed to placate the public.

It would be best for me to behave like Caesar's wife — above suspicion or reproach. So please let me pay for the use of your apartment."

My friend shook his head. "Corruption's a very fatal thing," he said. "There are far too many bent coppers around. But we have to be sensible in tackling that problem. A lot of corruption — and probably the worst of it — occurs outside the purview of government, within private corporations, inside the hearts and minds of men. In any case, I can't accept payment from friends. The most I can agree to — if you're going to use my apartment — is for you to pay the housekeeper for whatever food or drink you consume and give her a tip at the end of your stay. Is that meagre enough as hospitality for you to accept with a good conscience?"

"I guess I might get away with that, if you would allow me buy you and your wife a nice dinner when I get back."

* * *

Armed with the blessing of discreet accommodation in Taipei, I made haste to invite the potential candidate for wife for a holiday in Taiwan. She readily accepted.

By then, I had been installed as the Deputy Secretary for Economic Services and the next step was to sound out the Policy Secretary. I did so orally, asking if I could be spared for five and a half days of leave. He saw no impediment. I had in any case months of leave to my credit. With some judicious fitting-in of weekends at both ends, five and a half days would be sufficient for an eight-day trip.

Having secured a nod from my boss, I paid for a couple of those cheaper non-alterable and non-refundable air tickets for the journey. I then complied with protocol by formally handing in a signed Leave Application Form.

But I got a shock when the leave chit came back — I had been granted leave but denied permission to go to Taiwan!

The ostensible reason for the refusal was that I was now a fairly senior official and if I were to go to Taiwan it could be construed in certain quarters as Britain attempting to play a two-China game!

The explanation seemed rather ludicrous and far-fetched; it cut very little ice with me. It was expected that the upper echelons of any bureaucracy would err on the side of caution whenever anything was in doubt. But since the British government had long abandoned the welfare of Chinese British subjects when they went under Chinese jurisdiction, why should it change its stance now?

If the government was as wary about appearances, then it should not have selected someone with political and business attachments to Taiwan like Fung Hon-Chu to lead the Hong Kong delegation to the plenary session of the United Nations Economic Commission for Asia and the Far East back in 1963.

Fung and the rest of the delegation, of which I had been a member, were instructed not to fraternise with the Taiwanese delegates attending the meeting. China was then still struggling to oust Taiwan from United Nations organisations. Fung nonetheless openly ignored that instruction. But there had been no fallout.

Secondly, as I have already said, I had been granted permission to visit Taiwan years earlier, when I was in the Labour Department, and had gone as a private individual. Nobody raised an eyebrow. I could not see how going there now with a lady friend and for romantic purposes could give rise to any political awkwardness.

But I was not prepared to argue the toss. The flight I had booked on would leave in under three days and I knew from experience that any argument with the bureaucracy could not be resolved within that timeframe. What was much more pressing was that I had to find a way to square things with the lady I had invited. I also had to inform my friend I would no longer require the use of his flat in Taipei.

* * *

I decided instinctively that it would be best not to attempt to tell the lady the whole truth. She would be unlikely to appreciate the labyrinthian nature of bureaucratic thinking and, given my reputation, would most probably suspect me of disengaging from her for another woman. Short of proposing marriage there and then, I doubted whether I could ever convince her of the real truth. And I was certainly not yet ready to leap into matrimony, given how little I knew about her and her actual circumstances.

Even if I had told her the real reason how our trip became unstuck, her natural reaction would be to suggest going someplace else. That would present me with fresh difficulties. I had already spent part of my budget on air tickets to no purpose. Paying for new air passages and expensive hotel accommodation elsewhere would force me to dig into reserves set aside for my children's education. Having lost such funds once in the *Singapore Herald* misadventure, I was loath to risk them again.

Besides, even if I were to offer the ticket made out in the lady's name for Taiwan — for her to go on her own if she chose — I could still not prove my good faith, because I had no hotel reservation to back me up. I had meant the use of my friend's apartment to be a surprise. To try and explain that would merely add another layer of suspicion.

In the circumstances, I decided to tell the lady that some urgent official business had cropped up, so I could not get away as planned. Our Taiwan trip would therefore have to be postponed.

Unfortunately, as I had expected, the lady was unconvinced. From the tenor of her questions, it became clear she sensed I was hiding something. She began cross-examining me on rumours she had heard about my public displays of affection for various other women.

The fact that she doubted my intentions was a disappointment. I responded by telling her she should judge for herself whether I was pursuing a meaningful relationship with her or just playing the field. Listening to idle gossip was no way to find out.

This caused her to leave in a huff, saying that she had set her mind on a holiday and if I was too busy to take her, somebody else easily could. I learnt subsequently that she did indeed go off on a holiday to Thailand, with a man much better placed financially than myself. Thus the die was cast. Our relationship went no further. Shortly after their return, she married him. I could hardly blame her for wanting to secure a bird in hand, before her best years were behind her, rather than wait indefinitely for me to pop the question.

In retrospect, I should be thankful for being refused permission to go to Taiwan. It probably saved me from a woman who, however bed-worthy, had a potentially bossy disposition.

* * *

After the collapse of that last matrimonial possibility, I grew more desperate for the welfare of my children. Time was running out; their emotional needs were becoming more pronounced. The only alternative I had was to spend more time with them, although I knew in my own heart I was no good at interacting with children, even with my own. Under the divorce settlement, I was required to make the children available to Man-Ying on four days a week, if she so desired. Time was of the essence. How was I to find more time for them, given all my work constraints? Soon, with their growing up, the whole situation would turn moot.

The pressure of work often meant I could seldom leave the office till six or seven in the evening. During my tenure at the Home Affairs Department, first as Deputy Director and then as Director, outside commitments could not be avoided. A senior official was expected to attend inauguration ceremonies or cocktail parties, to show the flag by cutting ribbons, giving speeches to graduating classes, drawing winning raffle tickets at charity functions, participating at anniversary dinners of civic organisations, *ad infinitum*.

An appointment as a Policy Secretary was another possibility, as I was now at the right seniority to be given such an appointment. But that would entail pressures of another kind — responding to urgent telegrams from Whitehall and spending long hours cleaning up the messes left by others. My brief attachment to the Housing Branch had given me a taste of the latter and how disheartening that could be.

Hence any further advancement within the bureaucracy, even in an acting appointment, would entail a drain upon the time and energy I might otherwise devote to my children. The irony in the situation was that I suspected my children might not be all that anxious to see more of me!

After Man-Ying's departure, I had tried to tighten household rules, to bring them in line with the ones I had myself been brought up under. For example, during my boyhood my siblings and I had to go to bed right after dinner, so as to be in good shape to rise early for school. I had tried during my boyhood to beat that system by surreptitious reading by torchlight under the cover of a blanket. In doing so, I had ruined my eyes.

In imposing a similar regime of bed by nine upon my sons, I was hoping they would not be as unwise as I had been. I would check occasionally to see that the lights in their rooms had been turned off.

They no doubt resented my rules and I was certain that, whenever I was away from home on evenings, they would stay up till much later, to watch television or to chat with schoolmates on the telephone. Ah Duen could hardly be expected to impose discipline on them and there was no one like my grandmother or my aunts to do any enforcement. Being around more often would provide greater opportunities to shape their values and to encourage them to think for themselves, even though they might not always appreciate it.

* * *

An incident occurred around that time to illustrate my difficulty in dealing with my children. When I was a boy in Singapore, children used to wear a pair of white canvas shoes with rubber soles for physical education classes. They were commonly just called tennis shoes. They no doubt descended from the compulsory plimsolls required by British schools earlier in the century.

But early in the 1970s, branded sports shoes known as trainers made an appearance in Hong Kong. Their arrival coincided with a relaxation of the dress code among schools. Children went wild over them because they looked more flashy and decorative. They quickly became very popular. The drawback was that they cost more than ten times the sum for an ordinary pair of white canvas shoes.

Inevitably, my youngest son, Tien-Kit, approached me one evening and asked for a pair of trainers. I judged trainers to be just another fad and not good value for money. Prices ought to come down after a while. It seemed just another quick money-gouging scam hit upon by commercial outfits, like the "glass belts" mania stirred up right after the war which had taken in both my Eighth Grandaunt and myself.

"Are your tennis shoes worn out?" I asked, pretending to be obtuse. "If so, I'll get you another pair."

"No, I still have my tennis shoes," Tien-Kit replied, a little shyly. "They're still good. But I'd like a pair of trainers."

"Why, if your existing pair can still be used?"

"Trainers are better."

"How so?"

"All my classmates are wearing them."

"That doesn't mean they're better," I said. "They might just be following herd instinct. Or their parents might just be failing to exercise sound economic judgements. You don't have to follow others. You should make your own decisions."

By then, Tien-Kit was beginning to get a little flustered. "Oh, Dad," he said, "you just don't get it. I want to be like my friends. That's the way things are these days."

"Well, help me 'get it'. Can you run faster in a pair of trainers than in tennis shoes? Can you kick a ball more accurately? Or what? There has to be a good reason. Just explain things to me so that I 'get it'."

Thereupon my son gave up and the conversation ended, leaving me unable to get across to my nine-year-old son that I was frustrating his desire because I loved him and cared for his intellectual development. I had named him Kit in honour of my old friend and mentor Hon-Kit, of whom I had not heard anything concrete for a quarter of a century, ever since he and his wife went back to China in 1949. My secret hope was that my son would grow up as selfless and patriotic as his namesake.

But Tien-Kit was a boy who needed a certain amount of coaxing. He had suffered a serious bout of encephalitis when younger and the after-effects still lingered. A woman might handle him better. But I had no woman to count on.

Another development soon forced my hand. Man-Ying decided to migrate. So my sons would be deprived of her attentions too. I could see the growing need for me to be home more. Ergo, I simply had to avoid getting promoted beyond my existing level.

On that line of reasoning, I wrote to the government stating that I wished to be withdrawn from any consideration for promotion because, as a single parent, I was not in a position to take on additional official functions. I needed more time with my children.

The reply that came back was cold and devoid of any commiseration or empathy. It stated that my request had been noted. But then it went on to point out, quite unnecessarily, that it would mean my acceptance of more junior officers being advanced ahead of me.

The letter was signed by the then Secretary for the Civil Service, an expatriate Staff Grade B Administrative Officer who was ranked below me in seniority. I considered the reference about being passed over both superfluous and an impertinence. I was disheartened that so arrogant and insensitive an officer should have been given the responsibility — among others — for enhancing the morale of the civil service. But then, though the man's heart and soul might be crippled by ambition, he was nonetheless generally recognised as one of the Governor's blue-eyed boys.

And though government claimed it had noted the fact I was a single parent to three children, it seemed to have had no hesitation in sending me away from home for half the time during the following year, to deal with the long-running Bermuda II civil aviation negotiations.

* * *

Life can be a funny thing. Very often, just when one grows resigned to coming against nothing but dead ends, something unforeseen and pleasant happens. This was the case after my aborted trip to Taiwan. I was invited by a friend to a birthday dinner and there I met a lovely married woman. For the purpose of this narrative, I shall call her C. A number of fortuitous events subsequently followed and before long we fell in love.

In recounting the story, I shall stick as authentically as possible to feelings and emotions. But I shall alter some of the actual circumstances to shield the identities of the people I am writing about.

Our initial meeting happened shortly before I had been transferred from the Home Affairs Department. She had attended the dinner with her husband. They struck me immediately as a very odd pair. The man appeared close to 40 and was working at one of the local universities in a non-teaching capacity. His features were utterly bland, commonplace and unemphatic; his nature was about as communicative as a lamppost's. He hardly entered into a conversation the entire evening and when he did his voice was strangely muted and toneless. He seemed overly preoccupied with some problem of his own.

His wife, on the other hand, was cheerful, out-going and as delightful as the first blush of spring. She had a spontaneous smile, which was the most guileless and fetching I had ever seen upon a woman's face. She was also willowy and graceful, with a slender waist flaring pleasingly into generous child-bearing hips. She could hardly have been more than about 21 or 22 but she carried with her that very special glow which often lingered with a woman after giving birth.

During the course of the evening, I learnt that she had indeed recently given birth to a son. She was a stenographer by profession, living with her husband and their son in the home of the husband's parents.

She appeared so lively and attractive that I had to restrain myself from casting my eyes in her direction. Life was thoroughly unfair, I thought. Some men had all the luck. How come the prospective brides introduced to me never exuded an air and a personality half as beguiling? If one of them had been, I probably would have secured a substitute mother for my children by now.

I speculated for a day or two afterwards how two such ill-matched people could have ended up as a couple. It must have been one of those old-fashioned family marriages, betrothed by their parents, or else arranged through a matchmaker, sight unseen. Beyond resenting the vagaries of fate, I thought no further about them.

* * *

Throughout my civil service career, I had made a point of spending the lunch hour socialising with friends or colleagues, in order to garner insights into what was happening in the wider world or in other parts of the bureaucracy.

When lunching on my own, I would just grab a quick plate of fried rice or noodles at the Hong Kong University Alumni Association Club or at one of the less expensive eateries in the heart of town. Thereafter, I would spend the rest of the lunch hour wandering around, trying to get a feel of the prevailing business mood and the tempo of the city. It would all be impressionistic, admittedly, but I had been used to doing that kind of reconnoitring as a reporter. That habit had been reinforced by Sir John Cowperthwaite's advice for policy makers to see things on the ground for themselves, instead of relying solely on abstract theories and equivocal statistics.

During my after-lunch walks, therefore, I would note the size of the crowds in the shops and restaurants and the mood with which shoppers went about their window-shopping or purchases. I was also fond of roaming through the side streets where hawkers, roadside barbers, bootblacks and others in lowly occupations earned their living. If I could find an excuse, I would engage some of them in conversation. I enjoyed talking to such people. Getting indications of prices at hawker stalls gave me a quicker sense of inflationary pressures than the long wait for the weighted components of Consumer Price Index to land on my desk.

Common people knew life at the sharp end. They were generally straight-talking, earthy and uncontaminated by too many social artifices. Psychologically, I felt at ease with them, because I had started my working life as a refugee at the age of 13, washing dishes and sweeping floors, trying to satisfy my belly. I was keen to know the current problems they faced, whether they were making sufficient to get by, whether they were being squeezed by triads, and so forth. Since I was now in a position with a little influence, I wanted to ease their lives if I could.

There was a thin middle-aged fellow, probably a reformed drug addict, I had struck up an acquaintance with. He operated as a shoeblack on the pavement of a side-lane. I would occasionally spend a couple of dollars for a shine, just for the sake of talking to him. Though there were a couple of other shoeblacks operating alongside him, he had no qualms over telling me whether there were drug pushers lurking around the neighbourhood or whether the police had been harassing him too much.

Getting my shoes shined.

He told me that he and his fellow boot polishers preferred the patronage of foreigners because they paid more generously, well above the going rate. None of them knew how to attract their custom, however. When they called out, foreigners usually ignored them, taking them for beggars or con artists.

"Grab their attention by spinning a good yarn," I advised him. "Exaggerate your virtues like corporations do with advertising."

"But how? None of us know their language," he replied.

"Repeat after me: 'Best shoeshine in town, Boss! No good, no pay.'" I made him repeat the phrases a few times until he got a passable intonation. Then I taught him a couple more phrases in English and pidgin.

When I next went by his pitch, he told me the hailing calls had worked.

Sometimes, when two or three foreigners were together, getting one of them to have a shine often meant his companions would give custom to his mates along the pavement as well.

The collective earnings of bootblacks would never figure in the mountains of GDP statistics produced by governments because they formed part of the shadow economy. Yet the briskness or otherwise of their business would be one of the earliest indicators of the wider society's propensity to spend. A man going through hard times would not dish out that little extra sum to get his shoes polished. But if spent, his decision would produce its own marginal effect on the velocity of money.

* * *

One day, about three months after the birthday party I went for one of my after-lunch walks and unexpectedly bumped into C. She looked a picture of loveliness, smiling as beguiling as when we first met, though — at closer quarters — I could detect beneath her outward cheerfulness an undercurrent of restlessness. Because of that, she gave me the impression of a high-spirited filly not fully reconciled to being bridled, trying at times to get the bit between her teeth.

We exchanged the customary pleasantries before I asked if she had had lunch. When she replied she had already eaten, I suggested a cup of coffee. We thereupon repaired to the lounge of one of the swankier hotels in Central.

I was a trifle uncertain as to how I ought to engage with her. She was treating me deferentially, as if I were an elder, which — given our respective ages — I definitely was. She seemed so innocent and young that I hesitated over treating her as an equal. She was younger than all the three girls Ping had fixed up for me as prospective mates. Yet she was already a married woman and a mother. Not being sure what I ought to do, I played it off the cuff.

During coffee, after we had exchanged news of the mutual friends at the birthday dinner, I mentioned that it must be a great help to have in-laws to help care for her child since both she and her husband were working. The remark must have triggered some private concern, for she turned more sombre.

"Yes, they're a great help," she said. "But they can sometimes be a great hindrance too. Local housing does not provide for a great deal of personal space; living on top of one another involves taking into account the preferences of others."

Upon hearing that, I jumped wrongly to the conclusion that there had been some friction between her and her in-laws. My mother's former plight came to mind. My mother too had been a stenographer and she had not taken kindly to subordinating herself to the wishes of my grandparents. That might have driven her to seek employment in Canton. The consequence was the eventual breakdown of her marriage.

I wanted to commiserate with C and to deter her from following in my mother's footsteps. So I said: "Well, there are always pluses and minuses in life. I grew up in an old-fashioned extended family and later spent almost ten years living with my in-laws. I have to say that, on balance, living with in-laws brings more advantages than disadvantages. I would certainly have found it impossible to cope without them. I'm an authority on extended families and in-laws. But basically, it's all a matter of learning a few survival skills, like stooping to conquer."

"Really?" C said, with a soft note of surprise. "I've heard you described as a very tough guy in government circles, full of bright ideas, a man who usually gets his way. I must get some pointers from you."

"Many stories about me are completely unfounded," I replied. "My so-called bright ideas — if I may use a cricketing analogy — get knocked for sixes. Once in a while, I manage a fluke. That's about it."

"Well, I've got no elder to tell me about extended families or in-laws. Marriage and motherhood are both new to me."

"I'm not sure my advice is worth much but I would be glad to answer whatever questions you may have. Unfortunately, it appears our lunch breaks are coming to an end. I imagine we both have to get back to our jobs. Here's my card. When you are free for another cup of coffee, please ring me. We can meet after work. Don't be worried if I'm a little difficult to get hold of, because I'm due for quite a bit of travelling on government business. But my secretary can tell you when I'm due back."

On that note, we shook hands and went our separate ways.

* * *

When old Stanford friends got news that I would be making trips to Washington D.C., a number of them invited me to visit them. But because of time and travel constraints, I could only accept two invitations during the year of Bermuda II negotiations.

The first was for a brief stay with a couple in Bethesda in Maryland. On another round, a week to catch up with a good friend in New York. She had married the chief executive of American Express and they had a magnificent apartment on Fifth Avenue, within sight and almost directly across from the Metropolitan Museum.

While planning the New York visit, my thoughts drifted towards Sharlee, as they often did at random moments, like when I catch sight of one of her paintings on my wall at home or when I come across an evocative passage in a novel I was reading. A few bitter-sweet lines would pull me back to Holland, to those stolen adulterous moments of guilty flesh. I would then begin to wonder what Sharlee might be doing and how far she had got with her painting.

More than ten years had elapsed since we had been in touch and the only address I had was that of her parents in Ohio. On an impulse, either out of nostalgia or resentment against the cruelty of karma — I knew not which — I decided to write to her. I told her I would be in Washington on a government mission on and off over the next few months; if she was anywhere conveniently located, perhaps we could meet.

A reply duly came back, accompanied by a contact telephone number. She explained she was now married and living in New Jersey but could easily drive down to Washington to meet me.

Since I would be spending a week in New York, and that city was livelier than Washington, I wrote back suggesting a meeting in New York instead, giving the dates I would be at a Fifth Avenue apartment. I promised to ring after I had arrived in Washington to finalise details. And so it was that we ended up meeting on the steps of the Metropolitan Museum, on a certain afternoon on an autumnal day.

* * *

Sharlee was already waiting in front of the museum when I approached on foot. She was standing on the uppermost step leading to the entrance, a little apart from the groups of students and youngsters enjoying the sun on the lower steps. She looked serene and poised, ready to be recognised. Her blonde hair had darkened a shade since I last saw her. It was now more stylishly coiffured and her apparel had also gone up-market. She did not quite fit the image I had been entertaining of a dedicated artist. Nonetheless, she remained reassuringly beautiful and desirable, having acquired hardly any additional poundage.

As I approached, I waved to catch her eye. She waved back. I negotiated my way up the steps but before I could even get within kissing distance, she cried out: "Oh, David! You haven't changed a bit!" Her voice was warm and excited, still carrying a note of youthful exuberance.

We kissed, deeply and tenderly, in public and without embarrassment. What had drawn us together in the past rekindled in me. "You're as delectable as ever," I murmured, "and amazingly more beautiful with the passage of years."

"Liar!" she said, in feigned chastisement, while her lambent blue-grey eyes sparkled with modest delight.

"No, perfectly true, my sweet. Scout's honour. You've mellowed magnificently, whereas I've merely learnt to play Dorian Gray's trick of doing my ageing elsewhere."

"Still as deft as ever with a repartee."

"Only when the lady before me is attractive enough to inspire me to the effort," I replied, inclining my head stagily. We were now standing comfortably together. I had one of my arms around her shoulders and she had one of hers around my waist. "And if the truth be told," I added, "I'd like nothing better than to carry you off somewhere right now."

"That's what I like about you. You're incorrigible and always true to form! Right now I'd rather catch up with news of your bosom pal, Sonni Pillai."

"Ah, Sonni. I've been in regular touch with him since The Hague. Visited him at least twice in Penang. He's now left the civil service in Malaysia to join ours in Hong Kong, drafting legislation in the Law Draughtsman's Office. An ideal man for the job, being a barrister by profession, on top of his experience as an administrator. It's a tricky thing, drawing up legislation that can be efficiently implemented.

"As to his love life, I fear he's at last been harnessed to marriage. Otherwise in fine fettle. I actually see a fair bit of him and his wife. She's a buxom Indian lassie less than half his age."

"How very nice for him," she said, nodding. "So you've been keeping up with him much more than you have with me."

I felt abashed. "I'm sorry. I couldn't with you, because it would have meant stringing you along under false pretences. I couldn't do that to you. I should have told you in Holland I was already married."

"You didn't need to. I figured that out for myself. For me, it didn't change a thing between us."

"But it mattered to *me*. I had nothing to offer back then; I'm divorced now but I still have nothing to offer. I've been stuck with bringing up three kids. You got kids yet?"

"No, too many questions still up in the air," she said. "You're wrong, you know. Everyone has things to offer — if only we were willing to pay the price or to make others pay the price for us. But let's not go into anything so terribly dreary. Just tell me, what *you're* up to, besides breaking feminine hearts? I want the truth, not that evasive hush-hush stuff you tried on the phone."

I sighed. "I'm up to no good, I fear. Playing a devious three-cornered game of civil aviation politics, if you must know. Pretending to be in step with the desires of my imperial masters in London, to grab more air travel for their benefit, while signalling to your people my own sympathies for their mantra of open competition and open skies. In playing one party off against the other, I'm hoping to strike enough balance in their conflicting interests to allow me to secure for Hong Kong a fairer share of the economic cake. A thoroughly cynical and disreputable undertaking.

"Deeply cynical and disreputable because, however the unseemly scramble might turn out, one thing is certain. Only vested interests will ever benefit, not ordinary folks. Every third world country is already starting its own flag carrier to crowd the skies, even as it rushes hellbent to manufacture traffic jams on its streets. Soon planes will fill the heavens, carrying millions of dullards all over the globe, to the detriment of the very air we breathe, to the torment of those who have to live under flight paths. And all for what? The sake of extra tourism dollars and some tarted up GDP figures for domestic talking heads."

Sharlee looked at me darkly.

"What can a hired mercenary like myself do, in a world rampant with crony capitalism disguised as democracy?" I blurted out in my own defence. "I can't change the system; I've tried. So I can only play the three wise monkeys to earn my keep."

"Oh," Sharlee allowed. From the tone of that single sound, I knew I had over-exposed some of my own frustrations and failures. If she were to remain anything like her former self, a whole series of "whys" would surely be coming my way.

I was not yet prepared to answer for my sins, at least not so soon after our reunion. In order to divert her, I interjected quickly: "I've never been inside the Met. Shouldn't we take a turn now that I'm here?"

"Why not," Sharlee answered, somewhat flatly. She then slipped an arm around one of mine and we entered the museum.

It was a weekday and visitors were sparse. We strolled unhurriedly among the exhibits, pausing now and then for a better view or to voice some pedestrian comment. But I was not really taking in most of them. My mind was elsewhere; I imagined hers was too.

It was an absurdity, a madness, for us to meet, I thought, as we wandered among the detritus of long lost civilisations, dead loves and forsaken ambitions. What could either of us hope to achieve by meeting at this belated stage? So much had happened since that glorious spring of 1965. We could not possibly, in the autumn of 1976, return to where we had been, to pick up again from where we had left off.

I recalled with an aching heart some of the wilder enthusiasms we had shared and rashly committed ourselves to. The artistic life, intellectual integrity, great causes, lop-sided fights for justice, the betterment of humanity and all the rest of that stuff. We had advanced those notions in good faith, under the intoxication of love, only to discover years later they were just so much tommyrot. Life had not turned out even remotely to resemble our fleeting dreams.

At least none of the dubious things I had done would ever end up inside a museum to shame me, I reflected. How could the mastery of a few aviation technicalities like route structures, break-even load factors, comparative catchment areas, Freedoms of the Air and such become immortalised? Why should any record of a whole string of negations be preserved for posterity?

As we strolled, I became aware that something equally troubling might be working through Sharlee's mind. Thankfully, she was keeping her introspections to herself.

After a while, we found ourselves before one of Gauguin's celebrated paintings of Tahitian women. We stopped to study it. I recalled something Gauguin had said about women from that part of the world. He had ascribed to them the serene virtue of being knowing in their naiveté. No wonder he took on so many of them as *vahine*s, or native child brides.

My reflections were interrupted when Sharlee said in a small voice, while staring at the painting: "Perhaps the women in Polynesia accept the realities of life more easily than women in the West. They're not lumbered by so many expectations. I gradually gave up painting, you know, after I got married."

"Don't feel disheartened," I said, trying to be consoling. "You're still young. There's time yet. If one had a true flame, it's bound to flare again. How long did it take Gauguin to go from stockbroker to painter and sculptor? He was quite old, wasn't he, when he abandoned his family for Tahiti?"

"I've been deluding myself with those sorts of alibis," Sharlee said, turning to look at me straight in the eyes. "But they haven't worked. My husband heads one of Fortune's 500. That comes with too many obligations, too much stuff to deal with. Home in New Jersey, house in Connecticut, villa in the south of France, cars, yachts, entertaining others and being entertained, always in the limelight living the American dream. My husband and I must now number among those you call dullards, flying all over the world to no good purpose. At least when you fly, you have some purpose, whether it's your own or somebody else's. What I want to know is when is your flame going to start burning again?"

I gave a hollow laugh. "I'm too old and spent, already 48," I said. "I'm not sure I ever had a real flame. I tested it out in London once; it fizzled. Even if I had it, too many years of turgid bureaucratic prose must have done me in by now. Can't write properly any more. Can't even produce a half-decent sentence to save my soul."

"Well, you'd better start getting back into practice. You promised me a story which you still haven't delivered. I'm holding you to your word. You're not going to force me to admit to another misjudgement, are you, of relying on your word?"

"You're a hard woman, Sharlee," I said, with a shake of my head, giving another hollow laugh at the same time to hide my embarrassment over being called to account. "I can't recall having promised any early delivery, have I? But I'll keep that promise; just give me a little more time."

On that note, we continued our way through the rest of the museum. By the time we re-emerged, the sunlight was retreating in advance of the dying day. Most of the young people had dispersed from the steps.

As we stood outside the entrance, we looked at each other, putting on tentative and ambiguous smiles. A mixed sense of both elation and melancholy seeped through me. I felt slightly heady, because I had received confirmation that a connection made long ago still mattered to both of us. But melancholy also, because in engaging with Sharlee again I had been forced to confront my own inner self and to realise I had failed to achieve that elevated plane of living we both had once grandly aspired to.

Disconcerted by that self-knowledge, my mind was left at sixes and sevens as I walked beside Sharlee down the steps. Upon reaching the street, I was uncertain what to do next. "Shall we go for a drink?" I asked, ambivalently.

Sharlee hesitated for a couple of seconds. "Perhaps I should be heading back," she said. "I have a long way to drive."

"Of course," I said, half-disappointed but also half-relieved. "I shall be in New York for a few more days. If you should happen this way, we could meet again."

"I'll check my schedule when I get home and let you know."

We studied each other affectionately but indecisively for a moment longer. Words began forming in my heart. I did not want to part from her again so quickly. But before I could get my sentiments out, I heard Sharlee say: "Kiss me again, David, before I go."

I did. But I think each of us was only kissing our own flesh-tethered memories.

Those decade-old memories held me fast, like a rebuke, as I watched helplessly as Sharlee moved towards one of the yellow cabs at the kerbside, to take her to where she had parked her car. She climbed in and then waved goodbye. There was some vague yet definite message conveyed in that wave. It seemed to insinuate she would be doing some hard thinking in the days ahead.

I sensed it was highly unlikely she would find time to come to New York again.

* * *

It was to be another 15 years, after I had retired from Hong Kong and taken up residence in London, before I got down to doing any serious writing. It was only then that I began working on the story I had long promised Sharlee. I never managed to get the finished product to her, however, because by the time I had finished the story, the telephone number at New Jersey she had given me had been disconnected. We had completely lost touch.

If she had happened to chance upon any of the 50 or so short stories I had subsequently published in magazines or over the airwaves, she would still be in the dark as to whether I had ever written the story I had promised.

* * *

Meanwhile, during one of those brief respites in Hong Kong which hyphenated my repeated journeys to London and Washington, C rang to take up me up on my offer of a cup of coffee after work. This came before my reunion with Sharlee. C said she wanted some advice on how best to get one's point of view across to elders in an extended family.

I was loath to get involved with the internal affairs of somebody else's family. But since I had off-handedly made the offer, I could only follow through.

When we met, C said she would like to learn my ways of bending in-laws to my wishes, as she wanted to do the same with hers.

That question embarrassed me. In reality, over the years, I had actually just gone along with the inclinations of my in-laws. They set the family routine, including the care and upbringing of my children. I was dependent upon them for financial help because my civil service salary proved inadequate to support my family. I therefore had little choice but to accept whatever they decided. If they had been harsh and vindictive, blaming me for breaching their trust or messing up the life of their daughter, I might have reacted differently. But they had been absolutely kind, considerate and understanding, and very easy to live with. Most importantly, they formed a sort of buffer zone, mediating the tensions between myself and my wife, so that we could co-exist without undue acrimony. I felt considerably in their debt.

I was naturally reluctant to explain the full situation to a young woman like C. So I just said: "Well, my in-laws had been very nice and sensible people and a pleasure to live with. They were also very caring grandparents. It was very rare for me not to see eye to eye with them on most things."

"If that was the case, how come you had to get divorced?" C asked. "I'm a bit confused. With such good in-laws, why divorce? Do you mind my asking the reason?"

"You're asking some damn awkward questions, young lady," I said. "My circumstances are unlikely to apply in your case. In a nutshell, I'm in my present pickle because my in-laws had been actually too good. You see, their only daughter and I had never really been in love. It had been only sex that tripped us up.

"She was a teenager at the time and I was 12 years her senior; I was supposed to be her guardian. After getting sexually involved, I — being rather old-fashioned — felt honour-bound to marry her, though both of us had reservations about each other. By the time we had our first child, it became obvious we were temperamentally completely unsuited. I told my in-laws it would be best for us to divorce. Their daughter was still young enough, I said, to start afresh.

"But they wanted us to salvage the marriage. Things should get better, they argued, once their daughter became more mature. They suggested another child as a means of cementing things. Because I was weak and filled with guilt, I went along. Things never got better, however. So here I am, divorced, and having to look after three kids on my own."

"I'm sorry," C said. "I had no right to pry. Thank you for sharing your situation. I hope telling it wasn't too unpleasant for you."

"It's all right. As I've said, I don't think my story has any bearing on your situation."

"But it has! I'm at the same point you had been in when you sought a divorce."

"Oh, really? Why? I had understood you've been married for just a year and a half."

"Wasn't that how long it took you to realise your marriage couldn't work?" C replied, looking skywards and blinking her eyes to resist a flow of threatened tears. "My husband's an only son. When our son came, he felt he had done his duty towards his family. He lost interest in me. He regarded me in the traditional Chinese way, as someone to look after his son and his parents. My in-laws had much the same attitude. They focused their attention upon their grandson. But I want more out of life than just that."

C's confession had been unexpected. I sympathised with her, trapped in circumstances beyond her resolution. My immediate instinct was to help her. But it was tricky for a third party to get in the middle of a marital dispute; I simply did not know quite how to respond.

"Divorce is a very big step," I cautioned, "especially now that you have a child. Have you talked this over with your parents or family? Or with marriage counsellors?"

"My parents passed away when I was about ten; I was raised by distant relatives," C said. "They've since migrated to Canada, so I have no close relatives around. But divorce is not the real issue. My husband and I do not love each other. Neither he nor his family would object to our splitting up."

"But British law does not provide for divorce just because of people no longer love one another. There has to be some compelling grounds, such as cruelty, desertion, adultery or the like."

"None of that applies with us," C said. "The heart of the issue is my son. I want him. But my husband and his parents also want the boy. I cannot give up my son. What can I do to keep him?"

I saw at once it was not a matter I could handle. "I suggest that you consult a lawyer before you do anything," I said. "Child custody issues are rather complicated. From what little I know, I think courts are not so interested in the recriminations of adults as the welfare of children. I can also understand the imperative of your husband's family to have a male heir to perpetuate its family line. The lawyer who handled my divorce is a pretty good one. She's very sound and sensible. I can introduce you. She'll be able to give you an idea of how things might develop if your request for custody is challenged."

"Is she expensive?"

"She'll be quite reasonable, if you're referred by me. Are finances a problem?"

"I hardly have any savings. After a divorce, I'll have to manage on whatever I can earn."

"If you have to work, how are you going to look after your son should you gain custody? Presumably you don't own any property, so you'll probably have to rent accommodation as well."

"No, sadly, I own no property. I'll have to engage a Filipino maid in addition, I guess."

"That'll make for a tight squeeze on a stenographer's income. A working mother using a maid to look after a child would not sound very compelling before a court, compared with the attention the child could get from a pair of committed grandparents. You'd better have a chat with my lawyer friend first."

With that, I provided C with the contact details of the lawyer and, within days, left for Washington for a further round of negotiations and, afterwards, a reunion with Sharlee.

* * *

I returned to Hong Kong in low spirits. I had destabilised — in all probability for the worse rather than for the better — the life Sharlee had established for herself. The reunion had also brought me retrospective regrets and a degree of self-loathing I had not experienced for some time. Everything I had attempted seemed utterly meaningless and pointless.

After an absence of three weeks, I rang C to find out whether she had fared any better with a lawyer advising her on her problem. I was surprised to find she had moved out of her marital home and had taken a single room for a month at the Helena May Institute at Garden Road.

The Helena May was founded in 1916 by the wife of the then Governor, Sir Henry May, with the object of providing affordable residence and welfare support for women and girls.

C was quick to explain, when I finally caught up with her, that she had not initiated divorce proceedings but had merely moved out of the family home to determine whether she could stand being separated from her son. I suspected that her lawyer must have advised her that custody was a chancy thing, given her financial circumstances, relative to those of her husband and in-laws. I could well imagine the loneliness and desolation she must have subjected herself to at the Helena May, after returning there from work each day. So I invited her to join my family for one of our unspectacular dinners prepared by Ah Duen at Palm Court.

She became an instant hit with my boys. They took her more as an older sister than as an elder, for her age and that of my eldest son were not that far apart. She hid well her own sadness during her visit and she soon infected the entire dining table with her cheerfulness. Seeing how she was interacting with my children made me realise she was exactly the kind of woman that both my boys and I needed in the home. If she was separating from her husband, then there might still be a chance for me.

I therefore invited her to come again two or three nights later. She again cheered us no end with her spontaneous laughter and her out-going nature. She took Ah Duen's indifferent meal in her stride. After the children had retired to their rooms at nine, C and I drifted out onto the balcony to take some air.

It was late October, about two weeks after the autumn equinox. The evening was pleasantly cool. There was what the *Old Farmer's Almanac* called a harvest moon, hanging as brightly as a lantern in the sky. Beneath it, the lights of the restive city seemed only to languish in inadequate counterpoint.

The one which caught our eyes most was the big neon sign on top of the Ocean Terminal across the harbour. It advertised one of the more popular Japanese consumer products. The rest were largely uncertain pinpoints of light emanating from the concrete cells that passed for human habitation, from headlights of evening traffic or from squatter area stoves heating up evening meals. They melded together somehow, undifferentiated, to cast a deceptive veil over the hardships and the mendacity of a fractured and hard-nosed city.

Here and there, protruding gloomily above the evening skyline, were the arms of gantry cranes idled for the night, appearing like grim signposts along the road to perdition.

C and I stood silently, resting our forearms on the balcony railing, while we took in the anomalous scene before us. Each of us must have been mulling over our own predicaments. Mine were dark and depressing, without hope. Perhaps hers had been too.

Suddenly, from out of the night, the plaintive notes of a Chinese flute floated towards us. Its melody was soft and melancholy, resembling a lament gently sighed. C and I turned and looked at each other. Without uttering a word, we fell spontaneously into each other's arms and began kissing furiously. It was inevitable for us to end up in bed.

* * *

In the afterglow of love, within the curtained darkness of my bedroom, I heard C murmur in a voice mellowed by a fresh understanding forged through the interaction of lips and skin: "What has happened to us?"

"I think we've fallen in love," I replied. C's beauty and youthfulness now seemed even more wondrous than before. I had now appraised her beyond sight, through the senses of sound, smell and touch, and she had been found delightful in every way. There was no longer any differentiation between us as elder or junior; just a simple case of a man and a woman bewitched, in love with each other.

"I'm doomed," C allowed, dishearteningly, after a pause. "I'll be judged a bad and immoral mother, unfit to have custody of a son."

"No, no! You're not a bad mother at all. In fact, you're the best of mothers, one fighting tooth and nail to be together with her son."

"But I've done wrong; it'll be held against me."

"There's nothing wrong about two human beings falling in love. It must be karma or fate that has brought us together. Let us just see where it leads."

C was not convinced. But at least I persuaded her to have dinner at Palm Court again the following evening. We reaffirmed our love but neither of us could get around that eternal conundrum: What ought to happen when an irresistible force came up against an immoveable object?

If fate had brought us together, then duty tore us apart. Within two days I had to emplane for London, for the next round of Bermuda II. I wrote her a letter on the plane, reiterating my love, and posted it the moment I landed at Heathrow. But what was the point of the letter when I could offer no solution to her quest to be with her son?

* * *

Upon my return from London, devastating news awaited me. C had decided during my brief absence to leave the Helena May to return home. She explained she simply could not bear to be separated from her child any more. I could relate to how she must have felt. The irreconcilable equation in our lives languished hopelessly before us.

She was fearful of seeking a divorce, lest she lost custody of her son. I was in a quandary, not quite knowing what I should do next. I wanted to marry her, to tray and make both of us happy. And to make my children happier too. But I could not marry her until she got divorced and she would not initiate proceedings without a firm and prior assurance that divorce would allow her to keep her child.

I tried to set out the stark alternatives. In doing so, I no doubt had allowed selfish considerations to colour my presentation. I emphasised how much I cared for her but I carefully avoided any suggestion she should just let her infant son go in exchange for a life with me. Though I knew that giving up the child would both satisfy her husband's family and be advantageous for me, I did not want to be held responsible for urging so fraught a decision. She would have to make that on her own.

I reminded her the price for remaining with her son would be living with a man she did not love and remaining part of a family which did not care for her. How many years could she endure such an imposition? I had once made a wrong decision at a critical juncture; the result was 11 years of a loveless marriage. A similar mistake should be avoided. Her son was in his infancy; he might have to grow up, like my children, in an atmosphere riddled with family tensions. Quite apart from that, was she prepared to throw her own life away? And what about *our* love and *our* happiness? Must our happiness be sacrificed for the sake of her son?

C said she had no answers to any of those questions, though she had been wrestling with them day and night. All she knew was that she loved me but she also needed to be with her son. She wanted both, with all her heart, but was completely at a loss as to how that could be attained.

We continued to meet nonetheless, because neither of us could bear the pain of losing the other. But the circumstances that had brought us together had altered significantly, had become more equivocal, and we had to tread more carefully.

From my point of view, when we began our intimacy, I was a single man in search of a wife, while C was a woman who had taken an initial step towards ending her marriage. She had vacated her marital home for a women's hostel. In the more sexually liberated temper of the age, such a relationship, if somewhat premature, could not be considered unreasonable or frowned upon.

But now, she was trying to reconcile herself to living with her husband and his family. On that account, our liaison began to take on the character of an adulterous affair; my wooing her could be construed as an act of alienating her from her wifely affections. Should her husband discover what was going on, he could sue for divorce and name me as a co-respondent. That would lead not only to an unholy scandal but to serious damage being done to C's chances of gaining custody should a divorce occur.

The only justification I could offer for my actions was the madness and desperation of love. I had hopes that love could somehow be sufficient for C to surrender the child and decide in my favour. There had been moments when I sensed she might be on the brink of giving way. Unfortunately, I was never allowed to press my suit to a conclusion during those moments. Duty always intervened to drag me away, to send me off to the farthest sides of the world and out of my reach for her.

* * *

When I returned to Hong Kong after two weeks, I was in a despondent mood. Another round of negotiations had got nowhere in terms of a satisfactory trans-Pacific route for a Hong Kong airline. The Americans had the better technical arguments — on traffic configurations, catchment areas, intermediate points, *et cetera*. And all the while the unresolved situation with C weighed upon me more heavily than lead.

Our meetings were now becoming more difficult and dangerous. The risk of exposure was ever present. With C living at home, her absences outside of her normal working routine invited queries. We had to resort to the odd stolen half-hour during lunch time or at the end of the day's work. We made love when we could; we talked incessantly in circles but found ourselves unable to break out of our predicaments. And then, all too soon, we had to part again.

* * *

Away from Hong Kong, my mind was tormented by our uncertain future. The existing relationship was too stressful and unhealthy for both of us. It could not continue. A resolution had to be found — one way or another.

In reviewing my conduct, I judged it less than worthy. It was not good enough to set out options for C and to refer her to a lawyer for legal advice. She was hardly more than a child, with only a secondary school education. She was vulnerable in more ways than one. Yet I had left the weightiest existential decisions squarely upon her slender shoulders. It was not the behaviour of a true gentleman. I should have shared that responsibility.

I had also not set a good example of honourable behaviour for my sons. So I resolved to tackle the issue afresh upon my return.

But events had moved on dramatically by the time I got back. C gave me news that she was pregnant. I was ecstatic at first. I thought the child was mine. That development should make it easier for C to give up one child for another. But C soon punctured my happiness by saying that, according to her calculations, the child had been conceived during my absence. It was her husband's.

I was dumbfounded. My immediate reaction was a surge of jealousy. How could she be having sex with a man she did not love when she was supposed to be in love with me? Once that blind rush of emotion had subsided, however, I understood how it could have occurred. After all, my second and third sons with Man-Ying had also not been born out of love. The second had been in obedience to the wishes of my in-laws to salvage our marriage and the third had been through a momentary seizure of animal lust. Each human being had its frailties. So had sages and saints.

The new situation robbed both of us of hope. There was no longer any prospect of sharing a life together, at least not any time soon. We went through a sad and affectionate parting. Afterwards, we kept in desultory touch over the next four decades, albeit always with a touch of sweet sorrow.

It was to be another 15 years, after C had been divorced and had remarried a second husband, that she told me how she came to be pregnant with her second child, another son. But the details of that story have to be left for a later volume of these memoirs.

CHAPTER 13

Water, Water, Water

AFTER MY RETURN TO HONG KONG at the conclusion of the Bermuda II civil aviation negotiations in mid-1977, I was unexpectedly appointed Secretary for Economic Services. This did not imply an elevation as such; nor had anyone judged me suitable for advancement. I certainly did not lift a finger to seek the post.

The appointment came by way of one of those fortuitous hiccups in bureaucratic life, an accidental largesse bestowed upon an officer who happened to be in the right place at the right time. In my case, it came from nothing more earth-shaking than my immediate superior, the Secretary for Economic Services, becoming due for home leave. Someone therefore had to keep his seat warm. Since I was his only Deputy, the task fell upon my unprepossessing posterior. That had the effect of earning me a few hundred extra dollars a month in "acting pay".

That feature in the system undoubtedly benefitted many officers whenever some high personage went on leave. For example, with the Financial Secretary going on holiday, the Secretary for Economic Services might be chosen to act on his behalf. As a consequence, the Secretary's Deputy would also move up a notch. Likewise, an Assistant Secretary into the Deputy's position, and so on down the line.

Over the next two years, for various unforeseen reasons, I ended up on several occasions as Secretary for Economic Services. That outcome was a natural development of the costly McKinsey re-organisation of the Secretariat launched by Sir Murray MacLehose. Under that new regime, Policy Secretaries proliferated like mushrooms around some rotting log. An inordinate number of Secretariat officers benefitted from "acting pay" as a result.

During the period immediately after World War II, the Secretariat had been much leaner and more centralised. All major policy proposals had to be cleared by both the Colonial Secretary and the Financial Secretary before going to the Executive Council for endorsement. Those two top officials, together with the Governor, represented the official voice of the government. They announced policies and answered for them, both within the Legislative Council chamber and before the wider public.

But the rapid rise in population spawned an increasingly complex set of social, economic and technological issues. That resulted in those two top officials becoming quickly overloaded, causing a bottleneck at the very apex of the administration.

In 1963, when I was first assigned to the Secretariat, a post of Deputy Colonial Secretary had already been created to ease the burden of the two top officials. The then Deputy Colonial Secretary, Geoffrey Hamilton, was authorised to clear some of the less controversial policy memoranda for the Executive Council.

By 1975, however, when I was next assigned to the Secretariat, the number of Policy Secretaries had multiplied so greatly that the lines demarcating their responsibilities had become blurred. Sometimes they even overlapped. That situation left ample scope for turf wars, one-upmanship, back-stabbing and ego-skirmishes.

That unhappy prospect was made worse by the steady loss of some of the more talented and level-headed officers due to retirements. Those promoted to fill their shoes were, unfortunately, too often of inferior calibre. That diluted management quality, brought a loss in mentoring capabilities for new officers and eroded the integrity and *esprit de corps* through large parts of the administrative service.

At the same time, the Governor decided in the early 1970s to delegate to Policy Secretaries the authority to put policy papers directly to the Executive Council and to appoint a few of them as members of the Legislative Council. The Secretary for Economic Services became one of them. The titles and honorifics sounded grand but they came with very little power to make fundamental changes.

The rationale behind such moves was never very clear. Sir Murray was never one to explain his decisions. Perhaps he just wanted Policy Secretaries to be in the legislature to serve as straw men, to take the heat in case a policy proved too controversial or unpopular. I was never much good at reading his mind.

* * *

The Legislative Council of the mid-1970s was a relaxed and clubby sort of place. It was overwhelmingly dominated by males but it had at least two or three women members. Just as in the case of Justices of the Peace, there were two categories of membership — Official Members and Unofficial Members.

The Official ones were senior civil servants like the Chief Secretary or Financial Secretary and heads of major departments. The Unofficial ones were chosen from the ranks of solid citizens who had a reasonable command of the English language. In other words, they were drawn from bankers, doctors, lawyers, educators, commercial tycoons and captains of industry, with the odd community leader from the *kaifong* associations or one of the better-known charities thrown in.

The Unofficials were by and large decent people, who had accepted appointments as a matter of civic duty. They were conscious of their responsibilities to the wider community rather than just serving the narrower interests of their own callings. They regarded their appointments as badges of public recognition and did their best to earn that status. For such selfless work, they naturally did not expect any recompense.

The working arrangements between Officials and Unofficials were cordial, soothed by mutual respect and honest co-operation. If they had differences, they would work them out quietly in the corridors rather than publicly in the chamber. That called for give and take on both sides. It was not difficult because they all came from pretty much the same social and economic circles and shared similar bourgeoise outlooks.

People also had not been so brash, uncivil and ego-centric back then. Most speeches within the chambers were bland and amateurishly delivered; sometimes platitudinous and soporific. No one spoke with anything resembling the passion and oratorical flourishes of a Demosthenes or a Cicero. The odd hackneyed joke or an over-stretched pun might be the best anyone could expect. If memory serves, the only demand for a division during the 1970s came over a Bill aimed at liberalising abortion laws. Two Catholic members had got slightly hot under the collar over that issue of conscience. The Bill passed any way.

Around 1975, Sir Murray had another public relations idea. He noticed that no matter how hard the government's publicity machine strived to put a gloss on the Legislative Council being representative of Hong Kong's stratified society, it could not quite bring it off. He therefore decided that someone more solidly linked to the "grass roots" should be invited to join, to improve its image. He promptly ordered the Home Affairs Department to come up with names.

The order threw the department into a tizzy. It upturned the traditional way elevation to the upper crust had been done. The Secretariat for Chinese Affairs — the predecessor of the Home Affairs Department — had responsibility since the early days of the colony for keeping tabs on suitable citizens for political advancement. The word "suitable" implied a proven record in public-spirited endeavours, a reasonable command of the English language and no detectable symptoms of political awkwardness or traitorous inclinations.

In Hong Kong's cut-throat economic environment, it went without saying that any young person seeking to start a small business or to gain a footing in one of the more established professions had to spend many arduous hours simply to keep his or her head above water. There would be no time or energy left for getting involved in clansmen's associations, orphanages, Chinese temples and the like.

By the time a person could afford to engage in civic work, chances were that he or she had already arrived economically and socially, so to speak. Any former grass roots attachments would have been sloughed off, to stand four square among the *nouveaux riches*. It would only be then that a person would be noticed by the department. It was naturally a vicious circle. A genuine grass rooter who remained as one was about as rare as a person with a six-toed foot.

But thanks to the liaison work of an enterprising City District Officer in Kwun Tong, a young man named Michael Sze, one was found. A recommendation duly found its way back to Government House.

The candidate identified was Wong Lam, a former bus driver who had risen through the ranks to become a junior manager at the Kowloon Motor Bus Company. Wong had done voluntary work in running the Kwun Tong Sports Association. That was how the City District Officer came to know him. In spite of limited English, Wong Lam was appointed in 1976 and he soon proved a great success. He distinguished himself not only by working hard but also by being sensible and measured in his comments and pronouncements. He easily gained the respect of his fellow legislators.

One little unforeseen snag did crop up, however. It transpired that Wong Lam was a man of quite modest means. Working for the public good on the Legislative Council presented certain financial difficulties for him. The

Kowloon Motor Bus Company, which had hitherto employed him, could hardly be expected to continue paying his salary when he was spending most of his time on government matters.

Thus it came about that a stipend was introduced for those serving as legislators. In retrospect, it should be for reconsideration whether serving on the Legislative Council should be regarded as a kind of quasi-public service and be paid at the same level as a mid-grade civil servant. If the rewards were too generous, then any jobless person without qualifications or meaningful experience might chance his or her arm at getting selected on the basis of a gift of the gab or a thick skin.

* * *

The ability to meet Sir Murray's demand for a grass roots appointee to the Legislative Council was a vindication of the effectiveness and reach of the City District Officers scheme. It was only because it had an officer with the political nous of Michael Sze in place in Kwun Tong to identify a potential candidate.

A few years earlier, Sze had passed a rigorous recruitment process to become an Administrative Officer. He personified what City District Officers were meant to do by familiarising himself with the problems, aspirations, moods and personalities in Kwun Tong. He proved a thoroughly fine and talented officer and many more like him were needed by the administration.

And yet, in 1973, Sir Murray had issued instructions that the recruitment standards for Administrative Officers should be watered down so that "more bodies" could be found to fill vacant posts. Any less capable officer than Sze would probably not have unearthed a Wong Lam at such short notice. In the art of governance, quality always mattered more than quantity.

Anyone reflecting upon the Wong Lam episode would no doubt begin to detect certain incongruities and illogicalities in some of the administration's initiatives and policies. For instance, if getting a grass roots person into the legislature was a good thing, why stop at one? The experiment with Wong Lam had been a substantial success. So why not more grass roots members? A fisherman from the people living on fishing junks perhaps, or a female factory worker doing double shifts in one of the colony's growing hive of factories. After all, more than one fig leaf would be required to disguise the unseemliness and exploitative nature of neo-liberal capitalistic politics.

The legislative stipend that had been put in place represented more than what any grass roots person could normally earn. A fisherman might have observations about diminishing fish stock and marine pollution while a female factory worker might comment at first hand on the real impact of International Labour Organisation conventions on protecting women and young persons in industrial undertakings.

The passage of a law in 1972 making Chinese an official second language would also remove the old argument about legislators needing to know English. What was the sense in having two official languages if one had to be restricted for use under certain circumstances? It could well be that many expatriate Official members would be left at sea if people began speakong in Chinese. They would then have to rely on an interpreter, just as most of the population had to do for long decades.

Ever since the founding of the colony, Chinese brought before a court to face allegation for various crimes had to face proceedings conducted in a language alien to them. They could only gain an inkling of what they were up against through court interpreters of limited skill. It was not until 1976 that the first Chinese lawyer managed to get appointed as a Supreme Court judge. It seemed about time expatriate policy makers got a taste of their own medicine.

What Sir Murray's private attitude might have been towards using Chinese as a second official language remains uncertain to this day. For the record, English appeared to have reigned supreme in bureaucratic dealings throughout his watch.

Naturally, facility in the use of any language had to be inculcation through the local educational system. This would require massive massive reform for the existing system was an unholy patchwork of government, private and aided institutions, riddled with histories of religious or political proselytising, and hardly restricted in their choice of language as a medium of instruction. Teaching standards also varied greatly in schools, as did the level of fees being charged.

The system had been overseen for decades by an Education Department headed by expatriates. Yet no systematic attempt had been made to rationalise and regulate such a colonist and lackadaisical system. One of its drawbacks was that students from poorer families would be disadvantaged because they would encounter difficulties gaining access to the better and more expensive schools.

Syllabuses were antiquated and quixotic. The teaching of modern Chinese history, for example, had been suppressed for decades. That might have been an automatic reflex for those in charge of education, built upon their centuries-long imperial policy of dividing to rule. Such an approach hardly encouraged the development of a sense of Chinese identity in the face of economic and political changes looming on the horizon.

My ancestors had always been intimately involved in the problems of education. My paternal great-grandfather has come to the colony as a teacher soon after its establishment whilst my maternal grandfather, Anglican Bishop Mok Shau-Tsang, was massively involved in providing education in Hong Kong and Kwangtung. A secondary school named after him is still thriving in Tai Po today. My Eighth Granduncle was the owner of a Chinese secondary school in Hong Kong and he had engaged my father to be its headmaster for a number of years.

I myself had been a secondary school teacher for two years but I had not been given much responsibility for dealing with education policies after entering the civil service.

* * *

It was in that semi-befuddled state, disheartened over my own inability to make any significant change to the society to which I belonged, that I found myself appointed as Secretary for Economic Services in June of 1977. Simultaneously, I was made a member of the Legislative Council under Royal Instructions.

* * *

I soon discovered that becoming Secretary for Economic Services necessitated my submitting myself to two sets of bureaucratic protocols — one very much out of the public eye and the other on full display.

The hidden one was known as "positive vetting". It involved a detailed security check on my private and public life, to determine whether I had committed peccadilloes and indiscretions which might render me liable to blackmail and to assess whether any secret information coming across my desk might be leaked to unauthorised persons or politically hostile parties.

I was therefore required to supply the Special Branch with a complete list of my family members, together with their dates of birth, current addresses and occupations. Next, I had to provide full details of the schools and universities I had attended and the qualifications obtained, together with relevant dates. And then my employment history, again with names of employers and dates. Finally, a list of all the clubs, associations and other organisations that I was or had been a member of, again with dates and details.

It was a thoroughly tedious exercise. I suspected what was really required were the names of organisations I had joined in a personal capacity, like the trade union called the Senior Non-Expatriate Officers Association and the Hong Kong Jockey Club. But out of a sense of mischief to inflict as much

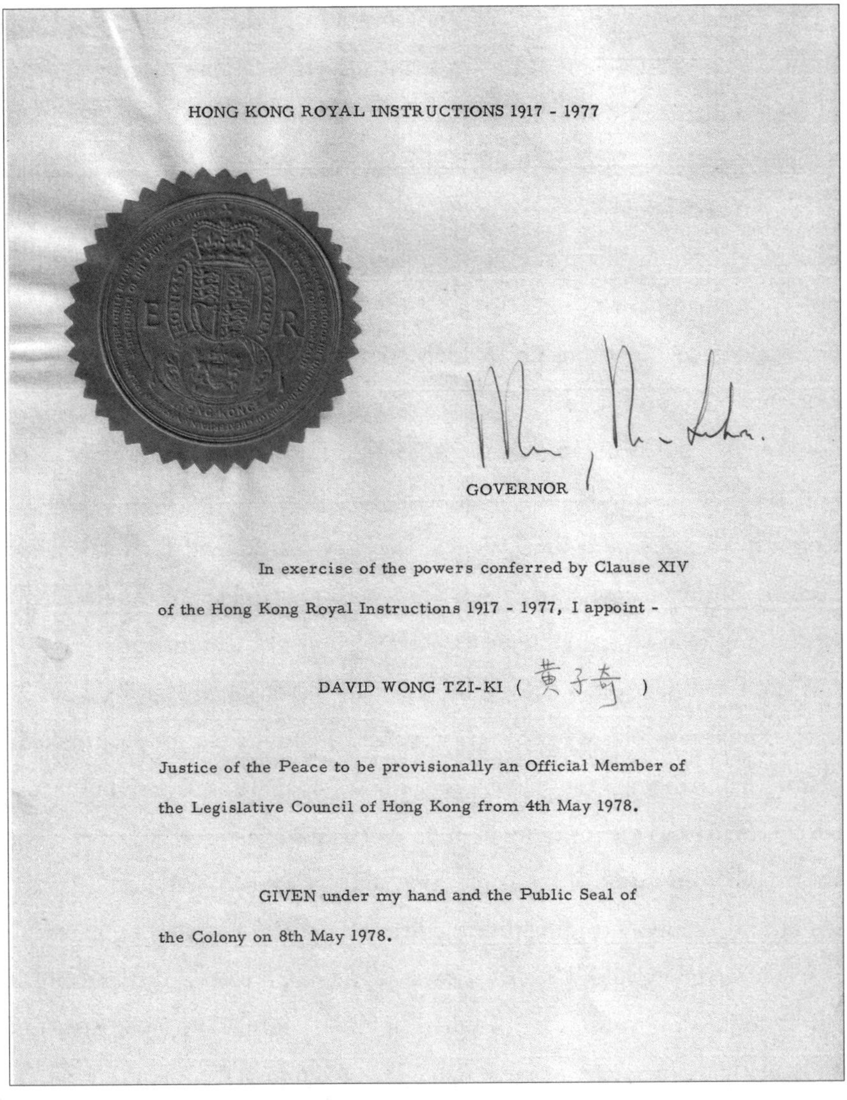

HONG KONG ROYAL INSTRUCTIONS 1917 - 1977

GOVERNOR

In exercise of the powers conferred by Clause XIV of the Hong Kong Royal Instructions 1917 - 1977, I appoint -

DAVID WONG TZI-KI (黄子奇)

Justice of the Peace to be provisionally an Official Member of the Legislative Council of Hong Kong from 4th May 1978.

GIVEN under my hand and the Public Seal of the Colony on 8th May 1978.

My first letter of appointment to the Legislative Council, signed by Sir Murray MacLehose under Public Seal.

work as possible on the so-called intelligence apparatchiks, I stuck in all the organisations the government had ever appointed me to, beginning with the secretaryship of the Hong Kong War Memorial Fund Committee.

The list was long indeed, running from membership on the Film Censorship Review Board and the Port Welfare Committee to being the Alternate Hong

Kong Representative on the Board of Governors of the Asian Development Bank. I also included my stints on management boards as diverse as those of the Productivity Council, the Export Credit Insurance Corporation, the Tourist Association and the Industrial Estates Corporation.

How that *pot-pourri* of facts demanded of me could possibly determine the likelihood or unlikelihood of my becoming a security risk was beyond me, unless the material was intended to form the basis for later interrogations. Otherwise, they might just as well have resorted to reading tea leaves or the markings on a tortoise shell.

Curiously, no demand was made for me to supply a list of my close associates or bosom friends, although both Mike Clinton, the Deputy Colonial Secretary, and the Defence Secretary had known for years I had been having regular social contacts with various members of the decidedly left-leaning Hong Kong Chinese General Chamber of Commerce.

Since I had not been asked about personal relationships, I felt I should be as reticent as possible. What could I have said about my patriotic journalistic mentor, Hon-Kit, and his wife Frances, for example, whose whereabouts had been a mystery to me for more than 28 years? And what of all those damsels I had been consorting with during my search for a wife? Neither did I want the Special Branch intruding into the lives of my *mah-jong* playing partners. It would certainly have been a betrayal of the confidences of friendship if I were to pass on to third parties their opinions and private thoughts. And particularly to operatives of some shadowy foreign intelligence outfit.

The efficacy of the methods used by such operatives had always appeared dubious to me. They often seemed unable to see beyond their own noses. How else to explain away such notorious cases like Burgess and Maclean and the Cambridge Five?

My own experience while undergoing the much lower level of vetting to join the Administrative Service had already demonstrated their ineptness. No one appeared to have taken any notice of my paternal grandfather's active involvement in the 1911 Revolution to overthrow the Ching Dynasty. Nor did anyone raise a question about my mother's work in the Canton office of Borodin, the Russian Comintern agent sent to China in the early 1920s. Of more recent vintage were the number of meals I had shared with the Soviet Assistant Cultural attaché in London's Chinatown. The least said I could get away with the better.

Experiences later on in my civil service career only provided more evidence of their general incompetence. I shall reveal details of those sorry episodes in a subsequent chapter of this book.

Shortly after I had supplied the information demanded, two middle-aged Chinese Special Branch officers asked for an appointment to see me at my office. For a moment, I was fearful they might ask for the names of political and sexual associates.

The honey trap was a staple in espionage. Few red-blooded males could resist the temptations of a beautiful woman for long. Men could often become just putty in the hands of a real beauty. My father had been a sucker for one for most of his life and in all probability I must have inherited a goodly batch of his genes. Before the officers showed up, therefore, I made up my mind I would refuse to cooperate on questions about my relationships with either women or close friends.

Each individual had to retain certain parts of his life as private and sacred. Governments should not be allowed to gain access to them in the name or national security or some other high-sounding purpose. If the Hong Kong authorities insisted upon my divulging all aspects of my private life, then it could go and find someone else to be the Secretary for Economic Services.

It transpired the Special Branch officers only wanted to ask a few supplementary questions on matters of no great moment. They then went away, apparently satisfied with my answers. I assumed I had passed because I had not been abruptly tossed out of the post.

As an aside, there had been strong gossip in Hong Kong that when Philip

Haddon-Cave was appointed Financial Secretary in 1971, he steadfastly refused to submit himself to positive vetting. One could only guess at why he should have taken that stance. Nonetheless he did acquire a knighthood, which came with the office, and was later promoted to Chief Secretary.

As another aside, it might be worth recording that in 1993, when Mrs. Anson Chan was the first Chinese to be appointed as Chief Secretary, there was still an attempt to limit her access to secret documents on the grounds she had not been positively vetted. Why that issue should have arisen in respect of Mrs. Chan when it had not been for Haddon-Cave is something readers will have to draw their own conclusions on.

In somehow sneaking through the positive vetting myself, I still had no illusion I would ever get to see any of those Whitehall communications marked "For British Eyes Only". But I did get to see a number of "Top Secret" documents, including a memo from the Commissioner of Police once every few months restricted to only the Chief Secretary, the Financial Secretary and the Secretary for Economic Services.

That memo listed the names of society notables currently under investigation by the police for alleged criminal activities. I imagined the three recipients of the memo were being alerted because they must have been deemed the most likely to officiate at ribbon-cutting and other business and community functions. It would not have looked right if one of them had been caught on camera clinking champagne glasses with a suspect only to have the culprit appear soon afterwards in handcuffs and charged with some serious crime.

Some of the names on the list surprised me. I was acquainted with a handful of them, though none had been a personal friend. So far as I could recall, the majority of those named were never actually charged or prosecuted, possibly due to insufficient evidence to prove crimes beyond reasonable doubt.

* * *

The second protocol I had to go through before I could take my seat in the Legislative Council was to publicly swear allegiance to the British Crown. That did not represent any philosophical or political impediment for me. While some diehard anti-colonialists might regard taking such an oath as an act of collaboration, I did not feel that way.

Although I was a Chinese nationalist of the small "n" variety and did not relish having to work for foreign masters in an alienated piece of my own country, I had already sold my toss when I signed up to become an Administrative Officer.

So far as I was concerned, the Chinese government had accepted the occupation of Hong Kong as a problem left over by history, to be tackled when "the time was right". Additionally, in 1958 the Chinese Premier, Chou En-Lai, had elaborated to the then British Prime Minister, Harold MacMillan, through private channels that any attempt by Britain to turn Hong Kong into a self-governing dominion like Singapore would be considered by China as "a very unfriendly act". In other words, China was prepared to see the city remaining a British colony until it considered the time appropriate for dealing with the issue.

Those unambiguous official Chinese declarations were good enough for me. I thought that any attempt by an individual citizen to buck that geopolitical reality would be pointless. It would be as idiotic as a Swiss Guard sacrificing his life for the Bourbons by defending a staircase in the Tulleries.

Furthermore, Britain had undertaken before the United Nations to rule all non-self-governing territories under the Union Jack in the interests of the people of those territories. In 1972, however, just as soon as China was admitted into the United Nations, the country insisted that Hong Kong and Macau be deleted from the United Nations list of colonies, making clear it would never countenance independence for either territory. Britain did not object to the Chinese move. So long as Britain kept broadly to its stated intentions, I saw little difficulty in keeping my oath of allegiance to the British Crown.

History has shown that even with the best will in the world, conflicts of interest between the metropolitan powers and colonies would inevitably arise. When Hong Kong became more industrialised, for example, its textile exports grew by leaps and bounds, threatening jobs in the mills of Lancashire. The British government could hardly ignore the complaints of its own voters. So restrictions had to be placed on the importation of Hong Kong textiles. But Hong Kong textile workers also had to make a living. So some appropriate level of restriction had to be worked out to satisfy both parties. That sort of occurrence was common in many other areas of inter-governmental relationships as well.

Sir John Cowperthwaite, as the Financial Secretary of the time, had fought legendary battles with Whitehall over such matters as cost-sharing for stationing the British garrison in Hong Kong and the Whitehall requirement for the colony to keep its reserves in Sterling when that currency was prone to instability and devaluation.

I myself, following another example set by Sir John, had had repeated tussles with London in the sphere of civil aviation landing rights. The approach I had adopted throughout was that I was being paid by Hong Kong taxpayers and it was my duty to fight for the best interests of the colony.

The one qualm I had over serving on the Legislative Council was that I would be placed in the unwelcomed limelight. While some of my colleagues might well enjoy that sort of attention, it went against my own grain. I much preferred remaining the traditional civil servant, faceless and anonymous, operating behind the scenes to serve up the most workable options I could think of for my political masters.

But in today's world of spin, propaganda, expediency, half-truths, total lies and the sped up nefarious engineering of consent, it is very difficult for a civil servant to remain somehow untarnished.

* * *

During the course of 1978, at the personal level I had to have one of those awkward conversations every father had to conduct with his son. No, it was not about the birds and the bees; rather it was about financing a university education of his choice.

My eldest son, Tien-Kuen, was completing his secondary education at the time and he expressed a desire to study architecture. He was the most intelligent of my three sons. But he had also inherited from me a streak of stubbornness and from his mother a disinclination to accept any opinion at variance with his own.

A couple of years earlier, it had been necessary for him to choose whether to enter the art stream or the science stream in secondary school. He favoured the science stream, simply because his maternal grandparents had planted in him the notion he should aim to become a doctor. They had encouraged that idea to console him over his frequent illnesses as a child. They said becoming a doctor would enable him to look after himself.

My observations told me that Tien-Kuen was not suited to medicine or to any other scientific field. He did not have that attitude of systematic doubt that was required. Moreover, he was of a squeamish disposition. He would panic at the sight of blood. Even the squawking of chickens frightened him. I doubted if he could handle the dissections of frogs and other small animals in biology classes.

I felt that the art stream would be more suitable for him. He was naturally fond of music, painting and reading. I suggested the art stream for him but he would not hear of it. So I allowed him to proceed as he had wanted. After three or four months, however, he found he indeed could not cope with the requirements of the science stream. He was forced to switch back to the art stream.

Against that background, his stated desire to study architecture also struck me as misguided. In an era when choking Stygian mega-cities were all the rage across the globe and when architects had to be largely in thrall to profit-gouging developers, there left little scope for architectural creativity. To my way of thinking, mega-cities were to people what carnivorous flowers were to insects. They both lure victims into their midst before devouring them.

But I feared that if I attempted such an exposition, my son would take it as another pouring of cold water on his choice of subject. He was, after all, still in his teens and there was every prospect that his mind had not been finally made up.

So instead of talking about any of the dehumanising uglinesses in modern urban life and the progressive abandonment of thousands of years of Chinese architectural traditions, I just said: "University should be no problem. There's a fairly respectable architectural faculty at one of the local universities. That should do nicely."

"I want to study in America," Tien-Kuen interjected quickly.

"But why? What can you learn there that you cannot learn here? If you're intending to practise here, local knowledge will be very important."

"Haven't thought that far ahead," my son replied. "I just want to study in America. You studied there; why shouldn't I?"

"Yes, I did study there. But I did it off my own bat. My father did not spend a single cent on me. I can support you for university locally but I can't afford financing studies in America."

Tien-Kuen turned sullen. "You're being very unfair, Dad," he countered. "How can you say you can't afford to send me to America when you can afford to lavish money on keeping racehorses? Isn't a son's education more important than keeping racehorses?"

I had not expected that line of attack. It jolted me a little. But because of his predisposition to see things only from his own point of view, there were things that needed to be aired sooner or later. The present seemed as good a time as any. So I took a deep breath and plunged ahead.

"When a man makes an assertion," I began, "he ought to be sure of his facts. It's true I've been keeping racehorses in partnership with Uncle Fung. But if you had investigated the nature of my hobby more thoroughly, you would have discovered that I never spent a penny on it. The reason is that I've been lucky enough to draw two good racing propositions. And I have also been prudent enough in managing them in such a way as to derive a small stream of legitimate income from them. I can show you the accounts I've kept for Uncle Fung, if you wish. Without that additional income, my financing even your university studies locally would have been a challenge.

"There is another factor you may not be aware of. Your grandfather has moved into a home for senior citizens in Singapore. I, along with some of my siblings, have to chip in each month to see that he can live out the autumn of his life in reasonable comfort. After that and our normal household outgoings, there's not much left in a civil servant's salary.

"It's also true, I have to admit, that if forced to it, I could dig into savings and borrow money for you to study in America. But that would be at the expense of your brothers. When the time comes for them to go to university, there will be nothing left. As a father, I have to be even-handed. I cannot ignore their interests. Nor my own. After retirement, I will no longer be entitled to live at Palm Court with a highly subsidised rent. Where would I find the money to put a roof over my own head?"

I paused deliberately, to give Tien-Kuen an opportunity for counter-arguments. But he only looked down glumly on the floor and said nothing. I had little financial room to manoeuvre but I suspected Tien-Kuen, being quite intelligent, had more than one strand to his strategy.

When he remained sullen, I summarised the existing position. "I'm sorry I can't meet your expectations," I said. "I wish it were otherwise. But I really believe it is better for you to attend university here, where our family has had its roots for the last four generations. The young always think the grass is greener elsewhere. That's often an illusion. If you insist on studying in America, then all I can give you is roughly what it would cost me if you were studying here, plus some pocket money and a small additional sum for incidentals. You'll have to find the rest yourself, through gaining a scholarship, getting a bank loan, doing some part-time work or whatever. That's the best I can do. Please think it over."

Tien-Kuen nodded and our conversation ended.

A few weeks later, Tien-Kuen told me he would accept my terms. He said his maternal grandparents had agreed to make up the difference.

That outcome was pretty much what I had anticipated. I did not know — and did not ask — how Tien-Kuen had sold that issue to his grandparents, then living in Dallas in Texas. He had always been their favourite grandchild. Having secured their backing, he accordingly headed for Texas the following year.

But, as I had anticipated, he did not end up studying architecture at all. He went in for linguistics instead and afterwards worked in academia in America and elsewhere.

* * *

At the beginning of 1979, I did another stint as Secretary for Economic Services and that made me an *ex officio* member of a powerful Secretariat body known as the Land Development Policy Committee. Land had to be at the heart of all major Hong Kong developments because land was a scarce commodity. The committee was chaired by the Secretary for the Environment. Other important players, like the Director of Public Works and the Finance Branch, were also on it.

At a meeting of the committee, a paper was presented suggesting approval for engaging consultants to study the feasibility of installing a reverse osmosis plant to augment the colony's water supplies. Reverse osmosis was then a technology just coming on stream, purportedly able to turn sewage into potable water.

Water had always been a critical resource for Hong Kong. When rainfall became erratic and drought conditions prevailed in 1955, piped water supplies had to be rationed to four hours every second day. It got even worse in 1963 and 1967, when supplies came for only three hours once in four days! Those had been very distressing experiences. In addition, the city had one of the highest per capita consumption of water for comparable cities in the world.

Therefore, to ensure adequate supplies, the administration began a programme of building reservoirs like those at Plover Cove in 1960 and at High Island in1969. But with the rapidly expanding needs of both the population and the industrial sector, it proved a losing battle. Suitable areas for reservoirs and catchment areas were running out.

Additional supplies, of course, could be pumped over from across the border. But a section of the administration could not reconcile itself to the decline in Britain's power. Moreover, framed by the adversarial attitudes spawned by the Cold War, it was strategically abhorrent to rely wholly on a Communist regime for a commodity as critical as water. Even for rice, a quota had been imposed to limit importation from China, in spite of such a move being contrary to the free market principles of capitalism.

The rice quota was actually just a flea bite so far as the Chinese were concerned. They had so many other levers of power to manipulate — if they were so inclined. This was particularly the case since they enjoyed dominant positions in respect of other daily necessities like fruit, vegetables, eggs, poultry and meats.

Nonetheless, an agreement in respect of water was somehow reached with the Chinese in the early 1960s, for them to supply water from the East River. The negotiations must have been confidential because I could not recall any account about them appearing in the media. I also did not know who had led the British side because I was not in the civil service at that time.

It transpired subsequently that the Chinese had been more than willing to supply water free of charge, for they regarded the people of the colony as compatriots. But the British insisted upon paying, lest the Chinese exploited the gift of water for propaganda purposes.

I suspected the leader of the British side must have been an expatriate, for he apparently had taken no account of the inauspicious funereal implications of "buying water." In ancient times, it was required of the eldest son of a family to fetch water to personally cleanse the body of his father before burial. He would draw water from some clear stream or spring nearby and make some symbolic payment for taking the water. So the act of buying water evoked rather unpleasant connotations.

Sometimes I could not help reflecting how two human beings, not tied up in the straitjackets of protocols and hubris of two opposing political and economic systems, would have handled a neighbourly gesture of a gift. Within Chinese culture, the only appropriate way of responding to a gift would be to accept it with due courtesy and to offer a similar gift in return. It had to be bad form to turn it into an arm's length commercial transaction.

The two human beings would also be one people, bound by ties of blood and common modes of behaviour. Hardly a single family in Hong Kong would be without relatives in Kwangtung Province and vice versa. Although governments could only be operated by individuals, it appeared that when they operated as officials, they could only bring out the worst qualities in the human personality. To coexist harmoniously implied the building of trust, not the creation of fears and suspicions. I supposed until mankind learn that, the world would continue to be in its present mess.

In any case, a deal was eventually done for initially buying 5,000 million gallons of water a year. Later the amount was increased and today China is regularly supplying in excess of 70% of the water required by Hong Kong. However, suspicions about the Chinese still bubbled on regardless. Those fears caused the administration to build as an experiment the world's largest desalination plant near Tuen Mun. The plant became operational in 1975 but it soon proved economically unviable. It was mothballed, then dismantled and finally sold off to a Middle Eastern country.

* * *

It was against such a history that the proposal for a feasibility study for a reverse osmosis plant at Tseung Kwan O was tabled before the Land Development Policy Committee in 1979. The plant was projected to eventually supply 10% of the colony's water needs

The Secretary for the Environment then serving as chairman of the LDPC was a portly expatriate with thick rounded shoulders and rather loose and flabby jowls. He spoke with a slight stutter. He had risen to high office on a talent which I singularly lacked — the ability to agree always with the predilections and opinions of his superiors.

When I read the paper before the committee, several thoughts crossed my mind. First, feasibility studies, particularly on expensive projects, had a peculiar way of turning into highly recommended and thoroughly worthwhile projects after such studies. Great caution was therefore needed in examining them. I feared the reverse osmosis plant might turn into another expensive white elephant, just like the desalination plant.

Secondly, the project was not expected to come on stream till well after the New Territories lease had expired in 1997. Thirdly, no matter what the scientific evidence might be, the Hong Kong public would not take kindly to the notion of drinking reconstituted sewage. And finally, there was no mention in the paper of the Chinese position over supplying water. Even after the reverse osmosis plant had become functional, it would only meet 10% of the city's water requirements, against what was then being supplied from the East River.

So when discussions opened on the subject, I asked why the option of simply asking the Chinese for more water had not been included for consideration in the paper.

"We did ask the Chinese but they have refused to supply us any more than the current amount," the Secretary for the Environment replied.

"Then that should be stated in the proposal, for that would constitute a powerful argument for proceeding with this study," I said.

The Secretary for the Environment then half-mumbled his agreement.

But I was actually quite astounded by his revelations. I had no responsibility for dealing with the Chinese on an official level on any subject whatsoever. The normal channel was between the Political Advisor and the New China News Agency, which served as the *de facto* Chinese diplomatic mission in Hong Kong. But I found it hard to believe that the Chinese would refuse to supply more water. Something had to be seriously amiss.

If such a request had indeed been refused, then it could be a harbinger of some bigger and more serious move against the city. Of course, it could also be just a local aberration, like in 1962, when a regional commander decided to withdraw a Peoples Liberation Army unit from guard duties along a section of the China-Hong Kong land border for other purposes. That led to thousands of Chinese immigrants charging across that stretch of the border, to create chaos on the Hong Kong side. In either eventuality, I became deeply worried, though I could not figure out the kind of future in store. In my state of speculative ignorance, I decided it best to keep my apprehensions to myself.

* * *

The moment I got back to my office after the LDPC meeting, I rang my friend and favourite *mah-jong* playing partner Ip Yeuk-Lam. Ip was the long-standing Vice-President of the left-leaning and powerful Hong Kong Chinese General Chamber of Commerce. He had superb mainland connections because he was a prominent member of the Kwangtung Peoples Congress.

"Yeuk-Lam, I need you to do something urgently for me," I said over the phone. "Please contact your connections in Canton and see if you can sniff out whether there is some concerted political move afoot against Hong Kong."

"What's making you think so?" Yeuk-Lam asked.

"I'll come to your office after work and explain more fully. But please take your soundings as soon as possible."

* * *

"Everything's smooth as a mirror; can't find the slightest ripple of anything brewing," Yeuk-Lam said, when I arrived at his office later. "What's this all about?"

I then told him what had transpired at the LDPC that morning.

"Sounds quite implausible," Yeuk-Lam said, after I had finished my narrative. "I can double-check with Canton again tomorrow and touch base with the New China News Agency as well. If a request has been made, it should go through the NCNA; and if it had been refused, I would certainly have heard about it."

"Please do that. Something is beginning to smell here. Let's meet for lunch tomorrow, to see what else you might find out."

* * *

Over lunch, Yeuk-Lam confirmed that all his sources had denied having ever received any request from the British for increased water supplies. "Why this reverse osmosis?" he asked. "There's already a pipeline in place, complete with pumping stations. More water is no problem at all. What are the British playing at?"

"I don't know," I said. "But something funny's going on. The current chairman of the LDPC is an intellectual lightweight. He has neither the wit nor the guts to pull a stunt like this off his own bat. He must have had a nod from higher up, perhaps from Whitehall, if there's a British consortium behind the project."

"Why not challenge him to come clean?"

"How? I can't tell a senior colleague to his face he has lied about the Chinese refusing to give further supplies without producing compelling evidence. And I cannot use the facts you have given me without getting into serious trouble for breaching a host of Security Regulations. I'm not authorised to have dealings with left-wing organisations, let alone Chinese officialdom. Proceedings before the LDPC are also strictly confidential. I could be roasted alive for disclosing them. My main concern is to see this matter properly discussed and assessed and not to have public money wasted on another hare-brained scheme. And so long as Hong Kong remains lacking in good investigative journalists with a nose for sniffing out government secrets, such issues will forever remain hidden."

We discussed several ways of trying to get around the problem of disclosing the Chinese position without revealing the unorthodox way I had come by my information. But no story we could concoct seemed very convincing or plausible. Eventually, Yeuk-Lam asked: "Are you friendly with S.Y. Chung?"

"Yes, of course," I replied. "Known him for years."

Dr. S.Y. Chung was the senior Unofficial member on the Legislative Council. He was a mechanical engineer by training and had become an important industrialist. He had worked tirelessly for years to improve the welfare and livelihood of the Hong Kong people. In recognition of his efforts, he had been made a Commander of the Most Excellent Order of the British Empire in 1975 and had recently been awarded a knighthood by the Queen.

"S.Y. has a number of good friends in the General Chamber," Yeuk-Lam said. "How about we organise a small and cosy dinner to celebrate his knighthood? You and a senior member of the NCNA, both known to him, could be invited to join in. It could then be represented that the two of you fortuitously stumbled into a conversation about water supplies from China during dinner. Would that work?"

I thought for a moment. "It just might," I replied.

And so it came about that a few evenings later I attended a dinner party at the Chinese General Chamber Club to celebrate S.Y.'s knighthood. Mr. Ki Fung, the Deputy Director of the New China News Agency also attended. It was indeed a small party, consisting of no more than eight or nine people. Yeuk-Lam arranged it so that Mr. Ki and I would be seated next to each other.

I ought to make clear at this point that neither S.Y. nor any of the other participants — except Yeuk-Lam — had the slightest inkling of what Mr. Ki and I were up to.

* * *

When I got back to my office the following morning, I wrote what was known as a confidential "loose minute" to the Governor, routing the message via the Political Advisor.

The Political Advisor of the time was Mr. David Wilson, who later became Lord Wilson, after serving a stint as Governor of Hong Kong.

I said in the minute that I had attended a private dinner party the previous evening and happened to find myself seated next to Mr. Ki Fung, the Deputy Director of the New China News Agency. After a few drinks, I could not resist complaining to Mr. Ki about China's meanness in turning down Hong Kong's request for some extra supplies of water.

The Secretary for the Environment had stated at a recent meeting of the Land Development Policy Committee that the Chinese had refused to supply extra water. That had been the justification given for a proposal to engage consultants to consider the feasibility of constructing a reverse osmosis plant in Hong Kong.

Mr. Ki had reacted with astonishment to my remarks, I reported. He responded categorically that no request for extra supplies of water had ever been received from the British. Should such a request be made, China would certainly deal with it very sympathetically.

I, of course, had no responsibility for communicating with the Chinese or for maintaining local water supplies. It appeared to me that there might have been miscommunication or misunderstanding somewhere along the line. It might perhaps be in the public interest for whoever was responsible for such matters to investigate further and to seek clarification, following up with Mr. Ki if necessary, I concluded.

Neither the Political Advisor nor the Governor acknowledged the receipt of my minute or replied to it. But I nevertheless had gained my objective. Shortly afterwards, the proposal for engaging consultants for a feasibility study on installing a reverse osmosis plant in Hong Kong was dropped. A new agreement was instead completed with China for supplying increased quantities of water to Hong Kong.

* * *

I have recently heard rumours that the possibility of constructing a reverse osmosis plant in Hong Kong has again surfaced. Many circumstances must have changed since 1979, not the least of which would be the increased pollution of the waters of the East River. It might still be worth considering whether it would be more beneficial to Hong Kong in the longer term to invest in a reverse osmosis plant or to invest in helping the Chinese authorities to reduce pollution in the East River, since that remained the city's main source of water.

CHAPTER 14

The Cabotage Route

IN CIVIL AVIATION PARLANCE, a cabotage route is one providing regular air services linking two points within a single country. In the case of the United Kingdom, for instance, it might be a route running between, say, London and Glasgow. Such a route would normally be within the gift of the nation's Civil Aviation Authority to a domestic airline, with foreign carriers being barred.

The vagaries of ancient imperial misadventures, however, had left the route between London and Hong Kong as a cabotage route as well, at the dispensation of the British authorities. The reason was because a colony was considered in civil aviation terms as a part of the ruling state, hence just another "domestic" point. The route was thus awarded to the British state-owned carrier BOAC on a monopoly basis.

After World War II, when civil aviation was in its infancy, the regulatory regime was fairly ad hoc. It was not till 1972 that a Civil Aviation Authority was set up in Britain to formalise the right to register and license operators on the cabotage route.

As Britain gradually recovered from the ravages of war and as Hong Kong prospered and opened up more trading opportunities for Britain, traffic between the two cabotage points rapidly grew. Air travel ceased to be the preserve of the wealthy and the elite. An expanding middle class in both territories sought to enjoy the perks of the good life. Rampant advertising by the cult of conspicuous consumption soon gave rise to burgeoning hordes of the cola-guzzling and souvenir-hunting package tourists as well.

The state-owned BOAC, operating within a cosily captive market, was less than responsive to the changes taking place. The shortage of state capital as well as balance of payments constraints compounded the problem. In any case, the fact that the airline was still using flying boats in 1950 when other major airlines had already switched to more modern aircraft was a reflection of the laid-back outlook of its management. It was not surprising therefore that the company did not achieve profitability till late in the 1960s.

Faced with that situation, the airline tried to squeeze additional income out of existing customers. In the circumstance of the time — if my memory for details has not faded as badly as some old sepia photographs — the rough rule of thumb for measuring a passenger flight's break-even point was held to be just under half of its fare-paying seating capacity. Or, to put it another way, a passenger plane could theoretically fly off half-empty and still turn in a slender profit. Every extra fare-paying seat occupied above that point would be added jam. A service regularly flying with a near-full load of paying customers would be sending its managers singing all the way to the bank.

In order to secure that desirable outcome, BOAC resorted to keeping the number of flights on the route static in order to boost load factors. To do so in the face of growing demand meant a better chance for getting bigger loads. Some flights might be fully booked and customers needing to fly might be forced to travelling on flights not entirely convenient for them. But in a monopoly situation, customers had little alternative.

BOAC was stingy in other ways as well. When other airlines flying in and out of Hong Kong on more competitive routes began providing free alcoholic refreshments, BOAC stuck to serving only free soft drinks on the cabotage route. Passengers who desired alcoholic refreshments had to pay extra. A charge was also levied for the use of headphones to listen to in-flight music or to watch other forms of entertainment.

It stoutly resisted the emerging long-haul practice of other airlines in handing out complimentary gift sets made up of a toothbrush, a tiny tube of toothpaste, a cake of soap, a plastic comb, a face towel and an eye shade. Its pre-packed airplane meals came close to being uninviting for many Asian travellers. For example, the wedges of English Cheddar meant to round off each meal were often left untouched on trays.

But its dismal record for punctuality was its greatest defect. If one of its flights arrived or departed strictly on schedule, it became almost a cause for celebration. Public complaints sprouted as abundantly as crocuses in spring. They were given voice even in the colony's Legislative Council. Virtually everyone who had ever travelled regularly on BOAC ended up with some horror story to tell. A joke of long standing currency was that the initials BOAC stood for "better on a camel".

In 1971, BOAC began a rebranding exercise. It merged with British European Airways to form British Airways. By 1974 BOAC was dissolved. But the change in name hardly brought better service on the increasingly heavily used cabotage route.

I myself have had several trying experiences while flying on government business. One flight I took had to make an emergency landing in Madras because of engine failure. It took four days for a replacement engine to be flown out from London and to be fitted. My enforced stay in a middling Indian hotel left me with only one pleasant memory: I had somehow developed an enduring fondness for spicy Madras curries.

In 1978, I was on another flight to London when another engine failure occurred, necessitating yet another emergency landing. This time the landing was in Teheran, right when the city was in the midst of strikes and violent demonstrations aimed at overthrowing the Shah.

Because of the chaos, the airport authorities in Teheran did not quite know how to handle the emergency landing of a British aircraft. Perhaps they feared it might be a ruse, by either the Shah or the rebels, to fly in covert support. To play safe, the airport authorities refused to allow anyone to disembark pending instructions. All passengers had to remain on the aircraft parked on the airport tarmac, under the blistering Middle Eastern sun. Since the aircraft engines were malfunctioning, the air conditioning could not be turned on. The air in the cabin quickly became more fetid than the air inside an overcrowded Third World sweatshop. The only semblance of ventilation came from the opened exits for normal and emergency use.

As the temperature rose to oven pitch, children began to act up and cry. Many male passengers were not slow in discarding their jackets and shirts. Women passengers also began loosening their blouses and pulling up their skirts in a manner that was not quite ladylike and decidedly contrary to Islamic traditions. They would have gone further if the dictates of modesty had allowed. Only soft drinks were available to quench thirsts. No alcohol drinks could be provided. Bedlam soon reigned.

I had been scheduled to attend a meeting on civil aviation matters at the Ministry of Trade and Industry at 9.00 am on the following morning. I demanded of the purser that I be immediately transferred to the first available flight of any other airline leaving Teheran for London. The purser at first demurred, saying that many other passengers had made similar demands and it was not possible to meet them all.

I warned the purser, however, that if I missed the scheduled meeting with the Department of Trade and Industry the following morning, the repercussions would definitely be inimical to the interests of his airline. He consulted the captain and I was duly transferred to a Japan Airlines flight out.

But I had to leave without my luggage. I was told it would be delivered to my hotel after the plane itself got to London. Fortunately, I had my working papers in the briefcase I had as hand luggage. I gave the purser the address of my usual cheap but friendly bed-and-breakfast hotel in Sussex Gardens.

I managed to turn up at the Ministry of Trade and Industry in the nick of time but smelling as if I had spent the previous night on the tiles. My suitcase was not delivered till more than three days later. In the meantime I had to buy myself new shirts, underwear and toiletries. I could hardly imagine what my fellow passengers might have had to go through during that period.

My misadventures were by no means unique. Many other Hong Kong officials had been hampered by BOAC or British Airways delays in the execution of their duties.

My colleague Eric Ho, for instance, recorded in his memoirs, *Times of Change: A Memoir of Hong Kong's Governance*, that in 1950, when he was sent to London to be trained as an Inspector of Taxes, BOAC delayed his journey for two days in Cairo because of engine trouble. Later, in 1989, he got stuck for a whole day in Rangoon on an emergency landing due to another British Airways engine breakdown. On the second occasion, he had been on his way from Hong Kong to London, to transit to Oslo for textile negotiations with the Norwegian authorities.

* * *

Meanwhile, the economic advancements in Asian countries on the Pacific Rim caused their governments to establish state airlines as a symbol of national pride. A flag carrier, however, was too often an unsound investment. Governments could have often done better investing their limited resources in other nation-building endeavours like education and health services. If a country was developing satisfactorily, there would be no shortage of airlines from rich countries willing to fly passengers and freight into and out of such a destination.

Hong Kong was proof of that happy approach. There was no shortage of foreign airlines wishing to mount services to Hong Kong, except that Britain was reluctant to grant rights without getting something in return. The Hong Kong administration was content to leave a private company like

Cathay Pacific Airways to make the running on regional services in exchange for similar services by regional flag carriers. It noted with satisfaction that Cathay Pacific was thriving under competition, providing local employment opportunities and making a significant contribution to the wider domestic economy.

Over time, to control and regulate operators of air services based in Hong Kong, the government set up an independent statutory body known as the Air Transport Licensing Authority. It was given powers to "grant, revoke and suspend licences to carry passengers, cargo or mail by air for hire or reward on scheduled journeys." The Authority would also consider local needs such as capacity on particular routes, frequency of flights, the pricing of seats and other related matters. It was given the responsibility to look after the interests of the travelling public as well.

The Air Transport Licensing Authority, however, could not require a licence from aircraft registered elsewhere by some other competent authority and whose service had been subjected to air services agreements between governments. For such aircraft to operate in and out of Hong Kong, only an operating permit from the Hong Kong Director of Civil Aviation was required.

Before long, the state-owned airlines in regional countries started developing larger ambitions. They wanted — or at least their political masters wanted — the prestige of running long-haul services to the main European capitals. Being state-funded, they did not suffer from the same financial and other constraints as private airlines. London was high on their lists of favourite destinations. Former colonial links had something to do with it. In any case, a variety of long-haul routes were soon agreed between Britain and those countries.

As the number of long-haul routes grew between London and Asian capitals, Asian airlines naturally synchronised the schedules of their long-haul routes with those of their regional services, for ease of connecting flights to tap into potential long-haul customers from neighbouring countries.

By the same token, European countries also sought long-haul routes to a dynamic economic and financial powerhouse like Hong Kong. This sometimes necessitated an awkward three-cornered type of negotiations between London, the foreign country and Hong Kong.

Hong Kong had always been keen to have as many international services as possible for wider developmental purposes. But Britain tended to be more narrowly focused, on the balancing traffic rights alone. It would only grant rights if there were either compensating rights for British airlines or else payments in hard cash in lieu. Once rights had been obtained, European airlines would also co-ordinate their long-haul schedules with their short-haul European networks.

Those developments gradually ate into the traffic on the monopoly route for British Airways. Because a growing number of Hong Kong's travelling public found British Airways services unsatisfactory, they often flew on a Thai or Singapore plane to Bangkok or Singapore to take their direct connecting flights to London. Or else they would take a direct flight on Air France or Lufthansa to Paris or Frankfurt, before connecting with one of their short-haul regional flights to London. Though such truncated journeys might take slightly longer, at least they could travel in greater comfort, without jam-packed cabins, and with a better assurance of reaching their destinations on schedule.

* * *

With the arrival of Mrs. Margaret Thatcher at No. 10 Downing Street in 1979, her fascination with privatisation, market forces and other neo-liberal fixations led to the decision to open up the cabotage route between London and Hong Kong to competition between British airlines. Thus the monopoly granted to British Airways was lifted and other British airlines were invited to apply to conduct scheduled flights on the route. By then, other British airlines had arrived on the scene in the form of British Caledonian Airways and Laker Airways, the brainchild of Sir Freddie Laker who developed the Skytrain concept for budget travel.

British Caledonian was founded at the end of 1970, growing out of an earlier idea to expand Britain's aviation capacity with a "second force" independent of the state-controlled operators. It initially concentrated on developing passenger services across the lucrative trans-Atlantic routes. Little was known about the nature of British Caledonian services in Hong Kong. Laker Airways had its eye on bearded backpackers and the young and adventurous. They both wanted to fly to Hong Kong. But most in Hong Kong would prefer seeing a local company like Cathay Pacific given a chance on the route as well.

In addition, certain sections of the Hong Kong community had reservations over the type of people Laker Airways might bring. They held there were insufficient facilities to cater to budget tourists. The possibility of a growth in the number of seedy and illegally subdivided cubicles in buildings to accommodate their needs — like those being provided in Chungking Mansions on Nathan Road — worried them in the event of a fire. A fire did indeed occur at Chungking Mansions in 1970. The local attitude was predictably money-conscious and pragmatic. If outsiders had to flock in, why not go after the big spenders instead of tight-fisted backpackers?

Under the then existing rules, Cathay Pacific was considered a British airline. That qualified it to bid for a share on the cabotage route. Although the company had secured a trans-Pacific route to San Francisco, via Vancouver, during the Bermuda II negotiations, it saw at once that a route to London would be a far easier one to establish and make profitable. So Cathay Pacific put in a bid and I was sent to London to express the support of the Hong Kong administration.

Hearings were duly held by the Civil Aviation Authority in London. No one in Hong Kong was exactly sure how that authority normally arrived at decisions. But rumours soon flowed back through the bureaucratic grapevine that the CAA intended to award the route to only two airlines — British Airways, with its hub at Heathrow, and to British Caledonian, operating out of Gatwick.

Those indications — once confirmed but remaining still unannounced — came as a great disappointment for me. Implicit in that decision had to be my failure to persuade the powers-that-be in London of the economic and political importance into giving Cathay Pacific a fair crack at mounting a service. It went without saying that the news constituted an even greater disappointment for Cathay Pacific and its chairman, John Bemridge.

Bremridge soon found himself caught in an ethical bind. He had, since 1977, been made an Unofficial member of the Executive Council. Being an honourable man, he saw immediately a conflict of interests if he were to press the Hong Kong administration to do battle on his airline's behalf, even if that request came under the cloak of defending a wider Hong Kong interest. But he needed not to have worried because I had already decided to pick up the cudgel on the colony's behalf and — indirectly — on Cathay Pacific's.

It was clear to me that a public row would do nobody any good. With the inexorable approach of 1997, the political and emotional undercurrents in society were stirring. And yet, my reading of the available omens suggested that a mutually satisfactory resolution could not be reached without a degree of pressure from the public. The well-mannered exchanges of opinions through the sluggish bureaucratic machineries at both ends would not secure the desired result.

For me, Sir Murray was the fly in the ointment. I could seldom predict his reactions to any given situation. Of course, his responsibilities were infinitely broader than my own and he would have to juggle them according to his own judgement and priorities.

But if it came to some serious arm-wrestling with London, would he exert himself in the civil aviation sphere as determinately as Sir John Cowperthwaite had done? I seriously doubted it. He was too much of a protocol-observing diplomat. He would make the required gesture to London for local consumption, a weak and lukewarm one just enough to pass muster. But his heart would not be in it. If things turned out that way, then the prize would have slipped away even before the game had begun.

Sir Murray's relative lack of interest in this particular issue was understandable. It was not a thing of great moment for him. He had a far bigger hornet's nest to worry about. He had poked his finger precipitously into the feverish hives of corruption buzzing within the uniformed services of government, without first working through the possible permutations in a dynamic middle or end-game. He had chosen the police for his initial foray.

Shortly after Sir Murray's arrival in the colony, he had sought my opinion about corruption within the police. I had been circumspect in my reply, as any Chinese who knew his place ought to be. The police, just like other government departments, had been led by expatriates while the bulk of the rank and file was filled by Chinese. The usual impediments in language and culture patently existed, if not quite in spades then at least in clubs.

I did not know enough about the police, I said, and it would be far better if the Governor were to consult Administrative Officers who had served in that department. I had no idea whom the Governor consulted afterwards, nor the nature of the advice he had received. Hitherto, police corruption had been handled by an in-house unit within the police force. The results had been predictably unspectacular.

It had been well-recognised by society that the salaries of policemen on the beat, along with those of other civil servants, had been depressingly modest. Policemen had therefore over the years augmented their incomes by extracting bribes from those engaged in the so-called "victimless crimes" like illegal gambling and prostitution. Accordingly, the policemen and their families had long been able to enjoy a standard of living out of line with their official pay.

The syndicated nature of the corruption was so well organised that virtually every policeman up to at least the Godber level got regular envelopes stuffed with money.

In any case, the Governor decided in 1974 to appoint an Administrative Officer by the name of Jack Cater to head a brand new Independent Commission Against Corruption to tackle that long-standing scourge. Cater, later made a Chief Secretary, would be answerable only to the Governor.

It was unclear whether the Governor, before launching the Independent Commission, had ordered the Secretary for the Civil Service and the Commissioner for Police to review the police pay structure to reduce the temptation of bribes. Nor was it clear whether the police high command had issued warnings to staff unions that the old lackadaisical ways of dealing with corruption within the force was about to change. At least nothing had been openly revealed to the public.

I supposed it was only human nature for any new organisation to want to deliver quick and visible results. But it faced that old and recurring enforcement dilemma currently confronting the Chinese government — to tackle initially the tigers or the flies? Because flies were easier targets and could be found everywhere, the Commission's investigators went for the flies.

Suddenly, ordinary constables found their pasts catching up with them, while those higher up in the chain of command were left relatively untouched. The foot soldiers on the beat had to face not only imprisonment but also an immediate drastic cut in family income to cover the likes of mortgages, instalment payments for cars and the fees necessary to provide their children with the best education available. As the Independent Commission's investigators dug deeper and wider, morale plummeted.

By 1977, the writing was clearly on the wall. To avoid being sent to prison and placed among some of the very people they had helped put behind bars, half the force put their names to a petition to the government asking for an amnesty for past misdeeds. But Sir Murray turned the petition down. It was not revealed whether he had taken the decision off his own bat, because he was working according to his own game-plan, or whether he had been advised to do so by senior officials.

In either event, tensions within the force mounted rapidly. Six thousand policemen soon made a protest march on police headquarters. The then expatriate Commissioner of Police sneaked off through a back door to avoid confronting his own angry staff. The penny finally dropped within the administration. Someone had seriously misjudged the stakes in the game.

The next episode involved an armed group of policemen storming the offices of the Independent Commission Against Corruption and roughing up several of its investigative officers. The possibility of mutiny now filled the air.

Before turning down the petition for an amnesty, had the Governor and his advisors factored in such a possibility? Had consideration been given to using the British garrison to deal with a possible mutiny?

Those questions still remain not fully answered today. In 2005, Lord Owen, who was British Foreign Secretary at the time, revealed in an address at a meeting of the Overseas Service Pensioners' Association that Sir Murray had asked to see him in private in 1977 and explained that he had ordered the arrest of about 600 civil servants for corruption offences of various types. He now wished for an amnesty to be granted to at least 400 of them.

Sir Murray explained that unless that was done, he would no longer have the authority to govern and would have to resign within days. It was on that basis that Lord Owen agreed to an amnesty.

So it came about that Sir Murray announced a general amnesty in November, except for policemen who had committed the most serious offences. Sir Murray's decision was subsequently debated and, naturally, fulsomely supported in the House of Lords.

After the dust had settled, a mass purge of other corrupt civil servants outside the police force was carried out under Colonial Regulation 55.

For those unfamiliar with the arcane architecture of Colonial Regulations, I should explain that Regulation 55 specified that all officers held office only at the pleasure of the Crown. Should the Crown ever become displeased, then an officer can be got rid of without any further explanation or recourse. There used to exist other Regulations for dealing with an officer who might be accused of criminal or corrupt acts, such as bringing him to trial before a court of law. But Regulation 55 was often the Regulation of choice, for it obviated any washing of dirty linen in public and the judicial requirement to prove accusations beyond a reasonable doubt. No doubt Regulation 55 was a marvel of Anglo-Saxon law undimmed by the provisions of the Magna Carta.

Interesting questions have been left tantalisingly hanging in the air ever since. How did matters come to such a dangerous pass? Who had been calling the shots along the way? Had each move been a deliberate and calculated one? Or had the whole saga been played out by gut-feel and the seat of the pants?

To deny a petition for amnesty and then to be forced into an about-turn left a bad taste in the mouth. Would a government not lose its legitimacy to govern if it ever surrendered to violence? To give way before a violent mob would be an awful precedent to set. Any government allowing itself to be thus intimidated had to lose its right to govern. Sometimes, therefore, it had to be necessary to defend the security of a nation and its way of life by allowing blood to flow.

And after the tumult and shouting had died, why resort to Colonial Regulation 55 instead of bringing culprits in corruption cases before an open court? Had there been too many dirty deeds that could not bear the light of judicial enquiry?

The answers, I fear, would have to be extracted assiduously from whatever secret documents which might eventually emerge from the archives or from the accounts of those at the heart of such affairs. Those with a genuine interest in Hong Kong history would simply have to wait or else to start digging themselves.

* * *

Against such a background, I surmised that Sir Murray would not be enthusiastic over taking on Whitehall on a relatively unimportant civil aviation matter. Therefore, to ensure that a Hong Kong position be framed in terms I considered fitting, I decided to commit a little political arson, hoping that the flames ignited would be containable.

Without seeking the by-your-leave from anyone, I contacted some of my old journalistic friends and gave them off-the-record briefings on what was lying just below the public horizon. I told them London had intentions of freezing out Cathay Pacific of the cabotage route.

Hong Kong would make a formal protest as a matter of course. But it would strengthen the administration's hand if a few critical stories or editorials were to appear about rumours of the nature of the impending changes to the cabotage regime. Not to give Cathay Pacific a chance to compete would be regarded by local people as an unfair decision, given that airline's superb record in providing regional services. Cathay Pacific would naturally do its own lobbying.

None of my contacts needed any convincing over the unfairness of such an outcome. They all had experienced their own horror episodes while flying between Hong Kong and London on BOAC or British Airways.

* * *

After a media buzz had been developed, I drafted a confidential telegram for the Governor's consideration. In essence, the message welcomed the ending of the cabotage monopoly but drew attention to public disquiet over rumours of Cathay Pacific being denied an opportunity to compete on the route.

Cathay Pacific had earned its spurs through developing an efficient network of regional air services, the draft continued. It was therefore right and proper that it should be allowed to expand to the trunk-route stage of development, to provide more local job opportunities and to contribute towards the colony's growing economic sophistication.

Cathay Pacific was a well-respected and well-supported Hong Kong company, whereas British Airways had chalked up a rather unflattering record of delays and poor service. There was a real risk that the CAA's decision to restrict the route to only two United Kingdom-based airlines might be construed as some form of discrimination.

Public sentiments had been in flux in recent years. The former local political apathy over government decisions could no longer be relied upon. The amnesty granted to policemen in 1977 and the subsequent mass purges of other corrupt civil servants under Colonial Regulation 55 had divided public opinion. A significant section of the public was beginning to feel that the rule of law ought to be adhered to, regardless of consequences.

Now that a decision had been made to open the cabotage route to competition, it was important that the selection of airlines to serve the route should appear to be fair and even-handed. To deny Cathay Pacific a share might cause some to speculate whether the time has come for our own Air Transport Licensing Authority to have a say in deciding who should or should not be serving the cabotage route. Other awkward and constitutional issues might arise therefrom.

In the circumstances, it might be wise to ask the CAA to reconsider the matter before any public announcement, the draft telegram concluded.

The Governor, naturally, was not prepared to send off my draft as it stood. But he at least did cover the points I considered essential.

* * *

Whitehall's response to the Governor's telegram was to despatch the Assistant Under-Secretary of State from the Department of Trade and Industry to the colony for further discussions and to get an independent feel of public sentiments in Hong Kong.

The Assistant Under-Secretary was a middle-aged civil servant dressed in an off-the-peg suit. He had none of the sartorial elegance usual among Westminster politicians or mandarins. He was a lean man with sharp features, dominated by a pair of hard, humourless eyes. Those eyes were shadowed by the confidence of experience and cunning. He spoke with a high-pitched voice, which was quite unmarked by the plummy intonations handed down by elite public schools. The indubitable stamp of a red brick education was all over him. He had an air both intimidating and vaguely sinister, similar to a Fagin's. His Christian name was George.

But George was in fact rather quick-witted and quite a dedicated civil servant. He and I had crossed swords previously during negotiations over regional routes. He was wont to be not entirely scrupulous when it came to pressing the interests of those who paid his salary, just as I was not entirely straightforward when advancing the cause of those who paid mine. We both had a reasonable measure of each other. I supposed we were each in our own way a hired mercenary, trying to earn his keep.

George had been scheduled for separate sessions with Sir Murray, the Cathay Pacific management, the Director of Civil Aviation, the British Civil Aviation Representative in the Far East and a host of others. But, since I was looking after the wider civil aviation policies for Hong Kong, I became his first port of call.

George started off without preliminary frills and went straight on the offensive.

"One of your people has been leaking confidential information," he said. "There's no way the local media could have got hold of some of the material they've published. Someone has been trying to manipulate the news. It simply won't do. I shall be forced to complain to the Governor."

"By all means, George," I replied. "We have a free and rather unruly press here, not so much under the thumbs of media moguls as in some other places. No doubt His Excellency will direct me to investigate your complaint. I can assure you I will do my level best to bring any culprit to book. But it won't be easy. We live cheek by jowl here, on top of one another. One can hardly go to the toilet without somebody making a note of it. It's an ideal environment for gossip and insider trading. Every person who thinks he has locked away a dark secret or two eventually discovers that what he had taken for a Chubb safe was in fact a sieve, leaving endless vulnerabilities for others to exploit.

"Our Chinese extended family system compounds the problem, I fear. Did you know that in ancient times we used to have more than a hundred names to specify exactly the degree of kinship a person has in relation to all the other members within an extended family? Thank goodness we are becoming more Westernised these days, going in for nuclear families. Can you imagine what a bore it must have been to have to remember all those old family titles? China has now gone one better. Only one child per family. That should simplify things no end in future; farewell to brothers and sisters, uncles and aunts, cousins first, second or third removed, everyone gloriously autonomous and unlinked."

"Stop fencing, David. What is it that you really want?"

"Only a place in the sun, my dear fellow, nothing more than a legitimate ability for a Hong Kong company to grow and prosper. That had been my position when I called upon you in the DTI and later at the CAA; that remains my position today. I had assumed then we were all going to indulge in a fair and gentlemanly game of cricket, of the kind traditionally played on village greens, that is. Now it appears to have been a game of a different kind, with ball-tampering and other tricks."

"Everything has been above board, I can assure you," came George's stern and immediate response. "You know as well as anybody there cannot be a free-for-all. Capacity dumping will be bad for everybody. There's only so much traffic to go around. We have to see that a private airline like British Caledonian gets a fair go."

"We also want a fair go for everybody, including Cathay Pacific, which is after all also a British airline," I replied. "Nobody's asking for capacity dumping or a return to predatory pricing. There are ways to harvest traffic. British Airways has been losing passengers on the cabotage route to foreign carriers simply because of its unsatisfactory performance. I don't know whether British Caledonian will turn the tide.

"But your new boss lady believes in competition, market forces, survival of the fittest and so forth. Why not give Cathay Pacific a piece of the action, to see how that plays out? Or are you afraid that the United Kingdom-based airlines won't hack it in open competition?"

"Lots of things sound perfectly feasible in theory but don't work out in practice. Governments can't afford expensive mistakes. We have strong trade unions to contend with. A lot of jobs are on the line."

"There are all kinds of pressures at both ends. I understand all that. I know it's traditional for the UK to look at traffic rights as a self-contained issue. But once in a while, we *have* to look at the bigger picture.

"At this end, it is not just job opportunities at Cathay Pacific at stake but also those in the Hong Kong Aircraft Engineering Company. It provides jobs for our young people coming out of technical schools. I've had relatives working at HAECO since the mid-1950s, for heaven's sake. British pension funds have bought shares in both Cathay Pacific and HAECO. Their dividends go back to Britain each year to pay British pensioners and to ease the country's balance of payments problems. Wouldn't Britain like to see those dividends grow?

"Let's get back to specifics. Cathay Pacific has operated very effectively on its regional routes. It hasn't been blighted by the kind of engine trouble and emergency landings plaguing BA. Once a monopoly has been removed, there ought to be a system of rewards and punishments beyond the vagaries of an unreliable market, don't you think?"

"Cathay Pacific has never flown long-haul before," George said. "It'll find that presents a different set of problems."

"Precisely," I said. "Isn't it time to give the company a shot to see whether it can deliver? Besides, there are political dimensions here too, you know. We've had the Air Transport Licensing Authority for some years now. It's beginning to feel its oats. Since the cabotage route is now open for competition, some of its members might feel aggrieved if Cathay Pacific were not to get a look-in. They read the newspapers; most have travelled on British Airways. They're an independently-minded bunch, not a rubber stamp. All it would take to land us with a very hot political potato would be for one or two of them to pose the question on why they should not have a say on who should operate on the cabotage route."

"Has anyone raised such a question?"

"No, no! Nothing of the kind. It's just one of the possibilities that has flitted across my mind. Call it thinking out loud, if you like."

"Why do I get the feeling that someone here might be trying to plant that notion in their heads?"

"George! How can you ever think that? I have sworn allegiance to the British Crown. How could I undermine the interests of Her Majesty's Government."

George made a sarcastic sound. "You were far too friendly with the Americans throughout Bermuda II."

"They were a friendly bunch. A few of them and I just happened to share a few idiosyncrasies. Besides, being friendly got us Vancouver, didn't it?"

"Yes, but in a very unorthodox way, coming out of the blue at the end."

"Well, you've been in this game long enough to know that if something works, don't knock it. If you're afraid of someone planting subversive ideas into the heads of members of the Air Transport Licensing Authority, why not have an informal chat with some of them yourself, while you're here? You can then get a first-hand reading of their inclinations. I would be happy to arrange for you to have a cup of tea with some of them, if you so wish."

"How *very* kind of you, David. But it does rather have the flavour of something a spider might say to a fly."

"Relax, George. You're in my home town. I'm just offering normal Eastern courtesy."

"Well, let me think about it. Don't want to put you to any trouble. I should really talk to the Governor first."

"Of course, George. Whatever you wish is never any trouble for me. I'm always at your service."

* * *

Following the visit by the Assistant Under-Secretary of State, a further appeal was made in the name of the Governor to Whitehall, for the CAA to reconsider its decision to exclude Cathay Pacific from the cabotage route. For me, then, it was just a case of waiting with bated breath, to see if my risky indulgence in political poker could salvage anything from my failure to convince the CAA to give Cathay Pacific a slice of the cabotage cake.

Eventually, the Secretary of State for Trade and Industry, Mr. John Nott, did overrule the CAA and asked for the bids to be reconsidered. Then it became a matter of fresh CAA hearings in London, scheduled for November and December, and possibly into January if matters dragged on.

By then, rumours had begun to circulate that I might soon be transferred from the Economic Services Branch. That caused John Bremridge, the Chairman of Cathay Pacific, to ask the government to defer any transfer for me so that I could continue to represent the views of the administration on traffic sharing on the cabotage route at the CAA hearings. The Chief Secretary agreed.

John Bremridge must have had greater confidence in my persuasive powers than I had myself, for my words had apparently left no impression the first time around. Thus, at considerable inconvenience to my own maturing plans for early retirement from the civil service, I had to pack my bags for more journeys to the other side of the world.

The eventual outcome of those new hearings was that Cathay Pacific was granted permission to mount a thrice-weekly service between Hong Kong and London.

Meanwhile, British Caledonian also began services on the route in August of 1980. But it soon met with a series of financial setbacks, due to geopolitical and other factors. By 1988, the company had ceased to exist, swallowed up by British Airways. Cathay Pacific picked up some of the slack.

* * *

Gaining a slice of the action on the cabotage route for Cathay Pacific was but small beer compared with another set of looming negotiations. No one in the community took the cabotage route outcome as more than a vagrant breeze upon its fevered brow. The city had by then been sweating metaphorically for quite a while, over a mixture of anxieties, uncertainties and happenings beyond its control — the nerve-wracking prospect of China resuming control over Hong Kong.

Pressures had been building up steadily since January of 1976. The first inauspicious portent came in the form of the death of the Chinese Premier, Chou En-Lai, that tried and tested moderating rock upon which the diplomatic policies of the Chinese Communist government had been founded. By September of that same year, Chairman Mao Tse-Tung, the absolute ruler of the Chinese nation since 1949, had also hurried off to join Marx. A month later, his widow and other members of the so-called Gang of Four found themselves rounded up and stripped of power. Within the short space of a year, the political future of China had been turned upside down and inside out. The accompanying uncertainty that jangled throughout the nation also rippled around the chancelleries of the world. Hong Kong could hardly remain unaffected.

A short while afterwards, Mrs. Margaret Thatcher stormed into the British Prime Ministership in 1979, throwing yet another unknown into the political equation. She had struck many like some modernised and rejuvenated Britannia, out to tell China what was what when it came to the expiration of the New Territories lease set for the stroke of midnight on the 30th of June in 1997. The China-watchers and the Foreign Office apparatchiks had not been slow in warning the new Prime Minister that the colony could not be viable without the New Territories. But no one was really sure how the Iron Lady's thinking went.

In spite of the repeated pieties about human rights and the need to welcome refugees and migrants, Britain had been habitually slow and hesitant in accepting displaced persons of non-European stock. Its approach had often been viewed by its colonial subjects as oblique and crab-like.

Its intentions, however, had long been made plain to those residing in Hong Kong. While it valued the economic and strategic advantages of ruling the place, it did not want British subjects of the Chinese race to seek the right of abode in Britain. To guard against that possibility, parliamentary obstacles had been erected well ahead of time. Some outspoken Hong Kong residents had — with justice — characterised those precautions as acts of betrayal.

In returning the colony to China, Britain intended to include as bargaining chips the fate of the millions of "British subjects" living there. Conveniently for the British, the Chinese government claimed to speak for all who were racially of Chinese stock, wherever they might happen to be. The British, with a bit of moral fidgeting, was only too glad to fall in with that notion. Thus Chinese inhabitants of Hong Kong — unless they had a guilty conscience and could do a timely bunk — would be handed over like roads, canals, bridges and drainage systems upon the transfer of sovereignty.

The final vestiges of public delusion and wishful thinking had been stripped away by *realpolitik*. Those who had previously braved abnormal dangers to reach the mythical Pearl of the Orient finally had to stare their dark destinies in the face. They saw a return of their old desperations, poverty, alienation, guilts, griefs and failed ambitions. The city they had dreamt of as an answer to their hopes and prayers had turned out to be largely a collection of blind alleys. The place had been a mirage, appearing in disguise. It was in fact like one of those carnivorous flowers in the wild, out to devour both their dreams and themselves once they had been lured into its embrace.

For ex-Kuomintang soldiers who had fought and lost to the Communists, for the survivors of the Great Famine of the 1950s, and for the displaced from the Proletarian Cultural Revolution, the game was definitely up. Some had fought the Communists in Hong Kong too, in 1956, at the cost of many lives. Their refuge in an anachronistic British colony was coming to an end. They had to devise an exit plan.

For Kuomintang followers, boltholes in Taiwan were the easiest to come by. But it was a shaming choice. Not only had the island already turned into the hideout of choice for crooked Hong Kong coppers but its survival depended on the protection of the American Seventh Fleet. And how much reliance could be placed on the honeyed words of any foreigner?

So for the hundreds of thousands who wanted to play it safer, there was little alternative to queueing up at foreign consulates for visas and the prospect of a second passport. Those with no means of escape could only bewail their karma.

But the numbers seeking to leave, though impressive on the face of things, formed only a small minority of the population. A large core of the people, like colonial subjects everywhere, welcomed the impending reunification with their Motherland. Most considered the dignity of being ruled by their own kind preferable to living under foreign yoke, whatever the social and economic consequences.

Of the rest, there was at least the customary Chinese resignation or indifference. What did any change in rulers matted to them? Emperors had come and gone since time immemorial. The lives of the common people usually remained as hard and unforgiving as ever.

Indeed, such attitudes dovetailed with the views held by the Chinese government. When Mrs. Thatcher met the Chinese Premier Zhao Ziyang in 1982, before sovereignty negotiations were actually joined, she had entertained the hope of retaining significant British control over Hong Kong's commercial affairs after conceding sovereignty. But Premier Zhao soon set her straight. He told her two principles were at stake — sovereignty versus the prosperity and stability of Hong Kong — and China's position was that sovereignty had to be placed above everything else.

Of course, not only patriots and chauvinists favoured Chinese sovereignty. Fraudsters, mountebanks, international businessmen and other speculative types were also licking their chops. They saw re-unification as an entrée for garnering easy wealth. After all, what would those dull and unsuspecting mainlanders know about the wonders of conspicuous consumption, of corporate takeovers, leveraged buyouts, pyramid selling and ponzi schemes? Even if their machinations got exposed as frauds, victims would hardly complain. To do so would cause them to suffer further for losing "face" over being duped!

Such differences in perception and in expectations ran right through every sector of the community. Society was certainly divided, between the rulers and the ruled, the expatriates and the locals, the rich and the underfed, the go-getters and the resigned, male and female, young and old, masters and servants, creditors and debtors, radicals and conservatives, patriots and collaborators, those with their fingers on their abacuses and those with their heads in the clouds.

Cross-currents of culture, habit, identity and myths skewed things further, accentuating every contradiction and fallacy. The quietism of Eastern religions jostled with the proselytising enthusiasms of various Christian sects for adherents, for instance. But no matter the actual number clasping joss-sticks in their hands or wearing crosses around their necks, the prevailing god at the end was usually Mammon.

Racism was also a given between Europeans and Chinese, each considering himself racially and culturally superior to the other. A Chinese would regard a European as a "barbarian" or a "foreign devil". How could any sane Chinese not regard Europeans otherwise when he could see them ruining a delectable beverage like tea by adding milk and sugar? A European would return the compliment by regarding the Chinese as "heathens" or "expectoraters" or belonging to a "lesser breed without the law".

A further mixture of diehard snobberies and class distinctions remained alive and well within each race. Woe betide a member of one race marrying into the other. Before mixed marriages became fashionable, a European taking a Chinese bride would be branded as having "gone native" and was likely to lose his job or his career or both. Any Chinese woman marrying a European would be regarded within her own community as little better than a whore. Children from such unions would face discrimination from all quarters and would often have to exist in a twilight zone with fellow Eurasians.

A small Portuguese community also formed a little sub-group of their own. Many of them found a welcoming niche for themselves in the Hong Kong and Shanghai Bank. The bank was at that time the *de facto* central bank of the colony and its bosses sought after the Portuguese as tellers because they wanted to create the illusion the bank was solidly staffed by Europeans.

Beneath the bustle, the bright lights and the edgy energy of the city, there exists a thousand other subterranean zones with inhabitants nursing antagonisms and alienation not apparent to the eye of a visitor. If one were to be a fly on the wall at regular meetings of some clans, for instance, one would soon discover that quite ancient enmities and feuds with other clans still had not been entirely forgotten or forgiven.

But the city was, paradoxically, also a place with a high degree of civility, inter-dependence, generosity and absence of envy. The all-pervasive need to maintain face and not to lose it had something to do with that. A dogged "can-do" and get-up-and-go attitude pervaded and found ready expression. If a rickshaw puller could end up running a bus company, a bank clerk could rise to become the Executive Chairman of one of the biggest banks in Hong Kong, a plastic worker could transform himself into the richest property developer in the colony and a *kung fu* practitioner like Bruce Lee could turn himself into an international film star, why not the next man?

Until fairly recently, therefore, Hong Kong was not a place for moaners. It might sink itself into an occasional bout of mass hysteria or collective schizophrenia but such outbreaks usually corrected themselves within reasonable time.

For legitimate businesses or for crime, the city had an allure and a pull that went far beyond the mere smell on money. A goodly proportion of prosperous citizens — and even crooks — who had decamped for a second passport eventually found their way back. It went beyond commonplace nostalgia. Perhaps the place had a way of infecting the blood.

Even for those who had lived among the shadows, the place had a fascinating appeal. In 1961, it was estimated that there were 80,000 triad society members in the colony. The present number is unknown. What was clear was that the character of triad organisations had been changing in line with the times.

Triad life is now not so much about tough guys with tattoos shaking down the weak and the vulnerable. Like the Yakuza gangsters in Japan, the Hong Kong triads had gone up-market. A free-wheeling financial centre, reputedly the third biggest in the world, offered plenty of scope for money-laundering and other types of white collar capers. Triad leaders are now more likely to be found sitting in the boardrooms of banks and multi-national corporations, selling sub-prime mortgages, participating in the fixing of LIBOR and foreign exchange rates and, like Wells Fargo, opening fake accounts in the millions in the names of their unsuspecting customers.

One persistent rumour over the years had been that some of the top triad leaders were now in fact partners in law firms. The rumour had never been confirmed, although a number of lawyers had been sent to prison over the years for other criminal offences, like embezzlement. But a significant triad presence in law firms would make sense, since triad members were likely to have more conflicts with the law so long as Anglo-Saxon corporate law provided an abundance of loopholes for them to wriggle through.

Such white collar misdeeds had at least one positive result. Since little violence was involved in picking the pockets of wealthy victims, the average Hong Kong policeman, though steeped in the syndicated corruption of that era, was unused to combating violence when tackling crimes, regardless of how things might be portrayed in local gun-blazing motion pictures.

The average copper thus remains today a non-intimidating and unmilitarised figure, though not quite the idealised avuncular bobby on the beat of a bygone era. But things might be about to change, given that a new generation of badly educated and attention-seeking adolescents have been testing his forbearance, egged on by failed politicians and *agents provocateurs*.

Another aspect of shadowy life in the city concerned the refuge given to revolutionaries, dissidents and whistle-blowers from elsewhere. They often had to play ducks and drakes with a not very bright local Special Branch. Notable among them had been such national heroes like Sun Yat-Sen, Ho Chi-Minh and Jose Rizal. A more recent example was Edward Snowden.

In addition, at the fringes between politics and espionage, there lurked always a motley collection of spies and secret agents of all persuasions. They might masquerade as journalists, educators, publishers, diplomats or simply tourists. Among them might be found the odd Kuomintang spymaster with his network now decimated and running for their lives, or a Comintern leftover with switched allegiances now willing to offer his outdated spy-craft to any bidder, or a clean-cut Langley operative so out of place outside his Virginia suburbs that he could be spotted a mile off. There would be no shortage of self-acclaimed China-watchers too, ready to parley every snippet of rumour or information into cool hard cash.

But apart from spies and spooks, the colony was also attractive to a variety of outsiders seeking jobs, ranging from dubious ones in the financial sector to the hard slogs in domestic servitude. This development is reflected in the demographics. For an extended period after the war, the population had been stable at being 98% Chinese. In recent years, however, the number of non-Chinese has increased by several percentage points. No doubt a continuing sign of a healthy openness in the society.

* * *

I am constantly amazed by some of the accounts I read about Hong Kong written by people I call five-day wonders. By that I mean some of the commentators or journalists who fly in, meet up with cronies for a few drinks and then pronounce definitively about almost every aspect of the city's immensely convoluted and tangled life. Their ability to discover within five days the essences of the city can only be regarded as magical and supernatural! Everything from its ever-changing moods, the nature of its governance, its neuroses, dynamics, delusions, aspirations, griefs and incongruities to predictions about its social, economic and political future.

A few of those five-day wonders might speak some Chinese or hold a degree or two in Far Eastern studies from the School of Oriental and African Studies. But it would be rare indeed for them to stray far from the usual stereotypical thinking about Eastern peoples and cultures. Add to that farrago the usual quantum of disinformation, propaganda, gutter and chequebook journalism and the justification of a free press holding truth to power begin to sound pretty hollow.

Even long standing residents of Hong Kong often stumbled in trying to describe or explain the protean nature of their absurd and infuriating home town. Part of the reason is that most tended to move mainly within their own narrow professional or social group and their own comfort zones. The layered, segmented and contradictory nature of the city made for isolation rather than reaching out. The fear of losing face is also a strong inhibitor. Thus the city often gets explained in terms of tourist-speak, hackneyed myths and quotations from that almost mind-numbing official annual reports.

That last named publication would contain plenty of pretty pictures but over the years it has taken on more and more the character of a corporate annual report — strong on public relations appeal but factually obscured. It is usually smothered with an overkill in equivocal statistics and overworked platitudes. But, surprisingly, the government has managed to get away with telling the public very little about what had actually been going on.

To chronicle the splendours and sorrows of so muddled a place and with so extraordinarily resilient a people would be no easy matter. But officialdom should have tied harder. How would one describe a city with the potential of becoming as open and creative as Changan at the height of the Tang Dynasty and yet, if the Old Testament prophets like Isaiah and Ezekiel were still around, would invite their condemnation as a harlot city, for its many strutting vulgarities and its godlessness?

To undertake such a task would require someone with at least the touch of a Tolstoy or a Balzac. Once upon a time, during my swell-headed youth, I had fancied myself up to such a challenge. But a year in London in 1957, trying to earn my living as a scribe, brought me crashing back down to earth. Hardly any editor or publisher would touch my stuff. Stories about Hong Kong and the Far East simply had no audience.

Later, during an unforgettable spring in Holland with Sharlee in 1965, I still had a remnant of that delusion bubbling inside me. But now, after years of insufferable bureaucratic prose, I am truly done for. Not even K'uei Hsing, the Chinese God of Literature, could ever rescue me.

My hope is that one day some native son or daughter more blessed with talent than myself will emerge, to do justice in chronicling the spirit of this anomalous and endearing place of my birth.

* * *

Yet, back towards the end of the 1970s, the prospect of a messy negotiation between Britain and China over a piece of historical real estate was unsettling in the extreme for many people. They saw the dismal prospect of inhabitants being used as bargaining chips. Yet they remained impotent to affect so ignominious an outcome. The problem was that very few had the ear and the trust of both of the main protagonists, let alone the various sub-groups. Each sector tended to listen only to those it could trust and it was axiomatic that those it trusted were people who shared its predispositions.

As a Chinese civil servant, I found my position even more frustrating and invidious. I was being paid by Hong Kong taxpayers and the only side I could choose had to be theirs. But in order to serve them, I had to be in touch with all shades of opinion, as well as what I might glean from the main protagonists.

Yet, to sound out opinion among those most affected, I was hog-tied by security regulations. If I were to speak to someone who happened to be an office bearer in a left-wing organisation, for example, I would be required to make a long and tedious report to the government as to who said what to whom. Most of the conversations I had with others, like those with people in the Chinese General Chamber, would be confidences exchanged between individuals and friends and not between a government official and an office bearer of a left-wing organisation. Because I could often gain insights into Chinese mainland thinking from friends in the Chinese General Chamber, I usually ignored compliance with security regulations. Nor could I betray the confidences of friends by sharing them with foreign occupiers.

More absurdly still, the administration seemed to have written off Kuomintang organisations in the colony. It must have regarded them as a spent force. Or perhaps it did not want to appear to be pursuing any semblance of a two-China policy. In any event, the Kuomintang remained strong in certain quarters, especially in a number of key trade unions. Oddly, talking to their officials required no reporting under security regulations. I could never quite work out the rationale to justify such a head-in-the-sand approach.

Such was the predicament I found myself in. Yet what could I do to influence anything? I had little power and virtually no influence within the colonial bureaucracy. I had no illusion of how I was regarded by the hierarchy. I was a loner, a maverick, someone who could not be relied upon to act as a team player. Hence someone with too many question marks hanging over him.

Time and again, even when my judgement was accepted my immediate superior — as in the case of the Diaoyu Tai student demonstrations — the Governor ruled against me. More recently, I had to resort to subterfuge to frustrate the false narrative to justify that very questionable reverse osmosis project.

Naturally, I had no standing with Chinese officialdom either. Thus I felt often like a mere feather, waiting to be swept along by an approaching storm.

As I thought about the situation, I was reminded of something my paternal grandfather had said. I remembered him saying more than once during my boyhood, when he was enjoying pipes of opium with his associates, that so long as the Chinese remained disunited foreigners would always try to make trouble for the country.

The more I thought about the matter, the more I got the impression that my grandfather had vague expectations of me. But what were they? He never spelt anything out fully. I had strongly identified with being a Chinese but

I had never entertained anything so grand as playing a part in my country's destiny. As a local civil servant, I could do nothing about the sovereignty issue, for that had to be handled between countries and governments.

I knew the British had an immaculate record in practising the old Roman maxim of *divide et impera* or divide and rule. They had a penchant for drawing lines all over other people's territory — the Curzon Line, the Durand Line, the McMahon Line, the Sykes-Picot demarcations in the Middle East, concessions and settlements all over China, the partition of India *et al.*

So far as Hong Kong was concerned, disunity suited British purposes. People could be manipulated easier. But in truth, the British could not bring the segmented population together even if they had wanted to. Their devious politics had long ago eaten away the trust of many and few of them could overcome the barriers of language and culture.

The only slight advantage I had over them was that I had been more catholic in my friendships, developing connections across the entire social, political, intellectual and economic divides. Perhaps I could add a stitch or two to knit the community closer together to face a common destiny. It seemed worth trying. Perhaps that had been all my grandfather had expected of me. So thinking, I decided on an experiment.

I chose the sumptuously bourgeois setting of a race day buffet lunch in the Owners' Box at the Jockey Club for my experiment. My ploy would be to say that my racing partner and I had a horse running and, if it lived up to expectations, we would need help with the bubbly afterwards. I would make it a family occasion, because H.C. Fung and his wife, Charity, would be there.

For my first experiment, I chose an occasion when our horse, Free Lad, had a winning chance. I accordingly invited Ip Yeuk-Lam, his wife Suze, and his youngest son, Shing-Kwan, and his wife Maureen. My hope was that in sharing a meal together they might also discover some opportunity for doing business together, in spite of their different political allegiances.

Happily, on that occasion Free Lad did not disappoint. So I invited all the ladies to help me lead the horse into the Winner's Enclosure.

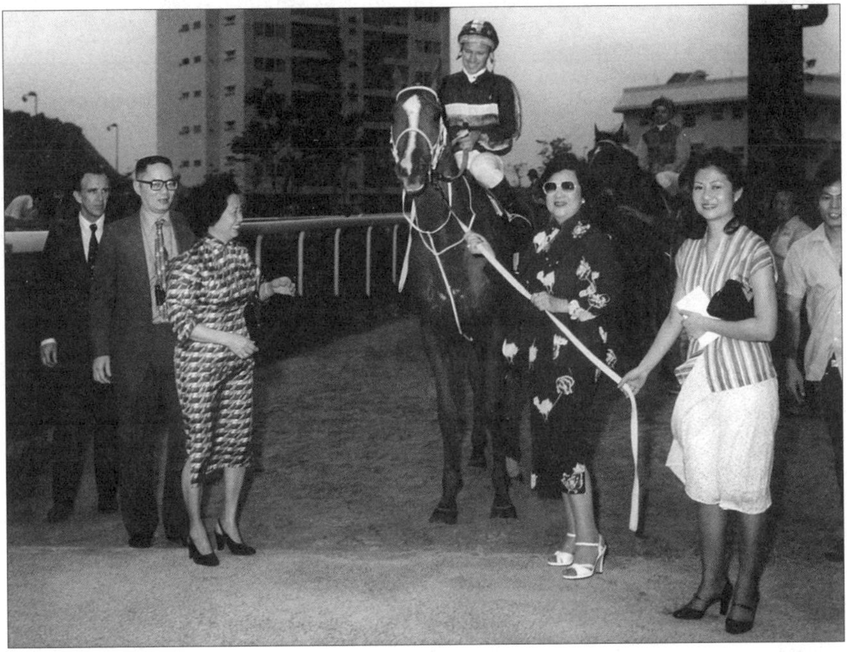

Leading in another winner at Happy Valley with the help of friends, from left, Mrs. Charity Fung, Mrs. Suze Ip and Mrs. Maureen Ip.

Unfortunately, that initial experiment did not quite work out as I had hoped. Although the ladies got along well enough —for they shared certain charitable interests — nothing happened between the men. The political divide between them proved too great to bridge. My grandfather had been right. We Chinese were a nation cursed by too many divisions. We were still as lacking in cohesiveness as Dr. Sun's tray of sand. So long as the nation remained in that state, it would indeed be exploited by others.

I had greater success later, however, when I put my former journalistic colleague, Leslie Sung, and Yeuk-Lam together. Leslie had once been quite anti-Communist because he felt his younger sister, Greta, had been wrongfully imprisoned by the Chinese for being an alleged British spy. Leslie and Yeuk-Lam happily got to deal with each other as rational and decent human beings. They got along well enough for all of us to take an Easter holiday together in Thailand some time later. A small step towards fostering a much needed unity.

As to Greta Sung's story, that would be left to the next volume of these memoirs.

CHAPTER 15

Crossing the Rubicon

DURING THE LATTER PART of 1979, shortly after my eldest son, Tien-Kuen, had left for Dallas, Texas, to join his maternal grandparents, my second son, Tien-Kay, approached me about his future university education. He expressed a desire to study chemical engineering after secondary school.

His choice surprised me. Up till that point, I had not noticed him displaying particular familiarity with the periodic table, let alone with Dmitri Mendeleev's role in its origins. His stated interest struck me as contrived, to justify being sent abroad since no local university offered a course in that field. He must have seen the position I had adopted with his elder brother and was trying to sound out his own prospects.

By the late 1970s, sending children abroad to study had become something of a fad among the *nouveau riche*, just as 40 years earlier colonial schoolboys who had devoured British boys' magazines like *Triumph*, *Wizard*, *Rover*, *Hotspur* and *Champion* used to dream of entering an English boarding school and emerging with all the panache of a toff.

Both fads smacked of that commonplace syndrome of regarding local ginger as lacking tang or of the grass being always greener on the other side of the fence. The laughable academic standings of some of the institutions children were being despatched to did not seem to matter a fig for some parents. Having offspring studying overseas was apparently deemed worthwhile enough in conferring bragging rights for themselves and some form of cachet on their children. The whole mindset was as misguided as the belief of some women that wearing six-inch stiletto heels would somehow bring greater grace and elegance to their movements.

Changing times and changing ambitions were probably also a factor. At the turn of the 20th century, most Chinese heading for studies in Europe, Russia, Japan or the United States had aimed at learning foreign ideas and new ways of doing things as not only a good in itself but also a means of helping to rejuvenate their country. Many had a solid grounding in their own culture.

By the second half of the century, however, the motive had become less lofty; it became more about personal ambitions, professional advancement or family enrichment. No doubt the more extreme forms of Western individualism and the instant gratifications associated with consumer capitalism offered had also infected their psyches.

I myself was very conscious that my early education in Singapore had infused me with too many alien values and colonial biases. That trend intensified after I had fled to Australia at the age of 12 to escape the Japanese invasion of Singapore. The net result was that I went through my entire adolescence knowing more about the deeds of Nelson and Wellington, Drake and Captain Cook, Hastings and Clive of India than I ever did about those of the Sung Dynasty General Ngok Fei or the Ming Dynasty Admiral Cheng Ho or even that premier Chinese sage, Confucius.

It was not till after I had entered the more intellectually stimulating academia of Stanford that I began pulling myself back to my roots, to delve more deeply and systematically into the half-forgotten teachings of Miss Nice in Canton and of Tutor Tam in Singapore. I gradually returned to the subtler Eastern habits and the more face-conscious requirements demanded by Chinese conduct.

I did not want my sons to go through that same unsettling cultural journey.

Education in Hong Kong at that time had remained far too Eurocentric, with the teaching of contemporary Chinese history and culture still being disallowed.

My boys were suffering the further disadvantage of not enjoying the usual benefits of the extended family. Their closest kin were far away. My father and most of my siblings were in Singapore; my mother in Vancouver. I was divorced from their mother and their maternal grandparents and relatives were in America and Europe. Their mother had also left years earlier for America. So they also had no close interaction there.

It was therefore difficult for them to acquire a sense of connectedness with their family and elders. I did send them one summer to Kuala Lumpur, to get to know my brother Francis and his family and to learn something of the Malaysian way of life from my friend Sonni Pillai and his wife. But such one-off trips did not go very far.

My hope was that if they could remain in Hong Kong till after their university educationl, they would at least be exposed to Chinese newspapers, magazines, films and television and hence absorb more of their own culture and feel less alienated and rootless.

Contrary to the prevailing fad of overseas education, I considered much could be gained from a local university. The best of them could hold their own against the best in the world. After all, both my grandfather and my father had been local graduates, and so had many of my relatives and some of my dearest friends. If I could persuade my sons to do likewise, it would also suit my pocketbook.

However, I realised that both the pressures of the milieu and the preferences of my children were against me. But I had a trump card: I had insufficient funds to grant their wishes — even if I had wanted to! And it would be unconscionable for either of them to approach their maternal grandfather for financial help. He was still assisting their eldest brother and he himself was approaching retirement.

But it did not seem appropriate just then to take Tien-Kay through my rather abstract philosophical considerations. He was only 16, temperamentally impulsive, emotionally insecure and still quite narrowly focused. He might well interpret any wider discussion as an indirect attempt to reject his request. He was bound to brood over that outcome, straining our all too tenuous relationship.

On that judgement, I told him he still had almost two years to go before university. It was far too early to consider the matter. I assured him, however, I would bear his choice of studies in mind. I was hoping he might change his mind about chemical engineering. If so, the chances of persuading him to pursue a degree locally might be improved.

* * *

Two or three weeks later, my third son, Tien-Kit, also approached me about his education. He and Tien-Kay were quite close, having shared a bedroom for many years. They must have gone over each other's hopes and aspirations before the younger one approached me.

I knew that he was having some trouble with the pressure-cooker nature of his schooling at the elite St. Paul's Co-educational School. It was a missionary school that both his elder brothers had attended. Unlike his brothers, however, he had year after year ended near the bottom of his class. It was not due to his being a loafer or a lad without ambition. He had suffered from encephalitis when he was young and that ailment had made him a slower learner than usual. Nonetheless, he had managed to do well enough each year to scrape through with a promotion.

Tien-Kit told me he was feeling disheartened at St. Paul's. His classmates looked down on him, he said, and whenever an examination or a test was due, they would lay wagers on who would come out at the bottom of the class. He was always one of the hot favourites. Some friends of his had left Hong Kong to attend a boarding school in Canada. They had told him studying there had been more agreeable and less demanding. Would it be possible for him to go to a boarding school there as well?

I empathised with him and tried my best to console him. I suspected that the presence of pubescent girls in his class might have added to his discomfiture. I told him the majority of Hong Kong schools and most local parents placed too much emphasis on examination results. That created a vicious circle. But I was not one of those parents. Tests and examinations were just snapshots, capturing a student's ability at particular moments in time. They did not necessarily reveal what a person might or might not really be capable of. A self-aware student should regard them much as twinkling amber traffic lights, cautioning him on changing circumstances ahead.

History was filled with people who had achieved great things after doing poorly in examinations, I continued. I cited as an example the Tang poet Tu Fu, who had failed not once — but twice — at Imperial Examinations. Notwithstanding those failures, he still managed to become both an exemplary public official and one of the greatest poets China had ever produced.

"You have not yet failed in any of your examinations," I asserted. "You may not have done as brilliantly as you would wish but your school is a highly competitive one. Wouldn't trying a little harder be the answer? If you need help on some subjects, both your Second Elder Brother and I are around to help."

"It's not as simple as that, Dad," Tien-Kit said. "I need a new environment, a place where I can make a fresh start, with the slate wiped clean. My classmates here have already nailed me as a loser, as someone who's never going to shine. That's depressing and hard to take."

"Well, why not try proving them wrong, particularly if there's a girl in the class who has caught your eye? Is there one?"

"No, there's no girl."

"Problems are never solved by running away from them, you know. They have to be surmounted. You're only 14, far too young to be going off by yourself into a totally alien environment. It'll be very confusing; I can testify to that from my own experience when I was your age. I'm therefore not yet prepared to expose you to that kind of learning curve. By going away you may be able to duck being teased here but you may well find more unpleasant forms of taunting elsewhere."

Tien-Kit looked sad-eyed and slightly embarrassed at my mentioning the possibility of a girl.

"You're a Chinese," I continued, not quite knowing how to get my concerns across. "We have our own ways of dealing with the problems in life. In foreign societies, you'll stand out because of your physical attributes, like the colour of your skin. Some foreigners may accept you for what you are but others will view you as a legitimate target for their own resentments and frustrations. When I was your age, I was spat on for no apparent reason by a total stranger in Australia and called 'a dirty Chink'. You may get that same reception. Can you take that in your stride?

"Before you head abroad, it would be as well for you to be more comfortable with your own culture and your own identity. Chinese spiritual and philosophical values have a lot to offer. Hong Kong may not the best place to pick them up. It's not a typical Chinese city; it's adulterated, alienated, corrupted and wrong-headed in many ways. But it's the only native place you have.

"Don't imagine a Green Card or a foreign passport will give you an alternative. That'll only be an illusion, probably just a ticket to a place you do not really belong and can never feel entirely comfortable in. At best you might just get an equivocal kind of hyphenated citizenship."

As I spoke, I watched Tien-Kit's uncomplicated face crumbling further with disappointment. Words! How inadequate they were to get the deepest feelings across! Without words, birds could fly instinctively in flocks, animals travel in herds and fishes swim in shoals, without smashing into one another.

But human beings, blessed with the gift of language, so often made a hash of things. They could seldom call into service the *mots justes* that Flaubert pointed to. How wonderful it must be to command a talent for painting or dancing or making music. One's feelings could then be expressed without resorting to words.

Tien-Kit was such a pliable lad. The image of him, standing silent and crestfallen, triggered a sudden helplessness in me. How could I tell him about my fears for his vulnerabilities without hurting him? His personality was still unformed. Facing peer pressure in a foreign boarding school, he was apt to experiment too early with alcohol, drugs or sex. In Hong Kong, I could at least keep an eye on him. Left to himself, anything could happen.

It came to me all at once that my outpouring of words might have struck him as a completely irrelevant spiel, just filled with embellishments and evasions sprouted by grown-ups and parents. All he would take away with him might be my unambiguous denial of his wish to study in a boarding school abroad, to possibly spare his blushes before the girls in his class.

My heart contracted with helplessness at that thought. I recalled my own boyhood, when I had nursed resentments of one kind or another against both my parents, simply because I could not understand what was happening to myself. It took years before I could grasp what had stood behind their then incomprehensible decisions.

If by some whim of Fate my life should be forfeited on the morrow, Tien-Kit would forever remember me as only the Great Negator, a father who had denied him everything, ranging from a simple pair of trainers to studying in a foreign boarding school. I dreaded leaving him with such a memory for the rest of his life.

Ultimately, he might also blame me for messing up my marriage; thus depriving him of motherly love he deserved. And to cap it all, I had failed to extend him the kind of fatherly love he wanted either. How impossible it was to communicate with another person, even if he happened to be one's own flesh and blood!

Not knowing what else to do, I placed a hand on Tien-Kit's shoulder and said: "Just give your school another try, my boy. I'm sure you can do better. I'll talk to your class teacher. Perhaps you need a part-time tutor."

* * *

Although I had told Tien-Kay it was too early to decide on his university education, I knew that was not really the case. Timing was of the essence. If the boy were to stand a chance of studying abroad at a time of his choosing, then I would have to initiate a process of disengagement from the civil service almost immediately. The reason was because I was bound by bureaucratic rules to give a year's notice.

At that time, the normal retirement age was 55, though the rules specified that an officer could apply for early retirement at 50. In any case, a year's notice had to be given. Otherwise complications in pension entitlements might come into play. Another rule specified that an officer could not, after retirement, take up any employment in the private sector relevant to his previous duties without first going through a cooling-off period of one year. Sir John Cowperthwaite, the former Financial Secretary, for example, had to wait for a full year after he had stepped down from office before he could take up an appointment as a consultant for Jardine Fleming, a Hong Kong investment bank.

The big financial picture was clear. My income came almost entirely from my civil service salary. I might gain an occasional windfall in the form of prize money from the racehorses I owned in partnership with H. C. Fung. That would come only if both the nags and the jockeys riding them lived up to expectations! But that was all.

Over the years, those two income sources had left me unable to finance my children's studies overseas. Nor had I been able to save a *sou* to put a roof over my own head after retirement, when I would no longer have any entitlement to heavily subsidised government quarters.

By failing to act promptly, therefore, I would in effect be allowing the regulations to move automatically towards the outcome I preferred, for I would definitely not have the funds to finance Tien-Kay for overseas studies when he finished secondary school.

If I had honestly believed that an initial overseas degree was essential to the future of my children, I might have gone into money-grubbing work sooner. But I had no such belief. Rather I believed the contrary; that their longer term interests would be best served by their growing up in Hong Kong and soaking up as much as possible of their Chinese cultural identity.

But self-interest also came into the equation. I was 50 years old. It was no time to cross the Rubicon, to trade in a challenging and meaningful career in the public service for a life requiring shady compromises and ethical ambiguities. The legal skulduggeries of Western corporate culture infiltrating local commercial life was quite repulsive. Was that too high a price to pay for accommodating the adolescent wishes of my sons?

Yet, I could not help experiencing some twinges of guilt. I had made too many mistakes in the past. I had brought them into the world knowing full well that my marriage to their mother was heading over the cliff. After siring them, I had also surrendered their upbringing to the mercurial moods of their mother, just to avoid conflicts in the home and to gain a semblance of peace And I had lost what little I had put aside for their education by investing in the ill-fated *Singapore Herald* venture.

After their mother and I had separated, I had perhaps tried to impose upon them too quickly a remedial and more stable domestic regime. It had been a fairly liberal one by the standards that I and my siblings had grown up with at our grandparents' home in Singapore. But my boys were not prepared for that rapid change. The main difference, I supposed, was that I and my siblings had no shortage of elders around to enforce the rules and to sweeten them with an occasional and unexpected act of affection or kindness whereas my boys had to be left largely on their own to follow the new rules. It was understandable, therefore, that I should have encountered resistance, especially from my eldest son. It took a while for my new regime to prevail.

But establishing reasonable order within the home did not equate with good parenting. I had inherited from my forebears a taciturn nature and I always found it awkward to communicate with my children on the abstract and philosophical plane. How could I explain to them all the complicated political, psychological and pragmatic factors which had caused me — a Chinese — to work willingly for a bunch of foreigners occupying a slice of my native land? The fact that my job came with a 3,300 square feet furnished apartment at Palm Court, a luxury far beyond the reach of the average salaried man, might lead them to surmise I had done so as a kind of dark and unspeakable *quid pro quo*.

My frequent absences on official assignments also rendered it difficult for me to bond with them. I must have come over as aloof and remote, just as my own father had appeared to me when I was their age. It was obvious that, lacking everyday contact with adults, their emotional development would have benefitted from a softer and more constant presence of a woman. To rely only on the faithful but illiterate Ah Duen was hardly adequate. Yet all my earnest attempts to get a suitable wife had met with total failure.

The fact I had not allowed them to enjoy another government perk must have compounded their misgivings. It concerned the use of an official chauffeur-driven car, a facility granted to every Policy Secretary or head of department. It was ostensibly for the purpose of taking him to and from office and for official engagements. General practice, however, sanctified its use by family members as well, like taking spouses on errands and sending children to school.

When I went into acting jobs as Director of Home Affairs and as Secretary for Economic Services, I also had the use of such a car. But I seldom took advantage of the facility. Naturally, I did not allow my children to enjoy that facility either. Their school was only a shade over a mile from our home. They could easily walk it or take a bus. I did not want them to get into a habit that was above their station in life. Yet trying to explain everything that lay behind my thinking would have taken more time and effort than I could spare.

For instance, Hong Kong had a reasonably good public transport system, operated partly by government and partly by private companies on franchises with profit-limitation clauses. Some 90% of intra-territory journeys requiring power-driven transportation were made on public transport. This compared with the alarming 85% of car-obsessed Americans driving to work each day. That meant that within the colony only plutocrats and those wishing to flaunt their wealth would go around in expensive road-hogging cars.

Since global warming, environmental pollution and hazards to public health were becoming big issues, I thought the government was setting a bad example by providing official cars for top civil servants. First of all, it seemed morally wrong that any civil servant should live in a style above that of their paymasters. Secondly, the most senior expatriate officers were already cut off from the ordinary folks by language and culture. There was no case for them being further insulated from the *hoi polloi* by moving around in metal contraptions set on wheels.

If I had my way, I would eliminate all official chauffeur-driven cars, with perhaps the exception of those assigned to the Chief Secretary and to the Financial Secretary. When Sir John Cowperthwaite was Financial Secretary, he used to drive himself around in a vintage MG sports car rather than use his official car. If other top officials wanted to drive to work, they should jolly well use their own cars also.

Since I had refrained from explaining my various considerations to my sons, I could hardly blame them if they read my prohibition as just another instance of meanness on my part. Thus misunderstandings accumulated between us.

* * *

The two conversations with my sons led me into a fair bit of introspection, particularly after I had slipped into bed but unable to find sleep. While delving into what someone had once called the dark night of the soul, I began to wonder if the course I was charting for my sons had been entirely honest and above board. Had I, in the fashion of so many other fathers, been subconsciously trying to shape them in my own image, as surrogates for my own aborted dreams? Acquaintances I had known as doctors or lawyers had often expressed the hope that their sons would enter the same profession as themselves and to do better in it. But what was meant by "better"?

That could hardly relate to my own ambitions. I had attempted journalism, teaching and fiction-writing and had failed to make a mark in any of them. Now I was a civil servant living at the economic margins and without any hope of meeting their wishes. I had never been even a good prototype as an obedient civil servant.

I had often failed to obey orders and had also failed, on occasion, to uphold the law of the land as I had been charged to do. My alibi for those failures was partly moral and philosophical and partly legalistic sophistry.

Chinese culture had taught me that human-heartedness ought to be at the centre of an individual's private life as well as his official one. In the case of an official, he had to behave as if he were the father and mother of the people he served. Merely following orders was not good enough. The Nuremberg war crimes trials had blown a gaping hole in that lame defence. A person could not do dastardly deeds simply because someone had ordered him to do so. He had to be personally accountable for his actions. That could create invidious choices.

In a previous volume of these memoirs, I had given examples of the choices confronting me when I was the head of the Labour Inspectorate, charged under local labour laws to protect women and children from exploitation. I provide herewith one further example from that period.

One day, I was cutting through a street side market to walk to work when I saw a stout and energetic woman selling fresh vegetables from a hawker pitch. She had with her two young girls, one around three and the other around ten. Girls of those ages had no business being at a roadside vegetable pitch, I thought. They ought to be in a kindergarten or a school. So I stopped a little distance away and watched the proceedings for a while.

The pitch was busy with shopping housewives and servants. The woman hawker was very efficient. She would weigh out a customer's purchase and agree on a price before passing the vegetables to the older of the two girls to tie them with a string and to collect payment. The girl was also an efficient helper. She appeared to be co-operating without coercion. It was a *prima facie* case of using child labour.

The orthodox thing for me to do would be to send one of my Labour Inspectors around to observe the activity and then to collect evidence and bring the case before a court. I of course knew nothing about the woman. She could be a widow or a woman abandoned by her husband. But in either case she was obviously trying to make a living and support her family. What good would it do to disrupt her life, to have a fine imposed on her and possibly to fracture her family by having her children taken into care?

My thoughts jumped back to the time I had to wash dishes at the age of 13 at Mr. Wong Sue's restaurant, in exchange for daily meals. What would have happened to me if Mr. Wong Sue had been a stickler for labour laws? How would I have ended up if he had chased me off for being underaged and unemployable?

It so happened that at that same time I had also become qualified as an Air Raid Warden under the rules of the Civil Defence Council in Western Australia. I had volunteered to patrol the streets of Perth at night in order to aid the war effort and I had been assigned to see that all the blackout regulations were being complied with. But I was paid nothing for that work.

Life seemed to be filled with moral hazards. Even when one followed some sort of vague moral compass, one was often left unable to read the direction it was pointing.

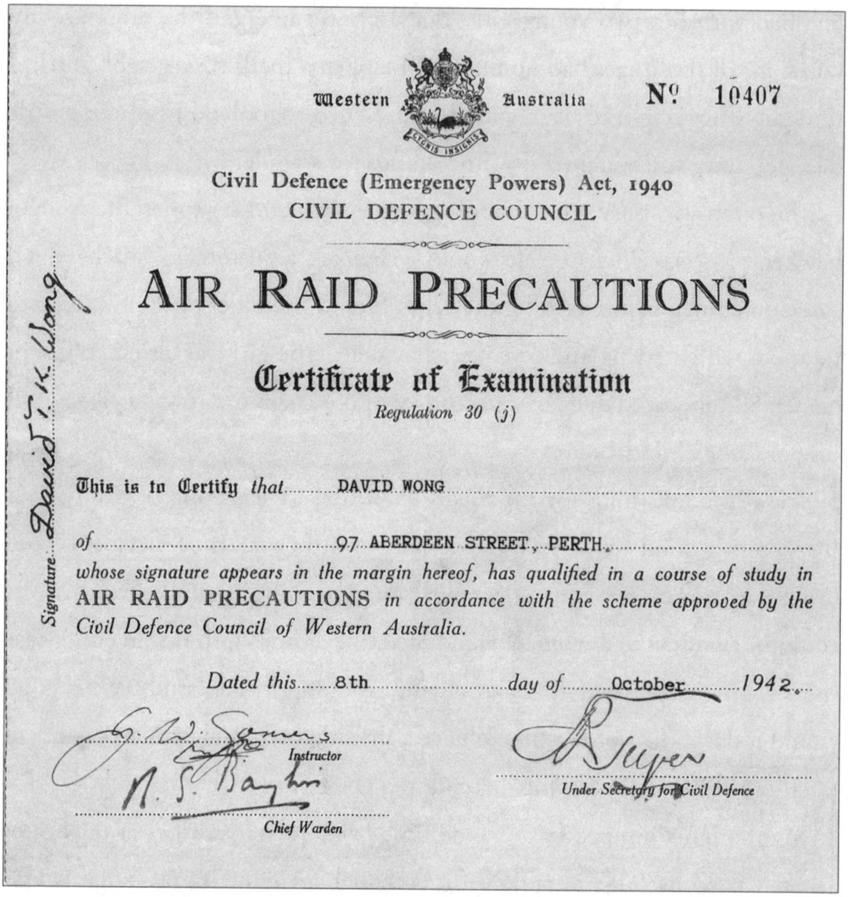
Western Australia No. 10407

Civil Defence (Emergency Powers) Act, 1940
CIVIL DEFENCE COUNCIL

AIR RAID PRECAUTIONS

Certificate of Examination
Regulation 30 (j)

This is to Certify *that* DAVID WONG

of 97 ABERDEEN STREET, PERTH.
whose signature appears in the margin hereof, has qualified in a course of study in AIR RAID PRECAUTIONS *in accordance with the scheme approved by the Civil Defence Council of Western Australia.*

Dated this 8th *day of* October *1942.*

Instructor

Chief Warden

Under Secretary for Civil Defence

Signature David S. K. Wong

Certificate for Air Raid Precautions Examination

In both instances, I had undertaken the duties of my own free will. But I could not figure out at that time — and after a lapse of 75 years I still cannot figure out — why it could be acceptable for a government to utilise child labour without payment but illegal for a child to offer his labour in return for food.

Sadly, up to the present day, far too many children all over the world still had to do the hard slog of harvesting cocoa or coffee beans or digging under appalling conditions for coal or gold just to earn enough to eat. In a perfect world no child should go hungry and no war would be fought. But how could such a perfect world be reached? So despairing over the state of the world as I saw it, I continued on my way to work and took no further action over the vegetable seller and her child helper.

After my two conversations with my sons, such recollections from my past kept riffling through my mind during my sleepless nights. A life like mine was certainly not what I would wish for my sons. I wanted to spare them my missteps and vicissitudes. But what was I actually trying to prepare them for? I was no longer sure.

They would certainly be growing up in a harsh and unstable world, full of the same problems and contradictions I had not managed to unravel or resolve. Was I being too unrealistic and over-protective in trying to shield them from reality? Would it not be better to cut them loose in the university of hard knocks? They might be better able to find accommodation with life than myself. Would it not be sufficient if they turned out to be reasonably hard-headed human beings instead of being hard-hearted ones?

* * *

But obligations towards my sons were not the only obligations I had to bear in mind. I also had responsibilities towards the wider Hong Kong community. Its taxpayers had paid my salary for the last 18 years and they had twice financed my overseas studies at The Hague and at Oxford respectively. I also had moral obligations towards several very fine expatriate mentors who had lavished their time on me and had passed on to me their collective wisdom in the art of governance. Their commitment to community service had also guided my path. It behoved me to repay their kindness by at least serving out my term. I could not, without due justification, shed such obligations as casually as a snake shedding its skin.

On the other hand, had I not reached the limits of what I could usefully do? I was one of the three or four most senior Chinese Administrative Officers in government; yet I had little in the way of actual power or influence. I had often wanted, in the spheres where I had been given responsibilities, to jolt the bureaucratic machine out of its established rut, to move it in fresh directions. But my views and suggestions had gone largely ignored or rejected. Hence I could count myself as no more than an inconvenient pebble lodged somewhere in the rut of the colonial machine.

Among current expatriate superiors, I had probably a reputation for being a loner, a maverick, and a poser of awkward questions. The few minor changes I had been able to bring about had been largely achieved through subterfuge, subversion and guile.

Perhaps it would be better if I were to leave after all. If I did, it might allow some of the camouflage covering colonial policies to fall aside, to reveal that Chinese officers had little say over most of the more crucial decisions. The public might then know who should be blamed for obvious flaws and for dodging all the big questions. The various strands in both my private and official lives seemed to have got as tangled as a Gordian knot and I was nowhere near being enough of an Alexander to cut through it.

* * *

Such nocturnal ruminations edged me a little closer to the banks of the Rubicon. But I still had too many doubts to cross it. I suppose I was still searching for some elusive personal justification, like that Taoist point of spiritual and intellectual equilibrium between the fluctuating forces of the *yin* and the *yang*. My psyche was still wrapped too much within a mixture of emotions, values, commitments, historical guilt, individual aspirations and quirks of temperament.

Over the years, a number of friends and acquaintances, being aware of my financial limitations in educating my children, had urged me to go after the material rewards of the private sector. But I doubted my suitability temperamentally. Indeed, I might not be the least bit marketable. I had seen many quite mediocre intellects striking it rich in business. But had I the stomach to sail dangerously close to the wind just to close a deal? Would any profit-minded employer allow me to dictate my own means of dealing when it came to making money for him?

Another worrying matter was the working culture inside many Chinese companies. Most had relatives lodged in positions with titles or in cosy sinecures. Blood was usually thicker than water and such relatives were likely to look to their family for instructions rather than any hired executive from outside the family. That could make for a lot of headaches. On occasion, money could also turn out to be thicker than blood and an outsider might quickly find himself in the middle of a family feud.

The only way to determine the lie of the land in any company would be to make soundings. Naturally, the starting point had to be H. C. Fung, the chairman of Li & Fung.

When we first met in 1963, he had tried to recruit me for the company. The firm was headed by his elder brother Fung Mo-Ying at the time. It was only after his brother had passed away that H. C. took over.

Li & Fung was founded in Canton in 1906 by his father and a Chinese merchant surnamed Li. The company operated as commission agents for trade between China and America, offering sourcing services and a linguistic bridge between buyers and sellers, in pretty much the same way as compradors in big British trading houses.

H. C.'s father sent him to establish a Hong Kong branch office before World War II. He bought a property in Connaught Road Central for that purpose. After the war, partner Li was bought out by the Fung family. The company later became publicly listed and also did some business as a principal, notably in the areas of firecrackers and Chinese handicraft. Following a public listing in 1973, it created a slew of subsidiaries to handle different aspects of its work, in line with the legal protection afforded by corporate law. The bulk of its activities, however, remained centred on agency work for mass consumer products on behalf of American and European corporations.

I took the tentative step of arranging a meeting with H. C. and quickly laid all my cards on the table. I reminded him he had been urging me to join his company for 16 years. Now at last I was prepared to give it a try, if mutually satisfactory terms could be arrived at. I had been forced to risk a change, I told him, because I needed extra money to send my sons to study abroad. I would certainly not be able to do that on my civil service salary. If he was still interested in my services, we could talk terms.

"You'd always be welcomed in Li & Fung," H. C. replied with alacrity. "You'll be making an excellent decision. The one thing I can promise you is that you'll be making much more than in government. We pay bonuses every year, for a start."

"Thank you, but I don't want to trade on our friendship," I said. "We both have to get something worthwhile out of any deal. I'm not looking for a golden transfer fee or a quick fortune, just a package that will not leave me any worse off than what I'm currently enjoying in government.

"You may be wondering why I should be willing to switch jobs without a significant improvement in my package. I'll level with you. I've never worked in business before, so I don't really know whether I can make any real profit on your behalf. I don't want to be greedy either. I've my own calculations.

"Right now, I only need enough to tide me over the expenses for my sons' education. If I retired prematurely, I can immediately draw my pension and convert a part of it into a lump sum. That should take care of the extra expenses for the next few years. I'm now acting as Secretary for Economic Services. Soon I'd be given a department to run and the salary and other perks that go with it. A package which gives me my present benefits and at the same time allows me to draw my pension is all I want."

"Put your mind at ease, David," H. C. said. "Doing business is easy. You'll pick it up in no time. What you're seeking is more than reasonable. If you join Li & Fung, I certainly will not treat you meanly."

"I don't want any misunderstanding between friends, H.C. Before you say 'yes' I have certain conditions you have to accept. First, I will not be a party to any transaction which I consider to be possibly illegal, not that I believe any of that sort of thing goes on inside Li & Fung. But there are just too many dodgy derring-dos happening in the private sector.

"Secondly, I know that you have kinfolk in various positions in the company. I'm not a very great respecter of bloodlines, you know. Anyone placed under my command has to work to my satisfaction or else he or she has to go. If you've got any relative you have a soft spot for, please don't place that person under me.

"Finally, if we agree to a deal today, it'll be at least a year before I can be available for work, because I have to serve out a year's notice for premature retirement. If you can't accept those conditions, I'll try somewhere else and we can still remain friends."

H. C. chuckled. "Don't worry, David; trust me. The conditions you seek should be no problem. I know your character well enough. You should have no problem with my kinfolk. Go and put in your notice. My eldest son, Victor, has recently returned from Harvard to join the family business. I'll get him to contact you so that the two of you can work out the terms in detail."

We shook hands and the deal was done, orally and without lawyers, in the old-fashioned Chinese way.

* * *

Once I had secured an agreement with H.C. I had to move smartly to disengage from the Economic Services Branch of the Secretariat, lest I got stuck with a cooling-off period of another year before I could start work at Li & Fung.

I could not risk leaving my next posting to the vagaries of the Civil Service Branch. It might well send me to another negotiating job in the Commerce and Industry Department for instance, and that would scupper any opportunity for me to work without a cooling-off period. I soon found a perfect excuse for moving into a posting without any possibility of a conflict of interest — a post in the General Post Office.

The Post Office was a microcosm of colonial society. The department was topped by four expatriate officers with British postal backgrounds — a Postmaster General, a Deputy Postmaster General and two Assistant Postmaster Generals. The rest of the 5,000 or so staff members, however, were virtually entirely Chinese. So much for the lip service paid to "localisation". The local staff had formed themselves into a number of active trade unions and staff associations. Recently, there had been one postal strike after another, ostensibly over working conditions and career prospects. Clear evidence of a breakdown of some kind in relations between management and labour.

It so happened that the Economic Services Branch had policy oversight in respect of the Post Office. I was aware of certain staffing problems in respect of the department's hierarchy. The Postmaster General had recently been promoted from his previous job as the Deputy. But neither of the two Assistant Postmaster Generals was considered sufficiently seasoned to be promoted to the post of Deputy.

Furthermore, the newly promoted Postmaster General was himself due to retire in January of 1982, which meant that whoever his Deputy might be would need to be ready to take the helm in two years' time. An outside recruitment for a Deputy was therefore necessary, with all the attending problems of morale within the leadership of the department while staff and management conflicts brewed lower down.

In the circumstances, I suggested to the Civil Service Branch that I take up the vacant Deputy's post at the Post Office *pro temp* and try to sort out its labour and management problems. That would take away the urgency of an immediate recruitment.

The Civil Service Branch jumped at my suggestion. It had its own reasons to be pleased. I would be the first Chinese to be among the top management of the department. Secondly, the Civil Service Branch calculated that once I had been installed at the Post Office, I might be persuaded to stay on and become the next Postmaster General.

The Secretary for the Civil Service sent me a letter in October of 1979 setting out those possibilities and offering me the choice of remaining in the Administrative Service or transferring permanently to the Post Office establishment. Since I had other plans, I replied saying I would consider his offer after I had started work at the Post Office.

Of course, the London hearings on the cabotage route intervened, to upset the best laid plans of mice and men. I was not appointed Deputy Postmaster General until the beginning of 1980.

As soon as it could decently be done after taking up my post, I sent in my application for early retirement, giving the required year's notice. The Civil Service Branch must have felt considerably narked by my move. Who could blame it? In the cat and mouse game with the branch, I had probably resorted to a ploy not sanctioned under Marquis of Queensbury rules. But the bureaucratic game was often a cut-throat business. From the MacLehose years onwards, if a person wanted a satisfactory career outcome, he could no longer rely on comradely feelings or any *esprit de corps* to secure him what he desired. He had to play his own hand the way he saw fit.

* * *

Meanwhile, once I had been installed in the Post Office, H. C.'s eldest son,

Victor Fung Kwok-King made contact and I met him for the first time. He was short and dumpy, taking after Charity, his mother, and he had an outgoing and glad-hand American approach.

He had acquired a doctorate from Harvard. His speech was peppered with modish business school jargon like "synergy", "mission statement", "paradigm shifts" and "economies of scale". He gave every impression of having already mastered all there was to know about the intricacies of leveraged buyouts, off-balance-sheet accounting and enhancement of shareholder values.

My guess was that his father must have instructed him that a deal had already been done and that what was needed was to tie up the small print prettily into a nice package. But somehow — perhaps because his speech was too earnest and his smiles too ready — he evoked for me an image of a hustling car salesman from Arkansas, trying to convince a customer a certain second-hand car sitting in the forecourt was truly the best bargain that could be had.

Over several meetings, we knocked into acceptable shape the detailed terms of my employment in Li & Fung. What we had ultimately agreed upon, I shall save for the next volume of these memoirs.

CHAPTER 16

The Q List

WHEN I WAS INSTALLED as the Deputy Postmaster General at the General Post Office at Connaught Place at the beginning of 1980, I was delighted to find myself in an office with a marvellous view of the harbour. The building had been completed only in August of 1976, as the colony's fourth General Post Office. It was on a prime harbour-front site that was worth a fortune, a mere stone's throw from the Star Ferry Pier.

The previous General Post Office, opened in 1911, had been an architectural wonder to behold. It used to be located at the corner of Pedder Street and Connaught Road Central. But it had to be surrendered to make way for building the Central Station of the Mass Transit Railway. Its replacement was externally not half as pleasing on the eye but it did come with a very spacious and up-to-date sorting office in the basement.

At the time I joined the department, there was a staff of approximately 5,000. Apart from the concentration at the General Post Office, they were scattered among 40 branch post offices around the colony. The oldest branch was at Stanley, opened in 1937. That branch is still operating today in its original building. The number of branches has since climbed, to approximately 130 I think, including the odd two or three mobile ones.

The departmental structure was then quite a simple affair. There were beneath the Postmaster General and his Deputy two expatriate Assistant Postmasters

General, one to head postal services and the other the telecommunications side. Most of the staff worked on the postal side. The telecommunications side was made up of technical staff who oversaw the two franchises granted for local and overseas telecommunications services respectively.

The local telephone franchise, valid until 1995, was held by the Hong Kong Telephone Company. The company was restricted to an annual return of 16% of shareholders' funds.

The overseas telephone franchise was granted to a Hong Kong subsidiary of Cable & Wireless. The parent company had its origins in a British company set up in the 1860s to provide cable links to various parts of the British Empire. With the steady rise of wireless communications, the different communication methods were merged into a single company in 1934, known as Cable and Wireless Limited.

Following the Labour Party's victory in the 1945 general election in the United Kingdom, the company was nationalised. Its domestic telecommunications monopoly was passed to the British Post Office while it continued to operate telecommunications services outside of Britain. One of its subsidiaries held a franchise for Hong Kong in return for a two percent royalty on turnover.

For some unclear reason, no profit limitation clause had been included in that franchise. That sometimes led to unseemly results. For instance, in 1992 the company made an annual profit of HK$5.6 billion on shareholders' fund of HK$12.2 billion — a whopping 47% annual return on capital. A veritable wet dream for a monopoly, even by the colony's freewheeling standards!

An announcement at the end of 1979 of my projected arrival in the new year as the Deputy Postmaster General caused a minor stir among the staff. They did not know exactly what to expect. I was not only an outsider but I would be the first Chinese to hold a top post in the department. The Postmaster General was on his last tour before retiring in January of 1982, so he was in a relaxed and happy-go-lucky mood. He was more than willing to give me my head. My priority was, naturally, to defuse the threat of another postal strike.

* * *

Staff and management relations within the department were not particularly harmonious. Otherwise there would not have been issues leading to repeated strikes.

I found that the administrative and clerical back-up for running such a large department was somewhat inadequate. So I requested the Secretariat to assign a Senior Executive Officer by the name of Wong Yiu-Wing to take over as the new Departmental Secretary. I had worked with Yiu-Wing in the Home Affairs Department before and had found him a highly efficient and capable officer. My request was quickly met and Yiu-Wing lived up to his record for sound bureaucratic reconstructive surgery.

Then it came down to familiarising myself with the large number of trade unions and staff associations within the department and to getting a feel of the personalities of their office bearers. The grades in the department ranged from the lowly postmen on the beat to clerical staff, manual labourers, night watchmen, Postal Officers, Controllers of Posts and telecommunications engineers and technicians. The interests of one group did not necessarily coincide with those of another.

The established way for the management to communicate with staff unions was to hold, from time to time, a general meeting wherein employment issues could be aired and thrashed out. That general meeting was called the Forum and all staff groups were represented. For practical reasons, based on the number of postal staff unions involved, the Forum was chaired by the Assistant Postmaster General in charge of postal services.

It was an unsatisfactory system because the chairman, being an expatriate, knew no Chinese whereas many union representatives of the lower grades knew only enough English to read the addresses on letters and other postal items. That meant that all discussions had to be laboriously filtered through an interpreter. That process provided ample scope for misunderstandings.

Furthermore, many of the issues raised appeared to be of a micro nature, like shift work, promotion prospects, the maximum weight of any mail bag being carried by a postman, the varying lengths of delivery beats, and so forth. A majority of those should have been resolved at a much lower level. To bring such matters before a large formal meeting took up too much of everybody's time. It also encouraged a "me too" attitude whereby a concession granted to one union engendered a similar demand from another.

After my arrival, I decided to take over the chairmanship of the Forum. I told the Forum that since Chinese had been declared an official language back in 1972 and since everybody except the Assistant Postmaster General spoke Chinese, proceedings would henceforth be conducted in Chinese. The interpreter would be retained to explain proceedings to the Assistant Postmaster General.

I further suggested that the Forum should be used for discussing major structural or career issues; minor tweaking of working conditions could more easily be settled in face-to-face meetings with representatives of the particular union concerned. The door to my office was always open and I hoped union representatives would make use of that facility. It was unnecessary to involve all unions in every discussion.

The pressing issue for the public, I emphasised, was the threat of another postal strike. There might well be certain disparities between the salary scales and promotion prospects for some postal workers, compared with those in other grades in government service. But management could not conduct talks under duress. The sooner union officials explained their dissatisfactions to me, without any threat of a strike, the sooner disparities could be examined and dealt with.

The union officials, after due deliberations among themselves, sensibly accepted my invitation. They called in separate contingents at my office. It transpired that there were indeed certain anomalies. The two sides worked through them, identified the ones enjoying mutual support, and made proposals for changes to the administration. The proposals were then left to work their way through the central bureaucracy.

* * *

Meanwhile, on the personal level, government approval for my premature retirement came through, setting off my required year of notice. The moment the approval was received, I sent in a further application for permission to take up employment with Li & Fung without any cooling-off period, arguing that overseeing postal services could have no bearing upon the core business activities of Li & Fung.

That second application was also duly approved. But then I sent in a third application to tidy up a technical detail. I would have, at the end of my year's notice, an accumulated leave balance of six months. From the time I stopped working till the end of my leave, I would still be technically in the employ of government and hence be entitled to the usual fringe benefits, like subsidised and furnished quarters.

But a "serving" officer could not take up employment in the private sector without permission. I wanted to start immediately with Li & Fung, without having to sit on my hands for six months waiting for my pre-retirement leave to expire. The money involved was, of course, a consideration. By working right away, I would be able to draw on both my full civil service salary and my Li & Fung pay at the same time. So I applied for permission to work in the private sector while on pre-retirement leave. That too was duly approved.

However, there was yet another bureaucratic procedure I had to comply with. It involved a once-in-a-lifetime decision on whether I wished to commute a part of my pension into a lump sum payment.

At the time I began contemplating retirement, the customary retirement age was 55 and an officer could opt for early retirement at the age of 50. A pensioner would also be entitled to convert up to 25% of his pension into a lump sum payment. The theory behind it was to give him some flexibility transiting from work into retirement. He might, for example, wish to migrate elsewhere, purchase a home, fund an overseas education of a child or grandchild, etc., for which a lump sum would come in very handy.

Any commutation would be based on an actuarial calculation that a pensioner would, on average, live to collect his pension for — if I can remember correctly — something like 14.2 years. A pensioner would naturally have to take his own health prospects and expectation of life into account. If he figured he could only live for a couple of years after retirement, then it would make sense to take the bird in hand.

Just before I was due to make my election, however, one of the factors in the calculation was changed. Instead of being allowed to commute up to 25%, a pensioner was permitted to commute up to 50%.

I believe the pressure for that change came from expatriate civil servants. They had made representations to London to guarantee their pensions in the event the colony could no longer meet its obligations after sovereignty had been reverted to China in 1997. They had been spooked by the deluded Whitehall belief that the place would fall apart at the seams both economically and commercially without British management.

London was thus caught up in the illogicality of its own presumptions. But the domestic calls on the British exchequer were many and it was reluctant to act as a guarantor for the pensions of ex-colonial civil servants. A compromise was eventually arrived at whereby a pensioner could commute up to 50% of pension as a lump sum.

That decision was, in my view, ill-advised and selfish, catering to a sectarian need without being mindful of its psychological effects on the general public confidence during a delicate time of transition.

I had not the slightest doubt that Hong Kong would continue to thrive and prosper, with or without the British. If it had not been for the need for ready money to send my two younger sons overseas, I would not have commuted any part of my pension. In the circumstances, I commuted only 25% of my pension and I have regretted it ever since.

Today, 37 years after my retirement, I am still drawing a Hong Kong pension and paying Hong Kong taxes. But I still have a long way to go to beat my grandfather's record of drawing a Crown pension for 41 years!

Since my retirement, the rules have been changed again and again. I believe the current retirement age is 65. I have no idea what the current commutation factors might be.

* * *

On the staff relations front, the proposed changes in the terms of service for postal workers were fairly swiftly agreed by the administration and the threatened postal strike was averted.

After the dust had settled, Sir Jack Cater, the then Chief Secretary, sent me a message, congratulating me on defusing the strike threat and asking if I would consider withdrawing my application for early retirement. He said the government could hardly afford to lose a senior officer like myself.

My reply was that I was in a financial bind. All my three sons wanted to study in North America and, much as I would like to remain in the public service, its salary structure would not enable me to meet the wishes of my sons. Even if I were to be promoted immediately to the rank of Policy Secretary, my salary would still fall far short of financing requirement. Hence I had no alternative except to leave for the richer pastures of the private sector.

There the matter reached a dead end.

* * *

The months of my retirement notice rolled by quickly enough. My involvement with staff unions and reorganising the administrative machinery of the department kept me busy.

Over the same period, I had several sessions with Victor Fung to fill in the details of my terms of engagement with Li & Fung.

By the time autumn came around, it was time for the Postmaster General to take his annual leave. I was slated to take over as Postmaster General, in addition to my duties as Deputy. Before departing, the head of department handed me the keys to the Chubb safe in his office and said: "Since you will be in charge of the department, you might as well look at some of the secret papers in the safe."

I accepted the keys. But I thought he was referring to papers detailing what everybody had long talked about in the tea houses and coffee shops, that is, of the British GCHQ or Government Communications Headquarters, in cahoots with the Americans, setting up surveillance posts at such places as Cape Collinson and Lei Yue Mun to spy on Chinese telecommunications.

Once I got around to opening the safe, however, I found myself proved entirely wrong. It became apparent that another well-established surveillance operation by the Special Branch was being conducted right under my nose in the General Post Office as well! So much for my blind faith over most of my life in the sanctity of the Royal Mail.

How could I have missed what was going on? It was true that doing my rounds of inspection in the basement I had neglected to go into every office there. I had been more interested in the workings of the modern sorting machinery and how individual postmen would bundle their letters and postal items in accordance with the routes they took on their delivery beats.

And it was in one of those inconspicuous rooms in the basement, during the dead of night, that certain postal officers specially selected by the Special Branch would steam open letters addressed to targeted individuals and photograph their contents, before re-sealing them for normal delivery the following day.

The whole operation revolved around a list of names and addresses drawn up by the Special Branch. For some unclear reason, the list was referred to as "The Q List". I could not figure out what the cryptic "Q" was supposed to stand for. Presumably it might stand for "Queer" or "Questionable" or "Quisling" or something of that nature.

The list was delivered personally to the Postmaster General from time to time, whereupon he would instruct the specified postal officers pre-selected by the Special Branch to photograph all communications passing through the postal system destined for those particular people or addresses. It required no imagination to conclude that a similar secret list would have been sent to the head of the Hong Kong Telephone Company, for all telephones either in the names of those people or located at those addresses to be bugged as well.

On the face of it, it appeared that the people in the Q List had been selected for either political or criminal reasons, though some element of collecting economic intelligence might be present as well. Most of the names were unknown to me, although a few could be identified as minor personages belonging to the cocktail cult, the odd banker, lawyer, accountant or businessman. Thankfully, no name of any close friend of mine had found its way into the list.

A feature of the list was that where the address happened to be a self-contained dwelling rather than an apartment, then the name of the target was not specified. Instead, all communications going to those addresses, under whatever name, would be intercepted and photographed.

Nonetheless, one of the addresses I came across gave me both a start and a chuckle. It brought to mind some of the stories of past bungles I had heard concerning the Special Branch. Those relating to the Vietnamese revolutionary hero and statesman, Ho Chi-Minh, were particularly memorable. That wily revolutionary had repeatedly led Hong Kong Special Branch operatives on a merry dance as he skipped in and out of the colony using multiple aliases. Once he even faked his own death while hospitalised, leading the Special

Branch to close his file and to report his demise to other spy agencies.

My own limited encounters with the Special Branch did not alter my opinion of its general ineptitude. Included in the Q List was an address in Victoria Road with which I had some familiarity. Its inclusion convinced me it had to be yet another Special Branch *faux pas*.

The address in question had been included probably because it happened to be the putative home of Fok Ying-Tung, the Hong Kong multi-billionaire businessman, philanthropist and highly-regarded advisor to the Chinese government on Hong Kong affairs. The irony of the situation was that Fok could hardly ever be found at there.

My familiarity with the address had nothing to do with Fok himself but rather with a couple of other members of his family. When I visited the Hong Kong Chinese General Chamber of Commerce club regularly to play *mah-jong* with friends, I sometimes bumped into Fok. His presence there was unremarkable for he was one of its most important personages. But we would merely exchange nods in greeting, without ever engaging in conversation.

Fok was born in 1923 in Poon Yu, where his family had a small boating business. His father was killed in an accident when he was about eight. He went to school in Hong Kong, but dropped out before finishing secondary school due to the outbreak of war with the Japanese. He then began working as a labourer.

When the Korean War broke out, the United Nations imposed an embargo on trade with China. Fok was among other patriotic Chinese in Hong Kong who set about breaking that embargo by smuggling vital supplies like medicine and machinery to China to support its war effort. Afterwards, as a reward for his risky services, Fok was granted a monopoly for exporting sand to Hong Kong. Since sand was a vital component in building construction and the colony was going through successive building booms, it took no time for Fok to make his fortune.

He then expanded into hotels, real estate, petroleum and casinos in Macau.

His links with the highest levels of the Chinese government flourished apace. The Chinese Premier Zhao Ziyang, for example, recorded in his secret journal *Prisoner of the State* discussions he held with Fok about developments in Hong Kong.

Fok was thus soon made a member of the Standing Committee of the National People's Congress and a Vice-Chairman of the National Committee of the Chinese People's Political Consultative Conference.

In Hong Kong itself, Fok's standing also rapidly grew. He came to prominence particularly as the "white knight" who rescued a crumbling shipping empire.

Fok Ying-Tung

During the heyday of the shipping boom of the 1970s, there used to be three shipping titans operating out of Hong Kong — the Pao family, the Chao family and the Tung family. Big money could be made or lost based on an operator's assessment of freight rates and hull values. The Tung family, operating as Orient Overseas under C.Y. Tung, the father of the first Hong Kong post-colonial Chief Executive, C.H. Tung, made the wrong forecasts and was soon in dire financial trouble. It was at that point that Fok entered the picture and saved Orient Overseas from bankruptcy.

In 1984, Fok established the Fok Ying-Tung Foundation to promote education, health, sports and science and it became the largest philanthropic organisation in the city. He became President of the Hong Kong Chinese General Chamber of Commerce from 1984 to 1988 and then again from 1990 to 1994. He was also President of the Real Estate Developers Association of Hong Kong and — because of his passion for soccer — President of the Hong Kong Football Association.

He passed away in 2006, from cancer, leaving three wives and 13 children.

* * *

My familiarity with the Victoria Road address stemmed from my friendship with Fok's eldest daughter, Patricia or Lai-Ping. I had met her in the 1960s, when she was working on an album of photographs which came to be titled *Hong Kong Through the Looking Glass*.

Pat was a superb photographer with a genuine passion for her work. She had studied in England, Switzerland and the United States and had taken courses in design and the photographic arts. Afterwards she was forever clicking her Hasselblad wherever she went.

We shared a strong attachment to China and its history and culture. Pat always had some excitingly ambitious project in China under consideration. It might be retracing the steps of the Tang poet, Li Po, climbing the Yellow Mountain and trying to recapture, through photographs, what the poet might have seen along the way. Or else Pat would head off to Tibet to give photographic substance to what an ancient Tibetan poem had described as "the centre of heaven, the core of earth, the heart of the world fenced around with snow."

Many parts of China had been still closed to outsiders at that time but Pat somehow always managed to use her father's connections to gain access to wherever she wanted to go. The result was two further fine albums — one in 1974 entitled *Faces of China* and the other in 1987 entitled *Quiet Beauty of China*.

I greatly envied Pat's ability to roam all over China. Ever since I had been denied permission by the colonial administration to visit Taiwan, I saw no hope of my being allowed to go to China so long as I remained in Crown service. I therefore derived vicarious pleasure in listening to Pat's accounts of the historical and scenic places she had photographed or visited. Whenever she was passing through Hong Kong I would grab the opportunity of having a cup of tea or a meal with her. Pat had, in the meantime, married a Dutch businessman and they had set up home in London, in a town house in Mayfair. So her visits to the colony became more erratic.

During one of Pat's stopovers, when I was working in the Home Affairs Department, she introduced me to her mother and asked if I could help her with a problem. Pat's mother was a lovely lady, a homely Chinese housewife of the old school. She was courteous, soft-spoken and slightly hesitant before outsiders. She came across as very much in the same mould as my beloved Eighth Grandaunt.

It appeared that Pat's mother had lost one of her more important official documents — a birth certificate or an identity card, I cannot now remember exactly which.

Like most Chinese housewives who had never had dealings with colonial officialdom, she was apprehensive over what might be involved in securing a replacement. She was fearful of having to explain before some haughty and intimidating European how her loss had come about. She herself was unsure of how the document came to be lost and she dreaded being tripped up by questions she could not answer.

I reassured her she had nothing to worry about. I would explain the problem to the department concerned, make an appointment for her to see an appropriate officer and shepherded her through the entire process. Everything went without a hitch. I was more than glad to be of service to so pleasant a member of the public.

* * *

Hong Kong was one of those tight, high-pressured cities sprouting a plethora of overlapping cliques of wealth, snobberies and charlatanism. In what other city in the world could a person find in the early 1970s four stock exchanges operating in fierce competition with one another? Or to find a stock index running up from 150 to 1,775 in a matter of a mere 18 months? Something did not smell right. It was almost inevitable that a few years later the chairman of one of the exchanges by the name of Li Fook-Shiu should be sent to prison for four years for corruption and accepting a reward while he was the chairman of one of the exchanges.

In such an *à gogo* business environment, anyone participating even marginally in its endless rounds of celebratory dinners and cocktail parties was bound — over time — to rub against the entire cast of colonial characters and hangers-on, ranging from philanthropists and physicians to predators and philistines. And thus it was that I became acquainted with Fok's second wife — through her unexpected participation in a *mah-jong* game I had been scheduled to play.

For a number of years, as I had explained in Chapter 4, I had been playing *mah-jong* regularly at the Chinese General Chamber's club with a group of close friends. The core of the group consisted of Ip Yeuk-Lam, a long-standing Vice-President of the General Chamber, Lo Yuk-Chuen, a jolly retired banker, referred to affectionately as Sixth Eldest Brother, H. T. Liu, a shipping magnate from Shanghai, addressed normally simply as Uncle Lau, and myself. We all commanded roughly the same level of game-savvyness and skill. Our challenge lay in how quickly we could suss out one another's strategies, feints and sucker traps and beating the rest to the punch. It was well known within the club that we did not welcome outsiders to our game, unless we happened to be one player short.

Yeuk-Lam was the one among us who had the most social and official engagements. So it was left to him to initiate a game whenever he had a free evening. He would do this through a staff member at the club, who acted as an informal convener, ringing around to form our ideal table. Sixth Eldest Brother, being a gentleman of leisure, was always available. Both Uncle Lau and I were equally keen to participate, unless one of us happened to be out of town or otherwise engaged.

The Chinese General Chamber was also a natural stamping ground for Fok because of his prominent business and political roles, though he was not a *mah-jong* enthusiast. He sometimes brought his second wife to the more ceremonial functions at the chamber. Why it should have been the second wife I did not know. Perhaps it was not even his choice.

The second Mrs. Fok soon began using the chamber club to entertain her own friends. In that way she came to know of the regular *mah-jong* games that Yeuk-Lam had set up for our selected group. She made it known she wished to join our game.

None of us was enthusiastic about any outsider butting in, let alone a woman. It was also not normal in Chinese etiquette for a woman to be playing *mah-jong* at a public venue with a group of men. Perhaps she merely wanted to establish her own standing among such influential old guards at the General Chamber like Yeuk-Lam. No one was sure of her real motives. But what we were all adamant upon was that we did not relish a feminine presence to cramp our style. We were sometimes given to using unparliamentary language when we got outfoxed by one of our group. Such language could hardly be escaping our lips if there was a woman present. The informal convener was thus instructed to come up with some creative untruths to explain his failures to fit her into our game.

But the second Mrs. Fok was a pushy woman, one not easily deterred. She would go directly to Yeuk-Lam to ask if he might persuade one of the players to give up his place for her, on the excuse she was at a loose end and itching for a game.

Now Yeuk-Lam was not only a consummate diplomat, but also someone brought up in the old school of Chinese social intercourse, never to make anyone lose face, especially the wife of so important a member. Yeuk-Lam would then contact Sixth Eldest Brother, an old friend of many decades, to explain his dilemma. Predictably, Sixth Eldest Brother, being the most obliging of gentlemen and a long-time friend, would gracefully indicate he had been thinking it was time for him to spend an evening with his collection of antique watches in any case.

It was under those circumstances that I found myself one evening sitting down to a *mah-jong* game with Mrs. Fok. The pleasure of the evening was decidedly not mine, for Mrs. Fok was not only a sub-standard player but one prone to talking far too much. After a second occasion when I found myself unexpectedly in a game with Mrs. Fok, I told the informal convener that in future I would be delighted to surrender my place at the table if Mrs. Fok wanted to play. After that, I never played with her again.

* * *

After I had become aware of the Q List, it struck me as ludicrous that the private correspondence and telephone calls of so many inhabitants at the Victoria Road address should be interfered with just for the sake of keeping tabs on Fok Ying-Tung's political or other activities. The whole operation was like episodes from one of those old Laurel and Hardy slapsticks — immensely amusing and full of comical mistakes hardly plausible in real life. How could any useful information be gained through such a clumsy and cockeyed operation?

For a start, the house at Mount Kellett Road, where the second Mrs. Fok resided, had not been included in the Q List. I did not know where Fok's third wife was located but I could not spot any likely address in the list either. What about Fok's various business offices and charities? Or his regular hangouts like the Chinese General Chamber? Besides, Fok himself was constantly on the move, in China and elsewhere.

I suppose the leading lights in the Special Branch, being all expatriates, would not know much about the psychology and ingenuity required of a man who has taken on three wives. Poor fellows! How could they know that by the time a man had acquired a third wife he was unlikely to be spending much time in *tête-à-têtes* with his first wife? Having lived with a polygamous grandfather during my boyhood, I had at least learnt that much about human nature!

If the Special Branch were trying to get its hands on, say, the minutes of meetings Fok had attended in the Chinese capital, would those not be delivered by secure courier rather than through the ordinary postal system? There had to be easier ways of finding out. What about by simply asking the man himself? By all accounts of those who knew Fok well, he was said to be quite a straightforward and decent man, with the interest of both Hong Kong and China at heart. If the Chief Secretary were to invite him to lunch at Victoria House or the Governor at Government House, who could say what useful information might be exchanged after tongues had been lubricated by a few shots of pre-prandial sherry. Or was Fok too much of a *persona non grata* for making such a mockery of a United Nations embargo and got off scot-free?

The world would never know what inconvenient truths might have surfaced if one of the parties had dared to initiate a conversation outside the confines of staid protocol.

And what if the Special Branch's surveillance of Fok had stumbled upon some wrong-doing or indiscretion by another member of one of his households? Would the information be filed away somewhere for later use against the person concerned? Or used as blackmail against the principal target? Would such shady ramifications be legal?

There was no documentation in the Postmaster General's safe which definitively addressed those questions. However, since the operation had been running for a goodly period, the issues of legality and public interest must have been already weighed carefully by the administration's legal and constitutional advisors.

All colonial regimes came fully equipped with draconian internal security regulations in case of mutiny or rebellion. Hong Kong was no exception.

Regrettably, far too many ex-British colonies had retained those harsh British laws after independence to keep their populations under control. British politicians frequently boasted of establishing the rule of law in far flung places but none seemed willing to praise the internal security laws they had bequeathed as well. Thinking about such issues, however, soon led me inevitably into the toxic fog rising out of yet another bureaucratic moral swamp.

In an open and accountable society, the privacy of its citizens should matter greatly and should not be invaded by third parties without judicial due process. Such intrusions could hardly be justified on the flimsy grounds of fighting crime or national security alone. If that was the case, then how should the claims of friendship stack up against the requirements of public duties? Should I reveal to Pat and her mother, for instance, that their letters and phone conversations were being monitored by governmental agencies without their permission?

But before I could work out the right answers, another surprising development set me back on my heels.

* * *

When I took over as Postmaster General, I chose to work from the Deputy's office using my existing private secretary, rather than to move office and break in a new secretary. The only exception I made was when I had to deal with some of the secret files in the Postmaster General's safe.

One day, I had gone down to the main hall of the General Post Office on a lower floor of the building to observe the staffing levels at the various postal counters and to determine how quickly customers were being served at each. After a while, I headed back to my office.

On the way back, I saw a couple of postal officers emerging from the ante-room to the Postmaster General's office. As we approached one another along the corridor, I asked if they had wanted to see me.

"No, Sir," they replied, rather sheepishly, before continuing on their way.

After they had disappeared from sight, I was tickled by a slight curiosity. I headed for the ante-room, where the Postmaster General's private secretary was located, and asked her what the two officers were after in her room.

"Oh, they were just collecting their pay, Sir," she replied.

"Their pay?" I said, puzzled. "But the Treasury pays all of us directly through bank accounts."

"It's for their night shifts, Sir."

"But officers on shifts get paid the same way. Why would they need to come here?"

"They're the people doing unofficial overtime, in connection with the Q List. Their overtime is paid in cash. I've been asked to handle those payments and I, too, get paid extra for that work. Our understanding was that the extra money need not be declared for tax purposes."

"Oh, yes, of course. Slipped my mind completely," I said, shaken, before retreating quickly to my own office.

* * *

Back at my own desk, I was astounded by my latest discovery. I had deliberately refrained from asking the Postmaster General's secretary further questions for fear of exposing my own ignorance and of finding more unsavoury surprises. Internal security regulations might put a legal veneer over rifling through people's mail and tapping their phones for the sake of fighting crime or protecting national security but I could not imagine how using some slush fund to fiddle on income tax could be justified.

The government had trumpeted the setting up of an Independent Commission Against Corruption to fight corruption in society and yet it was using improper practices to circumvent the law within its own administration.

And here I was, unwittingly supervising a part of that malpractice. How could I keep silent and do nothing?

But all the courses of action open to me seemed completely useless, if not actually dangerous. I could, for example, pretend to be upset and demand to know why my staff involved in operating the Q List were getting extra tax-free cash whereas I, as their head, was getting nothing. The trouble with that approach was that the next time the moneybag came around there might well be a sum earmarked for me! That would suck me deeper into the morass.

Any other form of protest would appear just as pointless. I was a bird of passage, holding the fort only temporarily, waiting for the substantive head of department to return from leave. Any protest I made could easily be put in a government pigeon-hole until after my retirement. That would render the entire matter irrelevant and moot.

I could possibly inform the Commissioner for Inland Revenue that I suspected some of my staff were not declaring all their income for salary tax purposes. But that would only land the staff involved in hot water. They were only doing what they had been told to do, as expendable pawns in a cynical game played by foreign puppet masters. Putting them on the spot would not resolve the inherent contradictions in the system.

Whistleblowing to some of my old journalistic friends was another option. But it would not take the administration long to zero in on the source of that type of security breach. I was bound by the provisions of the Colonial Regulations as well as the Official Secrets Act. The dreaded Colonial Regulation 55 could see me out on the street without a pension and without a recourse. Under the Official Secrets Act I could be prosecuted and imprisoned. What would happen to my children and their education then? I was almost home and dry, with a well-paid job and pension waiting for me. Was it worth risking all that on a vainglorious matter of principle?

I mulled my dilemma longer and more searchingly than I really needed to. That delay conveniently brought the Postmaster General back from leave.

The issue of principle was now clearly his to ponder rather than mine. Truly Shakespeare had it right all along. Conscience doth make cowards of us all.

* * *

With the return of the head of department, the time had arrived for me to leave. I was much humbled and moved by an initiative by the staff of the department to give me a farewell dinner. I was an outsider and not really one of them. I had been in the department for only a year and had actually met only a small number of the 5,000 or so. I felt deeply touched.

Giving thanks to Post Office staff at the farewell dinner.

In truth, I had done very little for them. I had merely simplified and improved the means of communication between staff and management. Perhaps I had boosted the confidence of the Chinese staff a little, by demonstrating that they could function with equal efficiency without being led by expatriates at the top.

The staff, after discovering my interest in antique Chinese seals, also clubbed together to present me with a beautiful and costly piece of seal stone known among connoisseurs as a "white hibiscus". I naturally sought the government's permission before accepting so fine a gift.

All in all, I left the department with a certain amount of regret. If circumstances had been different, I think I would have enjoyed staying longer in that department. But that was not to be.

* * *

Footnote:

In 1982, a little over a year after I had left the department, one of the postal unions went public with a complaint of discrimination. It alleged that while certain of its members were allowed to earn extra money by working overtime on night shifts, other members were not granted that same opportunity.

The response from the government was that the anomaly had been remedied. It scrapped the entire Q List operation altogether, obviating the need for Special Branch approved postal officers to perform the clandestine work. The swiftness with which the long-running scheme had been done away with suggested that it had probably been neither effective, efficient nor necessary to begin with. The whole matter thereby petered out without public fuss.

Once again, the editors and investigative journalists of the supposedly free press had apparently been fast asleep on their jobs. No one contacted the trade union in question to discover the nature and roots of its complaint. Neither did anyone probe the administration to explain the allegation of discrimination.

If somebody had, there might well have been quite an interesting story about just how much public money the government had been spending to photograph the letters of ordinary citizens and to tap their telephones to allegedly prevent crime and subversion. The results, presumably, could or could not be shown to justify the cost and effort. Either way, some additional public relations spin would have been required. If the results were meagre or questionable, why had the operation been going on for so many years? And if good results spoke for themselves, why suspend the operation?

The episode illustrated clearly why a free and independent press has to be vital to the health of any free and democratic society. The Fourth Estate has the responsibility to record, elucidate, educate and entertain, while at the same time holding governments and big public entities to account. This was of particular importance in a society driven by naked free market capitalism at one end and a cosy collection of franchised monopolies at the other. Without active and enquiring journalism, society would soon degenerate into a playing field for the rich and the powerful.

That role for the media is given added importance in the present age of general governmental incompetence, propaganda, bluster, disinformation, lies and deceit. The privacy, liberty and even lives of ordinary citizens are being sacrificed too often — possibly even willingly so — in order to protect society from some mocked-up or exaggerated evil. There needs to be openness and accountability for many of the deeds done by governments in the name of their citizens. Both independent media and whistleblowers have vital roles to play.

Recent events have shown how the mainstream media in many parts of the world, in a greedy search for quick profits, have descended into sheer gutter journalism. The American mainstream media, for example, are controlled by a group of five or six conglomerates and through their bad handling of the 2016 presidential elections, had produced the unintended consequence of having Donald Trump elected to the most powerful public office in the world. They seemed to have sunk even further below the abominable "yellow journalism" standards set in the era of William Randolph Hearst.

In journalism — as in other important fields of social endeavour like banking, the judiciary and government — public trust is of the utmost importance. Once that has been compromised or lost, the public would cease reading, listening or viewing what they have to offer.

Concerned citizens should, however, also be aware that people usually end up with the media they deserved. The advances in technology, the rising costs of production and the relentless concentration of media power in the hands of a few gigantic corporations are posing serious challenges to independent voices in the media in all democratic societies.

Just within my own lifetime, I had witnessed in Hong Kong the disappearances of two venerable newspapers due to the ravages of market forces — the *China Mail* and the *Hong Kong Telegraph*. The former had existed for 130 years and I had been accredited as its London correspondent for a year during 1957-58. So its demise in 1974 created quite some nostalgia and regret for me.

Ultimately, it is for ordinary citizens to decide what they want as their source for news, information and analysis. If they do not want to put up with a numbing diet of empty slogans, fake news, official handouts and celebrity tittle-tattle then they have to do something about it. Unfortunately, there is no such thing as a free lunch. If they want something with substance, something which would enhance their daily lives, then they will have to pay for it.

CHAPTER 17

A Summing Up

THIS THIRD VOLUME of my family memoirs covers roughly the second half of my 20 years of service as an Administrative Officer in the Hong Kong government. That period ran roughly from the autumn of 1970, when I was sent to Oxford to study the international monetary system, to the spring of 1981, when the need to meet my sons' wishes to study in North America forced me retire from public service to take on a more lucrative job in the private sector, as the managing director of an international trading company.

In writing this book, one can hardly escape the fact that much of one's time is spent in the trivia of quotidian existence. Events of real significance to one's personal or family life are few and far between. Rarer still are deeds with any social or political consequence.

Fortuitously, the period I have written about coincided with the tenure of Sir Murray MacLehose as the Governor of Hong Kong. That has enabled me to garnish my account with a few tales of a more general interest.

My relationships with Sir Murray, both working and social, had been quite limited. I was too far down the bureaucratic food chain to be much in his company. When we were in contact, however, we were seldom on the same wavelength. My views on the state of the colony and its problems were seldom on all fours with his, with the result that most of my suggestions were either ignored or rejected out of hand.

Sir Murray was the longest serving Governor in the colony's history. He held office from November of 1971 to May of 1982. His appointment had been the most unusual for over a hundred years, in that previous governors had been colonial administrators with experience either locally or elsewhere in the British empire whereas Sir Murray was parachuted in after a career in diplomacy. Presumably a person practised in those dark arts was deemed necessary during the twilight of empire. In any case, the end of the Chinese lease for the New Territories in 1997 stood like a giant "Stop" sign in the middle of the political highway.

Sir Murray was an impressive man, standing six-foot-three in his socks. He had a patrician carriage, accompanied by a softness of speech and a personal likability. He had an autocratic streak, however, which he disguised most adroitly in public. The governorship had given him a chance to leave a mark for posterity. That might have led him to become — in the words of one of my former colleagues — "fond of shooting first and asking questions afterwards".

Within the Hong Kong establishment, there had been misgivings when Sir Murray's appointment was announced. He was too much of an unknown quantity to the gin-and-tonic set. Many doubted whether he could handle a rambunctious Chinese population riddled with divided loyalties and who generally regarded Europeans as "foreign devils".

Apprehensions abounded within the local community as well. What was the temperament of this new satrap? Was he as approachable and down-to-earth as the one he was replacing — Sir David Trench — or was he a person given to imperious airs? As a representative of the British Crown, what was his mission? To prepare local opinion for some dubious Sino-British deal? But if things were ticking over nicely with the Communist authorities across the border, why appoint a diplomat?

I, too, shared some of those ambivalences. A diplomat seemed little more than a silver-tongued and better-mannered politician. Their kind had made decisions which festered like weeping sores long after they had departed. The Balfour declaration, the Sykes-Picot carve-up, the partition of the Indian subcontinent *et al* stood as ghastly reminders.

It seemed unlikely that Hong Kong would suffer a similar fate. The local population was simply too pragmatic a bunch. But with a diplomat of unknown temperament at the helm, the future could be quite hit or miss. I told myself I had to tread carefully as a civil servant. The terrain ahead could be more unstable and treacherous than I had anticipated.

This book represents my two cents' worth on that period of Hong Kong's history with which I had some marginal involvement.

* * *

A little background context might be useful before I attempt to sum up. Prior to Sir Murray's tenure, I had already served for more than ten years as an Administrative Officer, having signed up at the beginning of 1961. Prior to that, I had spent my first 32 years following a rootless and wandering life in a number of different callings.

Immediately after joining the civil service, I was assigned to work for David Baron, who was then the Director of Social Welfare. Baron turned out to be a very thoughtful, caring and supportive superior. He taught me how each officer could do some good even within a vast and impersonal bureaucracy. The energy and dedication he brought to his own duties and his concern for his subordinates caused me to reflect on how I, too, might make a similar contribution.

My previous interfaces with officialdom had left me with a range of negative impressions. Officiousness and heavy-handedness seemed the order of the day, mingled with ignorance, racism and bullying. It made me want to make some difference, now that I was part of the machinery.

Most people had little idea what public administration was all about, even though they enjoyed its benefits almost every day. The complexities of modern urban life were too interconnected for many to absorb. Everything was part of a larger but hidden design, ranging from night-soil collectors to the suited mandarins dealing with other forms of unpleasantness. It was only when things went awry, when rubbish remained uncollected or when essential electricity or water supplies got disrupted, that the public would notice that what had passed for normality had broken down.

My initial years in government service were eye-opening. It was bewildering at first; but I soon appreciated the complexities and the need for patience to bring about even modest changes.

The government decided in 1965, after I had competed my probation, to send me to the Institute of Social Studies in The Hague for further studies in public administration. The students there were largely made up of civil servants from less developed countries. My conversations with them gave me fresh insights into the different sets of challenges each of them had to facd.

In the poorer countries, people were more likely to be suffering from inadequate education, tribal allegiances, hierarchical rigidities, religious antagonisms, superstitions, immaturity, poor health and apathy. Their leaders might also be autocrats, dictators, oligarchs, kleptomaniacs, war criminals or mere stooges. Where elections existed, they might be rigged, manipulated, tampered with or simply bought or stolen.

The drive towards urbanisation threw up additional problems of enormous magnitudes for them, like the breakdown of the traditional rural family structures, environment degradations, the prevention of contagious diseases, isolation and alienation of the individual and the rise of a new and unfamiliar range of criminal activities.

The professional associations, trade unions, chambers of commerce, industrial bodies and voluntary non-governmental organisations which might otherwise help in the transformational process or provide meaningful checks upon misguided policies or political excesses were usually weak or non-existent.

As the months went by, I could not help commiserating with them. I was grateful that, by comparison, Hong Kong's problems were infinitely less taxing and more solvable.

Hong Kong had also been blessed immediately after the Second World War by having a large number of very able Administrative Officers on its payroll. Among them were David Trench, Ronald Holmes, David Alexander, Donald Luddington and Michael Clinton, all of whom had been actual war heroes, either highly decorated as such or mentioned in despatches. The crucible of war had somehow matured, humbled and humanised them. Having lived through quite unique and dangerous situations, they all became admirable people to work for.

In addition, Hong Kong also had the services of a few intellectually outstanding administrators, like John Cowperthwaite, Claude Burgess and Alistair Todd. Collectively, they helped shaped a tradition of dedication, fair-dealing and intellectual honesty.

It has been said that all bureaucracies had to be animated from some source, taking their spirit and character from somewhere. In my view, the post-war administration had undoubtedly derived both spiritual and intellectual nourishment from the officers I have mentioned above.

It was an enormous privilege for me to have worked for most of them. They collectively restored the reputation of the administration from the scandals and corruption of the 19th century and set the stage for developing a prouder and cleaner ethos in the 20th century. The opening up of the service to Chinese officers after World War II also helped to add cultural diversity.

Cowperthwaite, in particular, did wonders economically and financially for Hong Kong when he served as Financial Secretary from 1961 to 1971. He not only had a firm grasp of economics but also more common sense and unerring local knowledge than many gave him credit for.

Just one example would be sufficient to illustrate his approach to problem-solving. Talk of having a bridge or tunnel to link Hong Kong Island to the

Kowloon peninsula had been bruited around for decades but to no avail. Economic and environmental impediments stood firmly in the way.

In the late 1960s, however, a private sector consortium put forward a proposal to finance and build a 1.16-mile tunnel under the harbour. The proposal was based on a build, operate and transfer model.

In other words, the consortium would build and operate the tunnel on a 30-year franchise, after which the ownership of the tunnel would be transferred to the government. The proposal envisaged two lanes of motor traffic in the tunnel, one in each direction. The calculations of the consortium had no doubt been based on a minimum of capital outlay and a maximisation of returns.

But Cowperthwaite, as Financial Secretary, would have none of it. He told the consortium he would not consider a franchise unless the consortium doubled the capacity of the tunnel to two lanes each way. The consortium went away to mull its figures. It continued to lobby for its original plan. In the end, however, it agreed to what had been asked.

A Cross Harbour Tunnel Ordinance was therefore passed by the Legislative Council in 1969 and the project went ahead, with the public purse providing only the access roads. The tunnel opened in 1972 and it soon became one of the colony's most heavily used thoroughfares. The consortium earned vast profits, notwithstanding being forced to increase capital commitments well beyond its original projections. The tunnel was transferred to public ownership in 1999.

That episode undermined the myth that the private sector always knew better than civil servants when it came to making business decisions. I had no knowledge of what Cowperthwaite had taken into account when he made his démarche for the tunnel's capacity to be doubled. No doubt he must have studied the growth of vehicular traffic on the cross-harbour ferries operated by the Hong Kong and Yaumati Ferry Company. But he must also have factored in various intangibles, like the middle-class's obsession with private car ownership, the growth in the wealth of the community and the likely conservative projections supplied by the consortium. In whatever way he arrived at his decision, he had enough courage of his own conviction to call the consortium's bluff.

The way that Cowperthwaite and his contemporaries handled various issues reminded me of a passage from Herman Finer, a British political scientist. Finer once asserted: "If men and women are competent enough, they can give life even to inexact, confused, and rough-hewn demarcations. Personnel is the sovereign factor in public administration. Will and mind are first; they engender policy, and mechanism is subsidiary to function." How true!

If further evidence were needed to demonstrate the managerial capabilities of many Hong Kong civil servants, subsequent years showed that the Mass Transit system, the Hong Kong section of the Kowloon and Canton Railway and the two main bus companies in the colony had all been successfully run by ex-Administrative Officers. So also the management of the Daya Bay nuclear power station in Kwangtung Province, which continues to this day to supply a significant amount of electricity for Hong Kong.

* * *

One of the things that struck me while studying at The Hague was that hardly any of the Western literature on public administration ever made reference to China's long experience with running a vast territory. For example, the Chinese had long held the notion that public officials were there primarily to serve the people. Thousands of years before opinion polls became fashionable, wise Chinese kings and emperors had sent officials out to collect the folk songs sung by the common people, so that they could be acquainted with the joys and sorrows being expressed by their subjects through song.

They also had the foresight to set up an Imperial Censorate, whose members had the duty to criticise the policies and conduct of the government. Imperial

Censors were expected to function in much the same way as the modern independent media used to, before turning themselves into self-serving oligopolies controlled by the few. They used to criticise without fear or favour, beholden to no one. If their comments were cogent enough, they could bring down governments.

But Chinese Imperial Censors had no legal or constitutional protection. Their activities could only count on the moral support of tradition. It would be up to the emperor to listen to them and to take action, even if powerful personages or court favourites came under attack. Censors knew they could risk their jobs or their lives by expressing inconvenient opinions.

Most celebrated of all was China's imperial examinations system, which for over 2,000 years had been aimed at selecting the most meritorious candidates for public offices. Furthermore, to guard against favouritism, such officials would never be allowed to serve in their native districts. They would normally be rotated every three years to prevent them getting too cosy with local vested interests.

Since Hong Kong was a Chinese city, it was puzzling why the British had not taken greater account of China's experiences in organising its colonial bureaucracy. I therefore decided, after my return from The Hague, to see what I could discover by studying at greater length the history of the Chinese and Western systems of appointing public officials.

* * *

In the West, Alexander the Great was probably the first ruler to demonstrate the economic and political gains to be had from good organisation. But on the whole, Western writers from Xenophon to Machiavelli tended to concentrate on how a ruler could best retain his power. This was understandable because Europe was for many centuries made up of only principalities and city states, often at war with one another. Few had to deal with ruling any territory as extensive as China's.

In the 12th century, Frederick II made a number of promulgations on the subject and some writers later claimed he had issued "the birth certificate of modern bureaucracy". But actually a spoils system, based on nepotism, patronage and shifting alliances, prevailed long afterwards. Those with power basically issued licences to friends and supporters to make money, either in the form of a letter of marque to attack foreign shipping for plunder and spoils or through awarding an "office of profit under the Crown".

No one seemed particularly alarmed by such unseemly developments until around the middle of the 19th century. Then a German professor by the name of Lorenz von Stein raised the issue. He pointed out that public administration had to take into account other disciplines, like sociology, political science, administrative law and public finance. He was duly dubbed "the father of the science of public administration".

Around that time, Bismarck was considering the amalgamation of some of the Germanic states and Britain was starting to move towards some form of merit-based civil service. Thereafter, British appointments both domestically and throughout the empire went through a selection process.

Not to be outdone by Europeans, Woodrow Wilson, the future American President, penned an essay titled *The Study of Administration* in 1887 and brought the subject to greater academic attention. His supporters claimed he was "the father of public administration".

At the beginning of the 20th century, Brooks Adams, an American historian, held that a rapidly changing world environment was creating an unprecedented need for the administrative or generalising mind and that any failure to meet that need could lead to revolutions and even to the eventual dissolution of civilisation itself.

A whole range of other scholars soon echoed a similar view. For example, Charles A. Beard stated that: "There is no subject more important . . . than this subject of administration. The future of civilised government, and even,

I think, of civilisation itself rests upon our ability to develop a science and philosophy and a practice of administration competent to discharge the public functions of civilised society." Dwight Waldo, another writer, added in his book *The Study of Public Administration* that: "Administration is at the centre of our civilisation, and it is the big questions that civilisation is about, one way or another."

Thus the importance of public administration gradually became recognised in the West. But certain important administrative processes still remained either ignored or not fully analysed.

* * *

On the other hand, the massive Chinese literature reaching back for well over 2,000 years gave early recognition to its importance. The whole issue came to the fore soon after the first Emperor of Ch'in unified the country by defeating the rest of the feudal kingdoms in 221 BC. Conquering a vast land mass was the relatively easy part of his enterprise; administering it was much harder. The Ch'in Dynasty faltered in its attempts to do so and, coupled with its own cruel misrule, the dynasty collapsed after only about 15 years.

The Han Dynasty came into being as a result. The same problem had to be faced. It was a thinker by the name of Tung Chung-Shu who offered a solution based on Confucian teachings and their moral imperatives.

Tung lived approximately between 179 and 104 BC. He had some unfounded notions about Confucius being sent by Heaven to start a new dynasty but apart from that, he was largely responsible for installing a management system for the new empire.

He did this by writing a memorial to the Han Emperor Wu around 136 BC, suggesting that territorial unification was not enough. A unification of thought was needed as well, he argued, before recommending that: "All not within the field of the Liu Yi (Six Classics) should be cut short and not allowed to progress further."

Some might interpret Tung's words as a return to the failed authoritarian state doctrine already attempted by the First Emperor of Ch'in. But that was not the case. Confucian thinking had made progress after unification and had become more eclectic by amalgamating some ideas from other schools of thought. What Tung was trying to do was to gain pre-eminence for Confucian precepts, by making knowledge of them a prerequisite for those seeking official positions. He viewed governance as a moral undertaking.

Emperor Wu accepted Tung's recommendation and formally announced that Confucianism would be regarded as the official state teaching. The Emperor also decreed that those who were experts in other schools of philosophy should be ejected from government posts. But he did not specify any punishment for the teaching non-Confucian ideas on a private basis.

The moves initiated by Tung had far-reaching effects. They imposed not only an implied duty upon those carrying out official duties to take account of the Confucian virtues of human-heartedness and righteousness but also reinforced certain popular habits and values which have persisted in Chinese society till the present day. Examples would be the general cohesiveness of the family structure among large segments of the population and the keenness of parents to get their children educated.

Tung believed that man — contrary to the Christian belief that man was born in sin and needed to be redeemed by Christ — was born inherently good. But his natural goodness had to be developed through education, until it reached its full potential. Otherwise that inherent goodness would be wasted, like the proverbial seeds being cast upon stony ground. Government officials, Tung felt, should be teachers to cultivate the goodness in people.

Under his system, the selection of officials was no longer dependent upon wealth or noble birth or being well-connected but on merit. That merit would be determined through periodic public examinations, open to all, but centred upon mastery of the Confucian classics. That system made for more social mobility and the development of a new aristocracy schooled in a humane philosophy. Its members could thus be trusted with the affairs of state and with promoting the public good.

The examinations were conducted at four levels. The lowest was at the county level and then the district level. Those who passed those levels but failed to move beyond them might still gain some minor position as a clerk or village headman. Otherwise, they might become teachers. The provincial level was next and those who passed them often secured positions of considerable influence and power.

But the plum positions were reserved for those who could pass the examinations in the capital, held at the imperial palace where the emperor himself was theoretically the Examiner-in-Chief. Most emperors, however, delegated that duty to someone else. Those who passed at that level secured high positions and became important members of the bureaucracy.

* * *

The Han Dynasty came to an end in 220. What followed was another 400 years of armed conflicts, confusion and disunity. A series of different dynasties once again ruled over different parts of the country. Alien races who had penetrated the Great Wall reigned in the north. During that period of social instability and political uncertainty, Taoism revived. Buddhism also made great inroads after its arrival from India. It was not till 590 that the Sui Dynasty managed to reunify the country again.

But the Sui Dynasty began encountering the same problems of administrating so vast a territory. It updated some aspects of the imperial examinations system but its rule did not last long. It was replaced by the powerful and highly centralised Tang Dynasty. That marked the start of another golden age in Chinese cultural development.

The imperial examination system again became reformed and re-established in 622. A few years later the Emperor Tai Tsung ordered that a Confucian temple be established in the Imperial University and that an official edition of the Confucian Classics be prepared, together with the commentaries made upon them. The emperor then reaffirmed Confucianism as the official teaching of the state by commanding that its classics and commentaries be taught at the Imperial University.

The examinations at the capital were always gruelling affairs. The candidates had to turn up at dawn with their cold meals because they would not be allowed to leave until the examinations were over. Such examinations lasted for several days, with candidates isolated in cubicles.

The Confucian classics might be filled with moral exhortations, but that did not prevent some candidates from trying to cheat. As a precaution against favouritism, all essays written by candidates had to be copied by clerks before the copies were submitted to the examiners, lest the calligraphy of some candidates might be recognised. Subjects for essays were set, sometimes by the Emperor as the Examiner-in-Chief, and sometimes by the Prime Minister. Candidates had to expound on the subjects specified, with references to the classics and the literary allusions contained therein. It was rare for anyone to be sufficiently prepared for success at the national examinations much before the age of 30.

In addition, the passing rate was quite low. For example, it was recorded that in the 1889 examinations over 14,000 sat but only about 300 passed. Even that low pass rate could sometimes lead to problems in that the creation of civil service posts was slower than the number passing the examinations!

On the other hand, there was no bar whatsoever to any failed candidate presenting himself again at the next round. Hung Hsiu-Chuan, the leader of the Taiping Rebellion, had presented himself for the examinations four times and had failed each time. Had he been successful, the rebellion in 1850 which cost between 20 and 25 million lives, might conceivably have been averted.

There was another celebrated case of perseverance by a man named

Liang Hao who had lived during the Sung Dynasty. He kept turning up for examinations until he finally passed one at the age of 84.

It had also been recorded that in 1889, in Anhui Province, 18 of the candidates at the provincial examinations had been over the age of 90! It was therefore not uncommon for a grandfather, a father and a son to be all sitting for the same set of examinations at the same time. A sterling illustration of the practice encouraged in the old British maxim of "if at first you don't succeed, try, try again."

* * *

For a person to be acquainted with the nature of virtue was one thing; for him to live a life that was virtuous was quite another. Although all officials appointed through imperial examinations had, *prima facie*, to be steeped in Confucian ethics, quite a number of venal and self-serving ones held public offices. The sad truth was — and remains — that any combination of greed, arrogance, opportunity and force of circumstances could render human beings susceptible to corruption.

It ought not to be overlooked, however, that there had also been no shortage of officials living up to Confucian ideals. The stories of those righteous officials were the ones that the common people — generally referred to as the "old hundred surnames" — took to their hearts.

One of the earliest officials celebrated by them was Wat Yuen, who served in the kingdom of Chu during the period of the Warring States. Wat Yuen took office before the imperial system had even been instituted. When he realised his own inability to dissuade his sovereign from acting in a way harmful to his kingdom, he committed suicide by jumping into the Milo River clasping a large rock.

Wat Yuen also happened to be an exceptional poet and his long poem, "Encountering Sorrow", is still beloved by many today. The Dragon Boat

Festival, held each year on the fifth day of the fifth lunar month, continues to be celebrated by Chinese people everywhere, to honour his memory.

There had been many other principled officials throughout the ages. I have already made references to Chancellor Fan Chung-Yen of the Sung Dynasty and Chang Chu-Tseng of the Ming Dynasty in Chapter 6 of this memoir.

Fan wrote four essays against the decadent ways of his time and later submitted a ten-point petition to the throne suggesting, *inter alia*, the establishment of schools to train practical men for public service. He was much before his time. Chang, who held power for 14 years, instilled discipline into officialdom by insisting that each official should fulfil his duties according to his station in life.

Anyone with a reasonable knowledge of Chinese history can easily draw up his own list of admirable officials. There are many to choose from. My list would certainly include the Sung Dynasty official Su Tung-Po — a celebrated poet, prose master, calligrapher, painter, administrator, engineer, magistrate, Confucian statesman, Buddhist metaphysician and champion of the poor.

This is not the place to detail the many facets of Su's life or to trace the ups and downs in his tumultuous career. His public achievements ranged from the establishment of irrigation and sanitation systems in Hangchow and Canton to orphanages and hospitals wherever he found the need for them. His famine relief efforts and attempts to gain tax forgiveness for the poor were also exemplary.

His fall from imperial grace was just as spectacular, leading to his demotion, arrest, exile and being pilloried as the top name in the infamous Yuan Yu Partisans' Tablet. All the 309 people thus named and their children were forbidden by imperial decree from ever holding government office. It so happened that shortly after Su's death a thunderbolt struck the stone tablet erected at the palace and split it in two. But that is a story better told elsewhere. Suffice it to say that through good times and bad, Su never compromised his integrity or his principles.

It is not unreasonable that the standards set by people like Su should be the ones used nowadays to measure the performance of public officials. Whether today's younger generations know enough about such larger-than-life characters depends on their education. If Su's actions were brought to the attention of the young, I have little doubt he would attract many modern admirers, both for his courage and integrity as well as for his poetic and other talents.

Contemporaneous with Su was the great Sung Dynasty Prime Minister and historian Szema Kuang, who towered intellectually and morally above his generation. He was more interested in carrying out his duties than in personal power. He was also the author of the monumental *Mirror of History*, which recorded the history of China up till the Sung Dynasty. The work comprised 294 volumes plus 30 volumes of appendices and set the standard by which subsequent histories of China were judged.

Given China's long history, the odds must be that there had been many other honest and upright officials who went their way unsung and unremembered. The number might be far more than commonly imagined. Take for example some of the Imperial Censors who worked during parts of the Eastern Han Dynasty and the Ming Dynasty. They did their duty by holding truth to power and paid for their honest opinions with their lives. A number of them wrote their reports against official misdeeds without mincing words and then committed suicide because they knew that fate awaited them for daring to criticise powerful officials for corruption or for implementing misguided policies.

Apart from the Imperial Censors, other upright officials also often levelled sharp criticisms of government policies at a risk to their own careers. A flavour of such criticisms can be gleaned by quoting an extract from a letter Su Tung-Po wrote to the Emperor Shen Tsung.

Su was at the time only 32 and occupying a strictly literary post in the Department of History. He was against a scheme for forcing high-interest loans on peasants and he wrote: "In all things, great and small, one should not depend on force, but must observe reason and the nature of things. For in all things done according to reason one is bound to succeed, and in all undertaking against reason one is doomed to fail. Now your majesty has compelled the farmers to pay you high interest, and you have entered into competition with businessmen for profits. Is this in accordance with nature, and do you wonder that it has failed? . . . . If your majesty has the welfare of the people truly at heart, the people would show confidence in you despite all rumours; but if you are going only after revenue, the people can hardly be convinced by words. If a judge receives presents from a defendant and lets himself be influenced in his decision, people will only say he has been bribed; and if a man takes what does not belong to him people will call him a thief. That would only be calling a thing by its right name. Now, you are receiving 20 per cent interest from the farmers' loans, yet you are insisting that you are not making these loans for interest. How are people to believe you? . . . . A man is condemned by his acts and not by what he professes to do. . . . All this commotion is because the whole country is coming to believe that your majesty is looking for the revenue, while you maintain that you are only working for their good. While you insist that you are totally disinterested, the whole world thinks that you are avaricious."

Of course other officials might not have been as forthright as Su. When some found their work grating upon their consciences, they would simply use the time-honoured grounds of returning home to look after aged parents to seek the emperor's permission to leave. Such pleas, rooted firmly in the tradition of filial piety, were not ones that even bad emperors would dare to reject or refuse.

Such departing officials often left no historical mark, unless they also happened to excel in some other sphere of human activity. One such official was the Six Dynasties official Tao Yuan-Ming. He had served for ten years before becoming so disgusted by the in-fighting and corruption in the court that he decided to quit. Upon leaving, he coined a phrase which subsequently passed into common usage, indicating he was not prepared to "bow like a servant for five bushels of grain". He became a recluse after retirement and concentrated on writing poetry.

His poems did not make much of a splash during his lifetime. But when the most famous Tang poets, Li Po and Tu Fu, came along two-and-a-half centuries later and praised them, their praise elevated Tao to poetic greatness. Tu Fu, of course, was himself also a public official of great courage and character.

* * *

The Confucian principles instilled into Chinese civil servants did not end with the Revolution of 1911. When a republican constitution was being drafted, robust discussions on the role of Confucian teachings in the new republic took place. Eventually, it was decided that Confucianism should be adopted as a fundamental principle for ethical discipline in government. That new constitution, however, was never put into practice because the country soon descended into internecine war and factionalism again.

Nonetheless, Sun Yat-Sen continued to advocate his "Three Principles of the People" which relied heavily on Confucian ideals. Furthermore, when his disciple, Chiang Kai-Shek, ruled the country, he set out in his book *China's Destiny* in 1943 a programme for reforms which also laid heavy stress on Confucian principles.

Given the shallowness and muddled thinking about national education in contemporary Hong Kong, it might be worth quoting a passage from Chiang's book to provoke reflection.

The man who had spent much of his life fighting Communists said: "To cultivate the qualities essential to China's salvation means we must revive and extend the traditional ethical principles of our nation. The most important task is to develop our people's sense of propriety, righteousness, integrity and honour. . . . In China, loyalty in its highest sense is loyalty to the state; filial devotion in its highest sense is devotion to the nation. In both cases, one must be mindful of private and family interests in serving the public and the state. Obviously the existence of the state and nation is a prerequisite to individual existence. It follows that we should regard obedience to the orders of the government as something given of our own free will, and the service demanded of us by the state and nation as service rendered of our own free choice. Evasion or manipulation of the laws is not allowed by the government; the choice of easy duties in preference to what is difficult should not be approved by the people."

The Communists, meanwhile, were also giving thought on how to legitimise their rule. They took inspiration from a two-page essay written by Mao Tse-Tung in 1944 titled "Serve the People". The doctrine Mao expounded was that the Communist leadership should always be subordinated to and in sympathy with the masses of the people.

Since administrators and technologists were needed to modernise the country, the Communists decided that such officials should accept service to the public as the sole source of their authority and legitimacy. That implied that each one had to bear personal responsibility for his decisions. Mere efficiency in outcome was not enough; decisions had to pass the moral test of whether they served the people. After attaining power in 1949, the new government began putting that theory into practice.

The education system was re-organised to emphasise the need to serve the people and all secondary school students had to spend one month out of the school year to work on farms or in factories to guard against producing "educated snobs" seeking personal rewards or advancement like under Western managerial capitalism. Entry into university was also no longer a personal or family decision. A person wishing to proceed to university had first to secure nomination by his or her work unit, whereupon the candidate would then be vetted against other nominations from other work units.

The approach of trying to instil a sense of achievement through nation-building worked reasonably well for a couple of decades. Average productivity increased by nearly four per cent each year while wages and food prices remained relatively stable. Indeed, salaries at the upper levels were actually reduced in 1966. But contradictions began building up within the system and that set the stage for the Cultural Revolution.

The Communist emphasis on self-sacrifice and serving the people harked back in some ways to Confucian ideals, although certain other Confucians ideas came under attack for being feudalistic and impediments to socialist goals.

There was very early recognition by the Communists of the vital importance of trained personnel. Once they had attained power, they recognised that the country was vast and there was a lack of qualified people to do most of the work that had to be done. In order to jumpstart development, they set up an elaborate recruiting programme for trained overseas Chinese scattered around the world. They appealed to their patriotism, urging scientists, engineers, doctors, teachers and others to return to engage in the monumental task of reconstructing and modernising the Motherland. Apart from appealing to national pride, they offered generous employment terms, according to their qualifications and experience.

Many overseas Chinese responded during the 1950s — particularly those chaffing under colonial regimes — and China was thus able to make up to some extent the severe skill shortages in many spheres of national endeavour. Of course, quite a number who returned could not adjust to the austere lifestyle demanded of them and soon became disillusioned. But a great numbered stayed and made their contribution to China's modernisation.

Today, there appears to have been some overt promotion of Confucian values by the Chinese government. It is busy setting up Confucius Institutes in various countries across the globe to spread the teachings of the sage.

This brief and quite inadequate outline illustrates the fact that China, in spite of going off-track from time to time, had followed with consistency a philosophy of governance based on moral principles, with officials serving — in theory at least — as the father and mother of the people. How well those principles had been carried out over the centuries depended on the calibre and the dedication of the individuals holding office.

It seems strange that so many other civilisations should have failed to examine some of the Chinese historical practices and moral imperatives and, where appropriate, incorporate some of their positive features into their own public service systems.

Quite recently there has been talk in Hong Kong of starting a staff college to train senior civil servants. Such a project should have been started decades ago. Still, better late than never.

However, before anyone gets carried away, I would caution against following any model that currently exists elsewhere. It would be best if the staff college could begin with what ancient Confucian scholars called a rectification of names, that is, of using words with their actual meanings rather than employing a lot of flaky management-speak.

A Hong Kong college must also be rooted in local realities which the city's past educational system had, either by design or default, failed to impart to students. The college must first make up for that defect by bringing students a deeper awareness of China's cultural past, so that they can derive inspiration therefrom. A large dose of ethics and the histories of native Chinese philosophies would not go amiss, given the vital need for delivering both a caring and a corruption-free government. When all that has been absorbed, then there would be scope for comparisons with alien philosophies and other systems of governance and to select from them elements which might be worthy of emulating.

It might also be worthwhile for any local staff college to consider the range of different courses it might offer. For example, the successful completion of a basic course might be made a prerequisite before an officer could be confirmed to the permanent establishment. Likewise, the successful completion of a more advanced leadership course might be required for anyone seeking promotion to the directorate level. A reappraisal of the wisdom or otherwise of appointing officials on contract rather than on pensionable status should be carried out.

Lecturers at such a college should not be made up of pure academics but should also include retired top civil servants who have had long practical experience in navigating the slippery ins and outs of governance and had to decide not only between the good and the bad but also from a range of competing evils.

* * *

The British moves in the middle of the 19th century towards a merit-based system for selecting public officials naturally had an impact on Hong Kong. They resulted eventually in three Cambridge graduates being sent to the colony to serve as the first "cadets" in 1862.

It is important to point out that the British merit-based system was significantly different from the established Chinese one. First of all, the Chinese system was based on mastery of a particular philosophy, with all its attendant values and relationships within an established society. A successful candidate would be expected to conduct himself in accordance with the rules set by that philosophy.

The British system was not based on any political or religious creed but only on a candidate having acquired a decent university degree in a subject of his own choice. He would then be interviewed in the august chambers of the Foreign Office by a couple of eccentric old Etonians in pinstripes, who would probably ask him a few fay and esoteric questions on subjects of no great consequence.

Vacancies in Hong Kong had been quite limited for much of the 19th century and the early part of the 20th century, due to financial constraints. The odds on being selected, however, were still much better than those sitting through the rigours of an Imperial Examination in China.

After being appointed, a cadet did not have to follow any specific philosophical or religious orientation except to serve king and country. His decisions in whichever colony he might be sent could be made in accordance with his own disposition, save that he had to keep an eye out for any precedent which might have been established by predecessors before him. After World War II the cadets became known as Administrative Officers.

The second important difference between the two systems was that the British one was more firmly based on race than on merit. Although the Hong Kong administration had announced a policy of localisation in 1936, its implementation had been less than half-hearted. No Chinese was admitted into the Administrative Service till 1946, regardless of how many qualified or intellectually gifted Chinese candidates there might have been.

Even after that belated implementation of the localisation policy, the number of Chinese was still limited to one per annum. The ratio of roughly one Chinese to three expatriates prevailed till the early 1960s. That statistic hid a further disadvantage for locals because the whole selection process was conducted in the English language, which was not the natural language of local candidates.

For a long time, the official alibi for the low Chinese intake was that the local universities produced only a limited number of graduates and many of them had prepared themselves for other professions. That neatly sidestepped the fact that many Hong Kong students had gone abroad for studies as well and had returned looking for suitable employment. The more plausible reason for the low intake was because the British had reservations over the loyalty of locals in the face of rising irredentist sentiments in the 1960s. It was not until after the Sino-British Joint Declaration had been signed in 1984 that the recruitment of expatriate officers came to an end.

To be fair to the British, that precaution of keeping a conquered people in check was not unique among Western powers. When the Manchus conquered China in 1644, for example, they also insisted that every senior post occupied by a Chinese had to have a duplicate filled by a Manchu. Naturally, the Manchu counterparts, being political appointees, did not have to pass any competitive examination. The traditional Chinese system therefore became more corrupt towards the end of the Ching Dynasty. Some public offices were simply sold for cold hard cash.

The third difference was that the British system had no provision for demotions or other specified forms of punishments for inefficiencies or failures to function effectively. Indeed, since each officer had a personal grade, he would suffer no reduction in salary should he be assigned to a less important post. Unless he committed a misdeed serious enough to warrant criminal prosecution or action under Colonial Regulation 55, his pay and his iron rice bowl were secure. The worst that might be expected would be to be sidelined in some backwater.

The Chinese system was different. If an official performed unsatisfactorily, he could be easily demoted, fined, given a reduced salary, exiled or dismissed. If he fell out of favour with a foolish Emperor, he might suffer an infinitely worse fate.

* * *

After I had joined the administration, I was asked on three occasions during the 1960s to sit on recruitment boards for selecting local Administrative Officers. Those were interesting experiences which I had detailed in Chapter 6.

Much as I would have liked to see more Chinese at the apex of government service, I saw no merit in simply having more yellow faces for the sake of more yellow faces. Quality mattered. In my view, a local candidate had to be better than the average run of expatriate recruits because the colonial dice were already loaded against him. His performance would be placed under a microscope. If he performed well, that would be taken as a matter of course. After all, he had been selected by a panel composed mainly of senior expatriate officers. If he did poorly, knowing smirks would be exchanged to confirm the die-hard myth that local people were simply not up to governing themselves.

Very able local officers, like Eric Ho and Lai Ka-Wah, had failed in their initial attempts to join. Candidates sitting for the Chinese Imperial Examinations over the centuries had also regularly failed. So it was no shame not to make the grade on the first try. But it was important that those selected should be made of superior stuff.

The problem of governance was not just a matter of officers of one race *vis-à-vis* those of another. Good governance required a combination of brainpower, a questioning attitude and a sense of moral purpose. Hong Kong was a very competitive city; fortunes in other callings beckoned relentlessly. A candidate who had been turned down might head elsewhere and be lost to the public service forever. After all, civil service pay promised only hard graft and plain living. That was why I considered the ethical predispositions and the willingness of candidates to dedicate themselves to public service were much more important than their intelligence.

My approach, however, did not find favour after Sir Murray came on the scene. He wanted admission standards to be lowered, on the grounds that every candidate had to serve a three-year probation and anyone found inadequate could be tossed out before confirmation. I had grave reservations over his approach and made my reservations known. As a result, I was never again asked to serve on a recruitment board.

The repercussions of laxer recruitment requirements did not become obvious to Sir Murray till the end of his tenure, when he had to seek outsiders to fill key posts. In subsequent years, long after I had left the service, I derived a certain amount of satisfaction from noting that many of those chosen by the boards I had been on had reached the highest ranks in the government.

* * *

As I climbed the bureaucratic ladder, it became apparent that — contrary to public perceptions — administrators in key positions had some scope for creative changes within the civil service, if they were so inclined. Even minor tweaks to existing procedures could bring more convenience and benefits to the general public.

But there existed some issues which could only be tackled if entrenched orthodoxies were challenged. The inequality in treatment between local and expatriate officers was glaring, for instance. For a Chinese officer in a British bureaucracy to raise such an issue — unless done as a trade union representative — entailed risks of being labelled as a person with a racial chip on his shoulder. Likewise the heavy Eurocentric content in the educational system had the effect of de-culturalising and destabilising Chinese children.

And yet, curiously, there appeared to be many human traits common in the make-up of the ordinary Chinese and British peoples. For instance, both possessed a strong sense of fair play and were given to a range of eccentricities. Moreover, many maxims hallowed in both cultures were almost identical in meaning, as in "My word is my bond" or "Death before dishonour."

Notwithstanding such similarities, the lack of awareness by the young of their own culture and past hampered them in divining a meaningful future for themselves. And that fast-approaching future clearly presaged the ending of colonialism by 1997, if not earlier.

But there was no way for me to raise such fundamental worries because they fell outside my immediate areas of responsibility. To attempt to do so would mark me as a member of the awkward squad if not as a potential subversive.

Nonetheless, I could foresee conflicts arising sooner or later, when I would be forced to take a stand. I concluded that should such an eventuality arise, I would have to align myself first and foremost with the interests of the people of Hong Kong rather than those of the British Crown. After all, local taxpayers were paying my salary.

It came to me in looking back on my studies about public administration that hardly any Western writer had touched upon the kind of predicament I faced. The conventional maxim was that civil servants ought to be neutral and execute whatever instructions they received from their political masters.

My contacts with civil servants from other parts of the world suggested that my type of predicament was really not uncommon. There were simply too many low quality and dishonest politicians around. Besides, what if political masters had attained power through gerrymandering or rigged elections or military coups? Would they command enough legitimacy for career civil servants to obey? And what if power had arisen out of a war of aggression and occupation?

Career civil servants — by the very fact they had chosen their particular calling — had to assume some responsibility for protecting their own community's best interests. They were also more likely to have better information at their disposal and greater understanding of the needs of their own people. It had to be fitting for them, under those circumstances, to assume the roles of either grey eminences or initiators of resistance.

Such developments have emerged in many countries plagued by coups and civil wars in recent decades. Even in stable societies, crises of conscience could arise. For example, senior British civil servants resigned in 1956 in protest against the British, French and Israeli conspiracy to seize the Suez Canal from Egypt contrary to international law. A number of American government employees and investigative journalists have also risked prison to expose unlawful acts by their governments. Whistleblowing has become more commonplace with advances in technology. Three cheers for Wikileaks! Such developments ought to be encouraged and legally protected in democratic societies.

On the other hand, it should be remembered that every government has secrets that could not be disclosed till long after the event. For example, when one government enters negotiations with another government, it would be contrary to the national interest of both to openly disclose their respective negotiating positions. Even news of consideration being given to many government projects could be sensitive to markets.

But the sacrifices of high-minded civil servants and others in disclosing wrongdoings or corruption would lose much of their meaning if independent mass media were not receptive to carrying their disclosures to the wider public, so that the politicians and governments could be held to account, either criminally or the next time voters entered voting booths.

Unfortunately, government surveillance over the private lives of citizens has been steadily increasing at the same time that control of the mass media has slipped steadily into the hands of corporate oligarchs. Those dismal developments have given governments and corporations greater scope for distorting or fabricating facts for their own ends. How to secure greater personal liberties and to give the public access to impartial and uncensored news remain compelling challenges for free societies everywhere.

* * *

Thus I arrived at certain notions over the years of what the proper role of a civil servant ought to be. By the time Sir Murray MacLehose became Hong Kong's Governor in November of 1971, I was serving in the post of City District Commissioner for Hong Kong Island.

My first interface with Sir Murray came almost immediately and I have described what happened in Chapter 3. A remarkable outcome of that episode was that probably for the first and last time since the tramway system began operations in 1904, a sitting Hong Kong Governor had ridden on a local tram and rubbed shoulders with ordinary citizens.

The next thing I heard was that the Governor had decided to splash out HK$4.7 million to engage a firm of management consultants, McKinsey & Company, to re-organise and modernise the Secretariat. I, together with quite a number of my colleagues, doubted whether a management company would be up to dealing with the many contradictions and subtleties within a colonial occupation machine.

To me, Sir Murray's decision seemed a dismal augury for the future. The hard men in management consultancies were accustomed to crunching numbers, extrapolating from them, identifying efficiencies and squeezing out additional profitability. Public administration was not the application of a set of management tools, as some writers had suggested. Nor could it be a science, as others had grandiloquently claimed.

Administration — in my view — was an art, practised under haphazard and evolving circumstances. It involved some imagined future cluttered up with a mixture of intangibles, core beliefs, ancient traditions, modern abstractions and pure hunches. But human elements always had to be factored in. If some efficiencies could be attained only at the price of a loss in human-heartedness, then those efficiencies had best be lost. That approach called for sticking one's neck out and making individual judgements.

Given such early developments, I told myself to be prepared for the vagaries of a new broom. My hope was that in making a clean sweep he would not do away with too many of the good practices painfully accumulated over the decades.

* * *

My first difference of opinion with Sir Murray on a substantive policy issue concerned a matter which arose long before his arrival. It had its roots in the

1970 announcement by the Americans that they would end the occupation of Okinawa in 1972. In doing so, they intended to hand over to Japanese control also some uninhabited islands near Okinawa which had long been claimed by the Chinese, who called them the Diaoyu Tai Islands.

The American announcement provoked world-wide protests by Chinese students. Protests naturally occurred in Hong Kong as well. At first the local protests were small but momentum soon built up and the student leaders wanted to organise a much bigger demonstration at Victoria Park on the 7th of July in 1971. They sought police permission to hold the event but the police decided to bamboozle them with bureaucratic excuses to avoid creating a precedent for granting permission for such a politically tinged event. The background to that not altogether honourable decision by government has been set out in Chapter 2.

The net result was that an unlawful assembly took place and the police attempts to disperse the crowds led to rioting spilling out into the commercial areas of Causeway Bay. In its aftermath, the then Governor, Sir David Trench, instructed me to open a dialogue with student leaders to defuse the situation. I spent the next nine months conducting one-on-one conversations with more than 50 leaders of student unions and youth groups and reporting back after each occasion to Donald Luddington, the then Secretary for Home Affairs.

As time went by, the local student and youth leaders were left feeling confused, stitched up and let down by imperatives beyond their comprehension.

I could well relate to their frustrations. They were sincere, intelligent and idealistic lads, though naive and sometimes ill informed. Their colonial education had left them in a cultural state of semi-hibernation, with the plasticity of their identity being prodded this way and that by various parties but with none of them giving it a meaningful shape. They were being conditioned to some degree, like Pavlov's dogs or Skinner's rats, to a range of external stimuli which did not require them to think too much. They were thus left in limbo, vaguely perplexed as to why — as Chinese — they ought to defer to white men presenting themselves as figures of authority.

Their education had thus cut them off from any significant understanding of their rich Chinese heritage and had barred them from drawing perspectives or solace therefrom. Their hearts and minds seemed to be sending conflicting messages, with their native culture ill-learnt and a foreign culture ill-understood.

Dispirited and unsettled, they eventually decided to hold one final demonstration in May of 1972 — perhaps just for the sake of maintaining their collective "face" — before winding up their campaign. It would take the form of a march from Victoria Park to the Central district, to hand in protest letters to the American and Japanese Consulates-General. They therefore applied for permission to hold the march and, in order to avoid traffic disruptions and to preserve good public order, they also asked for a police escort along their route.

How their application was dealt with has been recorded in Chapter 3. I recommended that permission be granted but the government decided otherwise. But the march — now illegal — went ahead in any case. Nothing untoward occurred. Yet afterwards the government lacked the will or the courage to uphold the law by prosecuting the students. I thought failure to prosecute would bring the rule of law into disrepute. But nobody at the top of government supported my position.

* * *

With the ending of the local Diaoyu Tai campaign, my remit for holding conversations with student leaders came to an end. The meetings at Government House made plain the administration's unwillingness to engage with the growing restlessness and irredentist inclinations among the young. Such reluctance would only store up trouble for the future.

I therefore wrote to Donald Luddington, recommending that a senior

Chinese Administrative Officer be appointed to continue the dialogues with student and youth leaders. The city's population was growing younger, I said, and the colonial education system was not helping their search for identity. A matured Chinese officer could well nudge them towards a less nihilistic and confrontational path.

Unfortunately, before Luddington could consider my recommendation, he got "kicked upstairs" in May of 1973 — to become the Governor of the Solomon Islands. So far as I could determine, Luddington's successor as Secretary for Home Affairs took no notice of my recommendation and simply left it to gather dust in some Secretariat pigeon-hole.

It could be no more than idle speculation now to wonder how relationships between the administration and the various uncivil and slogan-shouting sections of the Hong Kong young might be today if the government had acted upon my recommendation 46 years ago.

* * *

Sir Murray MacLehose ended his ten-and-a-half-year governorship of Hong Kong in May of 1982 to general acclaim. He was popular and well thought of among the local population. Apparently well thought of in London too, for he was elevated to the peerage, with a seat in the House of Lords.

Every biographical summary of Lord MacLehose's tenure as Governor features a long list of the things ascribed to his efforts. Those lists project an image of a progressive, benevolent and caring ruler. They usually begin with his turning Chinese into a second official language. Then came his ten-year public housing plan, his extension of compulsory secondary education from six to nine years, his cleansing of the colony's environment, his stamping out of police corruption and so on.

On the face of it, those lists look very impressive indeed. But are they factually correct? Or had they been tarted up by clever press officers using the latest techniques in managing public relations and creating a positive spin?

I do not wish to begrudge any man his reputation, especially so long after that person has departed the scene and no longer able to speak for himself. Nor would I wish to stand in the way of anyone who wishes to maintain illusions about the deeds of colonisers and occupiers. All I care about is the historical truth for the people of Hong Kong, the place of my birth, the city to which I owed my working allegiances and the chosen home for my family for the last five generations. Myths can distort the thinking of subsequent generations; the truth — hopefully might set them a little more thoughtful and freer.

To the best of my knowledge, no forensic examination of Lord MacLehose's record as a Governor has yet been made. I hope some day an enterprising doctoral candidate would do a dissertation on the noble lord, setting out his fit and proper place in Hong Kong's history.

Until that day comes, let me throw a few random observations into the pot for those who might have an interest in local history and similar matters. Many developments in the city have been cavalierly and not always accurately attributed to Sir Murray. One of them is that he made Chinese into a second official language. That claim is, on the face of it, factually correct in the sense that legislation was passed during his governorship. But to leave that as a bald statement would give rise to a number of false imputations about Sir Murray's progressiveness.

The background to the move has been set out in Chapter 7. If that had been taken into account, together with Sir Murray's lack of concrete action to promote the spirit of that legislation, a truer measure of the Governor's attitude might be arrived at. Years after the passage of the legislation, the recruitment and promotion boards in some government departments still remained entirely composed of expatriates using only English.

* * *

When Sir John Cowperthwaite retired as Hong Kong's Financial Secretary in 1971, he left the public purse in a very healthy state. Sir Murray became Governor at the end of that same year. When he noted the hefty coffers, he swiftly announced a ten-year public housing programme.

But in doing so, he overlooked one piece of advice Sir John had consistently preached, that is, successful projects required not only money but also the right intellectual resources. By then, the more seasoned administrators were also retiring left, right and centre, leaching the bureaucracy of some of its best brainpower. That diminishing pool of talent left the housing programme with a forest of unanswered and perhaps unanswerable questions. If the programme had been even half successful, would affordable housing remain such a major problem in the city today?

Housing is a fundamental human need. It would be unwise for any government to approach the problem as merely a matter of putting roofs over people's heads. Actually, housing goes to the heart of where a society aspires to be in the future, in terms of family structure, environmental enjoyment, social cohesion, urban isolation and loneliness, care for the aged, public security, the upbringing of future generations, employment opportunities, transportation needs, foreseeable challenges like energy, water and food scarcity and so on. It is a quest for both physical and spiritual space, so that the individual and his family could grow and prosper.

A vision embracing all those various elements has still to be clearly enunciated by latter-day political leaders. They might begin by first changing the language. Why speak of new towns when what was really needed was the creation of new and closer-knitted communities to counter the reckless and dangerous drift towards alienating and unmanageable urbanisation?

* * *

Another intriguing conundrum also arose in respect of Sir Murray's decision to extend compulsory secondary education from six to nine years. Could it be considered an improvement for Chinese children to have nine years of a compulsory but misguided colonialist education instead of only six?

The objective situation of the time was pretty clear. Most Chinese parents had since time immemorial sought the best available education for their children, even if that education was not what they ideally would like. Colonial syllabuses have always been geared to producing pliant subjects capable of discharging the functions required by their foreign masters and their local mercantile collaborators. Producing thinking and questioning citizens was far from their thoughts. Thus those syllabuses, fashioned since the early days of the colony, had been in need of drastic revision for ages — and particularly with the advent of 1997. Besides, shortages in good schools and good teachers had been patent for a long time. All the top schools, be they government or aided missionary ones, had been lumbered with long waiting lists.

The Education Department, led for decades by blinkered expatriates, had a long history of appalling incompetence and scandals. If there was a genuine desire to provide high quality education, the first priority ought to have been replacing the leadership in the educational establishment.

In the absence of that reform, what could an increase in secondary school places amount to? A predictably lame result — the "purchase" of places from some private secondary schools. Many of the schools with spare capacity were known locally as "school shops" for they were considered educationally sub-standard. They took in students fast and furiously, so long as parents were prepared to pay the fees. So to go from six years to nine years of compulsory schooling would often mean three more years of an unsatisfactory out-of-date education.

* * *

A great deal of Sir Murray's reputation in Hong Kong and elsewhere has been associated with his establishment of the Independent Commission Against

Corruption in 1974. I have already dealt with how Sir Murray had handled some of the Commission's various initial hiccups in Chapter 14, so I do not intend to repeat myself. I would say, however, that while the ICAC has been successful in reducing certain more obvious forms of civil service corruption, it has failed to tackle others, like the dubious distribution of secret slush funds recounted in Chapter 16.

Neither do I believe the ICAC is adequately equipped to deal with the rampant money-laundering, tax evasion and international fixing of LIBOR, foreign exchange and other rates which affect countless millions of ordinary citizens around the globe.

It would require an enormous amount of naivety to believe that all the major international banks and other corporate entities forking out hundreds of millions in fines to European and American regulatory bodies for misdeeds to settle potential law suits did not have Hong Kong collaborators. How regulatory authorities can dig through all their off-shore subsidiaries, their off-balance sheet accounting and the other forms of legalistic trickeries they employ remain daunting challenges.

When one hears foreign economic gurus and fund managers wearing Armani suits praise Hong Kong as "one of the best cities in the world for doing business" one can be confident they are not talking about setting up *wonton* noodle stalls. They would be addressing those with big bucks, reassuring them that the territory's banking secrecy rules and the availability of the services of expert lawyers and accountants would ensure that their wealth and their activities would be as well shielded from prying eyes as if they were in Switzerland or the United States.

* * *

Some biographical accounts of Sir Murray also credit him for initiating the "Keep Hong Kong Clean" campaign, among other things. In actual fact, the

"Keep Hong Kong Clean" campaign was started by the Urban Council in conjunction with the 28th Exhibition of Hong Kong Products in 1970, well before Sir Murray took up his governorship. Sir Murray merely continued to support the programme. That is quite a different matter from initiating it.

Until a forensic study of Sir Murray's governorship has been done, it is difficult to comment meaningfully on his overall legacy. I would, however, like to refer briefly to one other aspect of Sir Murray's activities.

Sir Murray, at the start of his governorship, was so keen to recruit more Administrative Officers that he overlooked the risks of deteriorating standards. The danger was probably never brought to his attention by any of the bureaucrats at the top. The chickens came home to roost at the tail end of his administration in 1981, when he discovered he had nobody suitable in the service to fill the important post of Financial Secretary. He then had to break with tradition to secure the services of the Swire Group taipan, John Bremridge, to fill the vacancy. That represented one of Sir Murray's better decisions.

Bremridge was an excellent choice. He was a very thoughtful, decent and knowledgeable man who did Hong Kong proud in both the private and public sectors. Some wider questions which might be pondered under those circumstances include: Why had Sir Murray not thought of this deficiency sooner? Was he too blinded by the yes-men around him to see the need for better thinkers and more creative staff throughout the service?

There were plenty of civic minded and qualified Chinese in the private sector more than willing to give up their hefty incomes to serve the community. Why had they not been tapped? They would be admirable in such sectors as education and public works. In fact, they had already established a long tradition of serving without pay on the Executive and Legislative Councils and in various voluntary bodies for over a century. Had they been ruled out simply because they were of the Chinese race and hence could not be relied upon to serve British interests first and foremost? A question worth probing.

* * *

In governments, things often happen under their own momentum. A good idea may get out of hand, however, and turn into something quite bad. Take for example the sensible concept of legal aid for the poor. I can remember that the legal aid outfit started as little more than a man and a boy in an out-of-the-way office somewhere. By 1978, the Legal Aid Department provided legal aid for 67% of the population. I do not know what it covers now but it does appear a great many people are abusing the system by launching frivolous litigation.

The trend to settle disputes through legal remedies would appear to be contrary to the Chinese way of handling disputes. In the past a whole range of issues relating to family life, inheritances, adoptions, and so forth could be settled through customary practices. It seems a pity that respect for elders and for Chinese traditions are not what they used to be. Otherwise many disputes could have been mediated without resorting to courts.

Who is responsible for steadily wiping away traditional practices to substitute them with litigation? Is that a natural heritage of colonialism? Hong Kong society now appears to be becoming almost as litigious as America. A sorry development. A study of its roots should also be enlightening.

* * *

Oscar Wilde once said that everybody owed History a duty to rewrite it. Well, I have used up my two cents' worth on the governance of Hong Kong during the time of Sir Murray MacLehose. I will leave it to others to pick up any further narrative.

About the author

David T. K. Wong was born in Hong Kong and received his early education in China, Singapore and Australia. He has degrees in political science and journalism from Stanford University in America and a post-graduate diploma in public administration from the Institute of Social Studies at The Hague. Later, he also became a Fellow in Economics at Queen Elizabeth House at Oxford.

He worked as a journalist in Hong Kong, London and Singapore for a number of years before joining the Administrative Service of the Hong Kong Government. After retirement from public service, he became the Managing Director of an international trading firm for eight years before migrating to London to embark upon a writing career.

To date he has published four collections of short stories and two novels. His short stories, some of which have earned him a number of awards, have appeared in various magazines in the United States, Great Britain, Hong Kong and other Asian countries.

Many of his stories have been broadcast by BBC Radio 4 in Britain, RTHK in Hong Kong and other stations in Ireland, Holland, Belgium and elsewhere. A number of his short stories have appeared in anthologies.

He is now resident in Malaysia and is currently working on the fourth volume of his family memoirs.

He is the founder of the annual David T. K. Wong Fellowship in Creative Writing at the University of East Anglia in the UK. The Fellowship awards £26,000 to a successful candidate to write a serious work of fiction set in the Far East.

All Wong's fiction is available for free download at his website, www.davidtkwong.net.